THE
INSIDERS'®
GUIDE
TO

GLACIER

NCLUDING FLATHEAD VALLEY AND
WATERTON LAKES NATIONAL PARK

THE INSIDERS' GUIDE TO

GLACIER

NCLUDING FLATHEAD VALLEY AND WATERTON LAKES NATIONAL PARK

Eileen Gallagher, Frank Miele, Mary
Pat Murphy, Rima Nickell
and SusanOlin

The Insiders' Guide®
An imprint of Falcon® Publishing Inc.
A Landmark Communications Company
P.O. Box 1718
Helena, MT 59624
(800) 582-2665
www.insiders.com

Sales and Marketing: Falcon Publishing, Inc.
P.O. Box 1718
Helena, MT 59624
(800) 582-2665
www.falconguide.com

Advertising: Falcon Publishing, Inc.
150 W. Brambleton Ave.
Norfolk, VA 23510
(757) 446-2933
rwalsh@falcon.com

•

FIRST EDITION
1st printing

•

©1999
by Falcon Publishing, Inc.

•

Printed in the United States
of America

•

Publications from *The Insiders' Guide*® series are available at special discounts for bulk
purchases for sales promotions, premiums or fundraisings. Special editions, including
personalized covers, can be created in large quantities for special needs.
For more information, please contact Falcon Publishing.

ISBN 1-57380-132-1

Preface

Western Montana is an outdoor recreationist's summer dream and winter paradise. On warm sunny days the rivers are filled with the sounds of white-water rafters careening through deep river canyons where just hours before the quiet whip of the fly-fisher's line was the only sound to be heard. Hikers, trail riders, and mountain bikers seek solitude on nearby trails where birding and wildlife watching abound. When the winds begin to chill and the leaves of the aspens take on a golden hue, the elk begin their poignant bugling and hunters know the season is near. As soon as the sky, leaden with the color of winter, begins to drop soft ice crystals from above, skiers anticipate the first downhill run through fresh powder or a glide cross-country through a quiet forest.

Glacier National Park, with its knife edged peaks and alpine fields filled with the splendid colors of summer wildflowers, is the reason many visitors first explore the northwest corner of Montana. A drive along Going-to-the-Sun Road introduces the inhabitants of cars, vans, and RVs to the many natural wonders the park offers and entices many to get out of the car for a closer look from trailside. For some, the trip through the park is just the beginning of what will become a love affair with the entire region, and they simply have to find out more about Kalispell, the Flathead Valley, the Swan Valley, and the grand expanses on the park's eastern slopes.

One of the most special things about Glacier is that it is not only a National Park, it is part of an International Peace Park that extends into Alberta, Canada. A visitor to the Alberta Visitor's Centre in West Glacier, Montana, is a wonderful introduction to the offerings across the border, but a visit to the Prince of Wales Hotel by the shimmering Waterton Lake in the Canadian section of the Glacier-Waterton–International Peace Park can only improve on your impressions.

To the south of Glacier, the Swan Valley and the Flathead Lake area are serious recreation destinations in themselves and provide a charming introduction to Kalispell and the towns that serve as gateways to Glacier National Park and are home to a wide variety of people who share a deep affection for the things that make the area such an incredibly place to live and to visit. This area is renowned for its arts festivals and a tour of any of the sometimes quirky but always interesting museums and well-known area attractions—such as the Stumptown Historical Society Museum in Whitefish and even the House of Mystery near Columbia Falls—will add depth and insight to your western mountain adventures. A description of the wonders of this area would not be complete, however, without mentioning the major summer and winter playground—Big Mountain, one of Montana's premier ski resorts. At the foot of Flathead Lake is the Flathead Indian Reservation, home to the federated Salish/Kootenai tribes, and a visit to Polson or the other towns on the reservation serve as a great introduction to the history and culture of these native peoples.

On the eastern side of the park, the Blackfeet reservation contains a number of small towns that serve as a jumping-off point for park explorations and offer great opportunities for long and highly enjoyable views of Montana's famed Big Sky Country. A trip to any of the region's museums and even visits to some of the local restaurants and motels will serve as a fascinating introduction to the Blackfeet culture and reservation life.

The rugged terrain of the slopes split by the Continental Divide belies the fragility of the ecosystems supported here. Not only have mining, logging, and industry had their effect on the pristine nature of the mountain setting, recreational use has affected it as well. Those who venture out in their hiking boots or on their skis must take responsibility for their actions and practice "no-trace" recreation if the attractions that draw us into this relatively wild place are to remain for future generations. After all, it is the beauty of the scenery and the solitude that an untouched setting suggests that keep us entranced.

If a visit to Glacier Country just isn't enough—and more and more people have found that it's not—then the real estate and other relocation information located in this book will be just what you are looking for. From rustic log cabins in remote settings to elegant Victorian homes just blocks from downtown, this area offers something for all tastes. Helpful insights for retirees looking for a more northern exposure are also included, as is information about childcare and education for the younger set.

The goal of this book is to provide newcomers and visitors alike with information about the very best and brightest offerings of a very special place full of special people and establishments. The Insider's Guide to Glacier and the Flathead Valley will help you explore all of the finest offerings of this delightful region with detailed information on restaurants, accommodations, and recreation. If you're staying for a week or a lifetime, the tips, facts, and insights gleaned from Montana insiders put all the information you need for your Glacier adventures within easy reach. We wish you luck on your wanderings and hope that you will come away with lists of your own favorites, as well.

About the Authors

Eileen Gallagher

Eileen Gallagher works in Kalispell as an interior designer. She is also a writer and has written for regional and national magazines. Her articles have been published in *Country Home*, *Country*, *Log Home Living*, and *Snow Country* (now *Mountain Sports and Living*). Her specialty is feature articles on homes. She is also a freelance book copyeditor and was a reporter and photographer for newspapers in Washington and Montana. A native Montanan who studied journalism and home economics at The University of Montana, Eileen has lived in the Flathead Valley for the past 13 years with her husband, Roger Semler, wilderness manager at Glacier National Park. Before that they lived in national parks in Alaska, Washington, and Hawaii. She enjoys travel, antiquing, and playing with their Norwegian Buhund dog, Siyeh.

Frank Miele

Frank Miele lives in Kalispell, Montana, with his wife Michele and son Carmen. He has worked at *The Daily Inter Lake* newspaper in Kalispell since 1984, and is well-known for his movie reviews and his work on the *Flathead Business Journal* for many years. He recently edited the book *A Woman's Way West* by Montana author John Fraley, and has published poetry and criticism in a number of literary magazines. In earlier years, Frank had a misspent youth in New Jersey, New York, New Orleans and points west, including Bismarck, Tucson, Los Angeles and Missoula, where he studied in the acclaimed creative-writing program at the University of Montana. Since 1997, Frank and Michele have also run Home Grown Antiques, selling pottery and glassware on the Internet at http://www.homegrownantiques.com.

Mary Pat Murphy

Mary Pat Murphy is a free-lance writer and editor who lives on a small farm near Kalispell. She was born and raised in Kalispell and loves the beauty of her native state. She worked as a journalist in Alaska for 22 years before returning to her hometown in December 1995.

Rima Nickell

Rima Nickell visited Glacier Country first as a college student on a climb of Chief Mountain and nurtured a dream of returning here to live. She is now a permanent Flathead resident following several decades living elsewhere on the continent including the east and west coasts, Alaska, Canada, and Mexico. National Parks have been prominent destinations during her treks and volunteer activities that include nearly four months as a volunteer with the National Park Service in remote Alaska parks and preserves. She constantly explores Glacier Country by car, on foot, by bicycle, on cross-country skis and by various water conveyances. As staff reporter and photographer for the *Hungry Horse News* and *Whitefish Pilot* and now freelance writer, Nickell has become familiar with many of the area's people, agencies and issues.

Susan Olin

Susan Olin is a freelance writer and editor who has spent her summers working in Glacier National Park since 1988. She winters in Whitefish, Montana.

Acknowledgments

Eileen Gallagher

I would like to acknowledge my husband, Roger Semler, Glacier Park wilderness manager, for contributing his expertise on wilderness travel and safety, the wilderness ethic, and the Leave No Trace program for this guide.

I would like to thank the proprietors and dealers of the many wonderful Flathead Valley antiques stores for taking time to share their enthusiasm for collecting; this passion is what makes each of their businesses special.

Finally, I need to thank the many authors — past and present — who chronicled the rich history of our Valley. Their accounts enabled me to write this brief history of the Flathead Valley and Glacier Park, as I spent a fascinating winter pouring over the rich tapestry of tales, times and tidbits that wove the fabric of today's Flathead Valley.

Frank Miele

First and foremost, I need to thank my wife, Michele, for her support and encouragement through the many months that went into researching and writing this book. She provided many invaluable ideas that have been incorporated into my listings and also took over the hard work of lining up photos to illustrate the book when I became too busy to complete that task. As usual, she did a great job.

Secondly, a big hug goes out to my son, Carmen, who has exhibited patience rare in a 3-year-old, confident that one day the book would be over and that Daddy would be able to approach playtime with renewed vigor.

As for the many chambers of commerce and tourism promotion agencies that have assisted in compiling the information and photos used herein, this book would have been immeasurably harder to complete without you. Not all businesses of interest could be included in the listings, but we hope that the sampling provided will prove of assistance to all in promoting the wealth of opportunities for recreation, entertainment and enjoyment in the marvelous Flathead.

Finally, my involvement with The Insiders' Guide would not have happened at all without the generosity of writer Diana Blend, who suggested me for the project. Thanks to her for her confidence, and to Erin Turner at Falcon Publishing for letting me "learn on the job."

Mary Pat Murphy

Many people were generous with their time and information as I gathered material for the relocation chapter. I could not have completed the project without their help.

Rima Nickell

I am grateful to the many people who patiently answered my questions and guided my research. Steve Gniadek, wildlife biologist, and Tara Williams, botanist, of the Glacier National Park staff; Allen Rowley, Flathead National Forest public affairs specialist; and consultant Dale Gunderson, were indispensable in helping me with the plant and animal communities and other natural history information. Montana Department of Fish, Wildlife and Parks Public Information Officer John Fraley provided necessary information and resources about hunting and fishing. For their help regarding Swan Valley section, I thank Ann Dahl, Director of the Swan Ecosystem Center, Joe Yates, silvaculturalist with the Swan Lake Ranger District and Stewart Stadler, whose grandfather Lewis Orvis Evans began the Kootenai Lodge development. I am especially appreciative of the continuing assistance of all the kind librarians in the Flathead County Library reference department. My editor Erin Turner was more patient than I deserved and always helpful.

Susan Olin

I would like to thank my father and my friends for their support and their help with the research for this book. I would also like to thank the many people who shared their enthusiasm for living in Glacier Country and the Flathead Valley and their excitement about their businesses.

Table of Contents

Directory of Maps

GLACIER AND THE FLATHEAD VALLEY

GLACIER NATIONAL PARK

KALISPELL

WHITEFISH

Of course, it's probably because Glacier Country is somewhat out of the way that so many people choose to vacation or relocate here.

How to Use This Book

From the fertile Swan and Flathead Valleys to the breathtaking open expanses to the east of Glacier National Park, this guide to northwestern Montana's Glacier Country is designed to help you find what you're looking for and to introduce you to things you might never have imagined exist in this out-of-the-way place.

Of course, it's probably because Glacier Country is somewhat out of the way that so many people choose to vacation or relocate here. The wildness of this place is a major part of its appeal to residents and visitors alike. You may be surprised to find out how easy it actually is to get here and how much the area has to offer in addition to great skiing, fishing, hiking, and other winter and summer recreation opportunities. Even if those things were what drew you here, you'll be amazed at what a hike through a Douglas-fire forest to an alpine lake can do for your appetite; you'll definitely need a hearty meal when you leave the woods and you can indulge in one of the area's fine restaurants. And if carrying your tent and all of your gear to a backcountry campsite isn't exactly your idea of a way to spend a relaxing vacation, hints on great bed-and-breakfasts, cozy inns, downtown hotels, and even the more luxurious campgrounds (with running water and other amenities) may be more to your taste.

This book will help you get to Glacier and the Flathead Valley (see the Getting Here/Getting Around chapter) and help you make the most of your visit once you arrive. The Area Overview, History, Attractions, Arts, Kidstuff, and Annual Events chapters are designed to give you some general information about Glacier and the Flathead Valley that will encourage and inform your visit—if the rumors of great outdoor recreation and spectacular scenery weren't enough. Each of these sections, and the sections on Outdoor Recreation give general information about what can be found throughout the region while providing details about the highlights and pointing you to additional sources of information about a variety of activities.

Once you've exhausted yourself with a full day of horseback riding, rock climbing, or rafting, you'll want something to eat and a place to rest up. Later, you may want to sample one of Montana's many new microbrews in an old-fashioned saloon setting. If souvenirs or some comfortable hiking books are on your wish list, you may also want to visit the local hotspots for the latest in hand-carved grizzly bears or high-tech outdoor gear. In the market for Antiques? There are dozens of venues for you to explore.

The sections of this book containing information about accommodations, nightlife, restaurants, and shopping are grouped by geography. If you're basing your adventures out of Bigfork, all of the best-and-brightest options for an overnight stay, fine meal, hearty ale, or sturdy cowboy boots in town or in the immediate area can be found within a few

pages. Within each section are recommendations for a range of options from bed-and-breakfasts to RV parks and from kid-friendly hamburger joints to elegant dining rooms.

When your vacation comes to an end, and you just can't bear to leave all of Montana's wonders behind you, our handy relocation guide can give you information about real estate, health care, education and child care, and more. After you've settled into your dream cabin by the shore of Swan Lake, we're sure that

you'll continue to use this book to inform all of your Glacier and Flathead Valley adventures.

Please let us know what you think about this Insider's Guide to Glacier and the Flathead Valley. We'll be updating the book annually, and we want to hear from you about your own discoveries that you think should be included in the guide. Write to us at Insiders' Guides, c/o Falcon Publishing, P.O. Box 1718, Helena, Montana 59624 or visit our website at www.insiders.com.

Winter and summer, Glacier and the Flathead are marvelous places to visit, and residents will quickly tell you that living here has a vacation-like quality.

Area Overview

In Glacier National Park and the Flathead Valley, the seasons are dramatic, wildlife is abundant, and nature is your constant companion. Rugged peaks rise majestically over pristine lakes, streams gurgle through the lovely valleys, and clear rivers carry fast-flowing fresh water. The forces of nature are a dynamic part of the landscape, which influences the dynamic nature of the residents who call it home.

Winter and summer, Glacier and the Flathead are marvelous places to visit, and residents will quickly tell you that living here has a vacation-like quality. But nature and its visible beauty isn't the only draw of the valley—the arts, annual festivals, and myriad attractions such as golf courses, museums, and excellent dining, lodging, and shopping draw visitors here and are supported by residents. From the smallest village to the area's largest towns, you'll never know what delightful surprises you'll find under the restaurant sign or behind the bed-and-breakfast door.

The Lay of the Land

The peaks of Glacier National Park, carved out by ancient glaciers and dotted with those of more recent origin, is the center of one of the largest intact ecosystems in the United States. It's relative isolation from settlement has helped it retain its rich biological diversity, even though nearly 2 million visitors cross the park borders every year. The surrounding communities act as gateways to the park and its northern sister, Waterton Lakes National Park in Canada. Together, the two parks are designated the Waterton-Glacier International Peace Park—so named in 1932 as the first such park in the world.

With the two parks at its center, it is natural to conclude that tourism is the mainstay of the surrounding communities, and the knowledge that Flathead Lake, the largest natural freshwater lake west of the Mississippi River is Glacier National Park's neighbor to the west will only strengthen that conclusion. Kalispell's population soars every summer to accommodate visitors, as do the populations of Bigfork and Columbia Falls on the north end of the lake and on the way into the park, Polson at the south end, and Whitefish—winter and summer with the Big Mountain Ski Area—is a vacationer's playground. The Swan Valley, located on Montana Highway 83 is a less-visited, equally beautiful vacation getaway. Tourism benefits the Blackfeet Indian Reservation, with its stunning views of the Rocky Mountain Front, and the Flathead Reservation, as well.

Don't be lulled into the belief that these communities exist only for tourism, however. These are vibrant, exciting towns with active arts communities, thriving businesses, and stunning settings. It's no wonder that more and more people make the Flathead Valley home every year. Festivals and events abound, from North American Indian Days in Browning to the myriad arts festivals held in communities from Whitefish to Polson. Families who have lived here for generations and newcomers fill the seats at these gatherings. This is a place where community still means something, neighbors share sugar, and everyone talks about how to keep deer out of the garden—though they'd willingly let the deer feed on their flower beds if the option was losing the wildlife and scenery that makes up the wonder of the area.

Quirks, Foibles and Other Important Information

As you wander through Glacier Country, the Flathead, and the Swan on your adventures, there are some things that you should be aware may affect your journey, your recreation, and your safety. We cover a lot of these topics in close-ups and tips throughout the books, but there are still some good things to keep in mind as you hit the highway and head off to the park or out on the water.

1. This is a really large area—We don't call this Big Sky Country for nothing, and though residents in the area may think nothing of hopping in the car and driving a couple of hours to get to a particular restaurant or to find a trailhead, this book is arranged so that if you're in Whitefish, all of the restaurants, accommodations, and other amenities in the area are listed in the same section of the book. If you want to head off to a restaurant in Polson from Whitefish, figure out the mileage before you hit the road, and fill up on gas. Twenty-four hour convenience stores exist out here, but you can't count on them on every corner.

2. Our weather can change quickly—Even after a warm summer day, or while you're still out enjoying it, storm clouds can come up, showers will start, and temperatures will drop. Be sure if you're on the water or on the trail that you have appropriate gear to get you through a storm. Remember, too, that in winter the weather can be extremely cold; watch for signs of hypothermia when you're out recreating, and think about carrying emergency gear.

3. Heed road information—Going-to-the-Sun Road in Glacier National Park is generally closed from the end of September until early June because of snow, and other roads can become dangerous in winter weather, as well. Exercise caution, and call the state highway information number (800) 226-ROAD for information on road conditions if you're in doubt as to the safety of travel.

4. Make your reservations early—

Credit: VIAD Corporation

Majestic bighorn sheep excite wildlife watchers in Glacier Country.

Credit: Marina Cay Resort

A shining reflection of light on Flathead Lake is a true area attraction.

Credit: VIAD Corportaion

Glacier National Park offers splendid views and fine accommodations.

Though we expect visitors in the summer, the communities in this area and the facilities in the park are not unlimited in terms of the accommodations we can offer. Call early to reserve rooms and arrive early at camp-grounds to guarantee a spot. Some camp-grounds accept reservations as well, and that reservation may save you hunting in the dark for a spot to pull into and set up the tent.

5. We do have bears and mountain lions—Though you will be lucky to see these wild creatures from a safe distance, please remember that they can be dangerous and follow the precautions outlined on pages 232 and 280 to ensure your safety and that of your family. We also have an abundance of other wild creatures—they are beautiful to view, but remember that you are the visitor in

their habitat and treat them with respect. Respect for wildlife means giving them a wide berth. If your behavior changes the behavior of the animal you're watching, you're too close.

Please Tread Lightly

Throughout this guide, especially in the Outdoor Recreation chapter, we offer tips for being a responsible visitor to this somewhat fragile ecosystem. Let us take a moment here to emphasize that what makes this area special is its abundance of natural beauty, its biodiversity, and the people who care about both. The remoteness of Glacier National Park and the Flathead Valley, and the cushion provided by the reservation land on its west and south sides, has helped sustain that diversity for the hundred years or more that settlement has been taking place in this area. Still, with 2 million visitors coming into the park every year, there is strain on our natural surrounding . . . it's unavoidable. Please keep your impact as minimal as possible so that our valleys and peaks will remain as they are for generations to come.

Montana is remote, it's large, and it's mountainous, three things that make getting here and getting around a challenge for visitors and locals alike.

Getting Here, Getting Around

Montana is remote, it's large, and it's mountainous, three things that make getting here and getting around a challenge for visitors and locals alike, though it seems to get easier every day. It's not getting faster, though. Let's dispel that notion right off the bat. Yes, it is true that for nearly four years, Montana had no posted daytime speed limit. Instead, our highways operated under the "Basic Rule" which stated that drivers had to drive in a reasonable and prudent manner based on road conditions and traffic. However, this author knows from experience that tickets were still distributed by our diligent and prudent highway patrol. We have since gone back to standard daytime speed limits with the support of our residents. This chapter should help you get here by plane, by car, by train or by bus, and it will help you navigate our state once you're here. We still recommend a reasonable and prudent attitude to travel here—weather conditions, mountainous terrain, and long distances between services (like gas stations)—should always be kept in mind.

By Air

Montana has three fairly large International Airports—large compared to the tiny International Airport at Glasgow in our state's far northeast corner—at Billings, Great Falls, and, lucky for the visitor to the Flathead Valley, Kalispell. If you fly into Billings or Great Falls, you'll have to make other arrangements to get to the Flathead by car or by bus. From Billings it's 463 miles to Kalispell and from Great Falls it's 229 miles. There are other regional airports at Bozeman, Butte, Helena, and Missoula.

Glacier Park International Airport
4170 Highway 2 East, Kalispell 59901
• (406) 257-5994

Most people who fly in to visit the Flathead Valley will choose the Kalispell Airport as their destination. It's serviced by Delta, Horizon, Northwest and Skywest. Car rentals are available at the airport, and some guest ranches will arrange to pick you up there.

Great Falls International Airport
2800 Terminal Drive, Great Falls 59404
• (406) 727-3404

If you fly into Great Falls and rent a car to get to the Flathead Valley, be sure to visit the falls themselves to see what the members of the Lewis and Clark Expedition faced as they explored the Missouri River. The airport is serviced by Delta, Horizon, Big Sky, and Northwest.

INSIDERS' TIP

Plan ahead when traveling anywhere in Montana. Weather conditions, the distance between towns, and whether your car can handle mountainous terrain will all affect your trip. Carry emergency gear and keep your tank topped off.

Glacier National Park is still beautiful — but easier to get to than it was earlier this century.

Logan International Airport
Billings 59101
• (406) 657-8495

Billings is Montana's largest city, and it naturally has the largest airport. Car rentals are available and you can fly in on Delta, Horizon, Northwest, Big Sky, Skywest, United, and Continental. From there you may also be able to get a connecting flight to Kalispell.

Missoula County Airport
5225 Highway 10 West, Missoula 59801
• (406) 728-4381

Flying to Missoula is also a good option for getting to the Flathead. It's closer than Great Falls, Billings, or Helena, the next near option. Car rentals are available and the airport is serviced by Delta, Horizon, Northwest, and Continental. While you're in Missoula and at the airport, you may be interested in stopping at the Smokejumper's Training Center there to see how forest fires are fought.

By Car

Montana has 1,200 miles of Interstate and 5,400 miles of primary highways, but remember this is big sky country, and that just means

INSIDERS' TIP

Consider flying into Spokane, Washington, or Calgary, Alberta, when visiting Glacier and the Flathead Valley. Airfare is sometimes less expensive, though you will probably have to rent a car.

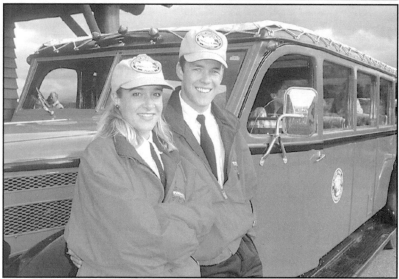

Credit: VIAD Corporation

Take a red bus through Glacier National Park for a spectacular view out the roof.

their long—not that it's complicated to find which one you need. There are three Interstate Highways, I-15 runs north and south, just to the east of Glacier National Park. I-90 runs northeast and southeast across the western two-thirds of the state, heading northwest toward Washington, and 1-94 connects Billings with eastern Montana and North Dakota.

If you're coming in from the west, you'll take I-90, from the north or south, I-15, and from the east, I-90 or I-94. U.S. Highway 93 runs the length of the Flathead Valley from North to South, starting in Missoula at Interstate 90 and winding its way north and then west toward Washington. This will likely be your primary travel corridor. Montana Highway 83 will take you through the Swan Valley—one of the most scenic drives in the state, U.S. Highway 2 will be your road into Glacier

National Park and across the Blackfeet Reservation, and you can choose to explore Glacier from that road or from U.S. Highway 89 or Going-to-the-Sun Road. Highway 89 dips to the southeast to meet up with Interstate 15 at Great Falls.

Montana travel information is available by calling Travel Montana at (800) 847-4868 or (406) 444-2654. For information on road conditions statewide call (800) 226-ROAD.

If you want to travel to Canada from Glacier and the Flathead, there are border crossings at Roosville (on U.S. 93, north of Eureka), open 24 hours a day; Trail Creek (at the northwest corner of Glacier National Park), open 9AM to 5 PM from June 1 to October 31, Chief Mountain (on Montana Highway 17, northeast of Glacier), open 9AM to 6PM from May 20-31 and 7AM to 10PM from July 1 to the

INSIDERS' TIP

Montana Highway 93 is one of the busiest in the state, particularly in summer as visitors and residents flock to the shores of Flathead Lake. The trip through the Swan Valley on Montana Highway 83 is a good alternative to this busy road.

Bus Tours in Glacier National Park

Bus tours provide an opportunity to see Glacier while leaving the driving to someone else—and along winding, narrow Going-to-the-Sun Road, that can be a real advantage! Two different tour operators offer guided trips through Glacier National Park and the immediately surrounding area. Both make stops along the way for visitors to take photos, stretch their legs, and generally enjoy the scenery.

Glacier Park, Inc. (GPI) offers tours which base out of their lodges, connecting the different areas of the park. Visitors ride in the historic red buses, built by the White Motor Company between 1936 and 1939. These vintage motor coaches have roll-back canvas tops that can be opened on sunny days for an open-air ride with views to the peaks above. The drivers provide a narrative during the ride and will answer questions for visitors. The red buses operate on a schedule that includes half-day and full-day tours to different parts of the park, including Logan Pass and Going-to-the-Sun Road, for prices ranging between $11.00 and $61.00. For more information, visit the website at www.glacierparkinc.com or contact GPI at (602) 207-6000. Reservations are required and should be made at least the day before you wish to tour; please call the GPI transportation office at (406) 226-9311.

Sun Tours operates out of the east side, picking up visitors at Browning, East Glacier, and St. Mary. These guided tours of Going-to-the-Sun Road—Natos'i At'apoo—highlight Blackfeet history and culture, and all guides are Blackfeet. Sun Tours operates small modern buses with large windows and air conditioning. Both private tours and tours of the Blackfeet Reservation can also be arranged. For more information, write Sun Tours, 29 Glacier Avenue, East Glacier Park, MT 59434, or phone either (800) 786-9220 or (406) 226-9220.

third Sunday in September; and Piegan (16 miles north of Babb on Montana Highway 89) open 7AM to 11PM.

By Train

AMTRAK provides east and west passenger service across northern Montana, making stops in Libby, Whitefish, West Glacier, Essex, Browning, Cut Bank, Shelby, Havre, Malta, Glasgow, and Wolf Point. The terminuses are Chicago on the east and Portland and Seattle to the west. The railroad follows Montana's Hi-Line, as U.S. Highway 2 is known, and a trip on the *Empire Builder* is certainly a romantic way to see this part of the state. Most boardings and deboardings occur at Whitefish; call AMTRAK at (800) 872-7245 for more information.

By Bus

Rimrock Trailways
• **(800) 255-7655**

Rimrock serves more than 60 Montana communities, including Whitefish, Great Falls, and Missoula. It also connects to points served by Greyhound Lines along I-90, including Missoula, Bozeman, and Billings.

Eagle Transit
• **(406) 758-5728**

Eagle Transit is Kalispell's City Bus. Call for schedules and route information.

Beginning about 1800 and continuing to 1820, traders and fur trappers sought adventure and wealth in the Flathead Valley, and their explorations would change the lives of the native peoples forever.

History

Just getting to the Flathead was enough to discourage many early-day settlers. Pioneers arrived on horseback or by horse and wagon, negotiating rough wagon trails that knifed through dense stands of virgin timber and up and down steep countryside. Fur trappers and traders preceded settlers in the early 1800s. But, of course, American Indians were the Flathead Valley's first inhabitants. Three main Indian tribes—the Kootenai; the Upper Pend d' Oreille, or the Kalispel Indians; and the Salish, known as the Flatheads—coexisted in the area and enjoyed the bounty the Valley offered. They hunted and fished in the area's many rivers and lakes and vied for territory with the warring Blackfeet Indians from the eastern side of the Rocky Mountains.

This country remains home today to the Confederated Salish and Kootenai tribes (Flathead, Pend d'Oreille and Kootenai). The Treaty of 1855 sliced Flathead Lake into two halves, with the southern half designated reservation land. The Flathead Indian Reservation, which comprises 1.2 million acres, extends south to Ravalli. The Confederated Salish and Kootenai Tribal Complex is in Pablo. On the east side of Glacier National Park is the Blackfeet Indian Reservation.

Beginning about 1800 and continuing to 1820, traders and fur trappers sought adventure and wealth in the Flathead Valley, and their explorations would change the lives of the native peoples forever. Canadian trappers and traders were some of the first to traverse the region, and Joseph Howse, one of the first white men to winter in the Flathead, was sent by the Hudson's Bay Company to establish the company's first fur trading post in 1810-1811. This post at the north end of Flathead Lake was called Howse House (or Howse's House).

In the footsteps of the trappers followed the homesteaders, hungry for land and a new start. A heavy influx of homesteaders populated the region throughout the 1870s and 1880s; many were European immigrants who brought their agricultural heritage with them. Some claimed land on the shores of Flathead Lake, despite its being reservation land. By 1909 former reservation land around Flathead Lake cost about $1.25 to $3 per acre.

The arrival of the Northern Pacific Railroad to Missoula, Montana, in 1883 was one of the major contributors to the region's growth. By about 1887 (some accounts say the early 1890s) public transportation was available from Missoula via a spur line north to Ravalli, south of St. Ignatius. From Ravalli passengers and goods were loaded onto overland wagons or stages and transported to Polson on Flathead Lake's southern shore.

From Polson steamboats offered passenger service to the north end of the approximately 28-mile-long lake, connecting with Somers and Demersville, two early settlements. The first steamer to begin crisscrossing Flathead Lake was the *U.S. Grant*, and by 1916 at least 16 steamers regularly traversed the waters of the lake, the largest freshwater lake west of the Mississippi. Besides containing roomy freight decks with booms, many steamboats featured upper decks with private cabins for travelers, and meals were taken in dining salons. The largest vessel, the *State of Montana,* was launched in 1889. It measured 150 feet long by 26 feet wide and was built for $25,000.

In the 1880s when agriculture boomed in the rich, fertile Flathead Valley steamboats hauled grain crops and potatoes to market. The temperate climate around Flathead Lake enabled the successful cultivation of fruit orchards. Many tons of apples were produced and shipped to out-of-state markets. In the early 1900s, the Bear Dance Ranch harvested 3,000 fruit trees and boasted 42 varieties of apples. Later sweet cherries were introduced to the Flathead and became a major crop, which they remain today.

Steamboat transportation on Flathead Lake thrived from about 1885 to the 1920s, but in 1917 when the Northern Pacific Railroad built a branch line to Polson, the ease and speed of rail transportation hastened the end of the steamboat era. The Northern Pacific was not the only railroad to shape the history of the Valley. It was empire builder James J. Hill's dream to build a railroad from St. Paul, Minnesota, to the West Coast. Some 6,000 men bent their backs surveying, grading and pounding in rails to the upper Flathead Valley to bring Hill's transcontinental railroad, the Great Northern Railway, west from the eastern Montana prairies through Marias Pass, which is located at the southern edge of Glacier National Park (elevation 3,220 feet). Hill's idea was to fill his cars with passengers going west. He heavily advertised the agricultural opportunities of the Flathead Valley and offered cheap fares for homesteaders. The railway played a prominent role in giving homesteaders access to the hinterlands of northwestern Montana. By 1891 the train carried passengers to Columbia Falls and then to Kalispell. By the turn of the century, the Valley was home to more than 700 farms.

Two Early Towns Have Their Day

Preceding other towns springing up in the north Flathead Valley were the communities of Scribner and Selish. But historians consider Ashley, a somewhat later arrival, the Valley's first real town. Established at the crossing of Indian trails near the Ashley Creek Bridge, it sat about one mile west of Kalispell's present-day business district, and some of Ashley's streets were incorporated into Kalispell when that city developed. The town was named for Joe Ashley, a trader who arrived in 1857, one of the Valley's first settlers, but it would die shortly after Demersville and Kalispell blossomed overnight.

Demersville was located a few miles south of Kalispell on the Flathead River and was founded by merchant T.J. Demers. The location came to be considered the head of navigation on the Flathead River. Demers set up his general store first in a large tent, and later in a log structure. With his death in 1889 the store was sold and became the Missoula Mercantile Co. But Demersville boomed from 1888 to 189l as steamboat traffic on Flathead Lake ferried the migration of settlers, their equipment and supplies up the lake to Demersville and points north.

Demersville was a hell-bent town, with an abundance of saloons and gambling. Hope was that the Great Northern Railway would lay tracks to Demersville so that it would gain the double advantage of both rail and water transportation. But when the Great Northern Railway extended its main line to Kalispell instead, most of the town folded up and moved to the new end of the line.

Bigfork

The first wagon trails through this part of Montana followed the west shore of Flathead Lake. Thus the Bigfork area on the east shore was slower to be populated than its west shore neighbors. The townsite perches on a bay where the Swan River spills into the northeast end of the nearly 200-square-mile Flathead Lake. The town was founded in 1902 when E.L. Sliter filed a townsite plat. (Some accounts say a year earlier.) He divided a portion of his 160-acre homestead into 11 blocks and about 95 lots. Sliter built the town's first hotel and general store and served as first postmaster. A 1903 photograph depicts Sliter's store, his hotel under construction and three saloons. Some early businesses were the Bigfork Mercantile, the Flathead Commercial Company and the E. J. O'Brien Hotel. The first restau-

Credit: Jana Goodman, the KM Building

Built in 1894, the Kalispell Mercantile "KM" Building is a downtown landmark.

rant built was Cheinies. A 1912 fire in Bigfork demolished many businesses. The Bigfork Light and Power Company constructed the first hydroelectric power plant at Bigfork in 1901. The plant, located on the mouth of the Swan River, harnessed energy derived from the turbulent waters and sent power and light to neighboring Kalispell. The University of Montana at one time operated its biological research station in Bigfork until the station was relocated to Yellow Bay in 1912.

Bigfork, with the surrounding area, has been known historically for production of exceptional fruit, because of the lakeshore's relatively mild climate. The first orchard is thought to have been planted by homesteader George Lakin in about 1885. City founder E.L. Sliter soon followed, clearing timber and brush and eventually accumulating more than 500 acres of farmland. When his orchards were in peak production, he had upwards of 5,000 apple, pear, plum and cherry trees. The area is famous for its cherries; the industry as we know it today originated at nearby Wood's Bay in the 1890s.

Just where the town acquired the name Bigfork is unclear. Henry Elwood reported in his book *Kalispell, Montana and The Upper Flathead Valley* that local Indians told Sliter that the site was the "Big Fork" of the Flathead Valley's rivers, hence the name. Later the U.S. Postal Service shortened the name to one word.

Since this little town was founded, almost a century has passed and Montana has again become a destination point. Appreciated as one of the last unspoiled spots to live, Montana enjoyed renewed popularity as a vacation and relocation spot in the late 1980s and through the early 1990s. The economy remains strong, and Bigfork has thrived, although it remains unincorporated. A tourist town— the summer population swells to approximately 10,000—it is a draw in itself, as well as an interesting stop for travelers on their way to Glacier National Park. Bigfork is listed in *The Great Towns of America: A Guide to the 100 Best Getaways for a Vacation or a Lifetime* by David Vokak.

It is home to the renowned Bigfork Summer Theater and performing arts center, fine art galleries, gift shops, superb restaurants and a world-class golf course. If you're traveling to Bigfork in mid- to late summer, don't miss sampling the region's sweet Flathead cherries.

Somers

The old company houses of this former lumber town on U.S. Highway 93 still are lived in, and time-worn dock pilings stretch out into Somers Bay; both are mute reminders that the quiet, historic community of Somers at one time enjoyed status as second largest town in the Flathead Valley. In the early decades of this century Somers existed as a bustling shipping and logging hub and passenger port.

Built on the northwest end of Flathead Lake, Somers grew up almost overnight. The Great Northern Railway needed ties to continue its railway expansion, and the abundant lumber in the area was responsible for an economic boom. In about 1900, James J. Hill, founder of the Great Northern Railway, contracted with John O'Brien of Stillwater, Minnesota, to build a sawmill capable of producing for the railroad at least 600,000 treated ties annually for 20 years. Additionally, 40 million board feet of lumber were contracted for each year. In turn, the Great Northern was to build a 10-mile spur track from its main line through Kalispell to the O'Brien mill site in Somers.

O'Brien purchased 350 acres of the Tom McGovern ranch and built the sawmill. The railroad recruited loggers from back home in Minnesota, offering them fare out to Montana for only $12.50. Besides Minnesota, other mill workers composing the labor force hailed from Sweden, Germany, Norway and Italy. Somers was known for the friendliness of these hardworking, diverse ethnic groups.

Operations at the mill began in August 1901, and a boomtown was born. The boom lasted more than two decades until the 1920s when virgin timber resources became less plentiful. Logging was done in winter because it was easier to haul timber over snow. Logs were cut, loaded onto horse-drawn sleighs and sledded to riverbanks or lakeshores, where they were stockpiled. In spring when the water was high logs going to the Somers mill were driven down the Flathead, Whitefish, Stillwater and Swan rivers to enter the head of Flathead Lake. Logs were towed by tugboat to a large pond in Somers Bay to be processed at the mill. The sawmill operated a planing mill for lumber, a sash and door division, and, for a time, a box factory. The Great Northern built the tie-treating plant and operated a power plant on the grounds to provide steam for all the operations.

Great Northern representative George O. Somers was in Somers during 1901 keeping track of the railroad's interests, the same year

the town built a post office. Both the new post office and the new town needed a name, and the well-thought-of railroad official was chosen as the namesake.

The Great Northern acquired the sawmill from O'Brien in 1906 when he left Somers. Eventually the name was changed to the Somers Lumber Company. Operating a day and night shift every 24 hours, the mill could produce 225,000 board feet of lumber each day.

The company employed most of Somers' 500 inhabitants. They all needed homes, which the company provided. According to Lou Bain and Frank Grubb in their book *Flathead Valley Yesteryear,* workers paid from $5 to $9 per month for rent. The lumber company furnished water and electricity. Workers were charged $1 per month for medical services from the company doctor.

In 1900 George Wilson constructed the first general store in Somers. The Flathead Commercial Company purchased it and did business there as the Normann and Smith Company. In 1933 Everit Sliter of Bigfork fame purchased the store interest of one of the original owners, and the store was named the People's Mercantile. Sliter became sole owner in 1937. Although not in the original location, the business still operates on Somers Road and today is a lumber and building supply center. The first hotel and eating house were under the roof of the McGovern ranch house in about 1900. The Somers Hotel and boarding house was constructed in 1901; also that year a company general store was opened by the Great Northern, and the post office was established.

Another historic Somers building is a popular restaurant today, which features fine dining. Tiebuckers Pub and Eatery is housed in the former office building of the Somers Lumber Company. Constructed in 1929, it shared space with the Great Northern, serving as its depot. The building has been put to many uses during the decades. According to the folks at Tiebuckers it's been a makeshift school, a mini-mall, a cafe and other businesses.

When growth was at its peak the Great Northern offered not only freight service, but twice-daily passenger service from Kalispell to Somers. Passenger traffic reached an all-time high about 1910 when the Flathead Indian Reservation, located at the southern end of Flathead Lake, was opened for homesteading. At that time passengers from either east or west were routed via the Great Northern to Somers, then ferried across Flathead Lake to Polson by steamboat, then carried south by the Northern Pacific Railroad—or vice versa. By the late 1920s traffic had dwindled considerably with the decline of the steamboat era, the advent of the automobile and the availability of public bus transportation, causing the Great Northern to abandon its rail passenger service.

Similarly, as Somers was no longer a transportation hub, the old order was passing in the lumber business. Plentiful timber was no longer available, and in 1948 the Great Northern regretfully shut down the vast mill.

As in days gone by, residents of the town and surrounding valley enjoy unlimited recreational activities on Flathead Lake. You can enjoy sunbathing or boating at the public park and boat launch at Somers Bay. The *Far West* offers boat cruises, some with meals, as well as private charters.

Nearby Lakeside, south of Somers, also makes available to travelers a public dock and park. The first settlers of Lakeside consisted of a group of Methodist church congregationalists, who in 1896 attempted to set up an educational camp. The Rev. W.W. Van Orsdel, known as "Brother Van," helped purchase some 240 acres of lakeshore property at Lakeside, reported historian R.C."Chuck" Robbin. The hopeful settlers called the camp "Chautauqua," namesake of the original Chautauqua site already established in New York state. Financial problems soon aborted the mission, and parts of the large tract were sold. John Stoner bought 25 acres and built a boarding house and opened Lakeside's first post office in 1901.

Lakeside nestles on the west lakeshore, where residents and visitors alike enjoy its spectacular lake and mountain panoramas. A growing village, Lakeside offers most services.

Columbia Falls

Columbia Falls, on U.S. Highway 2, reposes at the west entrance to Glacier National Park; travelers wind through Bad Rock Canyon to access the breathtaking and enchanting scenery of this renowned park. But like many Flathead Valley towns Columbia Falls grew up around the Great Northern Railway. Railroad tycoon Jim Hill decided in 1889 to extend the line from the eastern plains of Montana to Puget Sound, Washington, without the benefit of government land grants.

His major problem wasn't funding, but finding a feasible route over the Continental Divide through the Rocky Mountains. History records tales of other white men using the pass decades earlier. However, John F. Stevens, Great Northern railroad surveyor sent by James Hill to locate a passable route, is generally credited with discovering Marias Pass. In 1891 the railroad line was completed through the pass to Columbia Falls, then on to Kalispell.

The townsite of Columbia Falls had already been established several years earlier, as settlers were drawn to the area's good farmland and generous supply of timber. In addition, coal discovered up the North Fork of the Flathead River was mined in limited quantities and barged downstream through Demersville and onto Flathead Lake, then transported by the Northern Pacific Railroad.

The group of pioneers who established the village named it Columbia or Columbus. The first townsite was located down on the flats next to the Flathead River, but early settlers decided their town stood a better chance up on dryer ground and closer to the coming rails. Much of the town had relocated to the present site before the railroad steamed into town.

Although it is not clear how residents named the town Columbia, speculation has it being named for nearby Columbia Mountain, a long, horizontal mountain situated at the mouth of Bad Rock Canyon, a mile or so to the east. When first postmaster Jim Kennedy applied for a town name in 1891, he was declined the name Columbia since a town in Montana was already called Columbus. It was believed that such a similar name would cause confusion. Mrs. Kennedy actually named the town by tacking "Falls" onto it, although no falls existed there then.

With the railroad coming, a group of enterprising Butte, Montana, businessmen looked ahead to profit. Organizing the Northern International Improvement Company andspeculating that Columbia Falls would become the new division point for the railroad and land would be in high demand, they purchased the property from Mrs. Nellie LaFrombois, an Indian woman, for approximately $5000 and plotted it. Much of it was located in what would become the town's business district. Even railroad magnate Jim Hill thought the prices too steep, and he built the railroad on through to Kalispell, designating it the division point, instead. Kalispell citizens were sorely disappointed later when Hill moved the division point to Whitefish.

Moderate growth continued in Columbia Falls, the Valley's oldest town. Beatrice Macomber reports in *Columbia Falls Yester-Years* that in 1891 the small community sported 18 saloons, a general store, men's store, barbershop, flour mill, sawmill and lumber company and railroad depot. The year 1891 also marked the building of the town's first bank by James A.Talbott, prominent businessman who could be called the father of Columbia Falls. He and G.E. Gaylord, both members of the Northern International Improvement Company, built the sophisticated 31-room Gaylord Hotel, which burned in 1929. Talbott donated land for the first Episcopal church and first school, erected in 1892. Here he built his family home, a lavish mansion with eight fireplaces overlooking the Flathead River. Unfortunately, it was ravaged by fire in 1941.

A coup for the town, which in part made up for seeing the railroad division point given to Kalispell, was that Columbia Falls was chosen as the location for the "old soldier's home" in 1895, when Talbott's and the Northern International Improvement Company's offer to donate cash and equipment as well as acreage just outside Columbia Falls was accepted by the state board of review. Columbia Falls' bid was selected from among those of other towns throughout the state. The governor approved the decision, and the two-story structure was built for the sum of $9,985. Columbia Falls citizens also donated $10,000 toward the project. By the end of 1908 the home provided care for 88 residents. At first, the rules prohibited drinking and profanity, permitted smoking in rooms and required a bath at least once a week. Residents were signaled to rise at reveille and had to be in their rooms when taps played each night.

In 1909 citizens of Columbia Falls incorporated. The following year the modern amenities of electricity and telephone were

Flathead Valley and Glacier National Park Timeline

1810—Joseph Howse of the Hudson's Bay Co. spends winter of 1810-1811 in Flathead Valley, establishing company's first local trading post—Howse House—at north end of Flathead Lake.

1857—Trader Joe Ashley first to settle in upper Flathead Valley on Ashley Creek. In 1883 community of Ashley founded, one mile west of present-day Kalispell.

1862—Major gold strikes in Montana bring prospectors swarming to Glacier Park in search of mineral riches.

1885—First steamboat hauls freight and passengers up Flathead Lake, as the *Swan* sailboat is transformed into the *U.S. Grant* steamboat.

1887—Town of Demersville founded several miles south of Kalispell on Flathead River by Frenchtown merchant T.J. Demers.

1891—Great Northern Railway brings transcontinental rail service to the Valley. Great Northern establishes Kalispell Townsite Co. and names Kalispell new railway division point. Kalispell becomes Valley's leading town.

1893—Montana Legislature creates Flathead County from Missoula County.

1901—John O'Brien Lumber Company Mill built at Somers to manufacture ties for Great Northern railroad westward expansion. Somers becomes second largest town in Valley.

Guests enjoy an evening around the fire at Lake McDonald Lodge.

Credit: VIAD Corporation

1902—Townsite of Bigfork platted and filed by E.L. Sliter.

1902—Whitefish Townsite Co. established. Land surveyed and divided into lots.

1904—Main line of Great Northern moves from Kalispell to Whitefish for better routing by James J. Hill. Whitefish becomes new division point, which it remains today.

1905—Citizens vote to incorporate Whitefish.

1910—Glacier National Park created.

1910—Severe forest fires burn 3 million acres in Idaho and western Montana, including newly established Glacier Park.

1910—Flathead Indian Reservation opened for homesteading; Flathead Valley sees influx of pioneers.

1913—First of Glacier Park's Great Lodges built by Great Northern Railway at East Glacier.

1927—Great Northern depot is built in Whitefish and becomes symbol of Whitefish.

1929—"Half Moon" fire burns 100,000 acres, racing across Teakettle Mountain near Columbia Falls and into Glacier Park.

1929—First Great Northern passenger train, the famous "Empire Builder," passes west-bound through Whitefish.

1932—Waterton and Glacier parks become world's first international peace park.

1933—Dedication ceremony atop Logan Pass kicks off official opening of Glacier Park's scenic Going-to-the-Sun Road.

1935—Big Mountain's Hellroaring Ski Club founded.

1937—First golf club organizes in Whitefish.

1939—Izaak Walton Inn at Essex on south fringe of Glacier Park is built to serve Great Northern locomotives and rail worker crews. Filled with railroad memorabilia, the inn today caters to cross-country skiers and tourists.

1947—Big Mountain ski area incorporates and is run by Winter Sports Inc.

1950—A day's ski pass on Big Mountain costs $1.50.

1953—Hungry Horse Dam built. Structure is 564 feet high and is still the tenth-tallest dam in the United States.

1955—Anaconda Aluminum Plant built north of Columbia Falls. Today operated as Columbia Falls Aluminum Co., the plant produces aluminum for cans.

1960—Whitefish Winter Carnival is formed. Remains a big part of today's Whitefish winter scene.

1964—Huge flood hits north Flathead Valley and floods Evergreen. Sections of highway and rail lines wash away at Marias Pass.

1967—In unrelated incidents grizzlies in Glacier Park kill two campers in same night, which becomes known as the Night of the Grizzlies.

1976—Glacier National Park designated a World Biosphere Reserve.

1988—"Red Bench" fire burns 37,500 acres on west side of Glacier Park.

1990—Whitefish Stumptown Historical Society saves run-down railroad depot, restoring it much as it was when built in 1927.

1998—Blacktail Mountain Ski Area opens near Lakeside

installed in the town, and a sewer line was laid along Nucleus Avenue.

In its early years, the town's survival depended on the grain and lumber industries. Today, lumber still plays an important role in the well-being of the economy, with Plum Creek operating a sawmill and couple of plants in town and Stoltze Lumber Company running a nearby mill. Construction of the Hungry Horse Dam near the little town of Hungry Horse gave a shot in the arm to the economy in the early 1950s, and some workers stayed and put down roots.

Another industry important to Columbia Falls' economy has been the Columbia Falls Aluminum Co. north of town. Construction of the plant, originally the Anaconda Aluminum Plant, was completed in 1955. Today the plant employs more than 500 workers. Aluminum ingots-mostly for making cans-are processed and shipped to international markets.

Whitefish

When trappers penetrated the unexplored forests of the north Flathead Valley as early as the 1850s, they shared the long alpine lake that settles at the base of the Whitefish Mountain Range with Native Americans who lived in the vicinity. Trappers and early settlers came to call this lake Whitefish Lake, named for the rich supply of whitefish that had long provided a staple diet for the Indians. When a permanent town was founded in the present location, it also was called Whitefish.

By 1883 the first settlers, John Morton and Charles Ramsey, had hewn homes out of the primitive countryside, near the mouth of the Whitefish River. Ramsey also constructed a rooming house for hunters and anglers who came for the abundance of fish and wildlife at the lake. By the end of the decade lumbermen were lured to the Valley, but for a different reason—its dense timber stands. Loggers put Whitefish Lake to good use; nearby logs were cut and floated down the lake to the Whitefish River and then down the river to lumber mills in and around Kalispell. The first Whitefish sawmill was built by the Baker brothers, who played a prominent part in Whitefish's history. For a number of years logging and farming were the main livelihoods in Whitefish.

The early site of Whitefish—at the foot of Whitefish Lake—was moved to its present location to be nearer the Great Northern railroad. The Whitefish Townsite Company was established in 1902 by a group of four individuals, and the land surveyed and plotted. But it wasn't until the following year that articles of incorporation were filed for the townsite company. The Townsite Company hired loggers to cut the dense tree stands that spread over the townsite, and serious tree cutting began for the new railroad town. Although great progress was made, many stumps remained for a number of years after the trees were downed, earning the town the name "Stumptown." In 1905 townspeople voted to incorporate the village of Whitefish. The town council met for the first time, and the first census was gathered—the population of the boomtown was 950. Five years later citizens driving horse-drawn wagons down city streets still were forced to negotiate around tree stumps, so in 1910 the town council decided that prying out the offending stumps would be a good way for jail offenders to pay their debts. Thus, jailbirds carried out a major effort toward town beautification.

The Great Northern Railway main line had come to the Flathead in 1891. In 1901 Great Northern announced that Whitefish would be the new division point on the main line because it offered more feasible routing. In 1903 a spur line was added that linked Columbia Falls with Whitefish, and James Hill pulled division headquarters out of Kalispell, leaving that rival community fuming for years. The steel ribbon was rerouted in a more northerly route from Columbia Falls via Whitefish to Rexford, connecting to Libby and points west. Thus Hill eliminated the difficult current route, which crossed the Salish Mountains west of Kalispell. The "Columbia Falls Cutoff" was completed in 1904 from Rexford, Montana, to Whitefish.

Another reason Hill chose Whitefish as division headquarters was its proximity to Whitefish Lake. The lake provided a water supply for the railroad's steam-powered equipment, and crews of sawyers hauled out blocks of ice for Great Northern's icehouses. A natural means of refrigeration, the ice was used to cool fruit in the fruit express cars. Mechanical refrigeration later replaced the need for ice storage, and in the late 1970s the giant icehouses in Whitefish were demolished.

Whitefish Lake and River also provided citizens with water. Frank Baker and a Mr. Rile hauled wagonloads laden with jostling barrels of water down bumpy city streets to provide residents a water supply; cost averaged 25 cents a barrel. The Baker brothers (there were five) reportedly owned much of the land adjoining the town site. They gave liberally of their labor and money to help build a solid foundation for the fledgling town. Baker Avenue is named after them.

One of the town's first businesses was a tent saloon, with two entrepreneurs peddling whiskey to tree cutters clearing trees downtown on Central Avenue and Second Street. The town saw a building boom from 1903 through 1904. A mood of optimism prevailed. "By 1910, Whitefish had 1,479 people," Betty Schafer and Mary Engelter said in *Stump Town to Ski Town, a History of Whitefish*, "a business district primarily along Central Avenue and Second Street, a water system, a light and power plant, telephones, some wooden sidewalks, and a couple of crosswalks, some graded streets, some filled gullies." The council was discussing sewers and parking. Civilization, indeed, had arrived.

Almost a hundred years later many original downtown buildings remain in use, offering food, shopping and services in this thriving resort town. The charm of yesterday is all around, and visitors are invited to take a historical downtown walking tour.

The heart of Whitefish has always been the Great Northern Railway. (Later it became the Burlington Northern Railroad.) The first official passenger train cruised by the train platform in October 1904 westbound to Seattle. The steam-powered train was on time, and the town's citizens were on hand to cheer. At the same time, the city was formally proclaimed the railroad division point.

Beginning about 1913 passenger trains bound through Whitefish followed the southern boundary of Glacier National Park during daylight hours so that summer travelers could enjoy the scenery while crossing the Continental Divide. The daytime schedule remains thus today, even after Amtrak took over passenger service in 1971. The famous "Empire Builder" passenger train rolled into Whitefish for the first time in 1929, and today it still carries both east- and westbound passengers past the park.

The first train depot built in 1906 was replaced in 1927 with a building described as English Tudor style. The multi-story structure merged the half-timbered Tudor style with a Swiss-chalet look. The Swiss-chalet architectural vernacular was popular for the lodges being built at the time in Glacier National Park. By 1990 the aging depot needed refurbishing, and the Burlington Northern Railroad do-

nated it to the Whitefish Stumptown Historical Society for restoration. (The Burlington Northern Railroad was formed in 1970 from the merging of the Great Northern Railway, the Northern Pacific Railroad and numerous others.) The renovation of the treasured landmark returned its appearance and character to that of 1927, while adding modern amenities. Be sure to stop by the historical society museum located there—it's on the walking tour—to see the town's railroad history.

You'll see the "Rocky the Goat" logo, which the Great Northern chose for its trademark symbol in 1923. This author remembers as a child seeing "Rocky the Goat" emblazoned on Great Northern freight cars, a familiar sight for decades before the merger that created Burlington Northern ended Rocky's ride through the Flathead.

If the railroad was the heart of Whitefish, The Big Mountain was—and is—its soul. Hiking and huckleberry picking have long been pleasurable pursuits on this huge mountain. Snow-encrusted trees called "snow ghosts" are a famous winter oddity found up on The Mountain. Skiers using homemade skis found a way to ski the mountain as early as 1935, without the benefit of a resort company to hack out and groom trails. The Hellroaring Ski Club formed in 1937. A decade later—in 1947—two entrepreneurs from Great Falls and many interested Whitefish community members financed a fledgling resort operation called Winter Sports, Inc. Winter Sports still owns and operates The Big Mountain Ski and Summer Resort.

Big Mountain is buried in 330-plus average inches of annual snowfall and offers a wide variety of terrain—some 3,000 skiable acres—for great downhill skiing. The resort, just a snowball's throw from Glacier National Park, continues to be a popular draw and a continued source of economic stability for the small resort-and-retirement community cradled in the valley below.

Kalispell

Kalispell may have been cut off the Great Northern Railway's main line when the division point went north to Whitefish in 1904, but

Going-to-the-Sun Road

Going-to-the-Sun Road cuts through the heart of Glacier National Park, providing most visitors with their best access to the subalpine and alpine regions of the park. The road winds up from the forests of the west side and the prairies of the east to top out at Logan Pass. Magnificent views are standard fare all the way along this winding mountain road. In itself an engineering feat, the road was completed in 1932 and opened to the public in 1933.

Many interesting episodes illustrate the difficulties of building the road. Considering the amount of blasting that had to be done, the steep angles at which the rock was worked, the state of technology, and the harsh environment, it is probably a testimony

to safety that only three men died during its construction. But more than one man quit this job, even though it was during the Great Depression when work was so hard to come by. One story tells of how, during the construction of the 408-foot-long east side tunnel, workers had to shimmy down a hundred feet of rope over a cliff to get to the job site. Once there, the work included removing the excavated rock from the tunnel by hand—it was impossible to get any power equipment down the steep slope. In another case, when preparing to blast one particularly large cliff just east of the Loop (the hairpin turn on the west side), workers wore wool socks over their boots to prevent sparks! In 1931, a Caterpillar tractor slipped off the road and rolled 200 feet down the mountainside. Its operator drove it back up with only minor damage.

The difficult environment continues to affect Going-to-the-Sun Road today. Opening

Credit: VIAD Corporation

Cars flooded Going-to-the-Sun Road even in the early days of Glacier National Park.

the road over Logan Pass each spring is a major undertaking that begins in early April. Plows, a rotary plow, and a front-end loader begin their task of clearing the snow at low elevations, gradually working their way higher. The speed at which the road can be plowed depends on the depth of the winter's snowpack and spring weather conditions. Rain in the valleys can fall as snow up high, so that sometimes a stretch of road needs to be cleared more than once. Avalanches are inevitable in the springtime; avalanche watchers keep their eyes trained on the slopes above the road, looking for any sign of movement that could hazard the road crew and equipment. Fog can make it difficult to see above the road, making it impossible for avalanche watchers to assess safety and forcing plowing to end for the day. On occasion crews have had to plow their way home when an avalanche occurred behind them. As the plow crew works its way toward Logan Pass, the snow gets deeper and deeper. The last part of Going-to-the-Sun Road to be plowed is usually the Big Drift, which has measured as much as 80 feet deep when plowing began. The Big Drift must be surveyed each year so that the plows are sure they are plowing the road and not anything else! Going-to-the-Sun Road usually opens all the way over Logan Pass sometime between the last week of May and the third week of June. At that time the snowpack at Logan Pass Visitor Center is typically still about twelve feet deep. In the fall, the road is closed down from Logan Pass in sections, beginning the third Monday in October unless weather has already closed it. Stretches of Going-to-the-Sun Road are plowed all winter along Lake McDonald and St. Mary Lake.

Maintaining the 60-year-old road is a challenge too. Going-to-the-Sun Road is on the National Register of Historic Places, and preserving its historic character is one of the Park Service's goals. Over the last ten years, reconstruction of the road has begun and will continue for sometime into the future. Although modern technology has advanced far beyond that which built the road, reconstruction is still in a very difficult environment with a short season. In addition, visitation to the park—and the number of vehicles that drive Going-to-the-Sun Road—has increased well beyond anything that could have been imagined in the 1930s. Thus rebuilding the road is no small problem—it has to occur during the peak season of the short alpine summer, when people visit, animals inhabit their mountain homes, and plants must bud, flower, and set seed. You may encounter delays due to construction during your drive over the pass—ask at the front gate as you enter; generally delays are short. Should you be stopped, why not take the opportunity to turn off your car's engine, enjoy the view, have a snack, and step outside for a moment?

Logan Pass is the highlight of Going-to-the-Sun Road for many. It can be difficult to park here in the middle of the day; try coming before 10:30 a.m., or visiting in the late afternoon—daylight is long in the northern summer. Or consider taking the park shuttle up and back from lower elevation—leave the driving to someone else and you'll enjoy the view that much more! Both GPI and Sun Tours offer bus trips that stop at Logan Pass. However you arrive, you'll admire the Garden Wall, the Hanging Gardens, and the view in 360 degrees on both sides of the Continental Divide. You might walk to Hidden Lake Overlook—look for ptarmigan nesting under the boardwalk, as well as the goats—or perhaps strike off down the Highline for as far as takes your fancy. Or spend a few minutes with binoculars just scoping the slopes for mountain goats, bighorn sheep, or grizzly bears—all of which frequent Logan Pass.

Park statistics indicate that the average visit to Glacier National Park is about two hours—the time it takes to drive Going-to-the-Sun Road (see loop tour description in Attractions). But after that, the average visit jumps to four days—once you get a taste of this place, you'll want to come back for more. Going-to-the-Sun Road is the just the beginning.

the town did not go bust, as had other early towns in the Flathead Valley that were by-passed by the railroad. Kalispell managed to remain the financial and commercial hub of the Valley.

Back in 1891 when James Hill decided to relocate the division point from Whitefish to Kalispell, he sent Charles E. Conrad to find a site for Great Northern's facilities and the Kalispell Townsite Company. Conrad purchased part of a homestead on the west side of Kalispell. The land was surveyed, platted and recorded under the name Hill chose: "Kalispel," derived from the Pend d'Oreille Indian language. Kalispell has at least two meanings: "camas" or "prairie above the lake".

Land speculators had also bought up nearby ranches and homesteads and divided them into lots in anticipation of the railroad coming. In spring 1891 when newly divided lots came on the market, an unheard of $100,000 worth of lots was snapped up overnight. Inside lots on Main Street measuring 25 feet were priced at $1,000, while corner lots cost as much as $1,250. The next month the first building was constructed.

Everyone eagerly anticipated the coming of the railroad, and December 31, 1891, was a red-letter day for the town. Historian Henry Elwood quoted a special edition of *The Kalispell Graphic* newspaper: "After eight months of waiting anxiety, the most devout and earnest wish of the people of Kalispell is consummated. The iron horse has at last snorted in the Garden of Eden of Montana. The locomotive pealed forth its welcome sound to the people of Kalispell." A silver spike was driven to hail the triumph amidst a wildly cheering crowd, and the band played "Yankee Doodle." A parade, barbecue and public ball were all part of the festivities. The first passenger train steamed into Kalispell in summer 1892, complete with a dining car and sleeper, a colonist sleeper, a combination smoker and day coach and baggage car.

Kalispell enjoyed boom years from 1899 through 1901, with many residences and large brick buildings constructed.

Unfortunately, the status of being Great Northern division headquarters didn't last more than about a dozen years. Jim Hill in 1904 relocated the division point north to Whitefish because of the difficult route west of Kalispell over the Salish Mountains. It was a sad day when the last train, bearing Great Northern railroad crews relocating to Whitefish, wailed a farewell salute to Kalispell. The railway kept the branch line train connecting Kalispell with Columbia Falls, nicknamed the "Gallopin' Goose." But in 1950 the railroad discontinued that train, too, ending Kalispell's passenger train service.

Flathead County had been created out of Missoula County in 1893, and Kalispell had been voted county seat over Columbia Falls the following year. This helped to keep Kalispell stable when the railroad abandoned it. All county government business was conducted from Kalispell. By 1903 a permanent, three-story brick courthouse had been completed; it still is used today. (U.S. Highway 93 splits around it on South Main Street.) The town had a solid foundation—it had incorporated in 1892, and citizens had elected city officials. Water and electric light utilities were already created, as well as a post office and fire department. By 1904 a new city hall was operating, and progress had brought a library, hospital and numerous churches.

On the commercial side Kalispell counted at least three national banks, stores representing almost every trade—from meat markets to furniture, and from hardware to photographers—and several posh hotels, including The West and the Grand Central. The fertile farmlands and lumber industry surrounding Kalispell also provided the town a solid anchor.

The first buildings were mostly one-story structures built of wood. But building codes became stricter. "Because of fire codes, commercial-district buildings were later built of brick or other fireproof material," Kathryn McKay said in her book *Looking Back: A Pictorial History of the Flathead Valley, Montana.* "These brick buildings typically had corbeling or terra cotta decorations. Some earlier buildings had native rock pilasters, sills, and lintels. Cloth awnings shaded the shop windows, and most stores had recessed entries and glass block or leaded glass transoms." Several Kalispell-area brickyards furnished "common" brick, used locally.

Many of the historic downtown buildings

are used today. Among the noteworthy is the old Kalispell Hotel on Main Street, now the Kalispell Grand Hotel, built in 1911 to serve upscale travelers. In the early days rooms cost $2 per night. After being closed, parts of the gracious landmark were remodeled, including the lobby, and it was re-opened in 1991.

Just across the street stands the McIntosh Opera House, erected in the late 1890s. Its expansive upper floor served as stage for many kinds of entertainment—plays, recitals, music programs, dances, lodge meetings, wrestling matches and other events. The presentation "Uncle Tom's Cabin" drew one of the biggest-ever audiences—1132 people. In 1905 when it was pressed into service as a gymnasium, you could watch basketball games on the top floor. Although the dancehall-cum-basketball-court lies vacant today, the main floor contains a busy western store, while an antique mall sprawls in the basement.

Another prominent old building was the Kalispell Mercantile (KM Building). The mercantile originated in 1888 in Demersville as part of the Missoula Mercantile, and was first operated from a tent. The fine department store was known for its quality, variety, customer service and staff product knowledge, pointed out historians Lou Bain and Frank Grubb. In 1892 it was moved from Demersville to Kalispell, with its final location being First Avenue East and Second Street. Original store size was just 50-feet-by-80-feet, but the store eventually grew to eight times that size. Known as northwest Montana's largest store, the Missoula Mercantile offered groceries, hardware and paint, appliances, china, farm tools, plumbing, sporting goods, mill supplies, and even firewood. Eventually the name was changed to the Kalispell Mercantile, and over the decades many Kalispell residents vied for a chance to work at the popular store. Modern competition forced the store to close its doors in 1980. Various businesses have occupied it since. Today the historic structure is being restored to its turn-of-the-century character. Original stained glass windows were re-installed as part of an exterior facelift. Interior restoration that provides retail and business space is mostly completed. In 1999 a group of three local women formed the Kalispell Repertory Theater. It will occupy the former ballroom, with a stage and cabaret entertainment area, infusing the old building with new life. Early black-and-white photos displayed on first floor arcade walls are a timeline to the past.

Late in the 1990s two other treasured downtown buildings were renovated. The old Central School, opened in 1895, has been thoroughly overhauled, with pains taken to match original materials and to retain the building's integrity. The major renovation was made possible by $2.5 million in funds from the City of Kalispell and the leadership of the Northwest Montana Historical Society. From 1929 to 1969 the public school was the junior high. Then the Flathead Valley Community College took over the building. When the college moved to a new campus in 1990, Central School's doors closed. In 1999, heralding in a new century, the building has re-opened as the Central School Museum, A Heritage, Education and Cultural Center. Visitors are encouraged to stop by for a glimpse of the Valley's history.

Nearby at 15 Depot Park, off Main Street, stands the original Great Northern Railway Depot. The Kalispell Chamber of Commerce, among other businesses, operates from the depot. The chamber celebrated with an open house in December 1998, showing off newly refurbished offices and conference room. Respect for the depot's past was kept as the focus during the work, while a Montana-style casualness and comfort was incorporated.

These and other charming buildings are visible on the Main Street District walking tour. A second walking tour on the east side routes visitors by beautiful old residences, many built from 1900 to about 1920. Pick up a historical walking tour brochure at the Chamber of Commerce.

Not to be missed is the Conrad Mansion, built by Charles E. Conrad (see our Attractions chapter). James Hill had asked Conrad to take charge of the Great Northern's Kalispell Townsite Company, and Conrad is considered to be the founding father of Kalispell. A prominent businessman, Charles, with his brother William, established one of the town's first banks, the Conrad National Bank. Charles purchased 72 acres overlooking the east side of the Valley and built the Conrad Mansion.

The historic Central School building in Kalispell is now a museum.

Designed in the early Norman style, the mansion featured shingle cladding on the exterior. The unusual home contains 23 main rooms and eight fireplaces. The opulent house belonged to the family until 1975, when it was gifted to the city. The house has been restored, and turn-of-the-century antiques fill the rooms. Summer guided tours of the Conrad Mansion are available.

Today Kalispell remains the economic hub of the Flathead Valley. Tourism at nearby Glacier National Park continues to bring the

INSIDERS' TIP

Locals refer to the Flathead Valley as the Flathead, which derived its name from the Flathead Indians.

No one knows for sure how the Flathead Indians came by their name, although several theories exist. A popular one is that when famous explorers Lewis and Clark came across the Indians near Hamilton, Montana, they saw some visiting Chinook Indians from the West Coast. The Chinooks flattened their children's temples with headboards on their papooses (cradles strapped to the back to carry babies). The explorers mistakenly called them all Flatheads. Another theory has it that other Salish Indians (a group of Northwest Indians whom the Flatheads belong to) had wedge-shaped heads, and the Flatheads didn't; they had flat heads.

town a steady, if modest, income. Lumber and agriculture are still major industries. In the mid-1990s out-of-state retirees "discovered" the Valley; this continued influx has become a viable industry.

The Flathead has experienced a building boom during the mid-l990s. The January/February 1999 issue of *Mountain Sports & Living* magazine, formerly *Snow Country*, rated Kalispell the number one best mountain town in the country in which to live. The job market is not as glowing as the magazine reported, however. Montana ranks last place in the nation for average wages per job, a ranking the governor and others are striving to change.

Although the job market is frustrating for many, most of us stay here for all of the reasons we hold dear—beautiful scenery, outdoor opportunities, close ties to family and friends, fresh air, and not too much noise or overcrowding. Yet. We are seeing growing pains, but living in the Flathead Valley remains a treasured lifestyle. And Glacier National Park is an enduring reason for visitors to come.

Glacier National Park

"Here, serrated ridges and horn-shaped peaks reign over a jumble of turquoise lakes, waterfalls, cascades, river valleys, hanging gardens, and alpine meadows. Born of geologic and glacial violence, this random landscape couldn't be more perfect had it been designed and executed by Michelangelo. Like the ocean, its sheer scope has a way of putting humanity in its place."

—George Bird Grinnell, *Grinnell's Glacier: George Bird Grinnell and Glacier National Park*

Rivers of ice carved the craggy pinnacles of the Rocky Mountains during a succession of ice ages occurring during the past two or three million years. About 10,000 years ago during the last ice age an enormous cap of ice several thousand feet thick and miles long covered Glacier National Park's high country. As it melted, it heaved down the canyons, sculpting new shapes and gouging out glacial lakes. The melted remains of the last ice age have long since shriveled up. Today's "new" glaciers formed sometime after the last ice age ended. They are puny compared to the ice mantle that smothered the Park eons ago. In fact, they are shrinking—they are smaller than when they were mapped in the early 1900s. But Glacier Park remains an excellent natural setting in which to view the handiwork of glaciers.

The fierce Indian tribe of the northern plains who gained dominion over the others after the 1750s was the Blackfeet tribe. (The name Blackfeet came from an early group, who after walking through a burned-over prairie, met another tribe, who called them Blackfeet, explained C.W. Buchholtz in his history of Glacier Park, *Man In Glacier*. The name also may have resulted from the black color of the soles of their moccasins.) The agressive Piegan branch of the Blackfeet tribe protected its bison hunting grounds on the east side of the northern Rocky Mountains against other invading tribes, including the Kutenai, Flathead and Kalispel Indians, who inhabited the west side. These Indians traversed Glacier's mountain passes to hunt for buffalo every year on the eastern plains. The feared Blackfeet retaliated by crossing the mountains and viciously raiding their camps, further establishing their supremacy.

It was mostly the Piegan who regularly used the trails of Glacier Park. Although extremely war-like, the Blackfeet were a very spiritual people. They, and members of other tribes, revered the mountains of Glacier and Waterton parks, believing them home to the spirits. Many visited there to hold vision quests. In Glacier's northeast corner looms Chief Mountain, a lone symbol of the powerful medicine that Indians believe stirs in these mystical mountains.

Breaking the backbone of these crusaders of the plains was one unlikely factor—fashion. Plentiful in nearby mountain streams, the beaver attracted white trappers because it brought them top dollar for top hats. White traders and trappers established a permanent trading relationship with the Blackfeet by the 1780s, and the white man's foothold spelled the decline of the tribe. Captain Meriwether

Lewis explored the headwaters of the Marias River on the return trip of the Lewis and Clark Expedition in 1806. His party viewed the front range of Glacier Park's mountains, but for various reasons was unable to explore farther. The expedition stimulated additional interest in the Missouri region and Rocky Mountains, especially among the fur trade.

Finian MacDonald, a Scotsman, and two other traders were the first white men recorded to enter the lands encompassing present-day Glacier Park in 1810, Buchholtz said. Attacked by Blackfeet at Marias Pass, the party survived, but this episode convinced other fur traders to choose safer routes across the Rockies. By the 1850s more white men ventured into the area whose purposes included: government surveys to mark the international boundary between the United States and Canada; bringing Christianity to the Indians; and finding a transcontinental railroad route.

Major gold strikes in Montana in 1862 brought prospectors scouring Glacier's mountainsides in search of mineral wealth. Another rush to stake mining claims occurred soon after the Blackfeet sold the east side of the park to the federal government. Gold, copper, quartz—even oil and coal—attracted those hoping for a lucky strike. Despite the initial promise, nothing was discovered in sufficient commerical quantities, and soon after the turn of the century mining and drilling interest greatly waned.

The Blackfeet managed to dominate the area until the 1870s. By then the U.S. Army, episodes of smallpox, illegal whiskey proffered by whiskey traders, and the irrepressible surge of white men into their territory, all combined to break the power of the warring tribe. The decimation of great herds of bison, the tribe's main food source, brought quick starvation. (The shaggy beasts were annihilated by 1882.) Anticipating a flood of American homesteaders and hoping to gain peace among local Indian tribes, Isaac Stevens, governor of the Territory of Washington (which included the Flathead Valley and Glacier Park), talked the Kootenai, Flathead and Kalispel Indians of the park's west side into settling on a reservation on the southern half of Flathead Lake. Thus Glacier's west side became public lands. Two proponents of the

Blackfeet intervened in their welfare. James Willard Schultz, an American who lived among the Blackfeet, called their plight to the attention of George Bird Grinnell, prominent editor of *Forest and Stream* magazine. After Grinnell's visit to the reservation in 1885, his political influence helped increase government food and supplies.

In 1895 the Blackfeet sold the Ceded Strip—all of Glacier Park east of the Continental Divide—to the federal government. The remaining Blackfeet land—the Blackfeet Reservation—borders the east boundary of the park. Names of Indian legends and chiefs were given to many landscape features in the park by Schultz and Grinnell.

Protection for a Pristine Wilderness

When George Bird Grinnell visited the starving Blackfeet, he was introduced to the St. Mary Lakes region. With James Schultz and an Indian as guides, he hunted and explored. Excited about the area, the editor of *Forest and Stream* magazine returned back east and wrote a number of essays about his experiences. Grinnell returned many times. His articles extolled the exceptional scenery and wild game hunting out west, which appealed to wealthy hunters, who further exploited the area.

Despite this use of the resource, Grinnell—and a handful of other proponents—came to believe that this special place should be protected. By 1891 a national conservation movement prompted the U.S. Congress to allow establishment of national forest "reserves" (later called national forests.) Glacier Park was first protected as a forest reserve. But Grinnell's intent was to see the area established as a national park, and he lobbied to that end for 10 years. He was the most influential advocate in the founding of the park. Promoting his cause in a 1901 article in *Century* magazine, he bestowed the name "The Crown of the Continent" on the magnificent wilderness. His cause was furthered by the support of Great Northern Railway officials.

who saw tourism in the park as a way to promote use of their transcontinental train service.

By 1910 the period of heavy exploitation of the park's natural resources had pretty much ended. That year President Taft signed the bill to create Glacier National Park, and 1,600 square miles of wilderness were preserved. Today just over l million acres are protected within park boundaries. First superintendent was Major William R. Logan. Waterton Lakes Forest Park, to the north of Glacier in Alberta, Canada, already had been established in 1895.

The act that created Glacier Park called for "preserving the park in a state of nature." But attempting to please everyone, the U.S. Congress also mandated that the park provide a "pleasure ground for the benefit and enjoyment of the people." Indeed, early-day emphasis was mostly on the value of recreational opportunities. The act also permitted mining, private land ownership, railroad routes and harvesting dead and downed timber.

The Great Lodges

The Great Northern already carried passengers through the Glacier Park area before it was designated a park. To serve railroad travelers the first private accommodations were built at the foot of Lake McDonald. The tourist cabins, built by Milo Apgar and Charlie Howe, were the beginnings of the village of Apgar. Escorted tours were available on the sparkling lake. This was the beginning of early-day tourism in the park.

In 1895 George Snyder built a two-story hotel at the present site of Lake McDonald Lodge. Later John and Olive Lewis acquired the property. (Legend has it John won it in a poker game.) The Lewises moved the first structure and commissioned a lodge to be built on the original site. The structure was to be in keeping with the style and grandeur of the other lodges being built in the park, only on a smaller scale. The Swiss-style architecture was similar to Great Northern's lodges, which were constructed of stone and log. Opened in 1914 as the only private hotel in the park, the Lewis Glacier Hotel operated

several decades before it was purchased by the National Park Service and became the present-day Lake McDonald Lodge.

Soon after the park was established, the Great Northern embarked on a flurry of building construction. Setting out to create a playground for the rich, Louis Hill, son of railroad tycoon James J. Hill, directed the building of several huge, rustic lodges within the park to attract tourists. A networking system of lodges and eight backcountry chalets were spaced a convenient day's horseback ride apart. (Horses and boats were the main method of seeing the park's splendors.)

The Great Northern began an enthusiastic advertising campaign with colorful railroad timetables depicting scenes of Glacier National Park. "See America First" became its slogan. First-class scenery required first-class accommodations, Louis Hill believed, and the great lodges of the park provided every luxury. In this way the Great Northern became Glacier Park's first concessionaire. Concessions were managed and operated by a subsidiary of the Great Northern, the Glacier Park Hotel Company.

First of the extraordinary hotels, the Glacier Park Lodge, was erected in 1913. Almost immediately it proved inadequate to house the great number of park visitors. (An annex soon doubled the original size.) Built at East Glacier, the lodge served as eastern gateway to the park for arriving Great Northern passenger trains. It was modeled after the Forestry Building that was constructed for the 1905 Portland, Oregon, Lewis and Clark Exposition Sixty trees were used in construction of the mammoth lodge, which the Great Northern hauled from Washington and Oregon—only one or two per flatcar, since each weighed about 15 tons. Measuring 36 to 42 inches in diameter, the bark-covered Douglas-firs gave structural support in the lobby, while the cedars were incorporated into exterior verandas.

Equally as impressive was the Many Glacier Hotel. The park's largest chalet, it was a rustic showplace situated in breathtaking surroundings. It sat at the edge of a crystalline lake rimmed by chiseled peaks. Hill also built the Prince of Wales Hotel in Waterton (Canada).

Two of the park's original eight backcountry chalets remained in operation through 1992, and then they were closed by the National Park Service because of inadequate water and sewage disposal systems. Granite Park Chalet was upgraded and reopened in 1997, while Sperry Chalet is scheduled to re-open in summer 1999. The ninth chalet is outside the park's west entrance at Belton. Belton Chalet is being renovated under private ownership. Today the main chalet and two cabins are open to accommodate tourists.

The lodges and chalets enjoyed phenomenal popularity for several decades. When the automobile appeared on the scene, however, it precipitated long-term changes. Travel through this splendid wilderness was no longer the exclusive domain of the rich, but could be enjoyed by your everyday person with a "tin lizzy." Motoring became a popular way to see Glacier Park. Use of the backcountry chalets, previously only accessible by horseback or foot, declined. In response to a growing need, the National Park Service opened public campgrounds. Business at the chalets and lodges dropped off. In addition, railroad traffic decreased. All this added up to capital losses for Great Northern. World War II would sharply curtail visitation to Glacier, and many of the park's facilities would be shut down. Most of the backcountry chalets deteriorated badly and were never re-opened.

Going-to-the-Sun Road

A ribbon of road 52 miles long connecting the east and west sides of the park has for 66 years transported millions of adventurous travelers up Logan Pass over the Continental Divide—the backbone of the Rocky Mountains—and down the other side. The road seems to be merely an eyebrow of a trail chiseled out of limestone, which hugs the mountainside. Building it was an engineering feat, rife with challenges. Steep climbs, snow avalanches, falling rock and extremely steep dropoffs all contributed to the grueling nature of its construction;. two men were killed from falls, and one from falling rock.

In 1933 when Going-to-the-Sun Road opened park visitation jumped a whopping 44 percent—mostly from automobile touring. Today, an average of 1.8 million visitors travel through Glacier National Park annually. The picturesque, antiquated road needs needs to be reconstructed if it is to continue to accommodate the volume of traffic that floods it every summer. Park officials report that work will continue during summer season of 1999 and for the next two or three years to upgrade the worst areas—Avalanche Creek and the West Tunnel to Siyeh Bend. The road will not close, but expect delays. Rebuilding parts of the road won't change its original appearance or character.

The Park Today

In 1932 Glacier National Park and Waterton Lakes National Park, its Canadian neighbor, were named the world's first International Peace Park. Only a strip cut through dense timber designates the international boundary line, and managers from both parks maintain a strong working relationship and spirit of cooperation.

During the 1960s wilderness resource conservation gained renewed public awareness and favor. The Wilderness Act of 1964 provided for large natural areas of Glacier and other parks to be delineated "wilderness," and prohibited further development. Because of its unique natural and cultural qualities, Glacier Park was designated a World Biosphere Reserve in 1976. As always, park administrators continue to struggle with achieving a balance between protecting the resource and public use of it.

By the late 1990s the national Leave No Trace program gained strong momentum among many government agencies. Implemented in Glacier Park, the program promotes responsible outdoor use ethics to the public to help us all preserve the pristine landscape of Glacier National Park.

The lakes and mountains of western Montana dominate the lives of all who have ever lived in or traveled through this region.

Attractions

54

"Give a month at least to this precious reserve. The time will not be taken from the sum of your life. Instead of shortening, it will indefinitely lengthen it and make you truly immortal."

—John Muir

So wrote John Muir of Glacier National Park, which he also called "the most care-killing scenery" on the continent. Even if you can't take a month to explore Glacier Country, you'll find that each day offers countless opportunities to enjoy this magnificent place.

The lakes and mountains of western Montana dominate the lives of all who have ever lived in or traveled through this region. The lakes and rivers have been travel routes for Indian canoes and nineteenth-century steamboats; prehistoric trails have become paved roads for commerce and travelers; the mountains are ancient places of worship as well as a place of unparalleled backcountry recreation. For us, living and traveling throughout Glacier Country today, the number of places to visit is huge—and it encompasses everything from theme parks to shops to historic buildings.

The "Attractions" represented here are chosen for one of a few reasons. Some offer a better view of the area—the gondola ride to the top of Big Mountain or Far West Cruises, for example. Others allow you to immerse yourself in the area's past, whether the history of the Plains Indians or a 19th-century logging town. Some "Attractions" are included because they are near and dear to the hearts of local residents—when you see the lines of folks in swimsuits waiting their turn at the top of the Big Sky Waterslide, you'll want to be there, too! The section closes with two driving loops that will take you through a good cross-section of Glacier Country—be sure to check out the book's recommendations for each community along the way. Although the

driving time for each of these routes is a matter of hours, each of them makes a great day-trip. And, like John Muir, you may find that a few days is not enough...

Although the information here is as up-to-date and complete as possible, things may change. It's always good to call ahead and confirm prices and schedules.

So explore Glacier Country, and don't hesitate to turn off the road when something intriguing comes along!

Columbia Falls to Browning, U.S. Highway 2

Big Sky Waterpark and Mini-Golf
P.O. Box 2311, Columbia Falls
• (406) 892-5025 • Located at the
junction of U.S. 2 and Montana 206

Hot summer day in the Big Sky? For kids of all ages, there's no easier, more fun way to cool down than to spend the afternoon at the Big Sky Waterslide. You'll hardly be able to decide where to go next—the Big Splash River Ride, the Seven-Story Geronimo Speed Slide, the Roller Coaster Bullet Speed Slide, or the four Twister Waterslides. And Water Wars—a catapulting water balloon game—get your little brother going on this! For the very young or mellower crowd, minislides and a huge whirlpool may be just the ticket.

And, should you prefer to stay *dry,* the Waterpark offers Miniature Greens Adventure Golf, a video arcade, beach volleyball, and a 1938 antique carousel that is quickly becoming a favorite. Bring your own picnic or pick up some snacks and drinks at the concession stand. Changing rooms have free lockers, and locks may be rented.

The Big Sky Waterpark is open from apoximately Memorial Day to Labor Day, 7 days a week. For full day admission to the Waterslide, the adult fee (ages 12 and over) is $12.95; ages 4–11, $10.95; a nonrider admission is available at $5.00. Twilight admissions—from 4:00–8:00 PM—are: adults, $8.50; ages 4–11, $7.00; and nonriders, $4.00. Admission to mini-golf for adults is $4.75; ages 4–11, $3.75. Tickets for the antique carousel are .75 each, 3 tickets for $2.00, or a book of 10 tickets for $5.00. Group rates are available; please call to arrange group visits in advance.

House of Mystery
7800 U.S. Highway 2 East, Columbia Falls
• (406) 892-1210 • Located just north of the junction of U.S. 2 and Montana 206

"Montana's only vortex"—a natural phenomenon, not understood by science, causes the laws of physics not to be broken, but, well, to be *bent*...you can grow or shrink by moving three feet forward or back...birds can't fly...trees grow in strange shapes and angles...and you can actually feel the strange forces at work...

In a few such places in the world, nature's laws seem to be suspended. Is it sun spots, geological faults, or crossed gravitational fields that cause these effects? No one really knows, but bring your camera and document your experience for the amazement of your friends and relatives!

The House of Mystery is a local landmark as well as good family fun. Cold drinks, snacks, and picnic spots are available as well as a gift shop and antiques. The House of Mystery is open from 9 AM to 9 PM, April through October. Entrance is $4.00 for adults (ages 13 and over), $3.00 for ages 6-12, and free for children 5 and under.

Hungry Horse Dam
Located just south of U.S. Highway 2 at Hungry Horse

At 564 feet high and with a crest length of 2,115 feet across, the Hungry Horse Dam dwarfs every other structure in Glacier Country. Water cascades over the spillway to drop as much as 490 feet into the South Fork of the Flathead River. The capacity of the spill-way is 50,000 cubic feet per second, and the reservoir has a total capacity of 3,468,000 acre-feet. The principal power benefit comes from the dam's storage of water from the spring run-off for later release when needed. On average, this water generates 4.6 billion kilowatt-hours of power as it passes through a series of 19 downstream power plants. The numbers are impressive—and so is visiting the dam.

Tours of the Hungry Horse Dam run 7 days a week from Memorial Day to Labor Day. The free guided tours leave the Visitor Center at the top of the hour from 10 AM until 4 PM all day long, with the tour itself lasting from 45 minutes to an hour. Visitors will walk across the dam and go down into the power plant to see the generators. Guides talk about the building of the dam, production of electricity, the Columbia River system, and fish and other issues. A movie is an option if the group wishes. The tour is handicap accessible.

Alberta Visitor Centre
West Glacier
• (406) 888-5743

If Glacier Country is part of your grand tour of the Rockies, the Alberta Visitor Centre in West Glacier is a great place to start learning more about Wild Rose Country to the north. And even if West Glacier is as far as you're going, the Alberta Visitor Centre is worth a stop in its own right.

Immediately, you'll be greeted by a life-size dinosaur...model, reminding you that Alberta is the home of the Royal Tyrrell Museum, which houses the world's largest display of dinosaur skeletons. Photos so large you'll feel like you're walking into the mountains introduce you to two jewels of the Parks Canada system, Banff and Jasper. The Calgary Stampede—which some have called a "Mardi Gras of the North"—comes to life in displays and pictures, and you'll discover historic sites such as Head-Smashed-In Buffalo Jump or the Frank Slide. And, for those who have always aspired to the Olympics, you can scream down the (simulated) course on a real bobsled from the 1988 Calgary Games—it doesn't take long but it's exhausting!

The copper-topped building houses a wealth of information about Alberta, its history, and its magnificent mountains. Although it is closed during the winter, in the summer its staff of friendly Albertans will answer questions for you. Even if you hadn't planned on going further north, you might suddenly put Alberta on your itinerary!

Marias Pass Memorial Square
Marias Pass is crossed by Highway 2 twelve miles west of East Glacier.

At 5,216 feet above sea level, Marias Pass is the lowest pass through the Rocky Mountains in the United States. Nevertheless, it was one of the last to be discovered during the westward expansion. Weather deterred some explorers, and the Blackfeet Indians, who controlled the region, would not lead exploring parties through an area they prevented other tribes from using as well. Explorer Meriwether Lewis of the Lewis and Clark Expedition came within 25 miles of the pass before a fateful encounter with the Blackfeet. Eventually the pass was named after the Marias River, which Lewis had named for his cousin Maria Wood.

Today you can pull off Highway 2 into a wayside rest and Memorial Square at the pass. Memorial Square commemorates the history of the immediate area. One statue is to John F. Stevens, chief surveying engineer for the Great Northern Railway, who located the pass in 1889. By 1892 the railroad was running trains over the pass.

The Theodore Roosevelt monument honors the president who made forest conservation a national policy and also marks the twenty-fifth anniversary of the U.S.D.A. Forest Service. Constructed in 1931, it is a 60-foot-tall obelisk sheathed in granite that was quarried near the state capital in Helena. Originally located in the center of the highway, it was moved to its present site in 1989.

www.insiders.com
See this and many other
Insiders' Guide®
destinations online.
Visit us today!

William "Slippery Bill" Morrison, a trader and prospector who had squatters' rights to 160 acres of land at the Marias Pass summit, is also acknowledged. He donated a portion of his land for Memorial Square, and, according to his wishes, at his death in 1932 the balance of his property was also given to the federal government.

The Burlington Northern Stewardship Plaque, dedicated in 1991, recognizes the Burlington Northern Railroad's commitment to responsible stewardship of the environment. The railroad runs through important habitat for grizzly bears, mountain goats, elk,

INSIDERS' TIP

You are in hypothermia country! Sometimes the combination of wind, moisture and cold can cause hypothermia, even when temperatures are above freezing. Hypothermia is life threatening. The symptoms a victim exhibits are progressive shivering, slow reactions, stumbling and clumsiness, slurred speech, confusion and loss of judgment. If hypothermia is untreated, coma and death may result within a few hours. Treatment should be immediate and decisive. Move the victim out of the weather to a sheltered spot; remove wet clothing and cover the victim; if necessary warm with another body. If the victim is conscious, administer small amounts of hot drinks. Many backcountry tragedies have occurred because hikers used poor judgment, induced by hypothermia. You can help prevent this condition by: dressing in layers to regulate your body temperature; wearing good rain and wind gear, when appropriate; drinking lots of fluids and minimizing prolonged exposure to wind and rain.

and other animals. This route has been an important transportation corridor since the arrival of the Great Northern Railway in 1892.

Marias Pass is a great spot to take a break on your way across the Continental Divide. You might enjoy your lunch with a view of Summit and Little Dog Mountains, the peaks that dominate Marias Pass from the north. The slopes below these peaks offer one of the best places to view the Lewis Overthrust Fault anywhere in Glacier National Park (see Geology of Glacier National Park). The rest area offers public outhouses as well as a seasonal Forest Service campground.

Three Bears Lake, a level, 15-minute trail walk north of the tracks, was dammed by the Great Northern Railway and its water used to refill steam engines. This earthen dam from the 1890s was broached recently to prevent its failure; now the little lake's water runs again to both sides of the Continental Divide, as it did before the arrival of the railroad.

Browning

Scriver Museum of Montana Wildlife and Hall of Bronze
P.O. Box 172, Browning
• (406) 338-5425 • Located at the junction of U.S. 2 and U.S. 89

Bob Scriver has been called the "foremost sculptor in America today—bar none" (Dr. Harold McCracken, Director Emeritus, Whitney Gallery of Western Art, Cody, Wyoming). His bronzes of cowboys at work, Indians on the high plains, or animals such as bighorn sheep seem to freeze in time the essence of the frontier, and they are found in museums throughout the West. But Scriver lived in Browning, and here is the most complete collection of his work.

Scriver started as a taxidermist, and his intimate knowledge of the mountain animals shows not only in his taxidermy but also in the sculptures that followed. The museum boasts over 1,000 works altogether, grouped by theme. Taxidermied specimens include grizzly and black bear, moose, wolf, buffalo, and antelope—creatures of the mountains and plains that surround Browning. In addition to

Scriver's bronzes, the museum also showcases Scriver's books, including the *Rodeo* series and *No More Buffalo*, which focuses on Indian themes.

The Scriver Museum of Montana Wildlife and Hall of Bronze opens on Mother's Day and closes in late fall. Admission is $5.00 for adults, $2.50 for students, and $1.00 for those under 12.

Museum of the Plains Indian
P.O. Box 400, Browning
• (406) 338-2230 • Located at the junction of U.S. 2 and U.S. 89

Native Americans have inhabited this region for thousands of years. The Museum of the Plains Indian takes a closer look at this history through the art, clothing, tools, and other possessions of the peoples that have known the high plains so well. Each of three galleries presents a different aspect of the Plains Indians' lives. The historic gallery reaches into the cultures of the past with exceptional displays including traditional clothing, beadwork and quillwork, household utensils, and horse gear. These exhibits explore processes and skills required for daily life such as hunting, preparing skins for tanning, or clothing manufacture. A second gallery offers the 12-minute slide show "Winds of Change," narrated by Vincent Price and chronicling the way of life of the northern Plains Indians.

A third gallery features contemporary works of art by members of the northern plains tribes, including the Blackfeet. Over the winter months, the works of four different artists are highlighted in individual shows. During the summer months, selected works from the preceding winter's shows are presented in a combined show; many of these works are available for purchase.

The Museum of the Plains Indian is open all year round. From June 1 to September 30, it is open 7 days a week from 9 AM to 4:45 PM. Admission is $4.00 for adults, $1.00 for ages 6–12, and free for children under 6. For groups of ten or more, admission is $1.00 per person. From October 1 to May 31, the museum is open Monday through Friday from 10 AM to 4:30 PM and admission is free. The museum gift shop has an excellent selection of books and native crafts for sale.

Whitefish

Big Mountain Ski and Summer Resort

P.O. Box 1400, Whitefish
• **(406) 862-1900**
• **website: www.bigmtn.com**

Rocky Mountain High? Probably the highest place around you can get without hiking is the top of Big Mountain, at almost exactly 7,000 feet above sea level. On a clear day, you'll be able to see the Cabinet Mountains to the west, the Canadian Rockies off to the northeast, the peaks of Glacier National Park, and a magnificent view south to the Flathead Valley, including the Swan Range, the Mission Mountains, Blacktail Mountain, and Flathead and Whitefish Lakes. Summer or winter, it's magnificent.

The Glacier Chaser—Chair 1—offers access to the summit of Big Mountain both summer and winter. In the summer, gondola cars will lift you to the top in glass-enclosed comfort. The summer season typically runs from Memorial Day to late September, with the gondola operating from 10 AM to 6:30 PM during the shoulder season and from 10 AM to 9 PM during July and August. Round-trip price is $9.50 for adults; $7.25 for seniors (62 and up); $7.25 for ages 7-18; and free for children age 6 and under. In July and August the price is $6.25 for evening rides after 6 p.m. for everyone except children under 6, who ride free. Please note: for those who hike to the top (see Outdoor Recreation), the ride down is free.

In the winter, sightseers may ride Chair 1 with a foot passenger ticket. They will be loaded on the open chairlift with skiers and snowboarders. The detachable quad lift slows at both top and bottom so that loading and unloading are not difficult. Sightseers are welcome to enjoy the winter view—as well as something hot to eat or drink—in the warmth of the Summit House. Chair 1 operates daily during ski season—Thanksgiving Day to early April (please call to confirm, as snow conditions may affect operation of the lift at early

and late season)—from 9:30 a.m. to 4:20 p.m. Foot passenger tickets are $9.00 for one round-trip ride.

In addition, the Big Mountain Summit House offers dinner on Wednesday and Saturday nights during ski season (see Whitefish: Resorts). Gondolas lift guests to the summit for dinner; cost of the ride is $6.25 round-trip in addition to the meal, but anyone with a ski ticket or pass valid for that day may ride the gondola free of charge.

Great Northern Brewery

2 Central Avenue, Whitefish
• **(406) 863-1000**
• **website: www.blackstarbeer.com**

For those that know their beer...take an afternoon to visit Whitefish's Great Northern Brewery and Tasting Room. Built in 1994 by Minott Wessinger, the great-great-grandson of Oregon's Henry Weinhard, the brewery was located here to take advantage of the area's excellent water. The brewhouse is built in a gravity-flow arrangement and is mostly automated; for its size it is one of the most complexly designed operations in the country. A photo display describes the brewing process.

The Great Northern Brewery is currently producing six beers—Black Star Golden Lager, Black Star Black Lager, Black Star Amber Export, Wild Huckleberry Wheat Lager (a local favorite!), Wheatfish Hefeweizen, and Big Fog Amber Lager—as well as occasional seasonal brews such as Snow Ghost Special Edition Winter Lager. The Tasting Room—which boasts a spectacular view of Big Mountain as well as of the brewery—is open from 12–6 PM, Monday through Saturday, in the summer, and from 3–7 PM, Monday through Saturday, in the winter. Souvenir items include a unique zip-on neoprene bottle case that not only keeps your beer cool, it floats, too. . .

Stumptown Historical Society Museum

Whitefish Railroad Depot, 500 Depot Street, Suite 101, Whitefish, MT 59937
• **(406) 862-0067**

Even if you don't arrive in Whitefish by train, you'll want to make a point of visiting the historic depot. Like the train stations at West and East Glacier and the Izaak Walton

Geology of Glacier National Park

Glacier National Park is a geologist's dream: its rocks and formations vividly reveal the processes of formation. The park's geology could be the study of many years, but here's a four-stage thumbnail sketch to start:

Stage 1: Sedimentation. Glacier is mostly sedimentary rock, laid down approximately 2 billion years ago as silts and sands drifted to the bottom of the shallow ocean which then covered the area—the Great Belt Sea. Over time, these muds began to compress under their own accumulating weight. We see these rocks today in the brightly colored strata of the park: toward the bottom, the greenish-gray Apikuni mudstone or argillite; next, the reddish Grinnell mudstone (formed when the presence of more oxygen caused iron in the mudstone to oxidize; hence the red color); and finally the layers of harder limestone which make up most the peaks. Sometime later, magma from the earth's core expanded up through a weak layer in the sediments and spread out to form the black stripe seen running through some mountains: the diorite sill (also known as the Purcell sill). This intrusion of igneous rock is the hardest, most brittle rock in the park. In a few places it bubbled through the limestone layers and surfaced, still underwater, to form pillow basalts (such as are found at Granite Park).

Stage 2: Faulting and uplift. A mere 150 million years ago, major changes began again. Large plates under the earth's crust began to shift, with the North American plate and the oceanic plate just to its west starting to move toward each other. (Movement of plates is ongoing—consider the active San Andreas Fault in California, or the fact that the Himalayas are being pushed higher as the plate beneath the Indian subcontinent continues to ram into the Asian plate.) Eventually the pressure of the oceanic plate began to elevate the North American plate. Forces of compression became so great that a fold began to develop in the rock strata west of this area. Over tens of millions of years, pressure caused a huge slab of rock—at least 15,000 feet thick—to finally buckle, break, and slide as a unit some 50 to 100 miles to the east. These are the rocks of the Lewis Overthrust Fault which comprise Glacier National Park today. Evidence of faulting can be seen throughout the park in small ways—bent and angled rock strata—and on the big scale: at Marias Pass, for example, you can see where the rocks of the fault layer rode up and over the lower layers. And anywhere along the eastern front—where the mountains meet the plains—you'll be impressed with how suddenly the peaks stop and the prairie begins. That's the limit of how far the faulting process pushed this upper layer of rocks.

Stage 3: Glaciation. At this point, we have a huge slab of layered rock shoved out onto the plains, marked only by some gentle, relatively shallow drainages. Enter the Ice Ages! About 2 million years ago, the most recent period of glaciation began. The whole planet became just a touch colder...more snow fell in the winter, less melted in the summer. In the northern climes, snow began to accumulate. As the snow grew deeper and deeper, its nature began to change: under the pressure of its own weight, crystals in the bottom of the snowpack began to deform and to turn into ice; further pressure then changed their molecular structure so that they became almost plastic. Where the ice had formed on a slope, gravity began to pull it downhill. The moving glaciers scoured away at the little valleys beneath them, over time turning them into the deep, V-shaped valleys we see today. Other glacial features include hanging valleys, aretes, horns, passes, and cirques. These glaciers—for which the park is named—all melted away a good 10,000 years ago.

Stage 4: The Little Ice Age, the present, and the future. The current glaciers in the park are the result of the Little Ice Age. Geologists argue about when it started, but it seems clear that these glaciers reached their greatest extent probably in the eighteenth century. They are now receding very quickly—this is the time to see them! Global climate change has been studied from data collected at these glaciers, and is certainly an element in their disappearance. Blackfoot-Jackson, Grinnell, and Sperry are the largest of the glaciers today. Other factors affecting park geology today include the small but continual effects of wind and rain, freezing and thawing—all processes that tend to smooth out the rugged mountains. Slowly the peaks come down and the valleys are filled. Sometimes more sudden events dramatically change the landscape, such as avalanches and rockslides. In recent years an earthquake, centered on the Blackfeet Reservation, brought down a huge rockslide on Chief Mountain. Change is ongoing.

The Continental Divide also runs through Glacier National Park—the line separating watersheds flowing to the east from those flowing to the west. Look for Triple Divide Peak on your map—it's southwest of St. Mary at the end of the Cut Bank Creek drainage. This mountain marks the meeting of the Continental Divide with the Hudson Bay Divide, separating the park's waters into three: Those which flow north and east to Hudson Bay and the Arctic Ocean; those flowing south and east into the Missouri, the Mississippi, and eventually the Caribbean; and those flowing west, out the Flathead and Columbia Rivers to the Pacific Ocean. The Continental Divide is also a significant weather-maker: it stops the moisture from the Pacific with its wall of rock, so that more precipitation falls on the west side. The east side is drier and subject to the winds then rushing off the divide as they cool. The effects of these climatic differences are keenly visible in the park landscape—the west side supports lush forests, including a bit of true rain forest, while the east side is typified by open meadows and aspen groves.

Inn at Essex, it is built in the chalet style the Great Northern Railway developed for this area. Now owned by the Stumptown Historical Society, the building has been completely restored to its original 1927 appearance and is on the National Register of Historic Places. Be sure to check out the restored 1950s Great Northern Railway Locomotive 181 on display outside the depot.

Inside you'll find the Stumptown Historical Society Museum, devoted to illuminating Whitefish's past. You'll see Native American beading; handmade quilts from the early twentieth century; and photos and artifacts from the trapping, trading, and logging era that gave the region the name "Stumptown." Photos from the Great Northern Railway document its history—including wrecks and snowslides—and its tremendous influence. Train models, a telegrapher's desk, and dinner china with patterns exclusive to the Empire Builder service between Chicago and Seattle are a few of the objects that bring alive the railroad's impact on people across the north-

INSIDERS' TIP

Altitude sickness is a serious condition, marked by nausea, headache, loss of appetite and vomiting. It is relatively uncommon in Glacier country, as most peaks are below 10,000 feet in elevation. If you experience the symptoms the best remedy is to return to a lower elevation as soon as possible.

ern plains. Posters as well as calendar art commissioned by the Great Northern—including Blackfeet portraits from the 1920s by the German painter Winold Reiss—offer a unique account of the past. Many other objects represent other aspects of local history as well.

The Stumptown Historical Society Museum opens at 11 a.m., Monday through Saturday, year-round; please call to confirm hours of operation, as closing times and Sunday hours vary. Admission is free but donations are greatly appreciated.

Montana Coffee Traders
5810 Highway 93 South, Whitefish
• **(406) 862-7633, (800) 345-JAVA**
• **website: www.cyberport.net/ coffeetraders/mct1.html**

The story goes that, in about 1981, RC Beall was having a cup of the world's worst coffee in an all-night railroad café. As he contemplated how to make a living in this little town, the taste of the weak, stale liquid bothered him. Suddenly he wondered if selling a good cup of coffee might translate into a business...

Just walking into Montana Coffee Traders will tell you why this once-small operation has flourished: the rich aromas of coffee permeate the establishment. A Whitefish institution, Montana Coffee Traders has grown to a major business that roasts and sells coffee not only in Whitefish but in Monteverde, Costa Rica; Moscow, Russia; and Austin, Texas. Located just south of Whitefish on Highway 93—look for the covered wagon—Coffee Traders offers tours of their roasting facility. Depending on the group and interest, tours can vary from a quick visit to more in-depth "coffee education." In the store you can usually sample three or four brewed coffees; bistros and espressos are also available for sale. Coffee paraphernalia—from press pots and grinders to filters and dishware—is abundant, and, for those non-coffee-loving souls along for the ride, teas, baked goods, and various candies and treats are also thick. In short—indulge!

Montana Coffee Traders is open Monday through Friday from 8:30 AM to 5:30 PM and Saturdays from 9 AM to 5 PM Please call in advance for groups wishing to tour the roasting facility.

Whitefish City Beach
Whitefish Parks and Recreation
• **(406) 863-2470**

Located at the southeast end of Whitefish Lake; take Baker Avenue north over the viaduct, turn left at the light on Edgewood and follow signs to the lake.

All year round this little jewel of a park is a real asset to the town of Whitefish. With its spectacular views north and west, it offers a quiet retreat for walkers and joggers in the fall, winter, and spring. In the summer it's a hopping hub of activity: two docks go in, the buoys go up, lifeguards arrive, and swimming happens everyday, all day.

Whitefish Parks and Recreation runs a small concession that sells snacks, drinks, and ice cream. Bathrooms are available. Several small pavilions are available to rent; please call in advance. City Beach also has a boat-launching ramp and boat dock.

Whitefish Ice Rink
Whitefish Parks and Recreation
• **P.O. Box 158, Whitefish**
• **(406) 863-2470**

It's winter, it's cold, and you've been in the car all day...it's time to stretch a leg! Come out to the Whitefish Ice Rink and brush off your triple axel—or, maybe, just enjoy cruising the Zamboni-groomed ice to your heart's content. Take a break to step inside and have a cup of hot chocolate at the snack bar...let your legs relax a moment, then back to the ice! The Whitefish Ice Rink is outdoors and lit at night...evening skating—perhaps under a light snowfall—is a special delight.

Located behind the Saddle Club in Mountain Trails City Park, the Whitefish Ice Rink has open (public) skating sessions at specific hours morning, afternoon, or evening, every day of the week. The rink itself is open from 6:30 AM to 11:30 PM, but hockey leagues and skating classes also use the ice, so be sure to check on the schedule. General admission is $4.00 for everyone age 6 and up; admission is $3.00 for the last sessions on Friday, Saturday, and Sunday. Children under 5 skate free when accompanied by a paid admission. Skate rentals are $2.00 for all ages. The Whitefish Ice Rink operates from early November to mid March.

Credit: Flathead Lake Lodge

See Flathead Lake from the *Far West*.

Kalispell

Central School Museum
Northwest Montana Heritage, Education, and Cultural Center • Northwest Montana Historical Society
• P.O. Box 2293, Kalispell
• (406) 756-8381
• website: www.montanaweb.com/ museum

Built in 1894, Kalispell's Central School Museum is on the National Register of Historic Places and now houses the Northwest Montana Heritage, Education, and Cultural Center, opened in early 1999. It is a beautiful old building, newly renovated to high standards. Highlights of the Central School Museum include permanent and changing exhibits relating to the history of Central School itself; native nations of the area; the development of nonnative settlements; local industrial and technological development, including the histories of the logging, mining, and transportation industries in the area; Glacier National Park; and regional wildlands. The museum also has facilities for speakers, research, oral history, and genealogy, as well as public meeting rooms.

The Northwest Montana Historical Society operates the Central School Museum, which is open from Tuesday through Sunday. Please call for hours and admission fees.

Hockaday Museum of Art
Second Avenue East and Third Street, Kalispell
• (406) 755-5268

The Hockaday Museum of Art, located in downtown Kalispell, provides an intimate setting for displays by both local and nationally recognized artists. The permanent collection features works of Montana artists such as Russell Chatham, Ace Powell, Gary Schildt, and Bob Scriver. Exhibits change on a regular basis and may include everything from the work of local watercolorists or photographers to historic doll collections to sculpture in a variety of materials. The building itself, originally constructed as a Carnegie Library, is now on the National Register of Historic Places.

The Hockaday Museum of Art is open Wednesday from 10 AM to 8 PM; Tuesday, Thursday, Friday, and Saturday from 10 AM to 6 PM; it is closed Sunday and Monday. Suggested donation is $2 for adults; $1 for seniors; free for youth 18 years and under. On

Big Sky Waterslide offers can't-miss family fun.

Wednesdays admission is free for all. The museum gift shop offers an array of fine works by Montana artists (see the Arts chapter for more information).

Conrad Mansion
P.O. Box 1041, Kalispell
• (406) 755-2166 • Located six blocks off Main Street on Fourth Street East.

Step back in time—in the home of Charles and Alicia Conrad. Built in 1895, this Norman-style mansion reflects the wealth and elegance sometimes seen in the West in an era often known for its rough-and-tumble living. Charles Conrad, born and raised in Virginia, came west at the age of eighteen and built a fortune in trade and freight on the Missouri River. Later he moved to the Flathead Valley and helped to found the city of Kalispell. His herd of buffalo sometimes pastured on what is known as Buffalo Hill in Kalispell today. He and his wife Alicia established a reputation for hospitality and generosity in the new town; from the Great Hall, with its massive stone fireplace and oak woodwork, servants escorted notable guests upstairs to bedrooms with marble lavatories, sleigh beds, and canopied four-posters. Alicia Conrad Campbell, the youngest Conrad child, donated the mansion to the city

of Kalispell in 1975. Today all three floors, interior and exterior, have been restored to their original beauty. Inside you will see the Conrads' original furniture, clothing, and even toys; outside exquisite gardens surround the building. The Conrad Mansion offers a unique glimpse into the lives of the privileged in turn-of-the-century Montana.

The Conrad Mansion is open to the public from May 15 to October 15. Hours are 10 AM to 5:30 PM (May 15-June 14); 9 AM to 8 PM (June 15-Sept. 15); and 10 AM to 5:30 PM (Sept. 16-Oct. 15). Admission is $7.00 for adults; $6.00 for seniors; $1.00 for children 11 or younger. Please call in advance for groups of twenty or more; admission for such groups is $5.25 per person.

Woodland Park
Kalispell Parks and Recreation
• (406) 758-7718 • Located on Second Street at Woodland Park Drive, Kalispell

For a delightful afternoon in town, take some time to explore Woodland Park. In the summer you'll enjoy its formal gardens and rose beds for their beauty and fragrance. Both a swimming pool and wading pool are open to the public for a small fee; please check with Kalispell Parks and Recreation for hours.

To make a day of it—or for a bigger event—pavilions can also be rented in advance. When the lagoon freezes in the wintertime it is plowed and flooded for ice skating, which is open to the public free of charge. Kalispell Parks and Recreation also offers day activities for children in the summer months; please call for a current schedule.

Lawrence Park
Kalispell Parks and Recreation
• (406) 758-7718• Located at the north end of Main Street in Kalispell

Looking for some quiet time away from city busyness? Take a few moments to enjoy the out-of-doors here in town. While Lawrence Park also offers outdoor play equipment for children and pavilions to rent, it feels both a little more peaceful and "wilder" than Woodland Park (described above). Its paved path runs close to the Stillwater River and is sought out by walkers and joggers as well as bicyclists. Birders will enjoy getting out early in the day here to look for feathered friends. Because Kalispell Parks and Recreation runs all its public programs from Woodland Park, Lawrence Park is perhaps a more relaxed place for those seeking a quieter time outdoors.

Somers

Far West Cruises
P.O. Box 248, Bigfork
• (406) 857-3203 • Please note that while the office is in Bigfork, *Far West* cruises leave from Somers Landing, 1 mile south of Somers on U.S. 93 and 8 miles south of Kalispell. Look for the big boat!

It's hard to imagine anything more relaxing than an afternoon on the water—unless it's a dinner cruise on the water! The *Far West*, a 64-foot cruiser that carries up to 200 passengers, plies the waters of Flathead Lake daily. Its 1 1/2 hour cruises show off the Flathead Valley and its surrounding peaks as only a view from the lake can. A full-service bar is open for all cruises; juices and sodas are also available. The boat has an enclosed lower deck and upper canopy deck for inclement weather.

Flathead Lake cruises begin in late May or early June; the season ends in late September or early October. The *Far West* tour leaves the dock every day at 2:00 PM; evening cruises depart at 7:00 PM on Sunday, Monday, and Tuesday. Tickets are $8.00 for adults, $7.00 for seniors 65 and up, and $5.00 for children 12 and under. In addition to regularly scheduled cruises, be sure to ask about special trips such as brunch cruises, family picnic cruises, and dinner cruises. The *Far West* is also available for charter; please contact the office for details. Flathead Lake is the largest natural freshwater lake west of the Mississippi—30 miles long and 15 miles wide—and weather may occasionally cause cancellations for safety reasons. Reservations are encouraged; on some dates charters may preempt the cruise schedule.

Dayton

Mission Mountain Winery
U.S. Highway 93, Box 185, Dayton
• (406) 849-5524

Connoisseurs may not immediately think of Montana when they think of wine, but the Mission Mountain Winery has produced quite a few award-winning wines recognized at both national and international competitions. Primarily Pinot Noir grapes are grown at the Winery's Dayton location, but Mission Mountain also has vineyards in the Columbia Valley of Washington. Grapes grown there are crushed, transported as juice, and then fermented and bottled here in Montana. This family-run operation offers Johannisberg Riesling, Sundown (Riesling blended with Cabernet Sauvignon), Muscat Canelli, Chardonnay, Cabernet Sauvignon, Pinot Noir, and Pale Ruby Champagne.

The winery, located on the western shore of Flathead Lake, is open daily from 10 AM to 5 PM between May 1 and October 31. Stop by for a talk about the art and science of wine making as well as complimentary tasting, which includes special reserve wines available only at the winery. When the season is right visitors may also have a chance to watch harvesting of the grapes or bottling of the new wine.

Polson

Polson-Flathead Historical Museum
P.O. Box 206, 708 Main Street, Polson
• (406) 883-3049

From buggies to boats, from the (Kerr) dam to documents, the Polson-Flathead Historical Museum depicts regional history with great variety and depth. Homesteaders, steamboaters, cattle ranchers, city developers, Native Americans past and present all make their appearance—up to and including Calamity Jane, whose saddle is here. Polson's first building, a trading post, is restored and stocked as it was in the 1880s. Local histories described and illustrated here—of the Flathead Indian Reservation or the construction of the Kerr Dam, for example—provide insight into the broader history of the region and of the country at large. Local citizens, many of them descendants of early Montana pioneers, have made generous donations of family artifacts, documents, photographs, and even vehicles to enhance the museum's collection.

The Polson-Flathead Historical Museum is open between Memorial Day and Labor Day. Hours are 9 AM to 6 PM, Monday through Saturday, and 12 noon to 6 PM on Sunday.

Glacier National Park

Going-to-the-Sun Highway and U.S. Highway 2 Loop Driving Tour
Glacier National Park • West Glacier
• (406) 888-7800

Going-to-the-Sun Road in Glacier National Park has been called one of the most beautiful drives in the country on more than one occasion. This narrow, winding road leaves West Glacier, skirts Lake McDonald, and climbs from the forest floor up along mountain cliffs to summit at Logan Pass (6,646 feet above sea level), cross the Continental Divide, and descend again to St. Mary Lake and the wind-blown meadows of the east side. From St. Mary, turn south along U.S. 89, which snakes along the edge of the eastern foothills and offers views to both the mountains and

the prairie. At Kiowa Junction turn right on Montana 49 to head toward East Glacier, by way of Looking Glass Pass and huge views of the Two Medicine Valley. In East Glacier you'll meet with U.S. Highway 2 for the last 60 miles back to West Glacier. In its first 12 miles, Highway 2 rises gradually toward the Continental Divide at Marias Pass. At 5,216 feet above sea level, Marias is lower than Logan Pass, but Summit and Little Dog Mountains seem to tower over this wind-scoured, wild stretch of country. Once you begin the descent from Marias Pass, you'll be following first Bear Creek, then the Middle Fork of the Flathead River. These deep river valleys have a pristine lushness of their own. In no time at all you'll be back in West Glacier.

The total mileage for this remarkable tour is about 140 miles, and total driving time (in good weather in the summer and minus any delays due to construction) is only about 3-1/2 hours. Nevertheless this is a good excursion to give a whole day to, because you'll want to stop again and again to take in views, watch animals, and learn more about the park. Picnic areas are located at several scenic points along the way if you wish to pack your own lunch. Restaurants and other facilities are of course located at various points along the route (see the chapter on Glacier National Park for more details).

To begin at the beginning: parts of Going-to-the-Sun Road can be driven all year long, but as winter comes, the higher portions are closed to traffic. The road typically reopens all the way over Logan Pass sometime in June—it has occasionally opened in May—everything depends on the snowpack and plowing conditions. The road will close to traffic over Logan Pass on the Monday after the third weekend in October, unless it has already been closed by weather. This means that driving the full loop tour is generally possible only from sometime in June to sometime in early October. Please check with park visitor centers for conditions at the time of your visit. Snow has even been known to shut down the pass (usually briefly) in July and August.

Length restrictions have been imposed for vehicles traveling over Logan Pass due to the narrowness of the road and increasing congestion. Vehicles over 21 feet long may not drive over Logan Pass and are also prohibited from the stretch of Highway 49 between Kiowa Junction and East Glacier (they can, alternately, take U.S. 89 from St. Mary all the way into Browning and pick up U.S. 2 there for the trip back to West Glacier). If your vehicle (or vehicle and attached trailer) is over 21 feet long, please contact Glacier National Park for information on restrictions. Consider seeing Logan Pass with a Red Bus Tour or Sun Tour, or taking the shuttle up.

Having taken care of all that—most people will be able to drive over Going-to-the-Sun Road in their own car or truck when they want to, which is usually in summer. So sit back, roll down the windows, and enjoy! You'll be offered the park newspaper—tailored to answer frequently asked questions—in exchange for a $10 entrance fee at the park gate. Apgar Visitor Center is just two miles ahead and a good spot to stop for information; you might ask for a brochure called "Points of Interest along Going-to-the-Sun Road." As you leave the Apgar area and head up Going-to-the-Sun Road, you'll be immediately treated to views of the peaks at the head of the McDonald Valley. Or perhaps you'll have a moody day, with fog lingering close to the lake and permitting you only occasional glimpses of what's ahead...

Everyone has a different idea about where you "just have to stop" along the Road. It might be Lake McDonald Lodge, or Jackson Glacier Overlook, or an unnamed pullout along the shore of St. Mary Lake. Some like to pull off to read the roadside exhibits, which point out, describe, and explain prominent features. Others will incorporate short day hikes into their driving trip, perhaps the Trail of the Cedars, the Hidden Lake boardwalk, or the Sun Point Nature Trail. It's also possible to include one of the scenic boat cruises (see Glacier Park Scenic Boat Tours) as part of your itinerary. Whatever you choose, you can't go wrong.

Logan Pass—the Continental Divide—is the high point of the trip, often figuratively as well as literally. Expansive views stretch north to Canada; tiny alpine wildflowers bloom in the ancient rocks; ptarmigan have been known to nest under the boardwalk; and bears are often enough seen in the meadows surrounding the visitor center. If stopping at Logan Pass is a high priority, consider arriving there before 10 AM or after 4 PM—you'll have an easier time parking and a less crowded sub-alpine experience! The Logan Pass Visitor Center's huge glass windows allow visitors to enjoy the view even when it's nippy outside. Park Service naturalists staff the visitor center and will happily answer questions—

Credit: Flathead Convention and Visitor Bureau

Tour the Conrad Mansion in Kalispell and journey into Montana's past.

you might ask about "Alpine Talks" or short guided hikes. Glacier Natural History Association also offers sales of park-related books and other items. Keep in mind that between Lake McDonald Lodge and Rising Sun Motor Inn, no food or drink service is available. There is a phone at Avalanche, but then none until Rising Sun. Logan Pass Visitor Center has public washrooms and drinking fountains only.

You will no doubt discover your own favorite places along Going-to-the-Sun Road. As you leave the park at St. Mary, you enter the Blackfeet Reservation and will be within its borders almost until you reach Marias Pass on U.S. Highway 2. On the east side of the park, several side-trips are possible: Many Glacier is about a 40-minute, 20-mile drive north of St. Mary; a winding dirt road leads into the Cut Bank Valley of the park, heading west from U.S. 89 some 12 miles south of St. Mary; or you might wish to explore the Two Medicine Valley, a 7-mile drive west from Montana 49. Highways 89 and 49 are narrow, twisting roads that run along the foothills—take time to enjoy the scenery and drive carefully. You might choose to stay on U.S. 89 and

drive out over the plains to Browning to visit the museums, returning to U.S. 2 there.

Once you reach East Glacier, you'll be back on U.S. 2. This road is maintained all year-round. As you head back west, though, you may find your vehicle battling the eastside winds! Train cars have been blown off the tracks in East Glacier—if the weather is like that, perhaps it's time to look for a hotel room! Most likely, though, you'll get a milder dose of what the Continental Divide regularly dishes up for the east side. Soon you'll top out at Marias Pass (see Marias Pass Memorial Square, above), and once you drop down to the west side those winds will likely vanish.

Between Marias Pass and West Glacier, you are following the path of the Middle Fork of the Flathead River. The Burlington Northern Railroad, successor to the Great Northern Railway that opened this area in the 1890s, shares this narrow corridor. Chances are you'll see more than one train wending its way up or down the pass. Extra "helper"engines are added to each train as it leaves Spokane, Washington, or Havre, Montana, to head into the mountains. As you drive through the Middle Fork, you'll notice snowsheds over the railroad tracks at certain places. These avalanche sheds slough huge amounts of snow off above the tracks so that trains can keep running in winter.

About ten miles before West Glacier, you might keep your eyes out for Loneman Mountain, a double-topped mountain just across the river to the north. On its second summit sits Loneman Lookout, one of a network of fire lookouts once active in the park. These days most fire surveillance is done with small planes or helicopters, but these lookouts are still used when fire danger is high locally...and they make fascinating hike destinations.

The last few miles into West Glacier wind along a deep cut made by the Middle Fork of the Flathead River. The whitewater here draws kayakers and rafters...look for their brightly colored clothing and boats. Often they "take out" at the West Glacier bridge—wet, but smiling!

With a little luck, you'll be smiling too at the end of the day. And there's always more to come back and explore.

Glacier Park Scenic Boat Tours
Glacier Park Boat Company
- **P.O. Box 5262, Kalispell**
- **(406) 257-2426 year-round**
- **website: www.montanaweb.com/
gpboats**

Cruise through the mountains on glacially carved lakes of blue-green...watch for wildlife on mountain slopes...see vistas not visible from roads...and learn more about Glacier National Park's history, geology, flora and fauna. Glacier Boat Company invites you to cruise on Lake McDonald, St. Mary Lake, Two Medicine Lake, and Swiftcurrent and Josephine Lakes in the Many Glacier Valley. Each of the four locations offers several cruises daily that last from 45 minutes to 1-1/2 hours. National Park Service ranger-naturalists accompany some cruises and offer guided walks to places such as Grinnell Glacier, St. Mary Falls, and Twin Falls in conjunction with the boat ride. Boat trips can also be used as transportation to trails further from the park roads. And at the peak of the season be sure to ask about sunset cruises on these spectacular mountain lakes.

Glacier Park Boat Company also offers small boat rentals. Please call to check on cost per hour and availability of canoes, kayaks, rowboats, or small motorboats at each location.

Fares for cruises are $10 or less, with children ages 4–12 riding for half-price. Each location has its own schedule, opening in late May or early June and closing sometime after Labor Day. Glacier Park Boat Company has phone service during the summer at Lake McDonald (406-888-5727), St. Mary (406-732-4430), and Many Glacier (406-732-4480). Don't miss the boat! Please allow yourself a good ten minutes to park your car and walk to the boat dock.

Flathead Lake
Scenic Drive

Flathead Lake is the largest natural freshwater lake west of the Mississippi, and peaks surround it—a combination that makes for scenery as striking as you'll find anywhere. Although the changes in landscape are not as dramatic as they are on the Going-to-the-Sun Road/U.S. Highway 2 loop, nevertheless the ongoing change of perspective as you round the lake will continually surprise and please you. Sometimes the road runs close to the water's edge; sometimes it runs high through deep cuts made in the lakeshore bluffs. Parts of the valley are verdant and green, while others tend to be more open, windswept, and dry. The six units of Flathead Lake State Park—Wayfarers, Yellow Bay, Finley Point, Wild Horse Island, Big Arm, and West Shore (see Outdoor Recreation)—all offer opportunities to stop and do a little exploring. And various communities around Flathead Lake provide a wide range of services and points of interest.

The total distance around Flathead Lake is about 90 miles, and driving time (in good conditions in summer, minus time lost to any construction delays) is about 2-1/2 hours. You'll probably want to plan on at least a half a day though, and why not more? Bring a camera—you'll want to take frequent stops to admire the views.

We could begin at any point, but let's begin in Bigfork since it's right on the water. Montana 35 heads south toward Polson, rising and falling gently as it curves over the hills running down to the lake. Further south the road will actually run right along Flathead Lake for some distance. You'll also drive through the famous cherry orchards and no doubt notice the many roadside stands along the way—if it's cherry season, it's time to stop!

As you enter Polson, Montana 35 joins U.S. 93 at a t-intersection. Turning right will take you into the town itself; this might be a good opportunity to stretch a leg and take a break if you haven't already. The town offers a full range of services (see Polson section) as well as the Polson-Flathead Historical Museum (see page 64).

If you follow Seventh Avenue west out of town, signs will direct you to the Kerr Dam, about 8 miles below Polson. Completed in 1939, the Kerr Dam holds 1.1 million acre-feet of water at full pool; its construction converted Flathead Lake into a reservoir. Every year Kerr churns out more than one billion kilowatts of power. Montana Power Company pays rent to the confederated Salish-Kootenai Tribes for use of the dam. In 1989, MPC dedicated a new vista overlook and recreation area here. The overlook provides a spectacular view of Kerr Dam, the Flathead River canyon, and MPC's powerplant. The recreation area includes a boat launch, bathrooms, changing area, picnic tables, and drinking water.

Coming back to Polson, head north out of town on U.S. Highway 93. Immediately after crossing over the Flathead River, you'll notice the high-and-dry hills southwest of Flathead Lake. As you climb the steep hill leaving town this dry pocket will be left behind, but as you drive further north look off to the west from time to time and you will see more open grassland. Variations in rainfall, slope, and soil can have marked effects on the landscape within very short distances.

Soon you'll see two fairly large islands in Flathead Lake—Wild Horse Island, which is part of Flathead Lake State Park, and Cromwell Island further west, which is privately owned. Much romance surrounds Wild Horse Island, which is the home not only of a few wild horses but also bighorn sheep, deer, bald eagle, and the occasional black bear. One legend says that Indians once used the island to hide their ponies from marauding tribes...but no one really knows if it's true. The horses that inhabit the island today are courtesy of the BLM's adopt-a-horse program. The bighorn sheep population is doing well, and some animals have occasionally been relocated to other places where sheep populations needed some bolstering.

Soon the road will sweep around Big Arm, treating driver and passengers to an eastward view of the islands and across the lake to the Mission Mountains. During the summer months, the Mission Mountain Winery in Dayton opens a tasting room where visitors can sample select vintages. The vineyards are quite picturesque with their neat rows.

Continuing north on U.S. 93 toward Kalispell, the route passes through some huge road cuts in the bluffs along the western shore of Flathead Lake. Watch for the scenic pullout with its magnificent view—it's a good opportunity to stop for a few minutes and take photos. After you pass through the communities of Lakeside and Somers, look for the intersection of U.S. 93 with Montana 82. Turn right—east toward Bigfork—here. This last stretch of road will take you through the open farmlands typical of the Flathead Valley. You'll pass once more over the Flathead River, this time flowing from the north into Flathead Lake. The slow-moving water in the river here creates excellent habitat for many birds, from migrating swans to bald eagles. You'll reach the junction with Montana 35; a quick right turn and you'll be back to Bigfork in short order.

The scenic grandeur that lures tourists to the Flathead Valley also lures permanent residents, and many of the recent settlers have brought with them a wide variety of talents and interests that have fueled an artistic explosion over the past two decades.

The Arts

The arts scene is remarkably healthy in the Flathead Valley. Let's face it, Kalispell, Montana, isn't on anybody's short list of art meccas, but it would be easy to spend several days (and several thousand dollars) just visiting the galleries in Kalispell, Bigfork, Whitefish, and Polson alone. At one time, of course, you would have expected only to find Western art in the studios and galleries around here, but that has changed remarkably quickly. Today, many galleries in the area tend more toward the avant garde than the traditional, though you can easily find whatever you are looking for.

And that goes for theater, dance, and music, too.

The scenic grandeur that lures tourists to the Flathead Valley also lures permanent residents, and many of the recent settlers have brought with them a wide variety of talents and interests that have fueled an artistic explosion over the past two decades. Indeed, given the Valley's population base of fewer than 80,000, it is hard to conceive of the breadth of opportunities available here. But one look at the listings in this section will show that there is something for every interest, from foreign films to blues concerts to Western art.

In fact, the Flathead Valley was ranked 52nd in the third edition of *The 100 Best Small Art Towns in America* by John Villani (1998, John Muir Publications). Part of the reason for that is that most of the 2 million visitors a year to Glacier National Park pass through Kalispell and other Flathead communities and bring an influx of dollars into the local economy. During the summer months especially, that results in a healthy contribution to the arts through ticket purchases and actual art purchases.

Another part of the explanation is that Kalispell, Bigfork and Whitefish have all developed pride in their own artistic communities, so there is a hint of competition spurring each group to bigger and better things. An example of this can be found in the community theater scene. The Whitefish Theatre Company (WTC) started in 1978, about the same time that the Flathead Valley Community College's drama department was closing its doors. The success of the WTC goaded Bigfork into tackling its own theater project, and the Bigfork Community Players were born. When Kalispell actors grew weary of the commute north or south to perform, the Flathead Valley Community Theater was founded in the early 1990s, bringing the story full circle, as the new group is affiliated with Flathead Valley Community College, which once again has a dynamic and energetic theater program.

And when the various towns of the Flathead are not trying to one-up each other, they are working together synergistically to create art that is greater than the sum of its diverse parts, art that reflects the majesty of nature that is apparent everywhere here. An example is the Glacier Orchestra and Chorale, which draws members from across the Flathead Valley—from West Glacier to Polson—and sometimes beyond. Indeed, conductor John Zoltek arrived from the Seattle area a few years ago and immediately sensed something special about the orchestra and the environs. "I have a very strong connection to nature," he said. "And so I am delighted to have this opportunity to work and live in the Flathead. Because of the beautiful land that surrounds the area, it is a prime location for beautiful music making."

On the horizon in the Flathead Valley arts scene, meanwhile, is a high mountain. Not a literal one, though of course those are everywhere in the Flathead—but a project that looms large over the arts community, and indeed the community as a whole. That is the proposed ValleyDome, which could influence the direction of the arts scene for years to come.

The 10,000-seat arena, which would serve primarily as the home of a minor league hockey team, has been proposed for just north of Kalispell. Such a large facility would allow the Flathead to bring in major concert names such as Garth Brooks, and would no doubt be used on a somewhat smaller scale by local groups such as the Glacier Orchestra and Chorale or the Flathead Festival.

The positive effects are obvious. What changes might be wrought in the local mix of concerts and theater offerings are not yet clear, however.

In the meantime, with or without a ValleyDome, there is plenty to do for the arts-minded. What follows is a listing of some of the best the Valley has to offer in dance, music, art, and more. This summary is by no means complete, but includes a representative sampling from different communities and representing different styles. Do not expect to find every art gallery listed here. There are just too many of them, with a constantly changing lineup of exhibits, to be entirely inclusive. But it is easy to find additional galleries by stopping at any of those listed and asking where to go next. The Flathead Valley is tourist-friendly, and you won't have to look hard to find a helpful "native" who will point you in the right direction. This directory is just your starting point, not your final destination.

Museums and Art Centers

The Hockaday Museum of Art
Second Ave. E. & Third Street, Kalispell
• (406) 755-5268

This non-profit gallery and museum is a long-time hub of the cultural scene in the Flathead, and could perhaps even be seen as instrumental in developing a community spirit that has led to a range of artistic activities in the Flathead that go far beyond the Hockaday's offerings in the visual arts. Hugh Hockaday was an important figure in the

area's arts community for more than 20 years, and when he died in 1968, the Flathead Valley Art Association, a group of artists who had just begun leasing the 1903 Carnegie Library building, decided to honor Hockaday by naming the new art center after him. A number of his art works are included in the permanent collection. Over the years, the Hockaday has brought a number of high-quality exhibits to the Flathead, including recently work by Dana Boussard, who is best known for her large-scale painted and appliqued "fiberworks"; Russell Chatham, whose delicate watercolors depict the great wide-open spaces of Montana; Dale Chihuly, an internationally renowned glass sculptor; and Gary Schildt, a noted western artist and member of the Blackfeet tribe. Executive director David Lee Eubank is an artist himself, noted for massive, brightly colored oil paintings on canvas. When he began his tenure at the museum in 1997, he said, "We are hoping to stimulate some growth, and bring the Hockaday into the 21st century by increasing access for individuals in the valley. We hope to take art into the community." There is a $2 admission charge.

The People's Center
53253 U.S. Highway 93, Pablo
• (406) 883-5344, (800) 883-5344

The cultural center focuses on the history of the Salish, Pend d'Oreille, and Kootenai Indian tribes, but also has exhibitions of Native American art. The facility includes a learning center, exhibit gallery, and gift shop, and offers interpretive, guided tours on the Flathead Reservation.

Bigfork Art & Cultural Center
525 Electric Ave., Bigfork
• (406) 837-6927

This community-run, non-profit gallery exhibits artwork and crafts by local artists, with special showings in the summer. The center is open from April through December, with hours from 10 AM to 6 PM in the summer and slightly shorter in the spring and fall. In addition to the galleries, there is a gift shop that features local artwork and various made-in-Montana crafts.

Museum of the Plains Indians
Junction of U.S. Highway 2 and Montana Highway 89, Browning
• (406) 338-2230

The museum offers a comprehensive collection of Blackfeet Indian tribal artifacts, but in addition it also has a collection of art by Native American artists and craftsmen, some of which is available for sale. The museum is open year-round, with no admission charged.

The Studio
304 O'Brien Ave., Whitefish
• (406) 862-5929

The Studio is a grass-roots, community oriented, non-profit visual arts center. It aims to provide a place where children and adults feel free and confident to express their inherent creative nature and learn about the world of art. In addition to workshops, there are exhibits by local artists and a variety of classes and camps offered year round including art treks up the Big Mountain in the summer.

Galleries

Abbrescia Fine Art and Pottery Studios
12 First Ave. W, Kalispell
• (406) 755-6639

A gallery that carries the works of a Southwestern potter, a landscape oil painter, and a chain-saw artist, along with sculpture and historic etchings, might be considered somewhat eclectic, but in the case of the Abbrescia Studios, it's just a matter of keeping it in the family. Joe Abbrescia said the gallery opened in the early 1990s, when his family returned from an extended stay in Scottsdale, Arizona. "Essentially, this is our gallery, our studios and our showroom," he explained. "The gallery is mostly our own work. My wife, Sue Abbrescia, is a potter and sculptor. I'm a painter and sculptor, and our son, Tony, is a chain-saw wood carver. We have our studios in the back, and our showroom is in the front." Abbrescia's love of the genres also led the

family to include a sampling of "early American illustrators such as Joseph Lynedecker and Howard Chandler Christy and etchings by Whistler, Zorn, and others," he said. Abbrescia, who is also an art restorer and appraiser, is renowned for his paintings of Glacier National Park and has done one-man shows in Venice, Boston and elsewhere. His work, while very detailed, could almost be classified as impressionistic. Sue Abbrescia is noted nationally for her work making vessels, especially using a coil technique she adapted from traditional Southwestern methods.

Art Fusion
471 Electric Ave., Bigfork
• (406) 837-3526

Art Fusion features what owner Pamme Read calls "eclectic contemporary art with the emphasis on fun." The gallery represents more than 60 Montana artists and has the most colorful display space anywhere in the art world. As you enter the gallery space, your attention will be drawn first to the floor, where a variety of brightly colored ceramics vie for your attention, then your eyes will turn to the walls, where playful art features both landscapes and portraits. Among the artists represented are Louise Lamontagne from St. Ignatius, who paints impressionistic landscapes; Rebecca Harrison of Kalispell, who is noted for her glassworks; and Kirk Belding of Butte, who has a sampling of functional pottery with a bright and unusual trout motif. The gallery is open 10:30 AM to 6 PM six days a week, and is also open on Sundays with somewhat shorter hours.

Artistic Touch
209 Central Ave., Whitefish
• (406) 862-4813

If you are looking for three-dimensional art, especially crafted items such as jewelry, fiber and ceramics, then by all means stop in and meet Mary Kay Huff, the owner-proprietor of Artistic Touch in Whitefish. She opened the shop in 1987 and displays her own work and that of a variety of other artists. "I look for things that are unusual, things you might not see in other places," she said. The emphasis is always on quality, with a large helping of

Credit: Mark Ogle Studio

Craving the Fine Arts? Visit one of our many
studios and galleries.

local crafts and a smattering of fine art of regional distinction, especially metal sculpture. Mary Kay's adventurous spirit often brings a little something extra to the summer-long exhibits she puts up in the shop. "What we look for in shows is somebody whose work is interesting to begin with, and we ask them to do something they've always wanted to do for a show instead of just what they've been making money at." Examples of artists represented include Virginia Carter, who recently did a show of carved bricks in wall pieces that are raku fired, and Sarena Mann, who makes paper woman figures. Mary Kay herself specializes in silver- and gold-filled jewelry items, and has been experimenting with different colors of copper, as well as reproducing photographs on metal. Artistic Touch is open 10-5 Monday through Saturday and open on Sundays in the summer from 10-2.

Bjorge's Gallery
603 Electric Ave., Bigfork
• **(406) 837-3839**

When you ride down the hill into Bigfork Bay after turning off of Montana 35, one of the first structures that will catch your eye is Bjorge's Old Standard Gallery. Sculptor Ken Bjorge, along with his wife Tammy, converted an old-time service station into a comfortable gallery and studio space. Then, a few years ago, they built their home on top of the gallery, and the imposing three-story log structure is a perfect introduction to Bigfork's combination of artsiness and Western hospitality. "This place is just magical—it really is—and there's room for even more artists in Bigfork," confides Bjorge, who gave up a career as a lawyer and law professor, to move to Bigfork and start his mid-life adventure as a wildlife and Old West sculptor. Bjorge's work is exhibited in various states of completion in the studio, and new work can be watched taking shape under the hand and knife of the sculptor. Bjorge does many commission pieces, and often monumental-sized work, such as a pair of mountain lions, can be seen here before it is shipped to its final destination. The gallery, which is open from 10 AM to 8 PM seven days a week, also displays the paintings of Texan Oleg Stavrowsky and Montana artists Marnell Brown and Terry Mimnaugh.

Flathead Bay Gallery
303 U.S. 93, Polson
• **(406) 883-3951**

The gallery is owned by Russell and Barbra Stone and features paintings and sculpture by Montana and Western artists. A featured artist recently was oil painter Fred Fellows of Bigfork, who is a member of the exclusive Cowboy Artists of America and was named the honored guest of the prestigious C.M. Russell Art Auction in Great Falls for 1999. The gallery makes a refreshing stop for those who want to experience the great Western tradition not just because it specializes in Western, Native American and wildlife art, but also because it is housed in the beautiful KwaTaqNuk Resort on Polson Bay, a facility owned by the Confederated Salish and Kootenai Tribes. The gallery also has an unusual lifetime exchange policy on original art and limited edition prints bought there. If your tastes change, the Stones will exchange the work dollar for dollar for another piece of your choice or issue a credit note for the value of the art. Now that's customer service.

The Gallery
6080 U.S. 93 S., Whitefish
• (406) 862-5569

One of the special pleasures of visiting a new place is trying to find the unlikely treasures, places that don't look like much from the outside but contain the pearl you've been looking for. The Gallery, south of Whitefish, is just such a place. On the outside, it looks more like a carpenter's shop or a second-hand store. Just the unassuming name posted on a reader board above the entrance tells you that you have arrived at one of the Flathead's most unique galleries. Owner Jessie Deats says that her motto is "to allow almost any local artist to display their art, at least one or two pictures." If you are hoping to make a discovery of an artist whose work is still affordable, this 10-year-old gallery is a perfect place to start. "We probably have 50 or 60 local artists, as well as prints from Bev Doolittle, Mark Ogle and other better known artists," says Deats. Among the local artists represented are John Atkinson of Whitefish, who does realistic Glacier Park landscapes; Gladys Pilch, who specializes in smaller scenics; and Taryl Bodily, who does futuristic work. You can also find chain-saw art, pottery, photography and some sculpture. Most notable is the presence of oil painter Marvin Messing, whose surrealistic work is compa-

rable to that of Salvador Dali. The only notable difference in their artistic accomplishments is that Dali painted at a time when surrealism was popular, but Messing says he paints from the heart, not to be popular. "He's a sweet old gentleman who studied at the Art Institute of Chicago, and we are the only gallery that carries his paintings," says Deats. "They are all original oils and often have religious themes." The Gallery is open 10 AM to 5 PM Monday through Saturday most of the year.

Glacier Gallery
1498 Montana Highway 35, Kalispell
• (406) 752-4742

One of the most extensive collections of Western art in Montana can be found right here in the Glacier Gallery. "We have paintings and bronzes from the early 1900s and the turn of the century," says manager Sandy Noble. The gallery is owned by Dr. Van Kirke Nelson, a noted art collector, and was opened in 1969. Today, much of Nelson's extensive collection of Indian artifacts, and Charles M. Russell memorabilia is on display periodically for their historical value. Old West paintings by such famed artists as Russell, Edgar S. Paxson, Frank Tenney Johnson and Olaf Carl Seltzer are hung on the walls. There is also Southwestern art from Alfred Jacob Miller; an extensive collection of bronzes by Earle E. Heikka featuring pack trains and other Old West scenes; contemporary sculpture by Sherri Salari Sander, Tom Sander, and Frank Di Vita; and contemporary paintings by Charles Fritz, Gary Schildt, and Sheryl Bodily. In addition, Glacier Gallery carries prints and a variety of hand-thrown pottery by four local potters. The gallery is open from 10 AM to 5 PM Monday through Saturday.

Noice Studio and Gallery
127 Main St., Kalispell
• (406) 755-5321

Marshall Noice is typical of artists who are also gallery owners in the Flathead. He is accessible, voluble, and saleable. You will find a wide selection of his work at his downtown Kalispell studio and gallery, ranging from naturalistic photography to abstract oil paintings. But more importantly, you will usually find him.

That's one of the aspects of the Flathead art scene that is particularly rewarding for both the dedicated art collector and just the curious tourist.

Noice has been photographing Glacier Park for almost 30 years, and that is perhaps what he is best known for. "My fine art photography is black and white," Noice notes. "That probably stems from the summer of 1977 when I was fortunate enough to spend the summer working with (pioneering landscape photographer) Ansel Adams in California. When I want color I want more of it than photography can give me, and that's why my paintings and pastels tend to be very bold. If I'm interested in a literal image, nothing does it better than a photograph, so painting in a literal fashion doesn't capture my imagination." The gallery also carries original work by about 20 or more Montana artists, including sculpture and paintings by such noted contemporary artists as Rudy Autio, Sheila Myles, Nan Darham, Charlie Davis, Dave Shaner, and Michael Jones. There is also a sampling of Native American work. "We get people who are used to seeing art in San Francisco and Seattle and then are surprised to see the same kind of work here," said Noice's wife and partner, Jackie.

Mark Ogle Studio
101 E. Center, Kalispell
• **(406) 752-4217**

Mark Ogle has established himself in recent years as one of the premier painters of America's national parks. He has won most of the top artistic awards in the Northwest and Canada, and has frequently been among the top finishers in the National Parks Academy of the Arts annual painting competition. Glacier Park is his special love. "As the lower areas of the park see more visitors every year, it's refreshing to hike up where the air is thinner and the bears are free to romp around undisturbed," Ogle said. "We only see the tip of Glacier from the roads, and it's exciting to discover and paint some of the park's more remote regions. You find a different world up there, and it's a painter's paradise." He has also produced and sold oil paintings and prints of Yellowstone, Grand Teton, Yosemite, and Grand Canyon parks, as well as parks in

Alaska and elsewhere. His work is for sale exclusively in his own gallery, and even then it's hard for him to "keep in stock" since nearly 40 percent of his work is done on a commission basis. You can visit the studio and will frequently find Ogle at work on a new painting. He estimates he's painted more than 5,000 pieces, but he always has time to share his insights with visitors and he's a noted raconteur with a love of not just art, but the outdoors and the Western life.

Sandpiper Gallery
2 First Ave. E., Polson
• **(406) 883-5956**

The Sandpiper is a fine-arts non-profit corporation. The gallery features many wonderful displays, which rotate once or twice a month. In the past year or two, the gallery has devoted space to well-known local artists such as watercolorists Barbara Mellblom and Karen Leigh as well as to school-age artists, photographers, potters, woodworkers, and more. The gallery is open Monday to Thursday 11-4 and Friday and Saturday 11 to 3.

Bob Scriver's Hall of Bronze and Wildlife Museum
Junction of U.S. 2 and Montana 89, Browning
• **(406) (406) 338-5425**

This is the Old West in a nutshell, or at least in one building. The museum features hundreds of bronzes, a diorama of Western scenes, a life-size wildlife exhibit and many other pieces of art collected at the studio of one of America's foremost western sculptors, Bob Scriver. The museum is located in the Indian Country town of Browning, located on the Rocky Mountain Front east of Glacier Park. It is open from May to October from 8 AM to 5 PM Admission is $5 for adults, $2.50 for high school age students, and $1 for kids under 12.

Eric Thorsen Fine Art Gallery
547 Electric Ave., Bigfork
• **(406) 837-4366**

Oftentimes, its seems as though artists intentionally adopt an imposing or arrogant persona to keep themselves isolated from the demands of celebrity. Eric Thorsen is just the

James Welch, Montana author

As you travel through the Blackfeet Reservation, you drive through an area that has been inhabited for thousands of years. The Blackfeet Indians traversed the Old North Trail—which can still be traced in a few places where once thousands of dog-drawn travois made their way along the eastern front. Later the Blackfeet acquired horses and became known as the "raiders of the plains" for their fierce defense of their buffalo grounds. French trappers, Hudson's Bay Company traders, and Jesuit missionaries began to make their appearance as white civilization pushed westward. Smallpox and alcohol followed soon after, and eventually even the buffalo were lost. After such incredible changes, as well as those brought by the twentieth century, today the Blackfeet Nation numbers about 14,000 enrolled members, most of whom live on the Blackfeet Reservation.

James Welch, a Montana-born author of Blackfeet and Gros Ventre heritage, attended school on the Blackfeet and Fort Belknap Reservations. Later he graduated from the University of Montana, where he studied writing with the late Richard Hugo. Now a resident of Missoula, he has taken the history of the Blackfeet and other Indians of the northern plains as his subject in a number of fine novels. *Fools Crow* (1986), probably his best-known work, is set among the Blackfeet of the Two Medicine area in the 1870s, when white men are just beginning to influence the tribes significantly. It is probably the best reconstruction of precontact Blackfeet culture—or perhaps any precontact Indian world—ever written. Its protagonist, the young warrior Fools Crow, is born into the traditional world but will live to see it greatly changed.

Other works are set in contemporary times: two novels, *Winter in the Blood* (1974) and *The Death of Jim Loney* (1979), represent both hope and despair on the Highline—the high plains of Montana traversed by U.S. Highway 2. More recently, *The Indian Lawyer* (1991) spins the tale of a successful "Indian lawyer" in Helena, Montana, who decides to consider a bid for Congress. Welch's fiction speaks eloquently for those who find themselves still divided between two worlds.

Killing Custer: The Battle of the Little Bighorn and the Fate of the Plains Indians (1994), is a nonfiction account of that debacle that includes the Native American perspective. It originally grew out of work Welch did with director Paul Stekler for the PBS documentary "Last Stand at Little Bighorn," part of the American Experience series. As with his novels, here Welch provides a new depth to our knowledge of the past in his recapturing of Native American history. All these works are eloquent, thoughtfully crafted pieces that will increase your appreciation for what was once buffalo country and the source of a very different way of life. Welch's latest title is *Riding the Earthboy 40*, published in 1998.

opposite—a painter who is so affable and charming it's a miracle he gets any work done at all in his studio and gallery when he'd rather obviously prefer to be chatting with the customers. "Our focus is on people coming in and seeing the process of creating sculpture," he said. Thorsen and his wife Cyndy opened the gallery in 1993 and it displays almost exclusively his own work, which has gained a worldwide reputation for excellence among wildlife sculpture collectors. A public gallery is downstairs, and his studio is upstairs with several dozen works in progress scattered across a space that's perhaps 1,000 square feet. Every kind of wildlife imaginable is represented, whether it's bears, birds, or fish. In addition, Thorsen is now exploring the artistic possibilities of the human form, and he is working on full figure nudes as well as hands and heads. His naturalistic style is also gradually giving way to a more abstract work. Thorsen sells to collectors exclusively out of his gallery, sending the work worldwide. The gallery is open from 10 AM to 8 PM six days a week, and has shorter hours on Sunday. During the winter, the hours are also somewhat shorter.

Linda Tippetts Fine Art
10 Somers Road, Somers
• **(406) 857-3110**

Linda Tippetts is best known locally for winning $50,000 as the grand-prize winner in the 1992 Arts for the Parks contest for her painting "East Slope Tunnel on Going-to-the-Sun." That achievement certainly merits attention, but when you visit Tippetts' studio in Somers, you will discover that she has many more sides to her art. Yes, she does mostly landscapes, but not always of Glacier Park. She is a "plein air" oil painter, which means she paints whatever she sees on her travels, and she travels plenty. You'll find work from Mexico, China, and Portugal in her studio, as well as scenes from across Montana. In addition she does nudes and figurals for a change of pace, although everything is very distinctively in her own broad-brushed, muscular impressionistic style. She built her studio and home in 1995, just off of U.S. 93 on an imposing hillside in Somers. She shows her paintings only by appointment to serious collectors. "The collector enjoys seeing the work in a home," Tippetts said. "It gives them a better feel for what they can do with the art in their own space."

Dance

Northwest Ballet Company
1411 First Ave. W., Kalispell
• **(406) 755-0760**

The Northwest Ballet Co. is best known for their annual holiday presentation of "The Nutcracker" each Christmas season at the Bigfork Center for the Performing Arts. Carol Jakes, artistic director of the Northwest Ballet Company and the Northwest Ballet School in Kalispell, has choreographed and directed the show annually since the late 1970s in the Flathead Valley. The ballet company and school also perform other concerts during the year featuring classical ballet, ballroom dancing, and Broadway musical numbers. The ballet company is affiliated with the Dance Art Center run by Jakes.

Film

Whitefish Film Society
509 E. Sixth St., Whitefish
• **(406) 862-5994**

The Whitefish Film Society is only a couple of years old, but has already taken root as a beloved community institution. Under the directorship of Jill Zignego, the society has developed a mission "to bring alternative cinema to the Flathead Valley, especially foreign films and American independents," she said. Among titles that have been screened here are *The Full Monty*, *Mrs. Brown*, *Ponette*, *Life is Beautiful (La Vita e Bella)*, and *Fast, Cheap and Out of Control*. The films are shown the last weekend of every month at the Mountain Cinema in Whitefish's Mountain Mall.

Music

Flathead Valley Festival
Mountain Mall, 6475 U.S. 93 S., Whitefish
• **(406) 862-7708**

The Flathead Festival, which was begun in the late 1980s, is held annually in July and August. It features an array of concerts in a variety of genres as well as workshops and educational opportunities throughout the valley. The festival's performing artists and guest faculty have been drawn from the top professional ranks in both U.S. and Canada. The Flathead Festival started as a classical music festival under the direction of Kenyard Smith, conductor of the Montana Chorale. Then known as the Festival of the Rockies, the festival was pegged more as an educational experience for participants than a performance event. Through the years, the focus has shifted

Credit: Whitefish Theatre Company

A scene from *Little Shop of Horrors* — performed by the
Whitefish Theatre Company

somewhat, expanding in 1987 to include more jazz, then changing to a classical and pops format in 1988, when the name was officially altered to the Flathead Festival. In the early '90s, big-name entertainment became a standard offering, with such celebrity singers as Mel Torme and Jerry Jeff Walker making stops in the valley. Most recently, the festival has included top names in rock and blues such as Lynyrd Skynyrd and Robert Cray. Starting in 1998, the festival was divided into a Saturday Night Party Series and a Monday Night Classical Series. Many of the Saturday night concerts, in particular, are outdoors, and patrons typically wear jeans or shorts and bring picnic suppers or eat meals purchased at concession stands. Bring your own lawn chairs and blankets and prepare to enjoy an evening of music amid the splendor of the Rocky Mountains.

Glacier Orchestra and Chorale
P.O. Box 2491, Kalispell
• (406) 257-3241

This group was one of 12 orchestras honored nationally by the American Society of Composers, Authors and Publishers for excellence in programming of contemporary music. John Zoltek took over as conductor a

few years ago, and his dynamic mastery of difficult music has helped turn the orchestra into a showcase of fine talent. There are also frequent guest performers such as violin virtuoso Eugene Fodor or renowned clarinetist John Denman. The orchestra and chorale generally perform five concerts each season, starting in October and continuing through April. Each concert of the season is performed twice, on Saturday at Central School auditorium in Whitefish and on Sunday at Flathead High School auditorium in Kalispell. Get there early not just to guarantee a seat, but because Zoltek leads most shows with a preview lecture 45 minutes before the concert. The holiday concerts in December are usually sellouts, so plan to buy tickets early. The orchestra is also the parent body of the Glacier Youth Orchestra & Glacier Children's Choir, which perform throughout the school year. Shauneen Garner conducts the Glacier Chorale and the children's choir.

Wooden Music
P.O. Box 630, Bigfork
• (406) 837-5795

Wooden Music got started in 1992 when Whitefish resident and finger-style guitarist Larry Pattis decided he couldn't live without

The beautiful I.A. O'Shaughnessy Center is a favorite
performance venue in Whitefish.

seeing more of the acoustic music he loved. He scheduled appearances by Harvey Reid, Chuck Pyle, Greg Brown and many others. The past several years, in the wake of Pattis's departure to Salt Lake City, however, Wooden Music has changed from a one-man show to a one-woman show and is now run by Susan Morrow of Bigfork. The concerts, often held in Kalispell at the Outlaw Inn, remain of the highest calibre, featuring names such as Greg Brown, John Gorka, Cosy Sheridan, and the Drum Brothers.

Flathead Valley Jazz Society
Glacier Jazz Stampede
P.O. Box 2627, Kalispell
• (406) 862-3814

The Flathead Valley Jazz Society sponsors concerts and jazz parties throughout the year, bringing regional and local entertainment to the fore. But since 1994, the society has been best known for the Glacier Jazz Stampede, which has rapidly grown into one of the Valley's most anticipated arts events each year. The Stampede, which is held in the early fall, is a traditional jazz festival, and something more. Under the direction of unflappable, unstoppable jazz pianist Karla West, the festival draws some of the top names in the business, such as the Rhythm Rascals from Disney World in Orlando, Florida, Blue

Street Jazz Band from Fresno, California, and the Uptown Lowdown Jazz Band from Seattle, Washington, along with local groups such as the Don Lawrence Orchestra. Already the largest event of its kind in western Montana, it counts on local participation as well as the hundreds of jazz fans who travel from festival to festival in search of their favorite music. In addition to Dixieland, the festival always features ragtime music and has also included Latin jazz as well as the Big Band sound and modern jazz. The musicians perform on a rotating basis at four or five venues, usually including the Outlaw Inn, Cavanaugh's, the Elks Club and the Eagles Club.

Flathead Valley Blues Society
P.O. Box 219, Somers
• (406) 857-3119

Steve Kelley, the founder and president of the Flathead Valley Blues Society, is better known round these parts as Big Daddy. And when Big Daddy plays, people listen. He's the leader of a band called Big Daddy and the Blue Notes and is frequently heard as opening act for major blues shows passing through the valley. Most of the major blues concerts these days are actually sponsored by the blues society, with as many as 12 concerts a year bringing top names in Chicago blues and other blues genres to the valley. "There's a dual purpose to the blues society," Kelley said. "To perpetuate and support blues music, which is a true American art form, and also to provide alternative live music entertainment." Some of the top names to appear here recently include blues harp player Mark Hummel and Chicago blues giant Jimmy Rogers, as well as Andrew "Junior Boy" Jones, Larry Garner, and Coco Montoya.

Folkshop Music Series
221 U.S. 93 S., Ronan
• **(406) 676-5333, (800) 984-FOLK**

Folkshop Productions has been presenting concerts in the Mission Valley for more than 10 years, and has gained a reputation for excellence as well as for doing good works. "We were looking for a way to raise money for disabled employment, and this is the best fund-raiser we have ever had," said Chas Cantlon, executive director of the Folkshops. Local businesses sponsor the concerts by covering the costs, so every ticket purchased goes directly toward the Folkshop mission of hiring the disabled. Among the many popular shows over the past 10 years have been appearances by singer-songwriter Greg Brown, bluesman Spencer Bohren, folksinger Peter Ostroushko, and lots of bluegrass performers such as Special Consensus and Vassar Clements. The Folkshop series has also sponsored modern dance performances by the nationally renowned Ririe-Woodbury Dance Company and other repertory groups.

Flathead Community Concert Association
P.O. Box 894, Kalispell
• **(406) 888-5033**

When it was started several decades ago, the Flathead Community Concert series was pretty much the only top-name entertainment coming to the valley. Today, there are many more options, but the Community Concert Series has continued to be popular because of the quality of the entertainment provided. A membership drive is held in April for the entire series, but sometimes individual concerts have some room left over. Write to the address above for season ticket information, or call ahead to see if any tickets will be available at the door for particular shows. Performers in the series have included The New York Theatre Ballet performing "The Nutcracker," the Aspen Wind Quintet, the Welsh Male Choir, and harpist Carol McLaughlin.

Riverbend Concert Series
P.O. Box 237, Bigfork
• **(406) 837-5888**

If you'd like to enjoy a musical experience and still remain out-of-doors, then you can't do better than the Riverbend Concert Series, which is held on Sunday evenings in Bigfork's Everit Sliter Memorial Park every summer from June through August. Musicians range from well-known local acts such as the Don Lawrence Orchestra to classical guitarist Stuart Weber. Tickets are available at the entrance. In case of rain, the concerts move to the Bigfork Elementary School gym.

Nordicfest
P.O. Box 791, Libby
• **(406) (800) 785-6541**

Every year in September, the town of Libby in Lincoln County turns Scandinavian for the second weekend of the month. Nordicfest is a celebration of local and international culture. J. Neils came to the area from Wisconsin at the turn of the century to start a lumber mill. He brought with him many Scandinavian loggers and their families, and both logging and Nordic roots are remembered during the festival, which features a variety of musical and theatrical events as well as crafts and ethnic foods. A regular performer at the festival is the Don Lawrence Orchestra, the prominent Big Band based in Kalispell. Other performers over the years have been accordionist Myron Floren and other top names from "The Lawrence Welk Show." There is also continuous free outdoor entertainment at the bandshell during the daytime.

Theater

Bigfork Summer Playhouse
P.O. Box 456, Bigfork
• **(406) 837-4886**

Every summer, the Bigfork Center for the Performing Arts becomes the Bigfork Summer Playhouse as actors from across the United States come together to put on musicals and comedies. The Bigfork Summer Playhouse was begun in 1960 and has provided a training ground for hundreds of aspiring theatrical performers, technicians and musicians. It has been under the direction of owners Don and Jude Thomson since 1971. The playhouse offers four musicals and a farce every summer, and more than 3,000 people from throughout the United States apply to join the company each year. Expect a variety of musicals and musical comedies such as *The Will Rogers Follies, Grease, Cabaret* or *The Boys From Syracuse.* Tickets are cheaper for performances before July 4 or if purchased at the beginning of the season. The box office opens about the middle of May. Starting then, you can purchase tickets by telephone, mail or in person. Discounts are available for groups. There are no performances on Sundays.

Whitefish Theatre Co., Whitefish
1 Central Avenue, Whitefish
• (406) 862-5371

This is the oldest continuing community theater group in the Flathead Valley, performing since the mid-1970s. Under the direction of actress-director Jane Fellows for more than 10 years, the group presents four or five plays a year, often including touring productions by other companies and dinner-theater offerings. The company prides itself on a diverse season including drama such as *Waiting for Godot,* musicals like *The Music Man,* classics such as *A Midsummer Night's Dream,* family shows like *The Hobbit,* and comedies such as *Lost in Yonkers.* Recently the company moved out its stage at a local school to the new I.A. O'Shaughnessy Cultural Arts Center, and Fellows has announced her retirement, so more changes will be on the way. In addition to its own shows, the Whitefish Theatre Co. also sponsors performances of modern dance, ballet, Shakespeare in the Park, and a summer theater camp. New since the move is a concert series that has brought folk musicians Peter Ostroushko and Laurie Lewis to town.

Bigfork Community Players
P.O. Box 23, Bigfork
• (406) 837-1530

The Bigfork Community Players perform three or four plays every year from the late fall to the spring. In addition to enthusiastic casts, the plays boast of being produced in the

Credit: Hockaday Museum of Art

The Hockaday Museum of Art in Kalispell is a local treasure.

Bigfork Center for the Performing Arts, where every one of the 450 or so seats is a good one. Plays performed recently include the female version of *The Odd Couple, On Golden Pond,* Woody Allen's *Play It Again Sam, Crimes of the Heart,* and Tennessee Williams' *Cat on a Hot Tin Roof.* A new addition to the offerings is the annual Montana Community Theater Festival, held in the spring of each year, featuring as many companies as possible from around the state. The Players have also recently added a slate of children's theater workshops and productions to their calendar.

Flathead Valley Community Theater
777 Grandview Dr., Kalispell
• **(406) 756-3822**

The community college has also gotten into the act the past few years—theatrically, that is. Joe Legate, the head of the theater department, has been instrumental in reshaping a theater program that was quite active in the 1970s but eventually went into hiatus. Legate arrived in Kalispell in 1992 from North Dakota, where he had spent several years teaching at Dickinson State University. He has also worked in theater programs at Clemson University, the University of Southern Mississippi and the State University of New York. Though the theatrical program draws heavily from the students and faculty at the college, many of the shows also use other members of the community as well. Look for a broad variety of shows, from pure farce to high drama.

Down Home Productions
P.O. Box 1528, Bigfork
• **(406) 837-0244**

Mary Sullivan Slack moved here from California in 1994, and immediately jumped into the theater scene. Noted for her roles in community theater productions in California, once in the Flathead Valley she switched gears and became, primarily, a director. In the past few years, she has produced about 60 shows, including full-scale productions as well as reader's theater shows. Some of the titles the company is associated with are *Love Letters, The Gingerbread Lady, Jake's Women, 84 Charing Cross Road,* and *Lettice & Lovage.* The company plans an April 1999 startup date

for a new Kalispell Repertory Theater group that will be housed in the Central School Museum in downtown Kalispell, the home of the Northwest Montana Historical Society. "We want to do something in the summer, when there are lots of people here," said Slack.

The Port Polson Players
P.O. Box 1152, Polson
• **(406) 883-4691**

The Port Polson Players offer professional summer stock theater in the recently renovated Clubhouse Theater in the Polson City Golf Course at Boettcher Park on Flathead Lake. The company was begun in 1976 by Larry and Pat Barsness, who also started the Virginia City Players, in Virginia City, Montana, in 1948. The Polson group was purchased by Neal and Karen Lewing in 1983 and they have run it successfully ever since, adding a year-round community theater schedule to what started as just a summer-stock company. The larger-scale community theater offerings are usually presented at the Polson High School auditorium. Among the titles presented recently have been *Fiddler on the Roof, Oklahoma, The Miracle Worker, The Glass Menagerie, Forever Plaid, Nunsense,* and *Pump House Boys & Dinettes.* The Lewings also write a children's show every year, including adaptations such as *Sleeping Beauty* and original titles such as *Fortune's Fables.* The box office can be reached at 883-9212 from June through September only.

Venues

Bigfork Center for the Performing Arts
526 Electric Ave., Bigfork
• **(406) 837-4886**

This 450-seat facility in Bigfork provides year-round entertainment. From May through August, the Bigfork Summer Playhouse offers musical repertory theater, while at other times throughout the year, it is home to productions by the Bigfork Community Players, the Flathead Festival, the Northwest Ballet and many other groups. The playhouse is noted for its comfort and for the great view from all the seats.

I.A. O'Shaughnessy Cultural Arts Center
1 Central Avenue, Whitefish
- **(406) 862-5371**

The people of Whitefish are noted for giving generously to community projects, and during a several-year campaign, funds were raised to build a new center for the performing arts as well as a nearby library building. The I.A. O'Shaughnessy Cultural Arts Center includes a 300-seat theater facility, which had its grand opening on July 4, 1998. The Whitefish Theatre Company holds a long-term lease on the building and is now focusing its schedule on the thrust stage, which has seating on three sides, plus a balcony. Concerts, dance, and other theatrical presentations will also be booked into the facility year-round. The seating can also be pushed back to accommodate other presentations such as the annual Halloween haunted house fund-raiser.

Literary Arts

Authors of the Flathead
Flathead River Writers Conference
P.O. Box 7711, Kalispell
- **(406) 881-4066**

The Authors of the Flathead group has been meeting for about 10 years and has just under 100 members. The group conducts a craft-of-writing workshop or a speaker's meeting on most Monday nights. A recording at 881-4066 has details on times, locations and each week's topic, as well as other upcoming activities. Each year, the group holds its annual Flathead River Writers Conference in early October at the Grouse Mountain Lodge in Whitefish. "The conference is getting an excellent reputation in writing circles from the Midwest to California and Canada," said conference spokesman Jake How.

The conference features a variety of writers, editors and agents. Recent guests have included Jack Sowards, author of thousands of television episodes and movie screenplays including *Star Trek II: The Wrath of Khan,* and Steve Chapple, a Livingston, Montana author who is noted for his book *Confessions of an Eco-Redneck* as well as countless magazine articles. The conference always includes editors or publishers who can help see new writers through the nuts and bolts of publishing. "The conference remains the most affordable of its kind in the northwest United States," said How. "The two days are crammed with speakers, panel discussions, and one-on-one workshops." Registration for the conference costs a little more than $100 for two days. Those interested in attending can call Dixon Rice at 755-7272 and request a detailed brochure and registration form. Registration is also available at the door.

Yellow Bay Writer's Workshop
Yellow Bay Biological Research Station, 311 Bio Station Lane (mile marker 17, Montana 35), Yellow Bay
- **(406) (888) 254-2544**

The annual Yellow Bay Writers' Workshop is held about the second week of August every year at The University of Montana's biological research station on Flathead Lake. It provides a thoughtful getaway at a scenic location in the company of other writers. The workshop faculty generally features four top writers, in addition to several special guests and readings. Previous faculty members have included humorist Ian Frazier, novelist Ron Hansen, naturalist Gary Nabhan and Kalispell's own David Long, a noted novelist and short-story writer. Special guests include editors and agents talking about the business of writing. Non-participants of the workshops may still attend readings and lectures throughout the week for a nominal fee per session. For a schedule, send a stamped, self-addressed envelope to the Center for Continuing Education, The University of Montana, Missoula, MT 59812, or call the phone number above. Participants in the workshop are selected after they submit a manuscript sample. Tuition and residency fees add up to more than $800.

Whitefish Reading Series
P.O. Box 1273, Whitefish
- **(406) 862-0805**

One of those remarkable success stories that make the Flathead such a fun place is the Whitefish Reading Series, a labor of love since 1993 by Patty Smith, who has single-handedly created a demand for great writing and great writers in the Flathead. She has plenty of help from a core group of volunteers, but without Patty, this pillar of the arts community would not exist. Often during the fall, winter and spring months, she arranges for as many as four authors a month to read, present slide shows and sign books to the generally rapt attention of a devoted audience. Venues vary, but the Rocky Mountain Lodge in Whitefish hosts many of the events. Authors presented in the past few years include novelist David James Duncan ("The River Why"), poet Patricia Goedicke ("Paul Bunyan's Bearskin"), local radio personality George Ostrom ("The Over the Hill Gang" and "Wondrous Wildlife"), and travel writer extraordinaire Tim Cahill ("Pass the Butterworms: Remote Journeys Oddly Rendered"), mystery writer James Crumley ("The Last Good Kiss") and Civil War novelist Jeff Shaara ("Gods and Generals").

Arts and Crafts

Bigfork Festival of the Arts
P.O. Box 237, Bigfork
• **(406) 837-5888**

The Bigfork Festival of the Arts, which is held the first weekend in August every year, features more than 70 artists, including some from as far away as Oregon, Washington and California. Booths feature everything from paintings, prints, jewelry, stained glass, and pottery, to wooden toys, wearable art and baskets. There are also a variety of food booths, including huckleberry milkshakes, German barbecue, and snowcones, as well as the usual hamburgers and hot dogs. Bigfork's main business street, Electric Avenue, is converted into a boardwalk for the festival, with opportunities for shopping both in the booths and in local shops, which sell everything from books to antiques to a wide variety of artworks. Musical performances throughout the day also provide entertainment, and there are activities for children at various locations.

Arts in the Park
P.O. Box 83, Kalispell
• **(406) 755-5268**

Ever consider doing your Christmas shopping in July? You can get it all out of the way at the popular Arts in the Park festival held the last weekend in July at Kalispell's Depot Park (located at the intersection of U.S. 93 and Center Street). The festival is a fund-raiser for the Hockaday Museum of Art and has been held ever since the museum was founded in 1968. It calls itself the oldest and best juried art fair in Montana. At the very least it is a darn good time. "We always expect a huge turnout," says David Lee Eubank, executive director of the Hockaday. "At least 10,000 people will come through the gates, maybe more." More than 90 artists and artisans exhibit works every year in numerous media such as painting, sculpture, pastel, photography, glass, jewelry, pottery, ceramics, weaving, wood carving, leather, metal, and more. A few artists will also be on hand to demonstrate how they go about making their creations, and there are the usual generous helpings of musical entertainment and food that make these arts and crafts fairs so popular.

Whitefish Arts Festival
P.O. Box 131, Whitefish
• **(406) 862-5875**

The Whitefish Arts Festival, which is held on the first weekend in July, has been held for about 20 years, and it never disappoints. The event is a feast both for the eyes and for the palate, featuring 80 artists from the Flathead Valley and beyond, as well as food vendors, local musicians and entertainers, and other fun. Up for sale will be every variety imaginable of paintings, woodcraft, pottery, original clothing and other handicrafts. The festival is held on the Central School lawn in downtown Whitefish, and is a fund-raiser for the Cross Currents Christian School, which can be reached at the number listed above. Admission is free.

Most antiques stores here keep the doors open year-round for those of us who search out the antiques experience no matter where we travel or what month of the year it is.

Antiques

Postcard-perfect scenery, soul-satisfying outdoor recreational activities and world-class golf greens all draw visitors to the Flathead Valley, but this corner of Montana yields another, perhaps unexpected, attraction. It is also known as the antiquing mecca of Western Montana. From Bigfork and Somers on Flathead Lake north to Whitefish and on to East Glacier in Glacier National Park, you can find dozens of antiques malls and shops—at last count they numbered 35, a fairly high number for a county with a population of just 73,000. Most antiques stores here keep the doors open year-round for those of us who search out the antiques experience no matter where we travel or what month of the year it is.

A logical way to antique the Flathead is to do a loop, beginning in Bigfork on Mont. Highway 35, then cross Mont. Highway 82 (known locally as the Somers cut-off road). At its junction with U.S. Highway 93, turn south and proceed past Somers to visit one of our listings there. Then do a short backtrack up U.S. 93 and proceed north into Kalispell. (If you begin in Somers, reverse the process.)

Kalispell has the highest concentration of antiques stores, so you'll want to plan extra time there to enjoy the pickings. Although space constraints limit this chapter to our top spots, be sure to visit other fine local antiques stores for more great finds as time allows. Many of them are interspersed along the way.

The listings here give a representative taste of what the Flathead Valley has to offer, and include contact information, days of business, and a general overview of what you might find. It's a good idea to call ahead to make sure the business you want to visit is open, though the beautiful drive to any of these locations may be worth a trip in itself. Generally, owners of the Flathead Valley's antiques stores are happy to open by appointment if you are looking for something special and cannot visit during regular hours. Call the number listed with each shop. Our top antiques stores are not rated numerically as to which are the best of the best, but are listed by location on our antiquing loop. We hope you enjoy your antiques tour!

Architectural Innovations
Showroom • 459 Electric Ave., Bigfork • (406) 837-2334
Warehouse • 7975 Mont. Highway 35, Bigfork • (406) 887-2328

Looking for a place to retire, Margrit Matter chose Bigfork after a vacation visit in 1991. Instead of basking in retirement today, however, she finds herself thriving on running not one, but two, antiques stores (the showroom and warehouse) in Bigfork, which she has called Architectural Innovations.

Established in summer 1998, both the showroom and the warehouse are open to shoppers. The warehouse, located on Montana Highway 35, contains the bigger selection of antique furniture and accessories. Margrit's discerning Old World Antiques furniture line, composed of European antiques dating from the late 1700s through the early 1900s, is a little out of the ordinary for this corner of the country. Through her West Coast ties to the construction and remodeling industry (in which she worked before relocating here) she is able to bring in fine imported pieces.

Besides being originals, furniture selected for her stores must still function properly and be in excellent condition. Here you might find a pine piece from Czechoslovakia, an oak armoire from England or Belgium, a carved bed of French walnut or cherry and original European and American artwork. You'll discover other quality pieces—hutches, wardrobes, dressers, settees, tables, desks and accessories in her beautiful displays. Also, look for salvaged architectural details.

Margrit is expanding to offer a home design center in the warehouse. She is adding custom furniture by local artists, kitchen cabinets, sinks, faucets and fixtures, lamps—old and new—and some European marble, slate and tiles. In addition, her customers can find wallpapers and fabrics to create a distinctive backdrop for their furniture and accessories.

The showroom in Twin Birch Square in downtown Bigfork is a grand location to shop for original antiques and accessories and at the same time gather ideas for floor and wall treatments from different styles and time periods. Margrit has created room vignettes showcasing European, Southwestern, Mediterranean, Art Nouveau, Victorian and Montana styles. Ceilings and walls have been plastered, faux painted, crackled, glazed and stenciled. Unusual floor treatments include using a latex-based stucco that is waterproof, in which different patterns have been imprinted, such as tiles and cobblestones. Look for the plastered Kiva fireplace with faux-stone accents, ledges and a hearth of Idaho quartzite rock.

Both stores are open year-round seven days a week during summer. After Christmas through Memorial Day they are open Monday through Saturday and closed Sundays.

The Osprey Nest Antiques
6090 U.S.Highway 93 South, Somers
• (406) 857-3714

Look for a couple of Osprey nests on tall platforms just off the highway approximately 2.8 miles north of Lakeside. They will signal your arrival at The Osprey Nest Antiques. Here a huge red barn from the late 1890s is settled comfortably on a low hill, sharing well-kept grounds with an old log cabin. Reminiscent of a New England country inn, the barn, with its wide porches and white wicker furniture, beckons you to explore the wide variety of antiques housed within.

Owner Karen Nagelhus, who established the business in 1988, says the store carries "everything from A to Z." She does feature a number of specialty items. Here you'll find quite a selection of Early American furniture from the 18th century, primitives from about 1900 and out-of-print and rare books. Handmade lace and linens and sterling silver pieces, including flatware, add their vintage grace to the furniture groupings. Karen likes to concentrate on purchasing furniture and accessories crafted of walnut, oak and maple woods. As you browse throughout the chock-full rooms, expect to find glassware, kitchen utensils, stoneware, jewelry, tools and Western memorabilia.

The Osprey Nest was photographed by *Architectural Digest* magazine in April 1991. The barn's rustic interior is all wood. The ceiling with its exposed wood rafters, the log posts and the rough-paneled walls all give the rambling building a cozy warmth. As you stroll from one room to another a grandfather clock chimes the hour in deep, mellow tones. The charming displays, filled with treasures from the past, seem to transport you into someone's cabin, offering a nostalgic reminder of days gone by.

The Osprey Nest is open year-round, seven days a week.

Somers Antiques
210 Montana Highway 82, Kalispell
• (406) 857-3234

At the intersection of U.S. Highway 93 and Montana Highway 82 look for the large signs advertising the Somers Antiques store. Entering the grounds, you pass by such things as weathered wheelbarrows and bicycles and a long row of timeworn dining tables that line the porch. You venture inside and are greeted by 6,000 square feet of antiques and collectibles displayed in a mercantile-type atmosphere. Crammed with items from a by-gone era, this store will yield up everything from blanket chests to cupboards, pine tables to primitive wood benches, and ice cream parlor chairs to Coca-Cola soda pop machines.

Owners Larry and Carol Ask, collectors themselves for 20 years, offer several specialties at Somers Antiques. If you are looking for oak or pine, they provide a large selection of refinished furniture. Filling the store are hundreds of old toys (some from Larry's personal collection), pedal cars, old bicycles, old tools and tins. Sporting paraphernalia, such as old fishing rods and golf clubs, mingles with other collectibles. You can find advertising signs, here and there a piece of Western memorabilia and many other treasures stashed away.

Unique country and cabin-type furniture can be had here, including a cowhide-upholstered oak chair, a handmade twig shelf and, if you're lucky, perhaps an old canoe converted into a bookshelf. Something you may not expect is a variety of Victorian-style lamps. Some of the floor lamps are old, but the table lamps are reproductions. Fringed and beaded shades, despite being new, impart a vintage look.

Somers Antiques is open year-round seven days a week in summer, from June to Labor Day. During winter the store is open five or six days a week, with some flexibility there. The store is always closed on Sundays in winter, and call if you're visiting any other day of the week to be sure they're open.

Fine Things
3593 U.S. Highway 93 S., Kalispell
• (406) 756-8925

Opened in summer 1998 Fine Things, located south of Kalispell, brings a different twist to the antiques business. Antiques and collectibles are, of course, offered for sale, but owners Lynda and Jeff Johnson provide a restoration service for antiques and other fine pieces. Jeff also builds reproduction solid wood furniture. He crafts a lot of English pine pieces and French armoires. If your tastes run to Victorian, Queen Anne, Adirondack or just plain rustic, he can build that for you, too.

Filling this unusual niche in the Flathead keeps the couple busy. But Jeff and Lynda continue to find time for occasional visits to her family in England (she's from Nottingham), where they buy antiques to bring back for the store. Old toys, Flow Blue and other china and "smalls" that they can carry easily have made their way stateside with the Johnsons in the past.

On the retail end, they don't specialize in anything particular—whatever takes their fancy. A gentleman's wig cabinet from the late 1700s stands along one wall, waiting to be restored. In the room up front you might run across a pair of cherry nightstands or an old dogcart. Lynda, who loves visiting with customers, will be happy to tell you about the history of various pieces.

Folk art pictures, painted by Lynda, adorn the walls. The self-taught artist often paints on the furniture, too. She especially likes to paint French Country and Victorian armoires

Credit: Osprey Nest Antiques

A lovely farmhouse, a small sign — all you need to start your antiquing adventures.

built by Jeff. Her attractive floral designs of roses add a distinctive look to the doors of the armoires. These pieces have become popular with her customers. Lynda's painting also freshens up dressers, tables and chairs gleaned from local garage sales. If a customer wants to bring in a piece of furniture or an accessory that needs a facelift, Lynda is happy to work her magic.

Although Jeff studied lathe-work under an English craftsman and restored antique furniture in Houston, Texas, he's mostly a self-taught furniture craftsman. The couple does the furniture restoration for the Conrad Mansion in Kalispell (see Attractions). Jeff noted that they do all work by hand the old-fashioned way in both the furniture restoration and construction, using non-toxic, EPA-approved products.

"Fine Things" is open year-round seven days a week in summer, beginning on Memorial Day. Approximately early October the store begins winter hours and is open Monday through Saturday.

Southside Consignment
2699 U.S. Highway 93 S., Kalispell
• **(406) 756-8526**

Thirteen antiques dealers and hundreds of consignors keep this 6,000-square-foot store on the south side of Kalispell stocked with antiques, collectibles and some new gift goodies.

Owned by Donna Kouns, the rambling store offers a wide assortment of items. A stroll through here might turn up an old baker's table, hutches, side chairs, kitchen kettles, crockery bowls and old utensils. If you collect teacups, you may find a new favorite. Sterling silver pieces, flatware and costume jewelry add their sparkle to the mix. Toys and books are interspersed among furniture and accessories. You might run across Western memorabilia, such as branding irons or Western tack, or even an old-fashioned wood cookstove.

The pickings at Southside Consignment aren't limited to the old. A Christmas tree with ornaments in a fishing theme, candles, cards and potpourri may be found here, as well as rustic log beds, tables and chairs for your dream cabin. To complete your cabin, look

for a handmade ceramic moose planter. They are very cute—for moose!

Southside Consignments is open year-round from Tuesday through Saturday and closed Sunday and Monday.

Timeless Treasures
132 Main St., Kalispell
• **(406) 752-4659**

An attractive window display will charm you into visiting Timeless Treasures antiques store, easy to locate on Main Street (U.S. Highway 93). Old music from the 1950s, 1960s and 1970s played on an old-fashioned record player greets you. Take a trip down music's memory lane with such greats as Frank Sinatra, Lena Horn, Billie Holiday, Johnny Mathis and Simon and Garfunkel.

Diversity is the key to this 2,000-square-foot shop, says Linda Heim, who owns the business with husband Jim. The store is host for 20 dealers to showcase their wares. Many dealers focus on specialty items and either own their own antiques stores or have booths in other local antiques malls, as well.

Old watches, estate jewelry, costume jewelry and hard-to-find books are found at Timeless Treasures. Glassware, including Depression glass, American-made pottery and dinnerware, is available here, as well. Old toys and pedal cars mingle with yesteryears' dolls and Victorian-style lamps with beaded and fringed shades. Some cowboy memorabilia can be found here, as well as collectible home decorator items. You may run across other unusual pieces, such as a 1930s Wurlitzer jukebox.

Downstairs in the basement the furniture section is ever-growing. A trip below might net a camelback trunk, a marble-topped table or an old church pew.

Timeless Treasures is a pleasant stop and stays open year-round seven days a week.

Kalispell Antiques Market
48 Main Street, Kalispell
• **(406) 257-2800**

Up the street on the corner of First and Main is a must-stop antiques mall at Opera House Square. Located in the historic opera house building, the mall is downstairs, tucked under a spacious Western clothing store. The

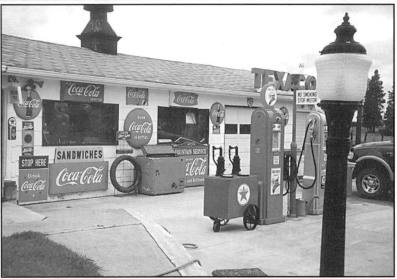

Credit: Stageline Antiques

Flathead Valley antiques come in all shapes and sizes.

market sprawls over 10,000-square-feet, making it the Flathead Valley's largest antiques mall, where thirty-five dealers display quality merchandise.

Every square inch bursts with interesting items to look at. If you don't want to miss anything, give yourself the better part of a morning or afternoon to wend your way through three long rooms with aisles and aisles of booths.

The store features a wide selection of antiques and collectibles reference books, if you are looking for antiques guides.

Proprietors are brother and sister Lee and JoAnn Eslick. Roseville pottery has long been a specialty at the Kalispell Antiques Market. In fact, Lee says it's the largest collection he's seen. He also claims the best selection of vintage rhinestone jewelry in the Valley. Another specialty at the market is handmade primitive furniture, which might include a pie safe with punched tin doors.

A large selection of Western Americana books can be perused here. Depending on availability, you might run across books by noted Montana authors A. B. Guthrie, J.W. Schultz and Frank Linderman.

Western memorabilia items come in, but go out quickly, since they remain ever popular in the Flathead. One unique furniture set was a children's Western card table with brands and cowboys decorating the top. Old hunting and fishing sporting goods come and go quickly, too, since many locals decorate with sporting goods memorabilia.

Adding to the mix are original oak pieces, many from the late 1800s to early 1900s. Antique furniture might include a sideboard, buffet, dining table with chairs or glass-fronted bookcase. Other interesting collectibles range from old linens and teacups to vintage paper goods, and a host of other items.

The market welcomes visitors year-round seven days a week.

Back In Time Antiques
278 4th Ave. E. N., Kalispell
• (406) 756-3714

Turn east on Idaho (U.S. Highway 2) and then turn north on Fourth Avenue East North. A brightly painted buggy advertises the store, which is tucked behind in the alley.

Owners Mark and Dawn Ingraham constructed the building and opened the business in summer 1998. Its plain facade doesn't prepare you for the surprise inside. The entire interior was designed as an attractive back-drop to showcase the antique furnishings. It appears that you have stepped into a well-appointed parlor from days gone by. Old-fashioned, warmly colored wallpaper in maroon and green covers the upper walls. The wainscot below is painted, and this simple finish highlights the well-displayed furnishings. A rose-colored carpet with a rose motif further replicates an old-time atmosphere. Mark and Dawn even ring up purchases by hand on an ornate vintage cash register by National Cash Register of Dayton, Ohio.

Hanging as a focal point on one wall is an old window from a local sheriff's office. A scene painted on it by local artist Leonard Miller depicts two girls in a meadow. The painted piece is special enough that Dawn hangs no other artwork along the wall.

If you're searching for oak accessories and furnishings, this store caters to you; most oak pieces date from the late 1800s to about the 1920s. At Back In Time, the owners hunt for furniture with cabriole legs and claw feet. "Mark loves claw feet," Dawn says.

Most of the store's inventory is composed of china hutches, buffets, dressers, tables with chairs, desks and accessories. Dawn has had old sofas with matching occasional chairs reupholstered with fabrics that coordinate companionably with the vintage surroundings. Most of the couple's "finds" for their store come from close to home, between Missoula, Montana, and the Flathead Valley.

Back In Time is open year-round seven days a week during summer. In winter—after early November—the owners close on Sundays, until approximately Labor Day when they open again seven days a week.

Glacier Antique Mall
3195 U.S. Highway 93 N., Kalispell
• (406) 756-1690

Return to U.S. Highway 93 and head north out of Kalispell. After 4 1/2 miles you will see the Glacier Antique Mall on the east side of the highway.

On the grounds are two log buildings. The larger cabin functions as a summer art gallery. The other log building is the oldest-known homestead in the Flathead Valley, according to owner Jim Browne. Constructed in 1883 of Western larch logs, it sat near the slough off Montana Highway 82 near the present day Ramada Inn. Jim moved it to the grounds of the Glacier Antique Mall about a decade ago, where it serves as a storage shed.

Jim, with his wife Patty, manages the large two-story mall. They invite you to fill a cup with coffee and browse through this store-house of the past. The imposing stone fireplace emanates a cheery warmth during winter. Allow yourself an hour or two to see both floors. You will find a little bit of everything here. The mall, which opened in 1988, houses 8,000 square feet of antiques and collectibles. Filling the space keeps the 12 dealers on the hunt for special antiques and collectibles.

Bronzes from a foundry located on the grounds are for sale here, as are bronzes by well-known Montana artist Ace Powell. Some of his oils and watercolors have been available here, too. Other art by Montana artists has included oil paintings by Harold Von Schmidt and oil and watercolor paintings by Gary Carter, as well as a Tom Lovell graphite drawing of Vikings. The valuable piece was sketched as a working drawing from which to paint the subject in oils. The oil painting was purchased by the National Geographic Society to illustrate an article on Vikings, Jim notes.

If you're decorating in a rustic style, you may get lucky here and pick up an old pair of snowshoes or skis or other Western memorabilia. Look for Early American and primitive accessories, such as trunks, crocks, even a wood butter churn. Indian memorabilia is displayed here; you might run across a circa 1850 Spirit Chest such as the one owned by Sioux Indian leader Crazy Horse.

Other merchandise ranges from dishware to fine china and from old postcards and paper goods to quality costume jewelry. The wide array of furniture might include a log

Artistic displays double the fun of browsing in antiques shops.

bed and rocker, a fainting couch, an oak cabinet with leaded glass and an ornate marble-topped buffet with carved hutch.

An oak Kimball player piano made the journey from Chicago, where it was built in 1915, to the Flathead Valley. The roundabout route was by way of Utah, where the piano belonged to a Mormon family, according to Jim. You might be able to convince him to pump the pedals to produce some lively tunes. Music rolls for the player piano are still being made today, he notes.

One of the mall's most unusual treasures is a stained glass window. In past years it illuminated the Nun's Chapel at St. Patrick's Hospital in Missoula, Montana, Jim says. Pieced from stained glass in 1890, it depicts St. Patrick of Ireland with a staff in one hand and a shamrock in the other, standing on snakes. According to legend, this patron saint drove all the snakes out of Ireland.

The Glacier Antique Mall remains open year-round seven days a week.

Stageline Antiques
2510 Whitefish Stage Rd., Kalispell
• (406) 755-1044

Continue north on U.S. Highway 93. At Milepost 118, turn east on Tronstad Road. Drive to its intersection with Whitefish Stage Road, turn north and go approximately one-eighth of a mile to Stageline Antiques on the west side of the road.

This pleasant country setting was made for a country store, and that's exactly what owners Bob and Chris Tolbert have created. For three decades they have amassed a collection of antiques guaranteed to thrill not only your child, but the child in you. This is the oldest antiques store in the Flathead Valley.

Coca-Cola buffs will want to make this a must stop. Coca-Cola and gas station signs

INSIDERS' TIP

Several of the antique dealers in this area also maintain sites on the Internet. One such site belongs to a dealer at Timeless Treasures, who offers American dinnerware, glassware, and pottery at http://www.homegrownantiques.com.

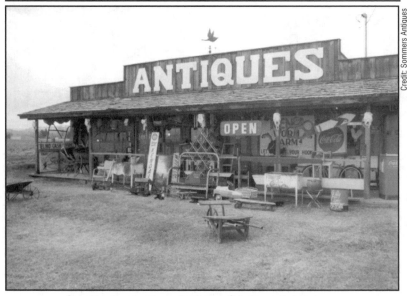

Searching for an antique wheelbarrow? Antiques of all kinds are available in the Flathead Valley.

crowd together on the exteriors of the garage and store. (The Tolberts collect Coca-Cola advertising themselves.) Old gas pumps on the grounds, restored by Bob, stand as a reminder to the era of Mom and Pop stores.

Inside expect to see tools of the trade from way back when—scales, bean counters, an old drugstore cabinet, even an old post office window that says "General Delivery." When the Tolberts opened the store in 1968 they carried antique wood-burning kitchen cookstoves; you'll still find wood- and coal-burning stoves today, dating from the late 1800s to the 1920s. Stageline Antiques would be a place to search for soda fountain items and game room collectibles, such as a 1955 Rockola jukebox.

Old toys and cars from the 1920s through the 1960s fill glass cases. A 1955 Ford Crown Victoria car—in pink—was an eye-catcher. Tins, boxes and pedal toys all share space here, as well. Bob restores pedal toys dating from the 1920s through the 1950s. If you want to take home a unique brass lighting fixture, Bob has a restored collection of those, too. Another highlight here is the hand-carved wooden carousel horse from the 1890s. The country store is open year-round six days a week, Monday through Saturday.

Cock-a-doodle-doo!
12 Lupfer Ave., Whitefish
• (406) 862-0776

If your whimsy is folk art, your penchant is for primitives or your heart beats for American country, you should stop at Cock-a-doodle-doo! in Whitefish. What better symbol for Americana than a rooster crowing to one and all the delights of this treasure-cluttered antiques shop?

Indeed, the cheeky rooster on owner Karen Ryan's business card won her a spot in *Victoria* magazine on the calling card page, which features interesting business cards.

Karen has relocated what was a Kalispell business to a new shop right next door to her Whitefish home, just off Baker Avenue, where she plans a June 1999 opening. Karen's shops are always marked by the scent of candles and potpourri, which welcomes you at the door. In winter, she keeps a pot of tea warming to keep take away the chill from die-hard antiquers.

From shelves to floor, her artfully arranged

displays burst with American country appeal. An old cupboard with cracked paint, decoys, crockery and old quilts add their homespun flavor. Plates, cups and saucers line shelves, and a 1930s metal bed fills a corner. If you've been looking for a gate-leg or drop leaf table, you may find them here, with peeling paint or newly painted. Karen collects 1930s and 1940s tablecloths—you may spy them rolled up and tucked in a crock or basket. An old church pew displays more treasures. Expect a few wooden architectural details from old buildings, including old window sashes. Karen also searches for birdhouses and other garden items for her shop. In addition she has added more country gift items to her inventory.

Merchandise is artfully stacked, piled and layered, but Karen encourages peeking, probing and handling!

Cock-a-doodle-doo! is open year-round on weekends and evenings. If it's closed of an evening, just go 'round and knock on Karen's door.

How about a simulated bobsled ride, a trip in a gondola, or the ultimate in summer fun — traveling to a high mountain pass and making snowballs in July.

Kidstuff

For a kid visiting the mountains in summer, what could be more fun than skipping rocks and splashing around in the cool water of lakes, creeks, and streams? How about a simulated bobsled ride, a trip in a gondola, or the ultimate in summer fun—traveling to a high mountain pass and making snowballs in July. In winter, the snow is the thing. Skiing, snowboarding, sledding, ice skating—and snowballs—will keep Mom and Dad out in the cold along with the kids. Hot chocolate might entice you to come inside long enough to get warm, and then you're out the door again.

Glacier National Park and the Flathead Valley both offer myriad activities for kids. Glacier isn't all that accessible in winter, and many "attractions" in the area close up from late September until May or June, but summer brings the excitement of fast-moving water and the possibility of huckleberries. The Flathead is famous for its winter activities, making both seasons equally ideal for a visit to Northwest Montana.

The following are our suggestions for some of the most kid-friendly activities in the area; let interest, ability, and stamina be your guide.

A

Avalanche Lake Trail and Trail of the Cedars

On Going-to-the-Sun Road, about 5 miles east of Lake McDonald Lodge, is one of the best short family hikes in Glacier National Park. The trail leads from the Avalanche picnic area and campground about 2 miles on a gentle slope to a clear glacial lake. On a very hot day, you may be tempted to splash a bit in the water at the end of the trail, but remember that it is fed by meltwater from the glacier above and can be frigid. There is a wide shore at the lake, and there can be a crowd.

If the two-mile hike seems a bit much for your group and you just want to stretch your legs, the 1-mile, wheelchair accessible Trail of the Cedars is a good choice. It starts from the Avalanche picnic area and heads through a grove of trees with trunks of 4- to 7-feet in diameter. An interpretive brochure is available to help you interpret the sights and sounds of the forest around you.

B

Big Mountain

In summer or winter, Big Mountain is the place to be in the Flathead Valley. It doesn't have to be January for this ski area to be fun and exciting; some of the summer activities are really the most fun of all.

Hiking and mountain biking are available on the mountain for any age and all ability levels—you can either bring your own bikes or rent them there. Even hiking boots can be rented. Special programs for kids are available; call 406-862-1995 for more information.

Two other kid-friendly activities are the gondola ride to the Summit House and the Environmental Education Center. The gondola—called the Glacier Chaser—makes the trip to the top, 2,000 feet of vertical gain, in about 10 minutes. A restaurant and picnic area are located at the Summit House—though you can feast on the views. The Environmental Education Center, run by the USDA Forest Service has interpretive displays on wildlife and habitats, complete with a children's activities corner.

Of course if these activities don't interest you, there's also horseback riding, wagon rides, barbecues, telescope stargazing, a catch-and-release fishing pond, concerts, festivals, tennis, and golf.

Big Mountain is located on Big Mountain Road, just outside of Whitefish. To get there, take U.S. Highway 93 north through town and follow it when it turns west. Turn left right on Wisconsin Avenue and follow it all the way to Big Mountain Road, which is marked with a flashing yellow light.

C

Coram's Amazing Life-sized Maze

If wandering through the Super Maze at this popular Highway 2 attraction doesn't interest you, mini-golf, go-carts, and squirting bumper boats might catch your fancy. You can't miss Amazing Fun Center—though you may miss the town of Coram if you don't look carefully—as you travel on Highway 2 to and from Glacier National Park and the Flathead Valley, you'll spot the giant wooden walls of the maze.

D

Depot Park

Stop to gather local visitor information at the Kalispell Chamber of Commerce office (located in the historic railroad depot) while the kids stretch their legs in this grassy park. There is a shaded area with benches, perfect for a picnic—and if you're lucky you'll catch a performance at the gazebo.

The park is located at the corner of Center Street and U.S. Highway 93 (Main Street) in Kalispell.

E

Elk

If you haven't seen these majestic creatures in the wild during your visit to Northwest Montana, make it a point to drive by or tour the Royal Tine Elk Farm. The 600-acre ranch has 100 elk, easily viewed through the fence

enclosure. Tours can be arranged by calling the owner, Justin Haveman, at 406-837-3557. Prices vary according to group size.

To get to the farm, drive 3 miles south of Bigfork on Montana Highway 35. You'll see the tall fence on the west side of the highway and, hopefully, the elk just beyond it.

F

Flathead Lake

Flathead Lake is the largest freshwater lake west of the Mississippi, and there are six state parks to enjoy along its shores. The fishing, picnicking, and swimming are great. Sailboats, motorboats, canoes, sailboards, and other watercraft are available to rent at several locations. Short cruises, evening cruises, and day trips are available from touring companies, as well. See the Kalispell and Somers and Polson chapters in this book for more information.

www.insiders.com

See this and many other **Insiders' Guide®** destinations online.

Visit us today!

G

Grizzly Bears

If you're lucky, you may see a grizzly bear while you're in Glacier National Park, but you'll see it from a distance. The scientific name for these 200- to 600-pound animals is *Ursus horibilis*—for a quick lesson in Latin, have the kids guess what the name means. A hint: *Ursus* is the name for the genus bears belong to.

Grizzlies come in a large variety of sizes and colors. They can be blonde, brown, or nearly black. You can distinguish them from black bears by their distinctive faces (their noses turn up at the end of a rather dished-in profile) and by the large hump between their shoulders.

Make plenty of noise while you're hiking the trails, to warn the bears of your presence so that they can get out of your way. Many people wear bear-bells (you'll hear them jingling throughout the park) and carry pepper spray in case of an encounter. See the close-

Credit: Flathead Valley Festival

Summer festivals provide great entertainment for kids and their parents.

up on bear safety in this book for more information.

H

Huckleberries

You'll notice huckleberry products—jams, jellies, pancake syrup, barbecue sauces, vinegars, and more—all over western Montana, but when you're in the Flathead Valley, you're near the self-proclaimed center of the huckleberry universe in the town of Hungry Horse. These small purple fruits are a true Montana delicacy, and it would be a shame to miss out on their juicy, messy goodness. At the Huckleberry Patch restaurant and gift shop on U.S. Highway 2 in Hungry Horse, you'll find all things huckleberry, including a very fine huckleberry pie.

Our Outdoor Recreation chapter has more information about seeking out the purple fruits yourself, though the location of prized patches is a secret passed down from generation to generation in some families. USDA Forest Service ranger stations in the area can give you a good idea of where to look if you're in the area at peak berry time—July and August. Be aware that bears are awfully fond of the berries, too. Make noise while you're picking and

INSIDERS' TIP

The most mysterious animal of all at Glacier National Park is a brown mountain goat...well, it has horns like a goat, but it's brown with a whitish rump patch....It's true: you'll never see this animal in a guide book: it's the *female* bighorn sheep. While most mammal guides include a picture of the bighorn ram—with its highly recognizable, curling horns—they usually neglect the ewe, which looks very much the same but grows a set of short spiky horns instead (which in fact look like the horns of a goat). In the spring and summer, the females with their young live separately from the bachelor bands of males, who thus are not around to provide a clue to what this exotic animal might be...

let the bears have the berries if they should happen upon you at their favorite patch.

I

Ice

To a certain extent, ice—really, really big and heavy ice—is what Glacier National Park is all about. Those peaks and valleys were formed by glaciers scouring the land and carving knife-like edges on the tops of mountains. In Glacier National Park you can play in the runoff from melting glaciers and you can actually walk out on glaciers yourself (given sufficient skill level and stamina in your group). One excellent place to see glaciers is the Swiftcurrent Valley on the east side of the park. Step out on the boat dock behind Many Glacier Hotel to view Grinnell and Salamander Glaciers, or take a scenic boat cruise and get a closer look from Grinnell Lake.

J

Jewel Basin

This hiking area in the Swan Mountains shines even in comparison to the recreation opportunities at Glacier National Park. There are more than 35 miles of hiking trails in the area, good for day hikes and short backpacking trips. This is a great place to introduce your kids to the backcountry experience.

The two best hikes for families are to Picnic Lakes and Birch Lake. Either are suitable for day hikes or short backpacks. The Picnic Lakes are 2.5 miles from the trailhead at Camp Misery on Forest Trail 8. Birch Lake is accessed from Forest Trail 717 and Forest Trail 7. A trail map is located at the parking area,

and a forest ranger is frequently on hand to answer questions.

To get to Jewel Basin, take U.S. Highway 93 7 miles south from Kalispell and turn east toward Bigfork on Montana Highway 82. Turn south at Montana Highway 35 and proceed to the flashing light, where you will turn east onto Montana Highway 83. At another flashing light, turn north onto Echo Lake Road. Signs will lead you to the Jewel Basin parking lot and trailheads.

K

Kehoe's Agate Shop

On a rainy day or even when you've just had enough scenery and fresh air, this little shop in what used to be the town of Holt is a great place to visit with the kids. In addition to the colorful polished rocks called agates, this rustic shop—built in 1932—has a collection of petrified wood, minerals, gems, fossils, and thunder eggs collected from all over the world.

To get there from Bigfork, turn west from Grand Avenue onto Holt Drive at the flashing yellow light. Signs will lead you to the agate shop in 2.3 miles. The road ends at the shop, so you won't miss it.

L

License Plate Game

Montana's Big Skies and steep mountains mean lots of roads and lots of time spent in the car. Luckily, we get traffic from enough places to make the time-tested license plate game for kids. See who can spot license plates from the most states and provinces. To make it more interesting, assign point val-

Credit: Johnson Communications/The Big Mountain

Dangle your legs from the ski lift for great family fun in summer.

ues to the states based on their area or population ranking using your road atlas. The winner gets to decide what activity to try next.

M

Mountain Goats

Though there are many places in Glacier country where you might spot one of these agile creatures, one of your best options is on U.S. Highway 2 three miles east of the town of Essex. There is a parking lot on the south side of the road, with a trail leading to an overlook at the end of the lot. On the steep cliffs above the Middle Fork of the Flathead River, you'll have a good chance of seeing billy goats, nannies and kids, as well as elk and deer. The animals are attracted to the mineral deposits on the cliffs—most of their time here is spent in licking the rocks.

N

National Park Service

The National Park Service offers guided hikes and regularly scheduled interpretive

Many Glacier Traditions

Many Glacier is one of those places people seem to return to year after year—and there are some good reasons for that! Beyond the natural beauty of the valley, two very different human traditions continue to please visitors here.

One goes back a long time—the tradition of hiring college students majoring in the performing arts at Many Glacier Hotel. Singers, instrumentalists, and actors and actresses make their way to a summer at the big hotel, offsetting their work as busboys, waitresses, and hotel clerks with evening performances for the guests. You may be

 treated to show tunes in the Ptarmigan Dining Room, or perhaps to a short harp or piano concert in the hotel lobby. And at the height of the season, the hotel sponsors its "Cabaret" in the St. Moritz Room—a full-scale production number presented later in the evening. Many Glacier Hotel, long ago dubbed the Showplace of the Rockies, continues that tradition today.

Another tradition has developed more recently at the Swiftcurrent Motor Inn—at the parking lot, to be exact! Each evening, a Park Service naturalist comes to the parking lot for the evening "Spotcheck." With a spotting scope set up in the median, the naturalist begins the evening's search for animals on the slopes above the valley—and there's almost always someone home. Goats can be seen on Mount Henkel or Mount Altyn almost every night; bighorn sheep make frequent appearances; more rarely elk or even soaring eagles are seen. Things really take off when the berries start to ripen in late July, however, because then bears—both black and grizzly—are sometimes seen for nights in a row on the open hillsides. Although the Park Service started this evening activity, it has taken on a life of its own. While everyone is welcome to view animals through the NPS scope, many visitors bring not only their own binoculars but spotting scopes and, in some cases, very large telescopes that allow others an amazing view of animals in their native habitat. Sometimes the crowd gets big—do be cautious about where you stand, remembering that you are in a parking lot and that cars may be moving through the area.

Credit: Glacier Orchestra and Chorale

The Glacier Children's Choir is a popular performance group.

talks throughout the park. You can see a schedule in the newspaper you receive at the entrance gate or call 406-888-7800 for more information on schedules and topics.

O

Óhpskunakáxi

The Blackfeet name for the area around Many Glacier Hotel is *Óhpskunakáxi*, meaning "waterfalls," and this is one of the best places in the park to see the tumbling water up close. One of the best short hikes for families is to Apikuni Falls, a 0.7-mile hike with spectacular mountain views, colorful wildflowers, and the occasional Columbian ground squirrel to interest you along the way. The falls and the potential to see small, furry pikas (small mammals that look like short-eared rabbits) reward the brief and enjoyable journey.

To get to the hike, take Many Glacier Road one mile east of the hotel to the trailhead parking lot on the north side of the road near Apikuni Creek bridge.

P

Polebridge Mercantile

If you have a four-wheel drive vehicle, a visit to Polebridge—where you can see part of the west that is still wild—is one your kids will truly enjoy. The trip up the North Fork Road is a bumpy and dusty one, but the fresh baked goods at the Polebridge Mercantile and the possibility of seeing bears, wolves, moose, elk, deer, mountain lions and fields of wildflowers make it worthwhile

Q

Shhh....quiet

Quiet hours in campgrounds mean that everyone gets a good night sleep and is ready for the adventures of the next day. Particularly at the campgrounds in Glacier National Park and at the busy state parks around Flathead Lake, crowds mean noise. Observing quiet hours from 10 PM to 8 AM keeps everyone happy and refreshed for the next day's events.

R

Redrock Falls

This easy 1.8-mile hike in Glacier National Park is a great one for stretching the legs and for seeing waterfalls in the Many Glacier area. There are sedimentary red rocks along the way—you can also see a burn area from a major 1936 fire on your way to splashing in the lake or admiring the falls. Be aware that the icy pools at the bottom of the falls are not ideal for wading. The rocks are slippery and the water is very, very cold.

To get to the trailhead, go to the parking area across from the Swiftcurrent Camp store in the Many Glacier valley. The hike starts at the parking area.

S

Skipping Rocks and Lake McDonald

Many an hour has been wiled away by children and adults skipping rocks, and the shores of Lake McDonald offer a great sport for this most serious of pursuits. Behind Lake McDonald Lodge is a boat dock—where you can rent boats and buy tickets for the guided lake tours—and beside the dock are some fine large rocks for sitting on, with the little skippers nearby. The time spent waiting for a table at the restaurant at the lodge will fly by.

T

Tyrannosaur at Alberta Visitor Centre

What could be more fun than visiting the Tyrannosaurus Rex skeleton at the Alberta Vistor Centre? How about admiring its teeth and then going for a simulated bobsled ride?

It may be hard to tear your kids away from the exhibits at this visitor centre, designed to introduce visitors to Canada's Waterton National Park. You don't have to cross the border to get there; the centre is in West Glacier on Highway 2. See our Attractions chapter for more information.

U

Umbrella Weather?

Though outdoor recreation is the area's main attraction, there are, of course, times when inclement conditions drive even the hardiest adventurers inside. Two great options for indoor family outings in Kalispell can be found at the Hockaday Center for the Arts and the Conrad Mansion. See our Arts and Attractions chapters for more information.

V

Vortex

The House of Mystery has got to be the strangest attraction in Glacier Country, and we guarantee your kids will love it. Located on Highway 2 between Columbia Falls and Hungry Horse, you'll see the billboards before you actually locate the small house where everyone has stopped. Why is it a mystery? The folks who run it claim that the area around the house is in a gravitational vortex, causing the trees to grow sideways. The odd angles of the house may convince you. . .though whether it's the work of mysterious forces or optical illusion is something your kids will have fun trying to determine.

INSIDERS' TIP

The short version is: Glacier National Park is not dog-friendly. Because of the presence of bears and mountain lions, dogs must be on a leash at all times in developed areas and along roads. Dogs are not permitted on trails at all. The major reason for this is that bears chase dogs...and dogs run back to their owners. Dogs also may not be left unattended in cars. Kennels are available in the Flathead Valley if you plan to backpack or do extended dayhiking in the park.

W

Wild Horse Island

You may not see wild horses at this state park in Flathead Lake, but there are plenty of other attractions to entice you to rent a boat so you can set foot on shore or board the *Polson Princess* for a ride around the island. The island got its name from the Flathead and Pend Oreille Indians, who used the island to protect their horses from raids by the Blackfeet. There are no facilities on the island, though the wildlife doesn't seem to mind. You may see the plentiful bighorn sheep, among others.

X

Xerophyllum tenax

The tall stalks with fluffy yellow heads that you keep seeing in campgrounds and throughout Glacier and the Flathead are called beargrass, but not because *Xerophyllum tenax* actually has anything to do with bears. Lewis and Clark—who skirted the eastern edge of this territory during their explorations of the Louisiana Purchase— named it bear grass because bears were often seen in its vicinity, and they assumed the bears ate it.

Now we know that the plant has more to do with elk, which eat the whole plant, and with mountain goats, which eat the parts untouched by winter's snow. Native Americans wove baskets and clothing from the plant.

The plants can grow to be 5 feet tall, and the fluffy head of flowers is generally about the size of a large fist. Be aware that the leaves, which lie in bunches close to the ground, are slippery. . .so watch your step.

Y

Yellow, pink, red, and purple.

Glacier National Park is full of wildflowers—and little ones are always tempted to pick them—encourage your kids to "take only pictures and leave only footprints." These wildflowers will please thousands of visitors if left in place.

Z

Good Night's Sleep

Get your Z's at one of the campgrounds in the area or at a hotel or motel. Tomorrow is going to be a big day.

Credit: Scott Spiker, The Big Mountain

Stretch short and long legs on our scenic trails.

Fiddling festivals, arts in the park, rodeos, powwows, and the ubiquitous huckleberry fill up our calendars of events and demand our attention.

Annual Events

At our annual events—big and small, on sunny days and in the snow—you can expect residents to come out in full force and visitors to join in on the fun. Fiddling festivals, arts in the park, rodeos, powwows, and the ubiquitous huckleberry fill up our calendars of events and demand our attention. The following listings, organized by month, are just a sampling of some of the more time-tested events we hold in the shadows of our glorious mountains and on the shores of our lakes.

January

Winter in Montana is cold, snowy . . . and wonderful. So we tend to spend as much time outdoors as possible, and our annual events reflect that tendency. Winterfest in Seeley Lake is one of the most consistent offerings, but you can find cross-country ski races, downhill events, snowmobile runs, and winter games of all sorts nearly every weekend.

Winterfest
Seeley Lake
• **(406) 677-2880**
• **www.seeleyswanpathfinder.com**
Located at the south end of the Swan Valley, the community of Seeley Lake comes alive for their annual celebration of winter. Activities include ice sculpture judging, dog sled rides, and snow softball, topped off by that mid-winter tradition—fireworks. The dates vary every year, so call the chamber of commerce at the number above or visit the website for information.

February

It's still cold out, so how about a nice evening torchlight parade and art walk? The folks in Whitefish cook up a special event every year in early February and have since 1960 —the Whitefish Winter Festival. Call (406) 862-3501 for more information about offerings in the community. For some reason, February also leads to thoughts of chocolates and other fine things to eat and drink. This is the month of wine and food festivals and chocolate fairs throughout the Flathead.

March

March may be spring some places in the world, but in the Flathead snow is still our main source of entertainment, not gardening. Be sure to check out local cross-country ski races and special downhill events. Also, this is a good month to catch performances and concerts at local theaters. Not everyone spends their winter getting frostbitten toes.

April

Well, in April the ski areas generally close and the snow recedes. Too bad. We'll have to venture elsewhere for our fun... how about a mystery weekend in Essex?

Murder Mystery
Izaak Walton Inn, Essex
• **(406) 888-5700**
Call the Izaak Walton Inn early to get res-

ervations for their Murder Mystery weekend. You'll arrive just in time for a crime, and then solve the murder before the weekend is out. Be sure to bring your cross-country skis; there may still be snow, and there are great trails out here on the southern tip of Glacier National Park.

May

Now it's starting to look like spring! You can celebrate the arrival of warm weather with a trip to the Cherry Blossom Festival at Bigfork, by hitting the water in a Kayak race, or by heading to an early performance of the Montana Old-Time Fiddlers' Association.

Cherry Blossom Festival
Bigfork
• **(406) 837-5888**
This area is famous for its cherry trees, and though the fruit usually gets all the press, this festival will surely make you think of the warm summer to come.

Whitewater Festival, Kayak Races and Parade
Bigfork
• **(406) 837-5888**
The water will still be really cold—and really fast—so bring your wetsuit and something warm for later. As much as we all love winter,

sometimes we can't wait for spring to come and water festival brings it all the earlier.

Montana Old-Time Fiddlers' Association Jam
• **(406) 889-3539**
This toe-tapping group of fiddlers of all ages performs at different venues throughout the Flathead over the summer months. Call for locations and dates.

June

Summer's festivals are just warming up in June, but there are plenty of offerings as the days get longer and warmer. Hit the water and the trail, but remember it's still early in the summer season and come prepared for all kinds of weather conditions. One of the most exciting events of the year—the opening of Going-to-the-Sun Road in Glacier National Park—usually takes place in June. It's a great time to see the park teeming with wildlife and showing its spring colors in banks of wildflowers.

Whitefish Canoe and Kayak Classic
Whitefish Lake
• **(406) 863-2470**
Bring your canoes, your kayaks, and your competitive spirit to this annual weekend of races on Whitefish Lake and Whitefish River.

Credit: Carl Wells, Flathead Convention and Visitor Bureau.

Royalty of the annual Whitefish Winter Carnival.

Credit: Hockaday Museum of Art

The community comes out for the annual Arts in the Park in Kalispell.

July

Make sure your spring yard work is done, because with all of the offerings of the season you won't have much time on the weekends to do much more than mow. Starting in July and continuing through August, this is our busiest time of year.

Whitefish Annual Arts Festival
Whitefish
• (406) 862-5875

Held on the lawn of Central School, this two-day event is filled with arts and crafts, food, and sidewalk sales. The whole community comes out for this event, and nearly everyone goes home with a locally made treasure. Sales benefit Cross Currents Christian School.

Flathead Festival
Whitefish, Kalispell
• (406) 257-0592

Every year, this music festival fills the Flathead Valley with classical music and fun summer offerings by well-known artists and those who deserve more exposure. The festival is held in venues in Kalispell and Whitefish—many of the concerts are outdoors, so bring a blanket or lawn chairs. Call for more information about this year's offerings.

Arts in the Park
Kalispell

This juried art show held annually in Kalispell's lovely Depot Park is a benefit for the Hockaday Museum of Art in Kalispell. Fine arts and crafts, entertainment, and food are featured.

KERR Country Rodeo
Polson

Bareback, saddle-bronc, and bull riding are all a part of rodeo action, and you'll find plenty of it here at the KERR Country Rodeo. The Northern Rodeo Association sanctions the event, so top performers are expected in all categories. Live country music is also a feature of the rodeo.

Montana Old-Time Fiddler's Contest
Polson
• (406) 323-1198

The Montana Old-Time Fiddlers meet all

over the Flathead Valley to "jam" throughout the summer, but this is the main event. Held at the high school in Polson, several hundred fiddlers of all ages and skill levels gather for this foot stomping gala. Admission is charged for the day and evening sessions.

Standing Arrow Powwow
Elmo
• **(406) 849-5541**

This is a great place to experience the culture of the Kootenai Indians, who share the Flathead reservation with the Salish Indians. The event is held at the Kootenai headquarters in Elmo, on the west side of Flathead Lake. Dancing is the main event of the powwow.

Arlee Powwow
Arlee
• **(406) 745-4572**

The 100th anniversary of the Arlee Powwow was celebrated in 1998, and we hope it goes on for a hundred years more. The even it sponsored by the Confederated Salish and Kootenai Tribes and takes place in Arlee, at the southern end of the Flathead Reservation. Dancing is the main feature of the powwow, and dancers wear traditional and non-

traditional costumes. Native American crafts, clothing, and food items—such as the delicious fry bread—are sold at the powwow.

Lewis and Clark Festival
Cut Bank
• **(406) 873-4041**

When you're on the Blackfeet Reservation, be sure to take some time to retrace the steps of two of the most famous and revered explorers in American History, Lewis and Clark. Cut Bank is near Two Medicine Fight Site—the location of Lewis' famed altercation with the Blackfeet. Events of this festival include a parade, costume contest, and more. Camp Disappointment, the northernmost point of the transcontinental expedition is 12 miles outside of Browning.

North American Indian Days
Browning
• **(406) 338-2230**

This nationally recognized powwow is the highlight of the year on the Blackfeet Indian Reservation to the east of Glacier National Park. Dancers and visitors come from around the country to the capital of the reservation at Browning; a parade and a rodeo are also held during the weekend. The Museum of the

Credit: Flathead Valley Festival

Jazz fills the air at the Flathead Valley Festival.

The highly popular Bigfork Festival of the Arts.

Plains Indians is located in Browning and will provide good background for your powwow experience.

August

Northwest Montana Fair and Rodeo
Flathead County Fairgrounds

A highlight of summer in the Flathead Valley, the fair stretches over the last two weeks in August and offers everything from farm animals and 4-H projects to llamas and carnival rides. In between are horse races, pro-rodeo competitions, fireworks displays, and exhibits of anything you can imagine. Yes, there's even a demolition derby.

Huckleberry Days
Whitefish
• (406) 862-3501

This annual ode to the tiny bright purple treasures we in Montana call huckleberries is filled with pie-eating contests, a huckleberry cook off, and an arts and crafts fair. Be sure to go home with a purple tongue.

Bigfork Festival of the Arts
Bigfork
• (406) 881-4636

Last year was the 20th anniversary of this event, held on Electric Avenue in Bigfork, and we predict twenty more years of fun music, good food, and fine arts and crafts.

Sandpiper Outdoor Festival of the Arts
Polson
• (406) 883-5956

Held on the courthouse lawn in Polson, this fine arts and crafts festival is in its 28th year.

September

Libby Nordicfest
Libby
• (406) 293-4167

A short distance from the main corridor of activity in the Flathead Valley, this traditional Nordicfest is worth the trip down U.S. Highway 2 for food, dancing, wood-carving workshops, and the extremely popular quilt show. They do serve lutefisk if that's what you're craving.

Flathead Quilters Guild Show and Quilt Auction
Flathead County Fairgrounds
• **(406) 892-5864**

This year marks the 18th anniversary of this extremely popular quilt show and auction. What a great chance to pick up a handmade piece of Montana history in the making!

October

Glacier Jazz Stampede
Kalispell
• **(406) 755-0592**

This Jazz festival is one of the largest in Montana, bringing visitors from around the country to hear strains of traditional and Dixieland Jazz over several days. Food, crafts, and sidewalk sales can also be found at festival venues.

November

In November we start gearing up for winter again, the ski areas open up, and we actually hope for snow. Kalispell is the first to offer a Christmas parade, and more will follow in the month to come.

December

The holiday season is upon us, and most communities offer lights and celebrations. Think snow at this time of the year; we want a white Christmas and a powder-filled New Year.

Night of Lights Parade
Columbia Falls
• **(406) 892-7529**

Holiday Parade, Art Walk, & Tree Lighting Ceremony
Bigfork
• **(406) 837-5888**

New Year's Eve Torchlight Parade
The Big Mountain, Whitefish
• **(406) 862-2900**

With Glacier National Park at its core, Glacier Country is a giant mosaic created over three billion years by natural forces.

Outdoor Recreation

This wondrous land in the Rocky Mountains—called by the Blackfeet backbone of the earth—this Jewel in the Crown of the Continent is a Mecca for outdoor recreationists of all stripes. In this chapter we'll guide you to some of the best and brightest offerings of the region's recreational opportunities, and give you some hints on keeping the area's pristine beauty intact for future visitors. We'll also guide you through some precautions that you should take when recreating in our great outdoors.

The Environment

With Glacier National Park at its core, Glacier Country is a giant mosaic created over three billion years by natural forces. Once a vast inland sea, the sediment and sea life deposited layers on the bottom that formed the limestone we see here today. Volcanic activity thrust up mountains to great heights, then suffered upheavals that slid the older layers over the younger ones.

This "block overthrust faulting" has created the steep rock faces on the east front and the somewhat more gentle slopes on the western side. The glaciers that retreated about 10,000 to 14,000 years ago sculpted the slopes more steeply, rounded other hills and filled in low spots with glacial till.

Nature's work continued over many millennia with storms, floods, wind, and fire. The resulting landscape became home to the plants and animals that compose the regional ecosystem.

The variety of plant and animal communities reflects the broad ranges of climate, geology, topography and soils. Elevations range from a low of 3,150 feet at the juncture of North Fork and the Middle Fork of the Flathead River to 10,466 feet at the summit of Mount Cleveland. These elevation differences alone influence different life zones. From the temperate rain forest of the Lake McDonald Valley one can go to conditions like the Arctic tundra simply by climbing to Logan Pass at 6,000 feet. The variations in moisture, wind, sun and shade at each elevation multiply the local microclimates.

The area we are looking at comprises three million acres of nearly unbroken wilderness. It is bounded by Waterton National Park on the north, Montana Highways 83 on the west, 89 on the east, and 200 on the south. It encompasses Glacier National Park and the Great Bear, Bob Marshall and Scapegoat Wilderness Areas in the Flathead and Lewis and Clark National Forests. A million acres are in Glacier National Park, 2.36 million acres in the Flathead National Forest and the remainder in state and private ownership. The Swan Range runs uncut by a road for a hundred miles.

Within this wild circle still remains one of the largest intact temperate ecosystems in the world. Virtually all populations of plants and animals—carnivores and herbivores, predators and prey and the plants that sustain them—remain almost as they were before Euro-American explorers and trappers first ventured here 200 years ago. In Glacier and Waterton National Parks alone live more than 1,000 kinds of plants, 25 major tree species, 264 bird species, nearly 60 kinds of mammals and 17 species of fish.

The larger predators include grizzly and black bears, mountain lions or cougar, gray wolves, coyote, fox and lynx, badger, marten and mink. Larger prey animals include moose, elk, white-tailed and mule deer, mountain goats and bighorn sheep. These are accompanied by their smaller neighbors such as beaver, snowshoe hare, pine squirrels, deer mice and meadow voles. Even the nearly exterminated bison that once roamed the plains by the thousands are represented by a penned herd in Waterton Lakes National Park. The Flathead River system is one of the few areas in the country that still support self-sustaining, genetically pure populations of native westslope cutthroat and bull trout.

www.insiders.com

See this and many other **Insiders' Guide** destinations online.

Visit us today!

The Continental Divide—The Great Divide—the north to south mountainous spine bisecting the region exerts a major influence on weather variations capturing rainfall from warm, moisture laden air masses moving in from the coastal states on the western side of the mountains. The mountains also restrict the westward flow of cold, continental Arctic air masses from east of the Rockies. The eastern slopes are dry, hot and windy and beyond them lies the vast upland prairie that once supported the great bison herds. In the high country weather can be extremely changeable and both sunshine and snow are possible any time of the year.

Water has been and continues to be another powerful force shaping the landscape and influencing habitat. The Flathead River's three forks drain Glacier National Park, thousands of acres of the Flathead National Forest, and part of British Columbia. The U.S. Congress includes 219 miles of these waters as part of the National Wild and Scenic Rivers System. Sometimes heavy spring rains, a deep mountain snowpack and warm temperatures that hasten snowmelt combine to swell one or more of the forks and the main river beyond their banks. The riverbed constantly changes as the waters eat away the bank some places and deposit soil and debris at others.

The Stillwater, Whitefish, and Swan Rivers wind their way through forests, agricultural fields and urban areas. The Saint Mary River heads north carrying Glacier's waters to Hudson Bay. Numerous swift mountain creeks carve through their rocky channels to forest and meadow below.

Disturbances to the land, both natural and human-caused, influence plant and animal communities. This landscape has evolved with fire as a constant force for change and renewal. Frequent low intensity surface fires kill the small trees and shrubs and leave the more fire-resistant trees largely intact. Many tree and plant species, especially the pines—ponderosa, lodgepole, western white and whitebark—and western larch depend on fire to perpetuate their life cycles. Lodgepole pine, which maintains its seed in fire-resistant cones for several years, is often abundant on sites where whole stands have been destroyed. Some seeds remain dormant in the soil for decades and sprout after a moderate fire. Aspen, huckleberry, fireweed and grasses quickly move in to regenerate the vegetation.

INSIDERS' TIP

Make sure your bicycle is in good condition, with lights and reflectors. Take a repair kit, pump and extra tire (you'd be amazed how often we've seen a biker walking the bike out of the trail with neither pump nor patch). Wear a helmet, stay alert for vehicles, road hazards and wildlife at all times. Observe the same advice about gear, water, food, etc. as for hikers. Because most grizzly attacks are provoked by bears that have been startled, be especially careful when traveling at high speeds, and make noise when traveling through timber and brush.

Grizzly bears and elk feed on many of these "pioneer species." Native Americans commonly burned prairies and pine-forest understory plants to improve grazing for deer, elk and bison.

Introduction of non-native species has also disrupted natural habitats, most notably fish and noxious weeds. Native fish have suffered from habitat loss, food competition and disease from the presence of these "exotics." Noxious weeds introduced largely by Euro-American settlers in crop or pasture seeds over the past two centuries, are so aggressive they have infested millions of acres, choking out native plants, and destroying fish, wildlife and livestock habitat. Spotted knapweed, leafy spurge and Saint-John's-wort are among more than a dozen noxious weeds targeted by weed control programs of all Montana counties. Landowners are responsible for eradicating weeds from their property.

Plant and Animal Communities

With abundance of streams, rivers, lakes and wetlands in the broad Flathead Valley, the riparian plants and animals form one of the area's major habitats. In valley bottoms about 3,000 feet in elevation black cottonwood, willow, alder and red-osier dogwood dominate the tree and shrub species growing along the waters, often mixed with a smattering of conifers and trembling aspen. Biologists estimate 82 species of wildlife may depend on these riparian marshes and forests including enormous numbers of migratory birds, eagles, and osprey. Spotted sandpipers bob along shorelines; red-winged and yellow-headed blackbirds share the cattail marshes and sloughs with muskrat, beaver and raccoons. River otters, weasels, and mink can also be found here. Even the rare northern-bog lemming has been spotted in Lake McDonald's marshes. White-tailed deer find good browse in the grasses, sedges and shrubs. The haunting cry of the common loon, long gone in many states, still adds its magical notes to nature's symphonies on large and small lakes across Glacier Country. The fascinating harlequin duck may be seen on the rushing cold, mountain streams in and around Glacier National Park during its breeding period.

From 3,000 to 4,000 feet, trembling aspen, paper birch and black cottonwood continue to dominate valley bottoms especially in riparian areas, often encircling grassy fields and forming a transition to the higher coniferous forests. Their yellow and gold autumn foliage stands out against the green of conifers. Also found here are serviceberry, chokecherry, mountain maple, red-osier dogwood, and alder. Wild geranium, arnica and Oregon grape grace the forest floor. This is habitat for white-tailed deer, moose and wolves. Montana's State Bird, the western meadowlark shares the open areas with LeConte's sparrow and the savannah sparrow. The low- to mid-elevation (3,000 to 4,000 feet west of the divide; 4,000 to 5,000 to the east) dry montane forest is typified by Douglas-fir, ponderosa pine, lodgepole pine and limber pine with understory species such as ninebark and mountain maple. These forests often have open crowns with a grassy understory that provides winter habitat for mule deer, elk and bighorn sheep. In stands of old growth, predators like the goshawk hunt.

The wetter mid-montane forest reflects the Pacific maritime weather influence in the lush growth of trees, shrubs, ferns, mosses and wildflowers. Western red cedar and western hemlock are common along with Douglas fir, western larch and spruce. The understory is typically luxuriant with many ferns, wildflowers, shrubs and mosses. This habitat is typical of the McDonald Creek drainage ranging from 3,100 to 4,000 feet. In the old growth forests live western tanagers, Swainson's and varied thrushes, Townsend's warblers, Hammond's flycatchers and brown creepers. Sharp-shinned and Cooper's hawks prey on birds and small mammals. The snowshoe hare is common and the lynx that preys primarily on this hare is reported to be returning. A magnificent stand of old-growth western red cedar can be seen at Avalanche campground and the shoreline of McDonald Lake's upper end. The 1910 fire destroyed a much larger population of this species.

In the sub-alpine forest (above 5,000 feet)

Credit: Flathead Lake Lodge

Trail riding is a popular Glacier Country activity.

spruce and sub-alpine fir dominate along with whitebark pine in higher elevations. Douglas-fir is common on south-facing slopes. Near the upper limits trees thin out and mingle with treeless communities, creating parklands with spectacular displays of wildflowers, mosses and lichens against a backdrop of breathtaking scenery. East of the divide subalpine fir and lodgepole pine dominate. Mule deer, pine marten and black bears inhabit these forests.

In the highest elevations the plants and animals of the alpine community have adapted to the long, cold winters and cool, short growing seasons. Only a few trees and shrubs can survive such as arctic willow, dwarf birch and fir, hugging the ground and stunted by the searing winds and frigid temperatures.

Mosses and lichens cling to bare rock, alpine bogs resemble a miniature landscape for a kingdom of little people. Alpine meadows astound the eye for a few July and August weeks with wildflowers of every color including heather, gentian, beargrass and glacier lily. The rare dwarf alpine poppy is unique to this area in both Glacier and Waterton National Parks. Grizzly bears dig for glacier lily and spring beauty bulbs. Ptarmigan, pika, hoary marmot, wolverine and mountain goat call this home. Big horn sheep graze in high meadows and golden eagles nest on the cliffs. Logan Pass, the Hidden Lake trail and the Highline Trail provide the easiest access to this habitat.

Remnants of the native grasslands that

once covered the Great Plains now occur mainly in broad arid, low elevation basins. Bluebunch wheatgrass, fescues and needlegrasses dominate these areas. Although primarily found on the park's east side, they move quickly into areas soon after a forest fire, as at Polebridge where the Red Bench fire decimated the forest in 1988. Wildflowers thrive in these grasslands, the blossoming peaking in May and June in the lower elevations. Common species are yarrow, fleabane, potentilla, cinquefoil, spirea, locoweed and lupine. Wild geranium is a major food item for elk and white-tailed deer. This is also the habitat for badger, coyote, savannah sparrow and chipping sparrows, northern harrier, and prairie falcon. East of the divide Two Dog Flat provides a splendid grassland wildflower display peaking in June, with pasque flower, lupine, Indian paintbrush, gaillardia, asters and shooting stars in abundance. Exotic weed species have infested many of these prairies especially east of the divide where forage grasses have been extensively planted for livestock grazing. Sagebrush, symbol of the romantic Western movie set, also grows in this environment and is common east of the divide, and found in a few spots west of the divide at Round Prairie and other areas along the Inside North Fork Road.

Glacier Country heavily depends on this wealth of natural treasures to support its economic activities including farming, ranching, timber harvesting, tourism, and outdoor recreation. Between 1969 and 1992, employment and personal income grew substantially because of these wildlands' attractions. People are striving to maintain their freedoms, and frontier lifestyles while also preserving the area's wildness, purity, clean air, water, and unlittered landscapes. Farmers and ranchers struggle to maintain their family operations as cities and towns expand outward to engulf them. Park visitors and area business people debate road access and development within the park. Families and businesses dependent on timber cutting in the national forests as well as wilderness advocates and forest recreationists apply diverse pressures to the Forest Service on such issues as road access and timber harvest methods and quanti-

ties. Despite these ongoing conflicts about how best to manage these lands and resources, local governments and private groups are working to achieve a balance between preservation and development, The Flathead Basin Commission, created by the Montana State Legislature in 1983 to monitor and protect Flathead Lake's water quality, has been working with Canadian, U.S., and state and local agencies to collect data and develop methods for guarding the waters in this important watershed. Volunteers monitor pollution levels on 30 lakes that flow into the basin. Landowners and managers are encouraged to use best management practices to reduce runoff into streams and rivers feeding the lake. Flathead County has initiated a water quality task force, which will be able to institute measures to protect the large, and so far unpolluted, aquifer underlying the Flathead Valley.

Private groups such as the Flathead Land Trust, The Nature Conservancy, and Montana Land Reliance work with private landowners to protect agricultural and wild lands from development and provide additional habitat for plants and animals. Organizations such as the Flathead Audubon Society, the Montana Native Plant Society, and the Glacier Institute conduct field trips, classes and meetings to educate the public about plants, birds and their habitats. The Flathead National Forest and Glacier National Park and Montana Department of Fish, Wildlife and Parks all have public adult and school educational programs. Through a variety of public meetings, forums, and workshops and active involvement in development and conservation issues, Citizens for a Better Flathead promotes "Smart Growth," so that population growth and development occur in such a way they do not unduly diminish the area's resources and values.

This chapter will suggest an array of possibilities for experiencing this immensely varied, fascinating country—from simply walking a few paces from your vehicle to see a stunning vista or look more closely at a wildflower to taking an all-day hike, a raft trip or ski tour into a wilderness setting. It will guide you to a few of the most special places and recommend other information sources to suit your needs and desires.

Nature Viewing

Fascinating plants and animals are everywhere in Glacier Country and are yours to view with only a little travel and effort. The many habitats are described in the environment section and give you a general idea of where they are likely to occur. Nature observation is particularly exciting here not only because of the uncommon creatures, but because so many are concentrated in a small geographic area. With the naked eye an observant person can see many of them. With binoculars or a spotting scope, the opportunities magnify wonderfully.

You'll probably want to see mountain goats, elk, bald eagles and grizzly bears—from a distance, of course. The many creeks, rivers, lakes and wetlands provide prime habitat for migratory waterfowl and songbirds, osprey and beaver, river otter and mink. Wildflower lovers will revel in the variety of species from the spectacular displays of color in the alpine settings along Going-to-the-Sun Road to the roadside plants everywhere in autumn. In this section we list a few specific places you'd most likely to see the starring attractions such as mountain goats or bighorn sheep. These areas include wildlife refuges and production areas and places to see wildflowers.

Wildlife-Watching Tips

You can make wildlife watching fun for yourself and safe for the animals you watch by observing a few basic behaviors. You'll enjoy the animals the most when you observe them undisturbed in their life activities. Wear subdued, natural colors. Be unobtrusive, move slowly and quietly and hide behind boulders or vegetation. Learn as much about them as possible before trying to observe them, such as where and when they are found. Most animals are usually most active and visible while feeding in early morning and late evening. Don't look directly into an animal's eye; that could frighten it away. Keep your distance; use binoculars or a spotting scope. If you're taking pictures, use a 400-millimeter lens. Don't feed the animals. An excellent pamphlet called *A Guide to Ultimate Wildlife Watching* expands on these points and can be obtained from the Forest Service or Montana Fish, Wildlife and Parks, addresses listed below. Also, look for the highway signs with the brown and white binoculars logo and the words "Wildlife Viewing Area," with an arrow pointing to the site.

Grizzly Bears

These large bruins originally inhabited the prairies along streams. Now they roam open woods and meadows foraging their diet of grasses, roots, berries, insects and occasionally young elk or deer. They also feed on carrion at kill-sites of mountain lions and other carnivores. In spring they are commonly seen grazing on the newly emerging vegetation at the edges of avalanche chutes along Going-to-the-Sun Road and in lower meadows in the St. Mary and Two Medicine Valleys. In July and August, look for them in the alpine meadows and at Logan Pass digging the bulbs of glacier lilies and spring beauties. They also frequent the park's west side along the North Fork. They are as fond of huckleberries as people and in summer and early fall you should expect to see them raking the berries into their mouths as they hurry to fatten up before going to ground for the winter. Always observe the "bear country" precautions described on page 232.

Rocky Mountain Bighorn Sheep

These large ungulates with the massive horns prefer high rolling valleys and high rocky slopes and cliffs on the park's eastern side where the winds keep them snow-free in winter. They graze on grasses, shrubs, and forbs and during harsh winters can be viewed in the lower valleys. Although sometimes seen on Going to the Sun Road, especially at Logan Pass in early spring, the best places to view them are on the east side, especially in the Many Glacier valley: Many Glacier Hotel, Pitamakan Pass, Ptarmigan Lake and the trail to Grinnell Glacier and at Haystack Butte. In the fall listen for the crashing of the males' horns during the mating season. A small herd of bighorns can usually be seen on a visit to Wild Horse Island (described on page 349).

Mountain Goats

One of the most easily-observed mammals in the park, these dare-devil cliff-jumpers favor precipitous slopes where they can evade predators. In the winter they seek south-facing slopes where they can forage shrubs, grasses, sedges, lichens, and forbs. In late spring Logan Pass is almost a sure bet for seeing goats, and they become traffic-stoppers on Going to the Sun Road where their white coats are easily spotted on the cliffs above the road. Hikers often encounter them at Gunsight Pass. Goat Lick, along Highway 2 near Essex, is another popular place. Goats hang out just across the Flathead River and are sometimes visible from the parking area or from the Goat Lick, a short trail walk from the road.

Elk or Wapiti

If you visit Glacier Country in autumn you might be lucky enough to hear the bugling of the male elk as they herd their harems and challenge other males during the breeding season. These larger cousins of the deer prefer coniferous forests interspersed with openings such as logged or burned areas and open grasslands bordered by shrubs and trees. They spend summers in high elevation mountain meadows where they are difficult to see. In winter, spring, and fall they may be seen in the St. Mary flats area near the park visitor center, at Two Dog Flats and the Many Glacier valley, and the southeast corner of the park near East Glacier. On the west side sightings have been reported in a wintering area along U.S. 2 east of Belton Hills, in the North Fork valley and in the grasslands along the Quarter Circle Bridge Road near Apgar. Check with a ranger about current sightings.

Gray Wolves

Wolves have made a comeback in Glacier Country after being virtually wiped out earlier this century. Park biologists believe two packs have established themselves in the park and at least two more in the national forest. Most sightings have been reported in the North Fork valley and it's possible to find their large paw prints in sand along the river and along the Inside North Fork Road at Hidden Meadow where they prey on small rodents. They shy away from people so consider yourself lucky if you actually get to see one. Do listen for them at night on the park's west side or in the Whitefish Range. There's nothing quite so thrilling as the wolves' evening chorus on a moonlit night in the Montana wilderness.

Bald Eagles

Even if you live where they are common, the sight of our national symbol always gives pause to the viewer. Its large size and bright white head against its dark body make it easy to spot. You may even locate a nest. Look for the birds near water, particularly along the North Fork of the Flathead River and major lakes including Lake McDonald, Two Medicine and St. Mary Lakes in Glacier National Park.

Pacific Harlequin Duck

For just a few weeks in mid-April until May we can watch the entertaining courtship of these small dark-gray and white ducks on the frigid mountain streams in and near Glacier Park. They return from their winter home on the Pacific coast to the same streams where they hatched, to mate and raise another brood. Their antics as they maneuver the rapids in the waters of McDonald Creek express their clown-like plumage. This is a rare opportunity and one that attracts many locals year after year. They are also seen in the Big Creek drainage.

Wildlife Management Areas (WMA)

Montana has set aside areas across the state to provide winter range for deer and elk and breeding areas for waterfowl and upland game. Besides helping maintain healthy populations of these animals, these WMAs are great places to view a variety of wildlife and plants. Some are closed during wintering and breeding seasons. Many wetlands are closed during the spring nesting season. Signs at parking areas and trailheads specify the closure dates.

Waterfowl Production Facilities— Somers Bay

The north shore of Flathead Lake is a duck and goose paradise and pretty close to heaven for the other species that dwell or pass through there. Starting at the fishing access on Somers Bay, where water birds can be seen almost anytime of year, there is a nearly continuous strip of meadows and marshes that extends east almost to Bigfork. It's a great place to see red-winged and yellow-headed blackbirds, flickers, geese, ducks and other waterfowl and the occasional deer. There are trails and small, informal parking areas. You can stroll in varied habitats or take a picnic and sit with the sun in your face and a breeze from the lake in your hair. This area is closed during the breeding season between March 1 and July 1.

Smith Lake Waterfowl Production Area

Located seven miles west of Kalispell south of U.S. Highway 2, this 1040-acre area encloses a lake and extensive marshes. It is a good area for viewing shorebirds, including phalaropes, yellowlegs, and waterfowl such as mallards, widgeons, pintails, and gadwalls. Also seen are Canada geese, grebes, gulls, tundra swans, and American bitterns that nest there. In the spring and fall look for sandhill cranes in the western grassy meadows, or Bluebirds nesting in boxes along the approach road. This is closed from March 1 to July 1.

Wild Horse Island (see description page 349.)

Bighorn sheep, mule deer, coyotes, bald eagles, ospreys and the remnant of a wild horse herd live on this island. The mature forests of Douglas fir and ponderosa pine and flower-covered uplands also support goshawks, coyotes, marmots, mink and numerous songbirds. Hiking trails lead to good viewing places.

Creston National Fish Hatchery

At this 74-acre hatchery located along a beautiful spring creek, you can see up to a million rainbow and cutthroat trout and learn how they reproduce in captivity. The facility raises and produces eggs for propagation in stocked streams and lakes. Birding for fish-eating birds is also excellent—osprey, great blue herons, kingfisher and magpies. Canada geese nest near the picnic area and the young can be seen in the summer. The hatchery is open daily from 7:30 AM to 4 PM.

Swan River National Wildlife Refuge

This 1,568-acre refuge is best seen by canoe, but a walk along Bog Road (generally impassible to vehicles) can yield sightings of some of its 171 bird species including bald eagles, great blue herons, Canada geese, wood ducks and yellowlegs. Keep an eye out for a glimpse of some of the large mammals found there seasonally including elk, deer, moose, and grizzly and black bears. The refuge lies at the southern end of Swan Lake. It is closed from March 1 to July 1. Signs on the highway alert you to the entrance road.

Wildflower Viewing

"There is no color known to man that is not reproduced from its most vivid hues to the most delicate tints by the plants and rocks of Glacier Park," writes George Ostrom in his recent book, *Glacier's Secrets*. He adds, "If I were a painter, I'd go bananas ten times a day running into this kind of arrangement of flowers, lichens, and colored rocks." He expresses so well the thrilling sensation of coming upon the plants in Glacier Country. People simply don't believe how stunningly beautiful they are until they behold them with their own eyes. Be prepared for spectacular summer displays in the alpine meadows, but don't overlook the cheering brightness of the first buttercups in early spring or the last of the Indian paintbrushes and others along the roadside. Because wildflowers are generally limited to a short blooming period, we suggest the months you are most likely to see certain plants and particular locations where they are known to grow.

May

Some of spring's first wildflowers appear this month in Wayfarer's and Lone Pine State Parks and on the Columbia Mountain trail near Columbia Falls, among them are buttercups, glacier lilies, blue bells and wild crocus.

June

Violets, pyrola, foamflower, and queen's cap bead lily come into bloom in the cedar-hemlock forests around Lake McDonald. Wildflowers of the prairies and foothills begin to peak in June. The more colorful members of the fescue-wheatgrass grassland such as yarrow, purple fleabane, Saint John's-wort, cinquefoil, spirea, lupine and wild geranium put on bold displays at many locations, notably at lower elevations along Going-to-the-Sun Road, in the Polebridge area and at Two Dog Flats on Going-to-the-Sun Road southwest of St. Mary.

July and August

The Danny On Trail on the Big Mountain, Jewel Basin and Logan Pass are prime areas for viewing the spectacular but brief displays of alpine wildflowers. At elevations between 6000 and 7000 feet blooms of every color include those of heather, gentian, Indian paintbrush, beargrass and glacier lily. At Logan Pass you may find the rare dwarf alpine poppy. Stop at the Flathead National Forest Big Mountain Education Center for information and nature programs on the Mountain.

August and Early September

Roadsides everywhere bloom in autumn. The backroads such as the North Fork Road, Camas Road, Hungry Horse Reservoir roads and open areas along national forest roads treat you to the last of the season's Indian paintbrush, goldenrod, asters and the beginning of the reds and golds of fall's trees and shrubs.

Huckleberry Picking

The area's exalted huckleberry is either more or less than you expect. For some people from wild blueberry country such as Maine, northern Michigan and Minnesota, the huckleberry is overrated. For those who have never tasted either, the huckleberry is an unsurpassed blue-black globe of flavor and aroma worth the effort to pick or price to buy.

The berries provided sustenance in lean times for travelers, including the Lewis and Clark exploration team in 1805, and both Indian and white residents during the depression, when whole families moved to the harvest sites and camped out, picking and preserving the berries. The huckleberry held both culinary and ceremonial significance for the Salish and Kootenai peoples who dried the berries for use in stews and pemmican.

The huckleberry industry which has grown in recent years, produces a hundred different products including preserves, pies, syrups, candies, and cosmetics, and most visitors take their huckleberries the easy way from the local purveyors, but if you want to try your hand at picking them yourself, here are some tips:

The best picking is usually found in areas opened up by forest fires, timber cutting or along old roads. You can tell where the berries are prolific by where a lot of cars are parked. Try forest trails and abandoned logging roads when accessible spots get picked over.

The huckleberry shrub prefers north-facing slopes between 3,500 to 7,000 feet elevation, in moist, acid soils typical of coniferous forests. It grows from a foot to six-feet tall and has short elliptical leaves. The white or pinkish bell-shaped flowers mature into small blue or black berries. They usually begin ripening from mid-July to mid-August, depending on the elevation and can be found on the highest slopes as late as October.

A battle of the berries may be in the making as humans take more and more of the harvest and grizzly bears are left with scarcely enough to fatten up for winter hibernation. In 1998, a lean huckleberry year diminished even more by determined pickers drove grizzlies in unusual numbers into residential areas in search of food and caused the deaths of several bears.

You can buy a map of huckleberry areas at forest service district ranger offices, campgrounds, and the forest supervisor's office in Kalispell at a cost of $2.00.

On the Trail— Hiking and Biking

Good, old-fashioned walking and bicycling are two of most economical and simplest ways to explore this vast area with its infinite variety of environments and hundreds of miles of trails. Truly there is a trail for hikers and bikers who want to leave their vehicles and steep themselves in this unsurpassed natural environment.

This section will introduce you to a few of the best, easy-to-reach, hiking and biking opportunities in Glacier Country and lists resources that can provide equipment, guidance and information.

Hiking

Hiking opportunities span trails of every description suitable for every type of walker, stroller, backpacker, and even the visitor in a wheel chair. The trails described here range from less than a mile to several miles, which can be accomplished in no more than a long day, even for slower sojourners. For short, short hikes in urban areas, check the individual city park descriptions. For longer day hikes and overnight and longer backpacks, consult *Hiking Glacier and Waterton Lakes National Parks* and *Wild Montana* (see our For More Information chapter). If you decide after you get here to do some backpacking, you can fin rentals and maps to assure a satisfy-

ing backcountry experience. Check the resource list at the end of this chapter.

Safety and Comfort

Good, sturdy shoes or hiking boots and proper clothing are a must for enjoyable, safe hiking. Even in midsummer when the hot, dry days resemble Arizona weather, in the mountains the weather can change quickly to penetrating cold, wind, rain, and even snow. When hiking or biking, always carry headwear, mittens, and bodywear that is warm and wind and water repellent. In the mountains, hypothermia is possible even in the summer. Also, carry more water than you think you'll drink. Keeping hydrated is critical to maintaining stamina and avoiding heatstroke in summer and hypothermia in winter. A small backpack or fanny pack stocked with a first aid kit, water, and high-energy snacks such as nuts, fresh or dried fruit and granola bars is indispensable for any but a few minute's walk from your vehicle. Be sure to pack out all food wrappers, as well as fruit peels and cores, because even though biodegradable, they attract animals—including bears—to the trailsides. Observe signs or rangers' warnings of bear activity and take appropriate precautions. (See page 232.).

Although you can drive to many of the higher altitude trailheads don't forget that at several thousand feet above sea level, oxygen is less available and people with breathing or heart problems should be cautious.

Hiking Opportunities

National Forest Trails

The hundreds of miles of trail are mapped and described in a packet available from the forest supervisor's office in Kalispell and the district rangers' offices.

The Big Mountain
Big Mountain Village, Whitefish

Big Mountain's summit provides an array of hiking possibilities with some of the most exquisite scenery in Glacier Country. Because the summit is snow-free only a few months, it's a treat to see the displays of alpine wild-

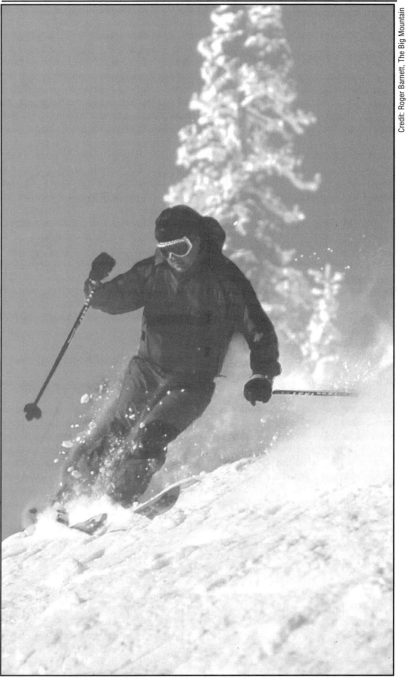

Credit: Roger Barnett, The Big Mountain

Downhill skiing reigns supreme in the world of winter recreation.

flowers and open meadows during July and August. Hiking season at lower elevations begins in June, but on the summit after July 1 and lasts into September. The lift stops operation in early October and begins again when the ski season opens at Thanksgiving.

The Danny On Memorial National Recreation Trail is one of the most popular hiking trails for people seeking easy accessibility, premier view and sections of varied length and difficulty. It was named in memory of a Forest Service silviculturist and nature photographer known for his beautiful pictures of the area, who died in a skiing accident on Big Mountain. It is actually six different hikes totaling 5.6 miles of varying difficulty and length. The more ambitious hikers ascend it from the trailhead right above the Chalet in The Village, a distance of 3.8 miles taking about two hours. Others ride the Gondola up to the Summit House and hike down. Two of the connecting trails are the East Rim Trail, which is a half-mile loop path along the summit, and the 3.8-mile Flower Point Hike back to the lift. Trail maps are available at the chair lift and the Summit House and Chalet at the Big Mountain Village.

Lone Pine State Park

Just 10 minutes southwest of downtown Kalispell, this Montana state park offers panoramic views from its trails of Kalispell, much of the Flathead Valley and into Glacier Park. The 0.75-mile Overlook Trail begins near the visitor center. It's a wheelchair accessible, self-guided interpretive trail leading to the Flathead Valley Overlook. The park also has 2.5 miles of multi-use trails for hiking, biking and horseback riding with benches along the way for resting and meditation. From Kalispell, go west on U.S. Highway 2 to Meridian Road, then south on Meridian to Foy's Lake Road. Proceed for four miles and turn left at the park sign.

Jewel Basin

This highly popular hiker-only area is noted for its beautiful scenery that features alpine lakes, mountain streams, meadows, rocky peaks, dense conifer woods and wildflower displays. There are trails for nearly every age and ability. Many hikers aim for the high peaks that dominate the 15,340 acre area, but open country on the lower slopes afford views for the more casual walker or those with children. Mountain bikes, dogs and horses are excluded. This area is being loved to death and forest service managers trying to protect the resource have introduced new regulations this year to help reduce visitor impacts: no dogs are allowed and groups hiking the area are limited to no more than 12 people. If you seek solitude, check with the rangers' office to see where there might be fewer people hiking that day. Located at the north end of the Swan Mountain Range between Kalispell and Hungry Horse Reservoir, the parking lot accessing the trails is reached by taking Echo Lake Road from Montana State Highway 83 and following the signs to Jewel Basin.

Glacier National Park

Most high elevation trails in Glacier Park are only hikeable in mid-summer after the snows have melted and into early fall, so be prepared to take an alternate route if ice and snow are still a factor.

Apgar Lookout Trail
West Side

This short but moderately difficult trail ends at Apgar Lookout at 5,236 feet and rewards you with views of Lake McDonald and the full length of the Livingston Range. It begins on a primitive road, then leads over switchbacks across the foothill, giving glimpses of Great Northern Mountain, and the Flathead Range and Swan Range. To reach the trailhead, turn just inside the park's west entrance at the sign for the Glacier Institute Field Camp. Follow it to the T, turn right, and go a short distance to a V intersection and take the left fork at the sign for Quarter-Circle Bridge. Go about a mile beyond the bridge and look for trailhead signs.

Avalanche Lake
West Side

This lovely and not-too-difficult 2-mile trek begins in giant old-growth cedars on the wheelchair-accessible Trail-of-the-Cedars boardwalk, then continues on a moderately steep trail along Avalanche George through well-timbered hillsides and emerges at the alpine lake nestled in a cirque among the peaks. For a first hike in Glacier Park, this is an especially satisfying one to take with a ranger-naturalist and these interpretive walks are scheduled regularly throughout the season. See the park newspaper for times and just show up at the scheduled time at the Avalanche parking lot.

Hidden Lake and Hidden Lake Overlook Trails
West Side

The 3-mile (6-mile round trip) hike from the Logan Pass Visitor Center to Hidden Lake conveys you quickly into Glacier's high country on a moderately easy trail. It climbs to Hidden Lake Pass where Mt. Reynolds and Bearhat Mountain dominate the skyline and Hidden Lake lies below. The 0.3-mile trail to the overlook drops nearly 700 feet to the north shore of the lake. Or you can go only the mile and a half to the Hidden Lake Overlook (3 miles round trip on the boardwalk) and observe the intriguing tiny alpine wildflowers along the way. Whatever you choose, this is a rare opportunity to experience an alpine ecosystem's plants and animals while savoring views of other Glacier high country. Interpretive information is available at the visitor center.

Emergency Gear

Glacier National Park and the surrounding wildlands provide unbounded recreational opportunities for the outdoor enthusiast. However, hidden amidst the scenic grandeur of the area are risks and hazards that can be deadly. Precipitous terrain, swift and cold water, wild animals and ever-changing weather are all factors that contribute to the wildness of the area.

It is important that you engage in outdoor activities that are compatible with the skill and physical capabilities of everyone in your group. Always evaluate your group and assess the hazards before leaving on your trip. Avoid traveling solo and advise family or friends of your route.

Responsible backcountry travelers are always prepared for the unexpected. Specific equipment that you bring should be governed by the type of outing that you engage in, but consider taking the following as standard emergency gear:

— Map and Compass. A topographic map of your area, as well as a compass.

— First Aid Kit. Being able to treat injuries and illness in the field can make a big difference in the well-being of someone in your party. Emergency medical services may not be readily available.

— Emergency Signalling Device. Be prepared to signal both aerial and ground search-and-rescue personnel. Helpful items include a whistle, signal mirror and an emergency signal that sends up smoke.

— Fire Starter. Your survival could depend on your ability to make a fire. Consider taking a candle and cigarette lighter. Fine steel wool or rubber bands make good fire "kindling."

— Adequate Food and Water. Calorie intake and hydration (enough water) are essential to your comfort and safety. Boil, filter or treat back-country water to avoid giardiasis. Carry extra high-energy snacks.

— Reliable Wind and Rain Gear. This is hypothermia country. A sturdy rain and wind parka and pants are a must to enable you to stay warm and dry.

— Bivouac Bag or Space Blanket. Be prepared for an unplanned night in the mountains. These items can help provide some protection from the elements. Carry a piece of insulated pad to provide insulation between your body and the ground.

— Layered Clothing. Dressing in layers of clothing allows you greater opportunity to regulate your temperature.

High technology has surfaced in the wilderness in the form of satellite phones. Many look at these devices as an intrusion into the "wilderness experience," while others consider the "dial-a-rescue" potential. Unregulated, these phones remain a personal choice. However, keep in mind that they could lead to a false sense of security—they can't take the place of common sense and appropriate skill.

Highline Trail
West Side

Little climbing and dazzling scenery await you here because you start at the top. The Highline Trail runs nearly 20 miles along the continental divide from Logan Pass into the Waterton Valley in Canada. It connects to several other trails going deep into the backcountry. The trail begins across Going-to-the-Sun Road from Logan Pass visitor center at 6,646 feet in elevation and runs level for the first 3 miles making it suitable for a short out-and –back trip for seniors and young children. Then it is a 7.5-mile, mostly downhill hike to Granite Chalet and another 3 miles to The Loop parking lot on Going-to-the-Sun Road. It's a nice all-day hike if you can shuttle with another car or have someone pick you up at the bottom.

St. Mary Falls, Virginia Falls and Baring Falls Trails
East Side

With trailhead parking areas along Going-to-the-Sun Road, the area offers interconnecting trails you can choose from to make a short hike to a single falls or hike them all. These hikes make a pleasant way to stretch your legs and view St. Mary Lake, its impressive surrounding mountains, and the creeks, gorges and waterfalls there. From the St. Mary Falls pullout you can hike the 1.2 miles to the falls then go the additional 0.7 mile to Virginia Falls. On your return you could hike past the pullout to Baring Creek and where it intersects the Baring Falls trail which begins steeply but rewards you with a cool place to rest at the falls after a short walk. The Baring Falls trailhead is located on Going-to-the-Sun Road about 0.3 mile west of Baring Creek. The St. Mary Falls Trail pullout is on the south side of the road about 6.5 miles east of Logan Pass and a mile west of Sunrift Gorge.

Ptarmigan Tunnel
East Side

Some of the best park scenery is yours on this popular east side trail. Allow a full day for this four-mile hike that begins at Swiftcurrent and follows one of the best-engineered trails in the park, which includes a tunnel blasted through the mountain. Go through it to a view of the remote Belly River drainage. Hikers often spot grizzlies along this trail.

Hiking Equipment Rental

Rocky Mountain Outfitters
135 Main St. Kalispell, MT 59901
• **(406) 752-2446**

This shop specializes in equipment, clothing, and information for the hiker and backpacker. They rent packs, hiking boots, climbing shoes and other items. They have a good selection of books and maps and will help you plan a trip and know the best places to go for people of all sorts of abilities.

Biking

Flathead County is striving to become a biker-friendly area, but it has a long way to go to be a real biker's Mecca. The county and its communities have been working to create a network of bike trails and bike routes that are envisioned to connect all the major populated areas within the decade. In populated areas a few short paved or hardened bike paths serve mostly the nearest residents. For vacationers who have brought their bikes and want a short jaunt in town, Woodland and Lawrence Parks in Kalispell have pedestrian-bike paths. There are also trail segments in Whitefish and Columbia Falls.

The new historical trail in Somers is especially attractive for families with young children. This 1.5-mile paved hike-bike path provides a friendly place to meet local strollers and bikers, young and old. You can't miss the trailhead in Somers with its large overhead sign announcing the Great Northern Historic Trail. Park along the road and enter the trailhead next to Tiebucker' Pub and Eatery (see the Kalispell chapter). You get panoramic views across the Flathead Valley to the Whitefish and Swan Mountain Ranges. The varied habitat along the open meadows, conifer covered cliff-sides and watery slough make it a great place for songbirds, waterfowl, small mammals and wildflowers. This new trail is well-used buy local families who stroll, jog, bike, roller blade or otherwise with non-motorized locomotion, which is the only kind allowed.

Mountain biking makes great sense in this great outdoor expanse, and that's the kind of cycling that's most popular. Here we list a few of the more accessible and popular bikers' destinations.

Biking in the National Forest

The miles and miles of national forest roads provide some of the best biking in Glacier Country because they can convey you into some of the most scenic and uncrowded areas of these wild lands. Bikes are allowed on all trails and roads, except in designated wilderness areas.

Tally Lake Ranger District

This district north of Whitefish has a network of easily accessible trails and roads suitable for individuals and families. Beginning mid-May to mid-June (depending on the year), bikers can spend the day biking picnicking, and observing the wildlife and birds attracted by Tally Lake, reportedly the deepest lake in Montana. The district and Glacier Cyclery employees have mapped ten good rides ranging from beginner to advanced difficulty levels. Mostly loops, they traverse a combination of singletracks and logging roads around the 4,800 feet altitude with little vehicle traffic. A local biker recommends the Reid Divide Trail as a "premier ride." It follows the ridge about ten miles on a surface of mostly softpacked forest duff before dropping down to the lake. Bikers have spotted varied wildlife including moose, black bear, and porcupines. By late September snow has usually begun on the higher trails. The map is available at the district office and Glacier Cyclery (see page 130).

The Big Mountain

Ride the gondola up to the top, then cruise down the trails on your bike. Over 20 miles of singletracks lead riders to stunning views of the Canadian Rockies, Glacier National Park, and the Flathead valley. Summit Trail runs on an 8-mile singletrack between the top and the Village. Another 12 miles of trails begins at the base of Chair 2. Twenty miles of trails lower down the mountain wind through forests and meadows accessed from the Outpost. No trail fees are charged, but there is an additional fee for bikes on the Gondola. Rentals complete with helmets and water bottles and trail maps are available at the hike-bike shop in the village.

Strawberry Lake Trail

The 10 bike trails at the north end of Jewel Basin have been mapped and can be obtained at Bikology (see page 130). The trails are routed on a combination of Forest Service roads and unmaintained trails with a beginner's loop, and experienced bikers say the main 20-mile loop will challenge even the strongest cyclists. It's perfect for those seeking a challenging route amidst the beauty.

Glacier National Park

Bicycling in Glacier National Park can be fun, but some roads are narrow and winding with little or no shoulder and are congested during the main visitor season. From June 15 to Labor Day, bicycling is prohibited from 11 AM to 4 PM daily on Going-to-the-Sun Road from Apgar to Sprague Campground and from Logan Creek to Logan Pass. There are no restrictions east of Logan Pass or on bikers traveling west. It generally takes about 45 minutes from Sprague Creek to Logan Creek and three hours from Logan Creek to Logan Pass.

Bicycles may be used only on established roads and designated routes. Bike travel is prohibited on all Glacier hiking trails excepts for the paved Apgar hike-bike path. Waterton permits biking on roads and has four hiking trails that bikers may travel.

Bike Rentals

Bike Easy
734 9th St. W., Columbia Falls
- **(4006) 892-2755**

"Soft rides for soft seats" is the motto of this new bike shop. They believe cycling is for everyone and their main interest is in having people as comfortable as possible. They rent mountain bikes by the hour, half-day or full day. The full day charge is $25 and includes a water bottle. There is an extra charge for the helmet.

Bikology Cycling Fitness
155 N. Main St., Kalispell
- **(406) 755-6748**

Bikology rents mountain bikes by the day and by the week. The $25 daily charge includes a helmet. They have trail maps, including for Big Mountain, and say that they will point you to some of their secret spots in the national forest, especially those near town.

Glacier Cyclery
336 E. 2nd St., Whitefish
- **(406) 862-6446**

These folks rent mountain bikes, touring bikes, and kids bikes by the half-day, full-day and week. The $20 daily rate includes a helmet and a water bottle you can take with you. They worked with the Tally Lake Ranger District to develop a map of the best trails on the district, and will steer you to the best local cycling areas on roads or trails. They also rent panniers, trailers, and car racks.

Horseback Riding

If a horseback trek in glacier Country is indispensable to your experience here, stables are handily located in and near Glacier national park. Outfitters offer different trips from one hour in duration to all day at a range of costs from $18 per hour to $125 per day. The season for horse riding in the park is short because of the wet or snowy trail conditions.

Muleshoe Outfitters
Apgar, West Glacier
- **(406) 888-5010, winter (520) 684-2328**

Muleshoe runs guided trips into the park's backcountry during the summer months from three stables in the park. The Apgar stable,

---

INSIDERS' TIP

Snow conditions on the east side of Glacier National Park vary considerably and winds can blow a cross-country ski route clear of snow at any time. Call the East Glacier Ranger Station for snow conditions at (406) 226-4473. Some routes cross onto the Blackfeet Indian Reservation. The tribe requires a free cross-country skiing permit obtainable at the tribal fish and game office in Browning.

which open July 1 is located just inside the western entrance. Another, located across Going to the Sun road from McDonald Lodge begins trips May 29 (406) 888-5121. The many Glacier stable opens June 5 (406) 732-4203.

Rawhide Trail Rides
12000 Highway 2 East, West Glacier
• (406) 387-5999

Located close to Glacier Park, this outfitter provides guided horse treks into the surrounding Flathead National Forest lands. They open mid-May and operate to mid-October, depending on the season's weather. They also offer backcountry overnight trips and saddle-paddle trips in conjunction with a rafting outfitter. They are easy to locate behind the covered wagons at Rawhide Trading Post

On the Water— Rafting, Kayaking, and Canoeing

A river runs through it, and creeks, sloughs, lakes and wetlands are abundant. In Glacier Country, wherever you look water defines the landscape. Trying to imagine it without alpine lakes mirroring the mountains, creeks rushing to the Flathead River, and Flathead Lake's azure expanse, is like trying to imagine the arctic without icebergs or the Sahara without sand. These waters give passage to treasured places difficult to reach by land. They bring exhilaration and excitement where they boldly rush through rapids or peace and tranquility where they quietly pool. There's a water adventure awaiting all seekers.

More and more opportunities become possible as local businesses seek to provide the best and most up-to-date equipment for the increasing number of recreationists attracted to these waters. Area kayaking and sailing events draw participants and spectators from near and far.

If you brought your canoe, kayak, rowboat or sailboat, you're set to hit the water. If you didn't, rentals are available and affordable. If you've never been on the water, now is the time to get your feet wet with one of the established and reliable guide services, whose staffs wants to give you nothing but a wonderful experience on their home waters.

Keeping Our Waters Wild and Wonderful

With more and more people discovering Glacier Country as a place to live and vacation, growing numbers of people are on the waters. The local, state and federal agencies charged with managing the resources for the benefit of ecosystems and the humans who live and play there, need the cooperation of visitors to assure they remain for generations to come. The primary agencies dealing with water recreation in the area are the Flathead National Forest, Glacier National Park and Montana Fish, Wildlife and Parks (FWP). They have lots of handy resource materials regarding regulations, maps and guides, and other materials to help make your water play safe and enjoyable. They are listed at the end of this section.

Warnings and Regulations

Glacier Country's streams and rivers vary greatly in their water conditions. High water from spring run-off usually begins in May and peaks in June on most river stretches. Always check with the agency in charge and scout the area as much as possible yourself. Whether you bring your own vessel or rent one, seek advice from local dealers, who usually get the latest scuttlebutt from local river runners about current conditions.

Glacier Country's changeable weather is particularly significant for lake boaters. High winds can descend quickly on Flathead Lake and small craft are advised to stay close enough to shore to return safely.

If you are floating in the fall, check on hunting seasons and take precautions in national forest and Montana state lands when going ashore and walking away from the water course. Trespassing on private land can sometimes be a problem. Public access areas are usually well defined, but many shorelines are a mix of public and privates ownership, which are not always well marked.

Power Boats

Montana boating regulations require all motorboats and personal watercraft (PWC) such as Jet Skis to be registered and numbered, including out-of-state boats used here more than 90 consecutive days. These regulations also apply to sailboats 12-feet and longer.

Children aged 12 years or younger must be accompanied by someone at least 18 years old to operate a motorboat or PWC of more than ten horsepower. Youths age 13 to 14 must have a Montana motorboat operator's safety certificate or be accompanied by someone who is at least 18. Persons renting motorboats or PWCs more than 10 horsepower must be at least 18. There are strict regulations regarding boat operation, including wake restrictions, launching and mooring, harassment of wildlife, waste discharge, noise limitations and others. Personal floatation devices (PFDs) such as life jackets, and other safety devices, such as fire extinguishers are required in most circumstances. You can pick up a copy of the regulations at Montana Fish, Wildlife and Parks. We recommend another helpful brochure available from the same offices: *Ethics, Etiquette and the River Recreationist*.

If you decide to go on a guided trip or commercial boat cruise, the U.S. Coast Guard advises that prospective riders are responsible for their own safety and should check out the operators of boat rides and cruises and follow these guidelines. Before leaving the dock talk to the operator about the driver or guide's qualifications and try to ascertain that the person in charge of your watercraft is not impaired by drugs or alcohol. Do they know first-aid and CPR? A smart skipper will take time to give passengers a review of safety equipment and rules of conduct. Check out the equipment for individual personal life jackets, radio, fire extinguisher and navigation lights and how to use them. If you had to, could you start, stop and steer the boat, or turn on navigation lights? Also, find out the trip plan, the route and return times.

Paddling Montana, by Hank Fischer, *Three Forks of the Flathead River Floating Guide* , published by the Glacier Natural History Association, and Flathead National Forest Map should be especially useful for planning your water recreation in Glacier Country. The map, besides showing, river and lake access on Forest Service lands, gives a wealth of information on all public lands, including lists of lakes, camping and other recreation areas with keys to services and opportunities at each. It's well worth its $4.00 cost. With these in hand, your dream water vacation will be a matter of a little research and decision-making. To get you started we offer a few suggestions.

Glacier National Park

Glacier National Park's lakes provide some of the best quiet and scenic paddling in the area and allow intimate exploration of shorelines seldom reached on foot. Even on the lakes where tour boats cruise, an unhurried day of gliding these crystal lakes can be nothing but pleasure.

The park doesn't charge fees for boating but does have regulations, a set of which can be had at headquarters or visitor centers. Canoes, kayaks and sailboats are permitted on all park waters except upper McDonald Creek between Mineral Creek and Lake McDonald. These areas are closed to all types of boating and floating to protect the harlequin duck. Personal watercraft such as Jet Skis are currently prohibited on all park waters. Privately-owned, motorized boats are prohibited except on Lake McDonald, and St. Mary, Two Medicine and Bowman Lakes, the latter are limited to 10- or less horsepower or less. Wearable personal flotation devices must be on board for each passenger and children must wear theirs while aboard. The park imposes both permanent and temporary shoreline closures in a few areas usually to protect breeding wildlife. Always check with a ranger to be sure what's in force during your stay.

Canoes, rowboats and low-power motor boats can be rented at Many Glacier, Two Medicine and at Apgar and Lake McDonald

Lodge on Lake McDonald. For those seeking a really quiet, pristine canoeing spot and don't mind traveling a long, primitive road to get there, we recommend Kintla Lake on the park's west side. It's a perfect jewel surrounded by heavily forested mountains, with no motorboats allowed and only a small primitive campground. But don't tell anyone else about it.

Area Lakes and Rivers

The larger and many of the smaller lakes have one or more easily reached boat-access sites. Flathead Lake State Park has them at each of its five units. Whitefish Lake State Park has a ramp on the southwest shore. Swan Lake's public access is located at the recreation area just north of the town of Swan Lake. Popular Forest Service access sites include Tally Lake northwest of Whitefish, Ashley Lake west of Kalispell, and numerous locations on Hungry Horse Reservoir reached from East Reservoir Road (turn off U.S. 2 at Martin City) and West Reservoir Road leaving U.S. 2 at the Hungry Horse Ranger Station. Motorized boats are permitted on these lakes, but check with Fish, Wildlife and Parks to see if waterfowl-nesting-season restrictions are in force in some areas.

Flathead Lake Marine Trail

Flathead Lake Marine Trail is designed specifically for kayaks, canoes, and small sailboats, with a network of access points and stopover areas. It would be useful for planning a day or multi-day outing around the lake, with stops at islands in the middle of the lake. It's a perfect opportunity to spot the famed Flathead Lake Monster. Campers pay overnight and vehicle-parking fees at Flathead Lake State Park. Between October and April, parks provide no drinking water. Pack-in, pack-out rules apply, and no pets are allowed at Wild Horse Island. Diamond-shaped signs mark landing areas. A trail map and guide is available from Fish, Wildlife and Parks.

The Flathead River

The Flathead River has a split personality. Each of its three branches, the North Fork, Middle Fork and South Fork, offer distinct environments and adventures. Some or all of these forks are included in the National Wild and Scenic Rivers, a total of 219 miles. The Middle Fork, where The River Wild was filmed, is suitable only for skilled rafters and kayakers or those with guides. The South Fork, which lies mostly in the Bob Marshal Wilderness, is only accessible on foot or horseback except for one section in the central part at Cedar Flats River Access. This fork has classes II and III waters with one gorge that is rated class V to VI, and must be portaged— definitely for the experienced. The North Fork arises in Canada and forms the western boundary of Glacier National Park. It has several public access points from both Inside and Outside North Fork roads. It flows clear and cold through conifer-covered mountains and is mostly suitable for intermediate floaters. During spring run-off, which begins in May and can last into July, fast currents and logjams offer thrills and challenges. The best conditions are usually from mid July to mid-August. The section between Polebridge and Big Creek is suitable for beginners only during low water and fair weather, and floaters should be watchful of riffles, log jams and narrow channels.

For the first-time or short-time visitor, the Flathead's best offering is its main stem below the South Fork's junction just above Columbia Falls. After spring runoff, it flows leisurely on the remainder of its journey to Flathead Lake through a braided channel among sloughs that provide habitat for waterfowl, raptors and beaver. It makes a good half- or full-day outing in good weather. Public access ramps are at Kokanee Bend, Pressentine Bar, and Old Steel Bridge.

Swan River

The Swan River careens northward 40 miles to Swan Lake from its three Mission Mountain headwater lakes, then gradually slows as it continues another 10 miles to its delta in Flathead Lake at Bigfork. The channel is heavily forested and bordered by abundant wildlife habitat. The upper Swan is narrow and even in its wider lower portions, log jams make it technically demanding and sometimes treacherous especially in high water. If the Swan's beauty makes you yearn

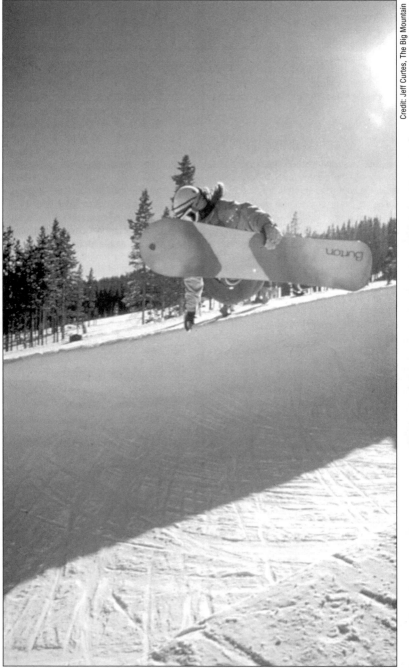

Snowboarding's popularity just keeps growing.

to put in your canoe, two stretches are worth exploring. In low water, two to three miles above Swan Lake the river slows and meanders apace suitable for beginners. Put in at the county bridge just above the Swan River National Wildlife Refuge, where waterfowl, shorebirds, deer, muskrat and other wildlife are often spotted. The Swan also attracts many streamside anglers, so you may see more people than you expected, but it's still a quiet experience. Local floaters favor the seven-mile trip beginning at the bridge east of Ferndale, which is easy enough for beginners during low water in August and September. Leave the final mile, the "Wild Mile," to the daredevil kayakers.

Swimming

Opportunities for water play are abundant in Glacier Country, whether it's swimming, wading, building sand castles on a river sandbar or collecting pretty, colored stones along the lake shores. It's generally an informal affair and often the kids play along the riverbank while Mom and Dad fish. Many of the numerous public access areas on lakes and rivers are free of charge and all you need is a bathing suit and advisedly protective footwear, as few area have sandy beaches. All units of Flathead Lake State Park charge a day-use fee that includes the use of shorelines, some of which have swimming areas roped off. For the most part you can swim anywhere on public lands and should take care you don't trespass on private land. The water is gloriously clean and clear nearly everywhere.

Popular swimming areas are Flathead Lake, Whitefish Lake City Beach, Foys Lake, Whitefish Lake State Park, Lake McDonald and Hungry Horse Reservoir. Woodland Park in Kalispell has a swimming pool, including a wading pool. Call (406) 752-6600, Ext. 274 for hours and season. Columbia Falls also has a municipal pool. To inquire about swimming there, call Columbia Falls City Pool (406) 892-3500.

Sea Kayaking Guides and Rentals

Glacier Sea Kayaking!
390 Tally Lake Road, Whitefish
• (406) 862-9010

Ocean-going fiberglass sea kayaks are stable crafts that anyone in moderately fit condition can operate with guidance for an enjoyable adventure around the shores of Flathead Lake. Glacier Sea Kayaking! offers a fun, supportive learning environment and group sizes are small with a high guide-to-student ratio. Trips are as leisurely as you need to explore the shorelines and islands and observe the wildlife. Children and photographers are also accommodated. The Flathead Lake headquarters is located just off U.S. Highway 93 in Rollins at the Big Sky RV Park Marina. The company offers half-day trips, full day tours, sunset and full-moon cruises. Half-day tours for 8 to 10 people cost $65 per person. Per person rates for smaller groups are higher.

Canoe and Kayak Rentals

Affordable Sports
2009 U.S. Highway 2 East, Kalispell
• (406) 756-5945

Canoe World (Bikology)
155 North Main Street, Kalispell
• (406) 755-6748

Rocky Mountain Outfitters
135 Main Street, Kalispell
• (406) 752-2446

Ski Mountain Sports
200 Wisconsin Avenue, Whitefish
• (406) 862-7541

Rafting Guides and Rentals

These folks love the rivers and want you to love them too. They also are passionate about keeping these waterways and the plants and animals living there healthy and happy for generations to come. They are all established companies with experienced guides. Their prices for half- and full-day raft and kayak trips are within a few dollars of each other, with similar equipment and services provided. Charges for half-day raft trips run about $38 for adults; $29 for children. Full-day trips cost about $72 for adults; $46 for children. Some or all gear is provided at this cost. These trips also have a scenic option that has little or no white-water. The companies also offer hike-raft, hike-horseback, extended wilderness trips, fishing excursions, fly-ins and other enticing combination packages, each distinctive to the company offering them. If you're single or a couple, expect to share a raft with strangers, from four to six others. The main tours feature some measure of white-water, depending on the month and melting snowpacks feeding the rivers. Scenic cruises provide relaxing jaunts on quieter stretches. Most companies require a four-person minimum for them, but nothing seems hard and fast with these folks. They want to give you the best deal they can. They are delighted to tell you about their menus of river trips. Check out their web pages for more detailed information.

Glacier Raft Company
6 Going-to-the-Sun Road (next to the Alberta Visitor Centre), West Glacier
• (406) 888-5454, (800) 235-6781
• grc@glacierraftco.com,
• www.glacierraftco.com

Celebrating its 24th anniversary this year, Glacier Raft Company is the oldest continuously operating raft company in Montana. It also gained prominence as host and technical adviser for production of the Hollywood movie The River Wild. Glacier Raft runs trips on the upper Middle Fork, main Middle fork, North Fork and main Flathead rivers. Eight riders on a raft is usual, with a minimum of four. Full day

trips include a barbecue lunch. They also rent inflatable kayaks for self-guided trips on the calmer stretches and provide shuttles.

Great Northern Whitewater
U.S. Highway 2, West Glacier
• (406) 387-5340, (800) 735-7897
• Email: whiteH20@digisis.net
• www.gnwhitewater.com

Great Northern's office is easy to spot one mile west of the Glacier Park entrance, by the red caboose on the hill. Now 22 years in business, Great Northern takes you down the Middle Fork of the Flathead River. They usually operate from mid-May into early October. In spring high-water they use larger rafts holding 10 to 12 people. Late season trips or when water levels are lower use six person rafts. Morning trips come with a complimentary breakfast. They rent inflatable kayaks for self-guided trips on the Middle Fork only.

Montana Raft Company and Glacier Wilderness Guides, Inc.
Box 935, West Glacier
• (406) 387-5555
• www.glacierguides.com

Now in its 16th, year Montana Raft Company and Glacier Wilderness Guides is the only company permitted to guide hikers in Glacier National Park. Its guides are knowledgeable about the area's natural history. During its season, from May 15 to September 30, it guides white-water trips on the Middle and North Forks of the Flathead River. It runs smaller rafts with six to eight people maximum, but a four-person minimum for the sce-

INSIDERS' TIP

Increasing levels of outdoor recreation are resulting in significant impacts on America's wildlands. The national Leave No Trace program promotes responsible outdoor use ethics. Please help minimize impacts to our wilderness by practicing these principles of Leave No Trace: Plan ahead and prepare; Travel and camp on durable surfaces; properly dispose of waste; Leave what you find; Minimize campfire impacts; Respect wildlife; and Be considerate of other visitors.

nic float. All its trips are guided and fees include all necessary equipment. All-day tours feature a deli lunch. It is located 1.5 miles west of the west entrance to Glacier.

Wild River Adventures
11900 U.S. Hwy. 2 E. (P.O. Box 272B, West Glacier, MT 59936)
• **(406) 387-9453, (800) 700-7056**
• **www.riverwild.com**

Wild River Adventures is entering its 15th year of guiding white-water rafting trips on the Middle and North Fork of the Flathead. The company also rents inflatable kayaks and rafts. Raft rentals cost $150 per day and they may require that you have a guide, depending on your experience and river levels. Prices include a full wetsuit package with everything else needed. Its season runs from May 15 to September 15. They are located one mile west of the west Glacier National Park entrance.

In the Snow— Skiing and other Winter Sports

Winter in Glacier Country revolves around snow—how much, what kind and how best to get out in it. Snow transforms the land into a winter wonderland and offers a menu of exciting outdoor adventures for young and old, and timid or adventurous. Deep snow and frozen waterways make accessible places in the park, national forests and lakes thaat are either difficult or impossible to reach at other times of the year. The possibilities range from a high mountain snowmobile tour to skiing in the silence of Glacier National Park's valley forests. For many insiders, winter is the best season and the reason they moved here.

Skiing, both Alpine and Nordic, becomes the central preoccupation in many people's lives and in the area's economic life. The same folks you see biking and hiking in summer head for the slopes after work and on weekends. Snowboarding has skyrocketed in popularity in just a couple of years. One of the things that makes the area so desirable is that the outdoor opportunities are so many and so close to the cities and towns. In fact, you can cross-country ski in town in Kalispell, and just a couple of minutes outside Whitefish.

As in other seasons, winter weather differs, often drastically, on either side of the Continental Divide. On the west side winters are generally cloudy, cool and wet. Only occasionally does the mercury dip below zero, as the cloud cover and moderating influences of Lake McDonald in the Glacier National Park and Flathead Lake keep temperatures in the teens and twenties. Areas east of the Divide tend to be much colder, less snowy, and more windy. Driving can be tricky as the high winds pile the snow into deep drifts on the roadways and you can experience whiteouts with near zero visibility.

Locals will generalize about the weather, then tell you there really is no typical winter. Take the last three seasons. The winter of 1996-1997 deposited 12 feet of snow in the Flathead Valley, and cross-country ski courses stayed open into April. Snow was sparse the following year, disappointing all skiers, snowmobilers, and ski resorts. In 1998-99 the ski resorts reveled in frequent powder showers and cross-country skiing continued well into March even at the lowest elevations.

Snow in the valley bottoms can be deep or disappointing. But even when there's little snow down below, you can almost always find plenty in the mountains above 5000 feet. The mountains receive about 80 percent of their precipitation as snow. While those clouds are hanging over the mountain tops blotting out the sun they are dropping snow on the peaks, amassing a snowpack that usually lasts well into summer. As late as June, I've seen bikers with skis or snowshoes strapped to their backs heading up Going-to-the-Sun Road (before it opens to vehicles) where they will stash their bikes and take off into the remaining high country snow.

With thousands of miles of forest roads and trails, backcountry snowmobiling ranks high on the list of winter activities. For the less ambitious or adventurous there are rinks for ice skating, in-town hills for sledding and tubing and even mushers who will take you for a dog-sled ride.

Winter Safety Tips

Don't let winter's soft, snowy beauty dull your awareness of its hazards. Lack of awareness and planning can be fatal. Whether you are snowshoeing, skiing, snowmobiling or hiking, when you're away from towns in Glacier Country, you are "out there" and you are on your own.

If you are venturing into the backcountry, travel with a partner, let someone know where you are going and when you expect to return, be sure you're in shape for the level of exertion you plan, check the weather and road conditions, and carry emergency-survival equipment and supplies.

The risk of hypothermia and frostbite hovers just beyond your mitts and parka, even when it doesn't seem that cold. It is the primary killer of outdoor enthusiasts. With hypothermia, a person's inner core is chilled resulting in slowing of mental and physical responses. Be alert to common symptoms—drowsiness and confusion. Once hypothermia has set in, external sources of warmth are necessary to restore the victim to normal. To stave off hypothermia drink plenty of liquids, stay dry, wear layers of warm clothing and snack frequently.

Frostbite can also mar your trip if you do not take the trouble to not only wear warm clothing but also to avoid exposed skin in freezing or windy conditions in which windchill becomes a factor. Be alert for whitening tissue and numbness in cheeks, noses, fingers and toes, which are especially prone to frostbite.

Avalanches

Avalanches can occur at any time during the winter. Snowmobilers are at greatest risk because their powerful machines can carry them into the highest and most avalanche-prone reaches. They outnumber other Montana snow recreationists in avalanche deaths each year.

An understanding of avalanche conditions is the snowmobiler's and skier's best defense, but if caught in an avalanche a survival kit can save a life.

Experts advise the following precautions:

- Avoid mountainous terrain after heavy snowfall or prolonged high winds
- Avoid crossing steep slopes and steep-sided canyons
- Keep to the windblown side of ridges
- Learn avalanche danger signals.
- Carry and know how to use transceivers, probe poles and shovels.

If caught in an avalanche:

- Try to keep calm and remember what to do
- Get away from your snowmobile, try to stay on the surface and "swim" toward the side of the avalanche
- As you stop, try to paw an airspace around your face.
- If you are a survivor, mark the place you last saw the victim, look for him or her downhill from there and probe the area. Unless help is close, stay with the victim and keep searching. A half-hour is all the time you usually have to save your companion's life.

For information about avalanche conditions contact Glacier Country Avalanche Center at (406) 257-8402, 800-526-5329 (Montana only) or check their website at www.montanaweb.com/avalanche. Our For More Information chapter lists some helpful books on avalanche safety, as well.

Downhill Skiing

The Big Mountain Ski and Summer Resort
Big Mountain Road, Whitefish
- **(406) 862-1900, 800-858-5439**
- **www.bigmtn.com**

The Big Mountain attracts winter sports enthusiasts from all over the U.S. and Canada. It is among North America's largest ski and summer resorts with more than 3,000 acres of skiable terrain and a view from the 7,000-foot summit *Ski Magazine* called the best in the nation. Snowfalls annually shower the peak with about 300 inches of the white stuff.

Especially renowned for its powder, the 51-year old resort offers a fine experience for every level of skier. Besides following the 67 marked trails, skiers can enjoy the freedom of open bowl and tree skiing. An atmosphere of celebration usually permeates the village area as skiers, snowboarders, tubers and sightseers buy their tickets, debark busses, and circulate between the lifts and slopes and the restaurants, pubs and shops. Just 5 miles from downtown Whitefish,"the village" attracts not only skiers, but locals and visitors, as well.

A variety of lifts, from a gondola and high-speed quad lifts to platter and T-bar will get you to your desired height and location on the mountain, whether you are a novice or schuss boomer.

The 1998-1999 daily rates were $40 for adults; $27 for ages 7 to 18 and for seniors aged 62 and older. The more adventurous can hitch a 12-person Snowcat ride to a summit ridge, then descend on skis through powder-covered glades. Make reservations with the Ski School. The cost is $80 per person.

Lighted slopes extend your skiing day Wednesdays through Sundays, December through March from 4:30 to 9 PM for $12. The $25 Family Fun Pass for families of up to six members admits them to the snow-tubing hill and lighted cross-country and snowshoe trails. The Big Mountain Ski School has many programs and rental equipment is available for alpine and Nordic skiing and snowshoeing. There is also a daycare center. The Big Mountain's ski season runs from Thanksgiving until the second week of April. The Shuttle Network of Whitefish runs the "Snow Bus" to the Bib Mountain Village from locations throughout Whitefish for one dollar per ride.

Blacktail Mountain Ski Area
P.O. Box 1090, Lakeside
• (406) 844-0999
• skiing@blacktailmountain.com, www.blacktailmountain.com

"Uncrowded, affordable and friendly" describe the features skiers find in Glacier Country's newest downhill ski area. The spectacular views and topnotch slopes on the summit of Blacktail Mountain make the 14-mile

drive through national forest from Lakeside well-worth the effort. As you reach the top on a wide, well-maintained forest service road vistas greet you across Flathead Lake and the Flathead Valley to the Swan and Mission Mountain Ranges. The road heads west from U. S. Highway 93 leaving just south of Lakeside. It takes 30 to 45 minutes to drive from Kalispell to the summit and lodge.

Blacktail first opened in early December 1998 after a flurry of construction to complete the 200-acre development on 1,000 acres of national forest lands. It straddles the mountain's 6,676-foot summit, which receives average yearly snowfalls of 250 inches. In a reverse of most alpine situations, skiers descend from the "base" lodge and pick up the lifts at the lower terminal some 1,440 feet below. The 24 groomed runs cover 13 miles of trails with a full range of challenges for every level of skier.

Blacktail attracts many people who seek affordable alpine skiing in a relaxed setting with all the necessary amenities. There's reasonably priced day care for the children, who can also take skiing or snowboard lessons from qualified instructors. You can also savor the views and the food at one of the two restaurants' new lodge, or have a hot drink in the lounge *after* you've conquered the slopes.

During Blacktail's season, from mid-November to April 1, it is open Wednesdays through Sundays and holidays 9:30 AM to 4:30 PM. It offers 2 double chair lifts, 1 triple lift, and 1 beginner's platter. Daily ski-rental package prices are $14 for adults, $10 for children, and $18 for snowboards and gear. Full day passes in 1998 cost $24 for adults, 15 for students and junior (8-18). Children under age under 7 and seniors over 70 ski free. Season and family passes are also available.

Cross-country Skiing and Snowshoeing

The Big Mountain Nordic Center
The Outpost Ski Shop, Big Mountain Road, Whitefish
• (406) 862-1900, (800) 858-5439
• www.bigmountain.com
Take to the wide trails hovering around

the 5,000-foot level that let the beginner enjoy the easy one and the advanced skier take the challenge of steep runs, all winding through conifer woods. These trails are some of the first in the area to receive snow.

The Outpost and Nordic Center, with its large parking area and activity area, are reached by the Big Mountain Road. Park your car and walk to the trailhead, which leaves just below the Outpost building.

Groomers sweep and set tracks daily on the 9 miles of trails with both classic and skating lanes. The 1.5-mile Weasel Trail is lighted for night skiing Wednesday through Sunday.

The ski shop sells the $5 daily cross-country passes, rents~skis and boots, and arranges lessons and tours. They also rent snowshoes and teach you how to use them. Snowshoe lanes and trails run around the cross-country area. The season extends from about Thanksgiving until early to mid-April.

Glacier Nordic Center and Outback Ski Shack
1200 Highway 93, Whitefish
• **(406) 862-9498 (November 1 through March 31)**
• **kalispell.bigsky.net/outback**

Located at the Whitefish Lake Golf Club, the center offers conveniently accessible, affordable skiing just north of Whitefish. Nearly 7.5 miles of gently sloping trails wind around the golf course with views of Whitefish Lake and the Whitefish Range. It's a perfect course for beginners and intermediates, but the racers in town also train there because its easy to get to for a noontime run. The Glacier Nordic Club sponsors the center and has the trails groomed daily for ski skating and track skiing. Nearly 2 miles of trail are lighted nightly making a pleasant after-dinner family activity. The more competitive go for the timed trials on Tuesday nights. Glacier Nordic Ski School offers instruction programs including classes for kids, seniors, skate skiing and classic skiing. The club asks a $3 donation, which, along with club memberships, covers the cost of grooming and equipment.

Outback Ski Shack rents ski equipment packages for half and full days (24 hours). Costs are $10 for a half day and $24 for a full

day for adults; children's are $8 and $10, respectively. Skiers with small children can rent a pulk (child-towing sled) for $5 per hour or $20 per day.

Glacier Ski School offers daily lessons at 1 PM in touring, skate skiing, and classic group.

The center trails are generally open from mid-December through mid-March. For more information contact the Glacier Nordic Club, P.O. Box 433, Whitefish, MT 59937.

Buffalo Hill Golf Club
1176 N. Main St. (P.O. Box 1116), Kalispell
• **(406) 756-4545**

Located a stone's throw from downtown Kalispell, the club opens its 27-hole golf course to cross-country skiers when snow conditions permit, usually from December 1 to March 1. Beginners and intermediate skiers will enjoy a relaxed tour on the gentle slopes, along the Stillwater with views of the mountains. Trails are occasionally groomed, but, if not, skiers soon have tracks leading to the best slopes and scenery. This is a perfect choice when you have only a short time to get your blood racing. Warm your toes and tummies with food and beverages at the cozy clubhouse. It's open 9 to 5, Mondays through Fridays throughout the year.

Izaak Walton Inn
Essex, MT 59916
• ⌐**www.vtown.com/izaakw, izaakw@digisys.net**

Thirty kilometers of scenic backcountry trials await you at this historic location on U.S., Highway 2 between West Glacier and Marias Pass near the Continental Divide. *Snow Country* magazine named the Izaak Walton one of the top 10 cross-country ski resorts in the Rockies.

The inn was built in 1939 to house winter snow removal crews working on the Great Northern Railway tracks. Railroad workers still stay there and the track complex behind the building evokes the excitement and romance of long-distance train ride through the west. Helper engines still push trains over the pass from the rail yard. Some vacationers, both local and continental, arrive by Amtrak train for their ski holiday.

Railroad buffs will enjoy the yard activity and memorabilia such as signal lanterns, historic posters and dining-car menus carrying out the inn's decor. Eighteen and a half miles of groomed and tracked trails appeal to beginner and advanced skiers on scenic slopes ranging from 3,000 to 5,000 feet in altitude. Lights on the Starlight Trail permit nightly skiing until 11 PM.

The high elevations, with earlier and heavier snows than most other areas, yield a longer season, from late November to mid-April. You often have the trails to yourself. This area is perfect for snowshoeing, and trekkers can take several trails that are marked specifically for them. Around every bend in the trail lies postcard view of distant snow-covered mountains or an intimate scene of a snow-banked mountain creek. A real favorite with advanced skiers is the half-mile loop along the Flathead River.

You can rent skis, snowshoes, and ski sleds here. They also offer ski lessons and guided trips into Glacier Park and the Bob Marshall Wilderness. A five-dollar daily pass admits you to all the trails, and an additional seven miles of trails awaits you on nearby national forest lands. See National Forest Trails, below.

Mountain Timbers Wilderness Lodge
5385 Rabe Road, Columbia Falls
• **(406) 387-5830**

This private bed and breakfast near Blankenship Bridge is increasingly attracting local skiers seeking a quiet, uncrowded tour with varied difficulties for beginners and intermediate skiers. The 9 miles of groomed, skier-tracked trails through second-growth mixed forest with views into Glacier National Park are on private land, but are open to the public for a small donation.

Glacier Wilderness Resort
U.S. Hwy. 2, at Milepost 163, Nyack Flats
• **(406) 888-5664**

Located 10 miles east of West Glacier, this year-round resort nestled in the conifer forests grooms 12 miles of national-forest trails leading right from their door, and they don't charge for the access. Beginner and interme-

diate skiers will enjoy these trails coursing about the 3,500 foot elevation. For the more adventurous skiers, ungroomed trails lead into the higher elevations and more challenging touring. For early season skiing, call ahead for snow conditions, as first snow dates vary from mid-October to mid-December.

Flathead National Forest Trails
The immenseness of the area and the vast network of Flathead National Forest roads beckon the backcounty skier to endless pleasure. Most of the roads remain unplowed and are used by both skiers and snowmobilers. The Tally Lake, Swan Lake and Hungry Horse districts offer groomed trails where snowmobiles are prohibited. Forest Service maps identify the roads suitable for skiing. Maps are available from the supervisor's office in Kalispell or the district offices. For general information call (406) 758-5200.

Round Meadows, Tally Lake Ranger District
Off the beaten track in the Flathead National Forest, 15 miles northwest of Whitefish, Round Meadows has nearly 7 miles of intermittently groomed trails open between mid-December 20 mid-March. Mostly beginner and intermediate slopes wind through woods and meadows. Snowmobiles and dogs are prohibited. Logging may restrict or close some trails. For information call the district ranger in Whitefish, (406) 862-2508.

Blacktail Mountain, Swan Lake Ranger District
Twenty-five miles of groomed or packed forest trails lead you along scenic ridges and slopes with panoramic views of Flathead and Mary Ronan Lakes and the Mission and Swan Mountains. Trailheads and parking area for the lower and upper runs are about 6 and 8 miles from Lakeside on Blacktail Mountain Road. At about 5,500 feet, this area offers 7 miles of easier and 18 miles of more difficult trails. Flathead County Recreation Department grooms the trails weekly. For ski condition report call (406) 758-5800. For area information call the Swan Lake Ranger District, (406) 837-7500.

Jewel Basin, Hungry Horse Ranger District

A spectacular and popular backcountry use area 15,349 acres of high mountains with 35 miles of trails, some suitable for backcountry skiing. Take Echo Lake Road from Montana 83 northeast of Bigfork and follow the signs to Jewel Basin. For information call the Hungry Horse Ranger District at (406) 387-3800.

Essex area

Several miles of touring trials lie along the Middle Fork of the Flathead River across on the from the Isaak Walton Inn. The Inn grooms the trails intermittently and has Forest Service trail maps.

Glacier National Park Winter Activities

Winter simply magnifies Glacier Park's special magic. The snow-covered roads become pathways into silence and into the heart of scenic areas away from crowds and cars. The season finds increasing numbers of skiers and snowshoers making the park their haven: new residents exploring their new home ground and conference-goers taking a day to recreate. Vacationers have discovered it as a way to unwind from the high speed and activity levels of the Big Mountain. The park prohibits snowmobiles anywhere within its boundaries. Check at park headquarters, (406) 888-7800 for snow conditions. A cross-country skiing brochure with map and descriptions is available the Apgar Visitor Center which is open winter weekends from 9 AM to 4 PM., (406) 888-7939.

Upper Lake McDonald

Going-to-the-Sun Road is kept plowed to Lake McDonald's upper end where it is barricaded. From there skiers and snowshoers take two popular routes: the 8-mile round trip through the cedar-hemlock forest along McDonald Creek to Avalanche Picnic Area or the 2-mile loop from the barricade to the footbridge across the creek and back downstream to Lake McDonald Ranger Station Road.

Apgar - West Glacier

Several routes lead from two parking areas here: at the horse barn reached by taking the first left off Going-to-the-Sun Road after the entrance station; and at the barricade on Camas Road just beyond the McDonald Creek Bridge. The trails range from 2 to 3 miles round trip to nearly 12 miles. The park brochure describes them in detail.

Polebridge

From the Polebridge Ranger Station parking area four popular routes follow either relatively level unplowed gravel roads into broad open meadows or lead to the hilly and sometimes icy 12-mile round trip to Bowman Lake. Several of these are especially suitable for families with small children. To reach the ranger station, take the North Fork Road leading from Columbia Falls toward the Canadian border, but check on road conditions especially after heavy snows.

St. Mary

From the special parking area near the Hudson Bay District Office (just south of the town of St. Mary) several routes, including

INSIDERS' TIP

Backcountry campers in Glacier country should carefully select gear to minimize bulk and weight, but maximize safety and comfort. Your comfort level will be greatly enhanced if you take clothing that keeps you warm and dry and that can be layered. Wear clothing next to the skin that wicks away moisture and dries quickly. Bring a portable camp chair to relax in comfort. An empty stuff sack can easily be converted into a pillow by stuffing it with extra clothing. Consider wearing gaiters to keep rocks, brush and snow out of your boots. Sometimes a mosquito net is a welcome commodity in the backcountry.

short loops, lead into level areas and rolling hills with views of St. Mary Lake and the Red Eagle Valley. Some are specially designated and marked.

Two Medicine Valley

Two Medicine Road, which remains unplowed, is used as a ski trail with several destinations, long and short, easy and strenuous through this highly scenic valley. Start at the end of the plowed road, usually 4 miles north of East Glacier near the Junction of Highway 49.

Wagner's Guest Ranch/Lodge

P.O. Box 218, Duck Lake Road, Babb
• **(406) 338-5770**
• **Waglodge@3 rivers.net**

East of Glacier, tourist activities come to a near-dead stop during the winter. The visitor is greeted by boarded up inns, restaurants and shops except for the Two Medicine Grill in East Glacier and Wagner's Guest Ranch in Babb. On the Blackfeet Indian Reservation, Wagners offers the only winter accommodations—including rooms, all meals and information for winter recreation in the area. If you're happy with unpretentious, down home comfort, Wagner's will suit you. It's located only 2 miles from world famous Duck Lake, renowned for its enormous rainbow trout. Ice fishing is popular and it's a short driving time to Glacier National Park's cross-country ski ares. Wagner's also rents an ice sailboat. With these activities and 350 acres of lands to explore by snowmobile, Wagner's makes a good winter headquarters east of the Divide.

Glacier Park Ski Tours

728 Kalispell Ave., Whitefish
• **(406) 862-2790, (800) 646-6043, Ext. 6043**

How'd you like to spend a day in Glacier's winter backcountry with a guide who'll safely escort you to prime locations and interpret the wondrous landscape you encounter. Put yourself in the hands of experienced guides skilled in winter mountaineering, avalanche safety and first aid. Owner Rusty Wells brings 17 years of guiding experience to the business and says people really appreciate being

able to go out with a guide who knows the natural history, the trails and how long it takes to travel them, and how to get to the best spots for scenery, wildlife, or terrific skiing. He has trips for just about every interest and ability: day tours, backcountry tours with overnights in an igloo and evening tours on full-moon nights. Day tours, including a meal, cost $40 per person for groups of 5 to 14 people, with higher per person rates for smaller groups.

Snowmobiling

This is truly a snowmobiler's paradise with more than 200 miles of groomed snowmobile trails and nearly 2000 miles of USDA Forest Service roads that can lead you into great hill climbing, powder play, and spectacular ridgetop views of Glacier National Park, the Flathead Valley and the Canadian Rockies. Snowmobile organizations are instrumental in keeping the trails maintained in cooperation with the Forest Service and groomed during the long season in the high country. They educate other riders about safety, outdoor survival and avalanche awareness to keep the sport enjoyable for all. One of the areas' most popular trails is the groomed Skyland-Two Medicine Snowmobile Trail that meanders along the Continental Divide, back and forth between the Flathead and Glacier Counties. Well-marked trailheads and parking areas border U.S. Highway 2 at the pass. Maps are available from the Snowgoer or the Lewis and Clark National Forest, see above.

Flathead Snowmobile Association

P.O. Box 5041, Kalispell
Randy Ek, president, (406) 756-3703, fax (406) 755-3703.

The Snowmobile Grooming Coalition, composed of area businessmen, supports the association financially through donations and fundraisers.

Cutbank Snowgoers

Box 301, Cut Bank
Lewis and Clark National Forest
1101 15th St. N., Box 869, Great Falls
• **(406) 791-7700**

The Cutbank Snowgoers grooms trails east

of the Continental Divide and the trails on Marias Pass that traverse both the Flathead and the Lewis and Clark National Forests.

J & L RV Rentals
30 Ninth Street East, Columbia Falls
• (406) 892-7666

You're not a skier but ache for a snowy mountaintop adventure? A guided snowmobile excursion is a good bet for an unforgettable experience in the Whitefish Range high country. J & L RV Rentals of Columbia Falls operates a snowmobile guide service under a special use permit with the forest and runs tours in conjunction with the Big Mountain and on their own. Guides are trained in avalanche awareness, CPR and first responder training.

At the Big Mountain, two three-hour tours leave daily from the Summit lift area, at 9 AM and at 1 PM. The charge, including a lift ticket, is $122 for a single rider, $133 for two, and no charge for a rider under 16 years old. A boots, gloves, and suit package rents for $25. Helmets and transceivers are mandatory and are issued at the Summit House at no charge. All trips are guided, but they provide plenty of free playtime (supervised) for fun. Call for reservations at (406) 862-2900.

J & L also offers rental equipment and guide service at its shop in Columbia Falls. Guides are optional, but first-timers are strongly encouraged to engage a guide. Rentals of machines and gear-clothing packages come with orientation about the equipment and directions to the area's snowmobile routes. Helmets and transceivers are mandatory. J & L will haul the machines to the main local trailhead at Canyon Creek Road, about five miles north of Columbia Falls on the North Fork Road. This trail system accesses the Whitefish Range trails from the opposite side of the Big Mountain and lead into a wonderland of high country tracks running north to Red Meadow within 15 miles of Canada. Half-day rates for single are $95, double $115. A guide costs $40 for up to eight machines. Full days cost $140 for a single, $150 for a double, and for a guide $75. They also rent trailers. Owner John Altenburg says people should feel free to call the shop for trail or other information. About a third of the people who come into the shop just seeking information, and that's fine with him because he just wants to see people out there having fun.

Other Winter Sports/ Activities

Dog Sled Rides

Dog Sled Adventures
P.O. Box 34, Olney
• (406) 881-BARK

Located 20 miles north of Whitefish on U.S. Highway 93, exactly 2 miles north of Olney, on the east side of the road, a half-mile past mile marker 147.

With a Montanan the 1999 Iditarod Race winner, dog sledding seems an appropriate way to spend a day in Glacier Country. Dog Sled Adventures takes you on a 1-1/2 hour trip along a 12-mile loop through the Stillwater State Forest with a team of fast and friendly Alaskan huskies and other breeds. Afterwards they pamper you with hot chocolate and cookies by the fire and exchanging of tall "tails." Wear warm clothes, including hat and mittens, and bring sunglasses. If it's very cold you will be encased in a warm cocoon of down and elk skins. After the trip you can pet the dogs. Reservations are advised. The cost is $60 for adults and $30 for children.

Ice Skating

Frozen lakes and ponds abound in Glacier Country, but you won't see many ice skaters on them, because snow is usually too plentiful to keep them shoveled, with the possible exception of the Blackfeet Indian Reservation where winds tend to keep lake surfaces clear. Skaters can take advantage of two public rinks. Woodland Park's rink has a warming hut and offers and rentals and lessons during December and January for children and adults. See Woodland Park in Kalispell attractions.

Mountain Trails Ice Skating Center
725 1/2 Wisconsin Avenue, Whitefish
• (406) 863-2477

The rink is just outside Whitefish on the way to the Big Mountain. Whitefish Parks and Recreation runs the facility, which is open for public skating on a variable daily schedule. It is also open Friday and Saturday nights from 6 to 11:30 PM and Sunday afternoons, from 2 to 7 PM It offers rentals, skate sharpening and instruction.

Sledding and Tubing

Some people enjoy sledding and tubing when conditions are right. It can provide inexpensive, convenient family fun when only a few hours are available. The Big Mountain has set aside a tubing area and families slide on popular hills in Kalispell, Whitefish, and Columbia Falls. Municipal recreation departments can guide you to sliding hills and places where you can rent equipment.

Hunting and Fishing

Hunting

The long-standing tradition of hunting wild game to fill the winter larder still burns strongly in Glacier Country as elsewhere in Montana. The homesteading way of life counted the harvest of meat and fish from the woods and rivers as a vital means of supplementing field crops or cash from timber. The abundance of fur-bearing mammals brought the first non-native people to the mountains and northwestern Montana is still one of the few places in the country where trappers can still trap wolverines, pine marten and some other species. Bird hunters find upland game birds here, especially ring-necked pheasant, Hungarian partridge and several species of grouse. Ducks and geese are abundant, with Canada

geese so common, that some hunters are calling them "flying carp."

Realistically, however, Glacier Country hunting is limited compared to other areas of the state. This is because well over half of the land is either in Glacier National Park, where no hunting at all is allowed, or on the Blackfeet and Flathead Indian Reservations, where only limited game-bird hunting is open to the public. National forest lands in Glacier Country are largely roadless wilderness areas and require backpacking or horseback to reach the game. The remaining, more accessible, national forest acres, state forests, state recreation lands and private lands do provide hunters with opportunities for white-tail, mule deer and game bird hunting. Hunters seeking a challenge can take home an elk if they are willing to stalk in steep terrain. Moose, bighorn sheep and mountain goat hunting permits are granted through drawings. Out-of-state-hunters tend to be few, perhaps because of the cost and difficulty in obtaining big-game permits which, except for black bear and mountain lion, are awarded to non-residents only through drawings.

For those who want to include hunting in their Glacier Country visit, a guided trip with one of the licensed outfitters provides a good option. A list of outfitters is available from the Montana Outfitters and Guides Association listed at the section end.

Licenses and permits are obtained from the Montana Department of Fish, Wildlife and Parks (FWP) offices or from license agents. People using Montana State Trust lands for hunting, fishing or simply walking must also have a state recreational use license also available at FWP and Montana Department of Natural Resources and Conservation. Regulations and dates of seasons change from year to year so it's wise to get a copy of the most current ones from FWP, the Flathead and Blackfeet Indian Reservations.

Fishing

Although not generally acclaimed as a "fishing destination," Glacier Country satisfies many anglers, both local and visiting, with food and diversion in scenic splendor that more than compensates for any deficiencies. A rich variety of lakes, rivers, and streams attracts a dedicated bunch of local anglers on a regular basis, rain or shine, cold or wind. Trophy lake trout, or Mackinaw, still thrill their catchers and send them home with either something to display on their walls or some great eating with friends and family. Fly fishers and catch-and-release enthusiasts will find some exciting fishing. This area still has a reputation for some of the best bull trout fishing anywhere.

Montana's Fishing Access Sites program provides recreational opportunities for residents and visitors. These sites have parking areas, usually either vault or flush toilets and are well marked with the brown and white, hook-and-fish logo on road signs leading from the main highways.

Fishing license requirements for Montana residents are as follows: under age 12, no license is required; youths 12 through 14 need only a conservation license; people aged 15 through 61 must purchase both a conservation and fishing license; and those 62 and older need only the conservation license. The conservation license costs $4; the fishing license, $17. Non-residents under age 15 need no license if they are with a licensed adult, but the combined catch limit is the same as for a single fisher. Anglers over 15-years old must buy a conservation license and a fishing license. The two-day non-resident fee for both is $15. Full-season licenses are $50. No license is required for fishing in Glacier National Park. Call (406) 888-5441 for information about fishing there. Resource agencies of the Flathead and Blackfeet Indian Reservations require permits to fish on the reservations.

Streams and rivers open for fishing the third Saturday in May and close November 30. Lakes and reservations are open year-round, with a few exceptions.

Catch and Release

In northwestern Montana catch-and-release is mandatory for bull trout except on Swan Lake, where the limit is one; bull trout are a federally listed threatened species. Pic-

tures and descriptions of this species are available at FWP and fishing shops. Some other species are restricted to catch-and-release on local streams and lakes. Check the current fishing regulations for such restrictions.

If you practice catch and release fishing, improve your techniques to reduce stress on fish. Use hook-removal tools and if you must handle the fish, use soft, wet gloves, or at least wet your hands.

—Use barbless hooks for fast-and-easy hook removal.
—Artificial lures and flies cause far less mortality than bait.
—Play the fish as rapidly as possible, not to its total exhaustion.
—Don't squeeze the fish or put your fingers in its gills when removing the hook. If deeply hooked, cut the line as close to the mouth as possible; don't yank the hook out.
—Release the fish only after its equilibrium is maintained. If necessary, gently hold the fish upright facing upstream and move it slowly back and forth.

In order to prevent both the introduction of non-native fish into new areas and the spread of disease, it is illegal to move live fish and aquatic insects, or to use live bait and to dump bait buckets.

Fishing the Lakes

Mountain Lakes generally are icebound until mid-June or early July. Trails to some may not be cleared until mid-summer or later. Inquire about conditions at the agency in charge of the public lands where the lakes are located or at local fishing-supply shops. Be prepared for biting insects and unpredictable weather. In Glacier National Park, Lake McDonald and Saint Mary Lake are more renowned for their beauty than for their fish. The best fishing lakes are said to be on the east side, but on either side the very best fishing is in the less accessible lakes that require a four to ten-mile or better hike. We've listed a few of those accessible by vehicle or a short, easy hike.

Flathead Lake

Flathead Lake seldom freezes over so year-round fishing does take place, attracting anglers seeking its renowned trophy lake trout as well as whitefish, and yellow perch. Somers Bay, Woods Bay, and state park units have boat launches. There is a small fee at the state parks for day use or camping. Parking areas are set aside for boat trailers. Somers and Wayfarers State Parks are handicapped-accessible.

Swan Lake

Swan Lake attracts many boat anglers who use the launch ramp at the state recreation area just north of the town of Swan Lake. There is little shore access. From May through October kokanee, rainbow trout, westslope cutthroat, and northern pike can be taken. This is the only place it is legal to take bull trout, the limit is one.

Echo Lake

Echo Lake is known for its large-mouth bass. Northern pike, yellow perch. Sunfish are also caught there. You can launch your boat at the state ramp at Echo Lake Marina. Parking and shore access are poor. Best fishing is spring and fall.

Tally Lake

On the Tally Lake Ranger District northwest of Whitefish, Tally—the state's deepest lake—is nearly 500 feet deep. The fishing is not the best, but its a perfect spot for a family outing when some members want to fish and others want to bike, hike or just picnic. There's a boat launch at the campground. Try your luck at the cutthroat, rainbow and bull trout, kokanee and northern pike.

Church Slough

About six miles southeast of Kalispell, Church Slough, a large oxbow lake, lies along Lower Valley Road. It is popular with local anglers for it yields largemouth bass, northern pike and yellow perch. A boat helps the catch.

Avalanche Lake, Glacier National Park

In a lovely alpine setting surrounded by mountain peaks Avalanche Lake is an easy two-mile hike from Avalanche Creek Campground on Going to the Sun Road. Cutthroat trout is the main species here and eight- to ten-inch fish are in good supply mainly in June and July.

Bowman Lake, Glacier National Park

The best time to catch the resident lake trout, kokanee, cutthroat, and bull trout in Bowman Lake is right after spring breakup and in the fall. The boat access ramp lies just beyond the campground. The campground is about seven miles from the Polebridge Ranger Station on a poor dirt road.

Kintla Lake, Glacier National Park

Continue on about 12 miles beyond the Bowman Lake turnoff on the Inside North Fork Road and you come to one the prettiest lakes in the park, with reasonably good fishing as well. Boat fishing is best, but shore fishing is also satisfying away from the road and campground. It has cutthroat, and lake trout, kokanee and some bulltrout.

Josephine Lake, Glacier National Park

June and July are best months to catch the brook trout and kokanee in this small lake just a mile-and-half walk from Many Glacier Hotel. If you have a light canoe or inflatable kayak, take it.

Sherburne Lake, Glacier National Park

Sherburne is the only park lake with northern pike, which reputedly get to be whoppers and can be a handful to land. They bite the best in August. There is a boat access ramp.

Swiftcurrent Lake, Glacier National Park

You could practically throw a line into this lake from your room at the Many Glacier Hotel. But for best results do your angling in June or July from a boat and try to bag some brook trout reputed to run about 10 inches.

Two Medicine Lakes, Glacier National Park

The beauty of these lakes—lower, main

and upper—makes it a joy to fish with fairly good chance of catching rainbow and brook trout. Most run under 15 inches. Best fishing is in June and July

Creeks and Rivers

The Flathead River system offers a wide variety of fishing opportunities. The other rivers have either poor fishing or poor access. The Stillwater and the Whitefish are slow and bordered by pastures and urban development, but there are a few places where people fish successfully for northern pike and rainbow trout in the spring. On the Swan River, the inexperienced boater or angler will have the safest, most satisfying experience with a guide. Brush and logs make it difficult and sometimes dangerous to navigate or wade, and private land ownership closes off a lot of the shore access.

Anglers seeking a more serious fishing experience in Glacier Country are advised to hire a guide or consult the extensive array of books about Montana fishing that give detailed descriptions of the waters, the fish, the lures or bait and techniques needed for best results.

Flathead River

The Flathead River system is vast and much of it, especially the Middle Fork and South Fork, lies deep in the wilderness, and that's where the most interesting fishing occurs, according to the experts. The North Fork, which is road-accessible along much of its way has bull trout, westslope cutthroat trout and mountain whitefish. The four-hour float from Big Creek to Glacier Rim is a popular float among locals. The main Flathead channel below Columbia falls offers reasonably good populations of westslope cutthroat, mountain-whitefish, rainbow trout from Columbia Falls to Kalispell, especially between Presentine and the Old Steel Bridge.

Fishing Charters

Flathead Lake charter fishing doesn't usually start up until early May when the lake is full. During the winter months into April, water

levels are so low the larger boats cannot get to the water. The Flathead Lake charters use downriggers to catch the Mackinaw lake trout that is the main species now caught and their large size makes them the preferred species with most anglers. The outfitters do not generally sell licenses, so to avoid delays call ahead and arrange to buy your license elsewhere the day before.

A Able Fishing
Marina Cay, Bigfork
• **(406) 257-5214**

Located in the motel-restaurant complex at the intersection of Grand Drive and Montana Highway 35, A Able has been running charters for 14 years. Owners Shorty George and Jeannie Goggins uses both large and small covered boats with bathroom facilities for their fishing charters on Flathead Lake. They take all comers including children and have had guests in their eighties. No experience is necessary to catch fish. On morning charters fish are guaranteed: no fish, no pay. Charter costs include all equipment and a snack or meal depending on trip length. Half-day (five hours) small-boat trips for one or two people are $200, for three or four, $235.

The full-day (nine hours) costs $325 for one or two; $335 for three or four. The larger boats are $25 more.

A-1 Fishing
559-1/2 N. Juniper Bay, Somers
• **(406) 857-2588**

A-1 moors its covered boats at the Lakeside Marina just behind Rosario's restaurant on Highway 93 at the north end of Lakeside. Managers Kathy and Craig Renfro have been running charters for 10 years. The experienced guides conduct charters generally from late April until early November, depending on water and weather conditions, but will take guests out at any season on request. Their 22-foot and 26-foot boats have on-board bathrooms. For their five-hour, half-day outings including all equipment, they charge $195 for 2 people, $235 for four. Full-day, eight-hour trips cost $325 for two, $375 for four. A sandwich lunch is available on request. They provide pop, and snacks and they guarantee fish or there's no charge.

Bagley Guide Service
Bigfork
• **(406) 837-3618.**

Owner Dusty Bagley has been fishing Flathead Lake 11 years and now takes others out to catch trophy lake trout. He offers half-day and full-day cruises for up to five people. Toilet facilities are provided on some boats. Call for current prices. Bagley's runs cruises year-round, depending on the weather. These charters operate out of Woods Bay Marina located about four miles south of Bigfork.

Lakestream Fly Fishing Shop
15 Central Ave., Whitefish
• **(406) 862-1298**

Lakestream's most popular trips are their driftboat floats down the Flathead River. They also guide anglers down the Swan River and on private lakes. They can take you where you are most likely to find cutthroat, rainbow and lake trout, pike, bass and whitefish by boat or as a walk-wade trip. Their jet boats get you through the meanders on the lower Flathead. Waders, rods, reels and other equipment are included in the trip price unless unusual gear is requested. Their experienced guides have the patience of Job and can assist you with either spinner or fly fishing. Their main goal is to show you a good day whether you catch fish or not. They charge $225 for half-day trips for two or three people, $300 for a full day.

The Northern Rockies Outfitter
7461 Hwy. 2 E., Columbia Falls
• **(406) 892-1188**

Owner Richard Birdsell offers guests a variety of fishing opportunities based on his nine years experience guiding and instructing fly fishing. Trips include Flathead River drift-boat floats for native cutthroat and rainbow trout, mountain-lake fishing and hike-in mountain stream fishing. Lake trips go mainly to the Badger-Two Medicine area on Glacier Park's east side for wade-walk or float-tube fishing. Half-day river floats trips cost $195 for two people, full-day, $285. Other trips cost $300 per day for two, with a $75 charge for each additional person.

Golf

Glacier Country golf courses don't have to toot their own horns. Lots of others are doing it for them. In April 1997, *Golf Digest* named the Flathead Valley as "the last best frontier of great undiscovered golf in the continental U.S." characterized by "terrific courses, excellent weather, welcoming locals, unparalleled natural beauty and prices that seem too good to be true."

You will find a course suited to your golfing goal whether it's to enjoy a few relaxing hours in the unsurpassed scenery with friends and family or to test your mettle on a tough 9 or 18 with other scratch players. The mild valley weather often means you can golf an extended season. It's not unusual to see players on the course in mid-December or mid-March. All the courses listed are open to the public. Consistent with a popular retirement area, several clubs are affiliated with a golf community. Some of the golf clubs and area hotels have teamed up to provide package deals for accommodations and course admission.

Yardages mentioned are for the men's white tee. Greens fees and cart rentals are quoted for 18 holes on 18-hole courses. Rates are for guaranteed advance, regular season. Two- or three-day advances cost a few dollars less. Cart rates are per person. All courses prohibit pets and metal spikes.

Flathead Valley Golf Association provides a central reservation service at (800) 392-9795.

Buffalo Hill Golf Club
1176 N. Main St.(P.O. Box 1116) Kalispell
• **(406) 756-4530**
• **sdunfee@digisys.net**

Buffalo Hill ranks consistently on *Golf Digest's* list of top courses and places to play. The 27-hole, target-oriented course keeps golfers returning to play in one of the most picturesque, natural settings anywhere. Along with spectacular views of the Swan and Whitefish Mountains and plays along the Stillwater River, golfers often see moose and other wildlife. The buffalo herd that belonged to the original owner is no longer there, but the name evokes its history. The original, stand-alone Cameron Nine, designed by Robert Muir Graves in the classic 1930's style, retains its push-up and multi-level greens on the par 35, 3001-yard course. The 6284-yard, par 72 Championship 18, offers challenges you can increase from the back tees. This course has the highest slope rating in the Flathead Valley. The rustic log clubhouse encloses the pro shop, and full-service lounge and restaurant. Greens fees are $37, cart fees are $11.

Eagle Bend Golf Club
279 Eagle Bend Dr. (P.O. Box 1257) Bigfork
• **(406) 837-7310, (800) 255-5641**
• **www.golfmt.com, golfmt@digisys.net**

Golf Digest has rated this 27-hole resort course the No.1. golf course in Montana and among the top 50 in the nation. Flowing in and around trophy-homes and condominiums, the original 18 holes enclose the natural features of rocky cliffs and mammoth outcroppings, stands of Douglas-firs and cattail marshes with landscaping in a skillful blending of human and natural developments. Views of Glacier's peaks and the Salish Mountains east of Flathead Lake provide a 360-degree scenic feast. The 6,189, par-72 course attracts high handicappers and scratch golfers who in a variety of challenges. The newest nine, designed by Jack Nicklaus provides a stand-alone course running along the lake and ponds. The pro shop, restaurant and Hap's Bar share the large clubhouse near the entrance. Greens fee is $54, cart fee, $14.

Glacier Park Lodge Golf Course
East Glacier Park

History and scenery combine to make this nine-hole golf course a unique experience. It was built in the late 1920s by rallroad magnate James J. Hill alongside the resort hotel that tied in with his goal of bringing eastern tourists to Glacier Country on the railroad he was constructing from Minnesota to the Pacific Coast. The course resembles others of that era designed by its New York golf-course architect. The par 36 course runs 3,300 yards with some unexpected tight and blind shots. Sitting east of the Continental Divide, Glacier Park Lodge experiences the vagaries of eastern-slope weather including stiff winds, but displays magnificent views from its fairways lined with lodgepole pine and quaking aspen. The season runs from mid-May to mid-October.

Glacier View Golf Club
River Bend Dr., West Glacier
• **(406) 888-5471,**
Tee times (800) 843-5777

Situated next to Glacier National Park, Glacier View Golf Course has earned its reputation as a friendly, family-oriented course. The 4,856 yard, par 68 course is characterized by open fairways and small greens. To create more challenges, they have gone to a three-tee system and roughed up the rough with water and sand. It's an ideal golf course for golfers looking for a way to combine Glacier

Credit: Marina Cay Resort

The Flathead Valley is becoming known for its beautiful golf courses.

Park touring with nine or 18 holes on the links in the same day.

Meadow Lake Golf Resort
100 St. Andrews Dr., Columbia Falls
- **(406) 892-2111**
- **www.meadowlake.com**

Although known for the premier natural setting and scenic beauty of its location just minutes from Glacier National Park, Meadow Lake is no pushover according to local golfers. Its narrow, tree-lined fairways and water hazards have created a difficulty that helped get the par-72 course rated as a "Top 500 U.S. Public Golf Course" by *Golf Digest* and a "must play" course by *Golf Magazine*. The 18-hole, mid season greens fee is $42, cart fee $13.

Northern Pines Golf Club
3230 U.S. Hwy. 93 N., Kalispell
- **(406) 751-1950, (800) 255-5641**
- **www.golfmt.com, golfmt@digisys.net**

This three-year old, 18-hole course combines traditional Montana-style courses and classic Scottish links with its tree-lined fair-ways and natural water hazards of the Stillwater River and a 20-acre lake. The lack of trees on the opening nine reveals its recent conversion from a 250-acre potato field. The 6,180-yard par-72 course is characterized by deep rough and lots of fairway mounding against a backdrop of the Whitefish and Swan Mountain Ranges. Greens fee is $43, cart rental, $14.

Polson Country Club
111 Bayview Dr., Polson
- **(406) 883-8230**

This vintage golf course situated on Flathead Lake's southern shore features spectacular views of the lake and the Swan and Mission mountain ranges. The original nine holes, opened in 1936, are short with tight, conifer-lined fairways and small greens. The decade-old front nine plays 300 yards longer in a more open setting. This nine along with a new one being developed will tie in with each other and the original nine, with its historic log clubhouse, will stand alone. The existing 18 holes measure 6089 yards with a par of 72. The greens fee is $28, cart rental, $22.

Village Greens Golf Club
500 Palmer Drive, Kalispell
- **(406) 752-4666**
- **www.montanagolf.com**

Affordability and superb greens-keeping attract many golfers to this seven-year old course in suburban Kalispell known for its fine bent-grass greens. Both nines on the 5,751-yard, par 70 course have an abundance of water, plenty of fairway mounding, ponds and white sand. Check out its all-grass driving range and full service pro shop and deli. Its all-season greens fee is $31, cart fee, $20.

Whitefish Lake Golf Club
Highway 93 North, Whitefish
- **(406) 862-4000**

Montana's only 36-hole golf complex is also one of its older ones. *Golf Digest* ranked the course among Montana's top five in 1996. With views of Whitefish Lake and the Whitefish Range, including Big Mountain, this tight, tree-lined course emphasizes accuracy over distance.

Whitefish Lake's establishment was a product of politicking during the 30s for the New Deal's Works Progress Administration. WPA would fund a landing strip and the citizens of Whitefish, who wanted a golf course and were willing to put up matching money. Pilots and golfers ended up sharing the green strips serving as both fairway and runway and the conflicts that flared between them are immortalized in the Stumptown Historical Society records. The log clubhouse lends its 1930s vintage atmosphere to the first-class dinner restaurant.

The North 18, par 72 course measures 6297 yards. The 6,144-yard South 18 plays at par 71. Greens fee $34, cart $12.25.

Flathead Lake State Parks

These state parks offer great venues for outdoor recreation, from fishing and wading to hiking and biking.

Finley Point
Located at the south end of the lake, this 28-acre park features a marina for boats up to 25 feet and 16 RV campsites.

Wayfarers
On the eastern shore, this park is located south of Bigfork and is a favorite place for swimming and camping. Thirty campsites are located here with seven tent-only sites.

Yellow Bay
Located on the eastern shore amidst the cherry orchards, Yellow Bay offers a wide beach for swimming, boating, fishing, and bird watching. One of the smaller Campgrounds, there are six sites including five walk-in tent sites.

Big Arm
On the western shore, this large park is a popular launching point for Wild Horse Island. There are 36 campsites, a nature trail, a hiking and horseback trail, and a mountain bike trail.

West Shore
Also on the western shore, the park's rock outcrops provide spectacular view of the lake and surrounding mountains. With 26 campsites, West Shore is popular with boaters and anglers.

Wild Horse Island
Hiking on this large island in Flathead Lake gives you the added benefits of a boat trip and visible wildlife including bighorn sheep, mule deer, bald eagles, and, of course, wild horses.

Resource Agencies and Organizations

Government Agencies

Montana Fish Wildlife and Parks
490 North Meridian Road, Kalispell
(406) 752-5501. Helena Headquarters:
1420 East Sixth Avenue, P.O. Box 200701
Helena, MT 59620, (406) 444-2535

Flathead National Forest,
Supervisor's Office
1935 Third Avenue East, Kalispell, MT
59901, (406) 758-5200

Glacier National Park
West Glacier, MT, 59936 (406) 888-7800
(general information), (406) 999-5441
(fishing information)

Montana Fish, Wildlife and Parks, Region 1

490 North Meridian P.O. Box 67, Kalispell, MT 59901 (406) 752-5501.

Montana Department Natural Resources and Conservation, Kalispell Unit

2250 Hwy. 93 N. Kalispell
(406) 751-2240

Confederated Salish-Kootenai Tribes

Tribal Fish Wildlife, Recreation and Conservation Division
P.O. Box 278, Pablo, MT 59855
(406) 675-2700 Ext. 1275, (800) 634-0690

Blackfeet Nation, Glacier County

P.O. Box 850, Browning, MT 59417
(406) 338-7276

Fishing Outfitters Association of Montana

Box 67, Gallatin Gateway, MT 59730
(406) 763-4761

Montana Board of Outfitters, Department of Commerce

111 N. Jackson, Helena, MT 59620
(406) 444-3738.

Montana Outfitters and Guides Association

P.O. Box 1248, Helena, MT 59624
(406) 449-3578

Other Resources

The Glacier Institute
137 Main Street, P. O. Box 7457,
Kalispell, Montana, 59904
• (406) 755-1211
• Email: glacinst@ digisys.net

This 16-year old environmental education institution offers many field courses on the plants, animals and ecology of Glacier Park and surrounding locale from February through September. For short-term visitors to the area a day-long or weekend workshop is a fine way to get off the beaten track and learn from experts about this fascinating ecosystem. Choose from topics such as Glacier's harlequins, owls of Glacier, Glacier's grizzlies and prairie wildflowers. They also offer affordable day-long field seminars for children ages six through eleven. Write or call for a course schedule.

Leaflets and checklists are available from Flathead National Forest Headquarters, 1935 Third Ave., E., Kalispell, MT 59901, (406) 755-5401. See our For More Information Chapter for a thorough list of books, pamphlets and checklists to help guide you through the area. Maps

Flathead Area Snowmobile Trails, Flathead National Forest and Montana

Department of Fish, Wildlife, and Parks. Topographic maps of Glacier National

Park, Flathead National Forest, State Parks Listed elsewhere.

The concept of the International Peace Park—an idea that has since been copied around the world—originated here in 1932.

Waterton-Glacier International Peace Park

Wildlife and natural processes recognize no political boundaries, a fact that is easily seen when we travel between the United States and Canada. Elk that summer within Glacier National Park migrate to the grasslands of Waterton Lakes National Park for the winter. Eagles fitted with tiny radio transmitters in Glacier have been tracked far into the Canadian north. Glacier began to recover its indigenous wolf population when a female wolf moved south from British Columbia into the North Fork valley and raised a litter of pups. Wind and water disperse seeds across the international border...all these are obvious examples of how the international boundary means little in the natural world.

The concept of the International Peace Park—an idea that has since been copied around the world—originated here in 1932. It was the brainchild of the Montana and Alberta chapters of the Rotarians, who recognized that the political line between the two parks sometimes interfered with managing the continuities between them. By designating the two parks as one International Peace Park, both parks and countries acknowledged the need to work together to maintain this incred-

ibly rich ecosystem. While each park retains control over its portion of the peace park, staff from both parks work together on joint projects including scientific research, resource management (including fire control), visitor services, and education. The Peace Park designation is also an opportunity to celebrate the beauties of this rugged landscape of mountains and lakes, on both sides of the border.

You can share in the International Peace Park experience in specific ways. The *International,* a large tour boat on Waterton Lake, runs cruises daily during the summer from the Waterton townsite to Goat Haunt in the United States. You'll mix with citizens from both countries as well as from around the world, and have a chance to look up and down the boundary as you cruise by. On Saturdays during the peak of the summer season, the International Peace Park hike departs in the morning from Waterton townsite. It's guided by naturalists from each of the two countries, and you'll hike the 8 miles from the townsite to Goat Haunt. Along the way, naturalists will talk not only about the natural landscape but about the differences and similarities between the two parks. Return is via the

The Prince of Wales Hotel in Waterton is a lakeside showplace.

International in the late afternoon. And each summer a "Hands Across the Border" celebration takes place, usually at the Chief Mountain Customs crossing. Check with either park's information centers for specific information.

The Waterton-Glacier International Peace Park isn't of significance just to Canadians and Americans, either. In 1995, the Waterton-Glacier International Peace Park was recognized for its value to the world through the World Heritage Site designation. This status was awarded based not only on the park's scenic, geologic, and ecological values but also on its cultural importance as an example of two agencies working together, across an international boundary, in the name of shared stewardship and peace.

Waterton Lakes National Park, Alberta

Waterton Lakes National Park sits just over the Canadian border in Wild Rose Country, Alberta. For those from the United States, visiting Canada is a fascinating combination of familiarity and foreignness...they speak the same language, they'll accept U.S. dollars

THE WILDERNESS CONCEPT

"If we are to have broad thinking men and women of high mentality, of good physique, and with a true perspective on life, we must allow our populace a communion with nature in areas of more or less wilderness condition."
——Arthur Carhart

No better place in America exists where one can realize the meaning and spirit of Arthur Carhart's words than the northern Continental Divide ecosystem. This region is home to huge tracts of protected wildlands, which straddle the divide. Glacier National Park lies at the heart of this wildland complex.

Glacier's proposed wilderness lands are managed in accordance with the Wilderness Act of 1964. This will assure that wilderness values are not impaired until such time as the U.S. Congress acts to include the Park's wildlands in the more-protected wilderness preservation system. More than 95 percent of Glacier's one-million-plus acres are proposed for inclusion into this wilderness preservation system.

Close-up

South of Glacier Park the Bob Marshall, Great Bear and Scapegoat wilderness areas adjoin to form the massive 1.5-million-acre Bob Marshall Wilderness. Additional wildlands in Canada's Waterton Lakes National Park (Alberta) and Akamina-Kishinena Provincial Park (British Columbia) adjoin Glacier's northern boundary.

The Wilderness Act of 1964 was the culmination of a uniquely American ideal "to secure for the American people of present and future generations the benefits of an enduring resource of wilderness."

Wilderness is intended to provide visitors with outstanding opportunities for solitude (Motorized access is prohibited.) and a primitive-type recreation. Wilderness areas are intended to retain their primeval character and appear to have been created primarily by the forces of nature. The wilderness is a place in which visitors can leave behind the pressures of modern society and experience risks, challenges and rewards on Nature's terms.

Maintaining wilderness as an enduring resource is the responsibility of all visitors. Ever-increasing use and cumulative resource impacts make it imperative for visitors to learn and practice "Leave No Trace" outdoor skills and ethics.

(though it's usually smarter to use a credit card or exchange cash at a bank), and things seem to happen in pretty much the same ways...but it's still so different!

You'll notice some striking differences between Glacier National Park in the United States and Waterton, its neighbor immediately across the border. For one thing, there's a town in the park. Waterton townsite is dominated by the spectacular Prince of Wales Hotel, built by the Great Northern Railway in 1927,

another part of the Hill enterprise. The Prince of Wales is well worth a visit, even if you don't intend to either stay overnight or dine there. Its lobby commands one of the most remarkable views in the Rockies: the vista down Waterton Lake, flanked by peaks on both sides (including Mount Cleveland, the highest peak in Glacier National Park). And, if you step outside to enjoy the view, chances are you'll experience the strong winds that buffet this building on a regular basis! During its

Credit: VIAD Corporation

Sure-footed mountain goats are a delightful sight in Waterton
Lakes National Park.

construction it was actually blown several inches off its foundation one night. Although the new structure was moved back into place, parts of the building have never been quite plumb since. Rumor has it that the top floors sway several inches during a good blow...for

more information on this historic hotel, visit the website at www.glacierparkinc.com or phone (602) 207-6000.

Waterton boasts quite a few other lodgings as well, ranging from bed-and-breakfasts to a hostel to both modest and quite upscale motels. One, the Kilmorey Inn, is open all winter and offers a variety of visitor packages. It also has a delightful dining room and bar, both open to the public year-round. For more information, visit the Kilmorey's website at www.watertoninfo.ab.ca/kilmorey.html, phone (403) 859-2334, or write to Kilmorey Inn, Box 100, Waterton Lakes National Park, Alberta, Canada T0K 2M0.

Shopping, a movie theater, and many restaurants make for a lively little town. You'll feel the European influence a little more closely here north of the border, with Scottish woolens, Irish lace, and china featuring pictures of the British royal family all for sale. On a warm summer day, be sure to check out the ice cream shops—they have lots of flavors, and every one is delicious! The Waterton Heritage Centre features historic displays and a fine collection of books, videos, maps, and souvenirs of the area.

For those who like to explore outdoors, Waterton offers a variety of activities. The cruise boat *International* heads down Waterton Lake several times a day to Goat Haunt in the United States; you'll see the docks as you drive into town (phone (403) 859-2362)). The same company also offers a water taxi to the Crypt Lake trailhead, across Waterton Lake; this hike is often rated one of the best in the Canadian Rockies. Be sure to plan for a full-day trip and check on trail conditions. In addition to hiking, some of Waterton's excellent trails are open to mountain biking; check at the visitor centre for details.

For more information on Waterton Lakes National Park, visit the website at www.worldweb.com/ParksCanada-Waterton/ or write Waterton Lakes National Park, Waterton Park, Alberta, Canada T0K 2M0. The park visitor centre may be reached at (403) 859-5133 during the summer season. The *Waterton-Glacier Guide*, published jointly by the two parks, carries a full listing of services at Waterton and may be requested from either park.

There are as many ways to explore the park as there are people to visit it. Be sure to stop at a visitor center or ranger station for information and a schedule of naturalist-guided activities.

Glacier National Park

"Scenery is a hollow enjoyment if the tourist starts out after an indigestible breakfast and a fitful sleep on an impossible bed."
—Stephen T. Mather

So complained one national park visitor to Secretary of the Interior Franklin Lane in 1914. Lane's reply? "If you don't like the way the national parks are being run, come on down to Washington and run them yourself."

Lane recognized his correspondent's name: Stephen T. Mather, philanthropist, mountain-climber, and self-made millionaire. What Lane didn't know was that, at age forty-seven, Mather was restless and ready for something new—and would eventually become the first Director of the National Park Service in 1916. It was Mather's vision of what the parks should be that set the tone for the early years of the new agency.

In Glacier National Park, which was established in 1910, the work of development—of opening up these then remote parts of the West to vacationing Easterners—was primarily accomplished by the Great Northern Railway. While Mather was still climbing mountains, rambling with the likes of John Muir, and making his own fortune, J. J. Hill and his son Louis Hill were literally the "Empire Builders" of the great northern plains. Once John F. Stevens located Marias Pass—the lowest route through the Rocky Mountains in the United States, and now also the U.S. Highway 2 corridor—in 1889, it took only three years for the Great Northern to complete its rail line from Chicago to Seattle, opening up vast territories for settlement. Louis Hill, in particular, had a vision: He wanted people to ride his train, and he was ready to build destinations for them. His slogan was "See America First," and he aimed it at wealthy Easterners who otherwise might vacation in Europe. He billed the Rockies as the "Alps of America" and developed a Swiss-chalet-style design for his enormous mountain hotels. Waitresses wore dirndls and bellhops wore lederhosen. Visitors could spend their time in the luxurious hotels, or head out on horseback to rough it—in groups of 50 or more. And the Great Northern built not only trails but also a system of backcountry chalets and horse camps. Mary Roberts Rinehart, a well-known novelist, gave the park further publicity in her account *Through Glacier Park in 1915*, with her vivid description of the "call of the mountains." All this dovetailed perfectly with Stephen Mather's view of how the western parks needed to be developed for visitors to enjoy them.

Most of the historic lodges and chalets that visitors still enjoy today were built between 1910 and 1920: Glacier Park Lodge, Many Glacier Hotel, Granite Park and Sperry Chalets, as well as the Prince of Wales in Canada (1927) and the privately built Lake McDonald Lodge on the west side of Glacier National Park. But the Great Depression and World War II brought many changes. The Many Glacier Chalets—but not the Hotel—burned in the Heaven's Peak Fire of 1936. The Gunsight Chalet was destroyed in an avalanche. Wooden structures, which included many of the original back country chalets such as St. Mary, Going-to-the-Sun, and Cut Bank Chalets, suffered neglect and were soon beyond repair. They never reopened after the war and were razed in the late 1940s.

And other things changed too. After World

War II, the family car became a reality, and most visitors began to drive to Montana rather than take the train. They didn't have as much money as those who had patronized the Empire Builder, and they found the big hotels too expensive. Gradually the park began to realize it had a new visitor—the middle-income family that arrived in a car. And so the motor inns were built: first Swiftcurrent, built before the war but later expanded; then Roes Creek Inn, now called Rising Sun Motor Inn; and finally the Village Inn at Apgar. In conjunction with the campgrounds, they provide a spectrum of accommodation that enables everyone to get a good night's sleep and a decent breakfast—and so to enjoy the unparalleled scenery and wildlife that bring us all here.

There are as many ways to explore the park as there are people to visit it. Be sure to stop at a visitor center or ranger station for information and a schedule of naturalist-guided activities. But whether you choose to drive Going-to-the-Sun Road in two hours, backpack for two weeks, watch birds, count goats, or take a swim in an excruciatingly cold lake, do leave your worries behind. Let the place work its magic on you.

Accommodations

The lodging at Glacier National Park covers a wide array of options: from historic lodge, to one-room cabin with a bath down the way, to high-mountain hostel. The recent history of what is now the park—the last 100 years—is reflected in its structures. You may want to check out the Two Medicine Campstore building just because it is the last of the Two Medicine Chalets, built at the same time as the Granite Park and Sperry Chalets, both of which still operate as lodging. You may want to trace the history of the Great Northern Railway through the lodges it built—Many Glacier Hotel was the largest hotel in Montana until very recently. Or perhaps the subalpine landscape will draw you into Granite Park

Chalet, built before World War I, which claims to offer the "best sunset in the park." These buildings often offer a view into the past as well as into the mountains.

Overall, lodging within the park can be found on a wide scale of prices. Make your reservations early—especially for the peak season of July and August, when most park facilities will be completely booked. At the same time, if you're in the area but don't have a reservation, it's still worth a phone call to check on space—cancellations do occur, and you may be able to find yourself a room with a view on very short notice. With the exception of Apgar Village Lodge, Granite Park Chalet, and Sperry Chalet (see page 171), all lodging within Glacier National Park's boundaries is operated by Glacier Park, Inc. (GPI), a concession under contract with the National Park Service.

Most facilities have an information desk where a staff member will be happy to help you with schedules for naturalist-guided activities, bus tours, boat tours and small boat rentals, the Going-to-the-Sun Road shuttle, the Many Glacier hikers' shuttle, and horseback trips. Each of the large hotels has a gift shop that sells film, postage stamps, huckleberry treats, books and maps, hiking snacks, and outdoor clothing, as well as a variety of souvenirs. Campstores are located at Swiftcurrent Motor Inn, Rising Sun Motor Inn, and at the Lake McDonald Lodge complex, and they carry a similar selection with the addition of limited food supplies, some camping equipment, and bundled firewood. The Two Medicine Campstore also has a snack counter that is well known for its fine huckleberry milkshakes. The descriptions that follow highlight the unique character of each location.

Glacier Park Lodge, Lake McDonald Lodge, and Many Glacier Hotel all have ATMs; all GPI locations have pay phones. Handicap-accessible rooms are available at Glacier Park Lodge, Lake McDonald Lodge, the Village Inn, Swiftcurrent Motor Inn, Many Glacier Hotel, and Rising Sun Motor Inn. Please be aware that the historic lodges do not have elevators to their upper floors; a bellhop will carry your luggage to your room, but if climbing stairs is a health concern, please mention this at the time you make your reservation.

Accommodation Rates

Keep in mind that some rates are based on availability. The average nightly rates for two adults at the hotels and motels listed in this section are indicated by a dollar sign ($) ranking in the following chart. Also, the hotels and motels in this chapter accept all or most major credit cards.

$	Less than $85
$$	$85 to $115
$$$	$115 to $150
$$$$	$150 and up

Hotels and Motels

Apgar Village Lodge
$ • Apgar Village
• (406) 888-5484

Apgar Village Lodge, located among old-growth cedar trees at the foot of Lake McDonald, offers a significantly longer season than any other accommodation inside the park boundaries. In 1999 it will open on May 1, giving visitors an opportunity to see Glacier National Park in spring. Although the upper elevations of the park will still be buried in snow and inaccessible to all but backcountry skiers, along the shores of Lake McDonald you'll be delighted to see the bright green of brand-new leaves coming out all along the shore. A walk in the woods will bring you the special pleasure of early-season wildflowers: trillium, glacier lilies, or even lady's slipper orchids. Like the GPI lodgings, Apgar Village Lodge will be very busy during the summer months, but it will stay open into the fall shoulder season. With a closing date of October 14, Apgar Village Lodge offers accommodations to those who like to travel in the fall, when the crowds are less and the days cool and crisp. You'll enjoy the contrast of the larch, which turn golden all along the slopes above Lake McDonald, with the blue of the sky and the startling whiteness of new-fallen snow on the peaks.

Apgar Village itself includes the west side visitor center, a backcountry permit office, a number of shops, a restaurant and other snack shops, and the amphitheater for evening programs at the nearby campground (some of these have shorter operating seasons than Apgar Village Lodge). A paved bike trail runs along Lower McDonald Creek back toward West Glacier, providing one of very few opportunities in Glacier National Park for biking off the roadways.

INSIDERS' TIP

At the peak of the summer—from mid-July to Labor Day—parking at Logan Pass can be a test of anyone's patience. The busiest times are from about 10 AM to 3:30 PM—on a few occasions, gridlock has occurred as people try to move in and out of the lot. Park rangers do their best to control the situation, but sometimes it's best just to avoid it. If your goal for the day is to see Logan Pass, check out the Visitor Center, and maybe hike out the Highline for a bit or go to Hidden Lake, consider riding the shuttle bus up and back down from either the east or west side. If you want to hike the Highline out to Granite Park and down to the Loop, try leaving your car at the Loop and picking up the morning shuttle to Logan Pass and starting your hike there. Or park at Avalanche and use the shuttle up and down...pick up a schedule at any visitor center. A little creative planning will lower your stress level too!

Credit: VIAD Corporation

The chalet-style lodges in Glacier National Park are beautiful inside and out.

Apgar Village Lodge is Glacier's only AAA-approved lodging facility. It includes 48 rustic cabin and motel units, all with private baths. Some have views of Lake McDonald or Lower McDonald Creek, but all are within footsteps of spectacular mountain vistas. Most cabins have a kitchen, and several barbecues and picnic tables are available to guests. Regular season rates range from motel rooms for $57.00 per night for two people to a cabin that will accommodate six for $120 to $210 per night. Value season runs from May 1 through June 20 and from September 15 through October 14; please call for availability and rates during these times. You can also write to Apgar Village Lodge, c/o West Glacier Mercantile, P.O. Box 398, West Glacier, MT 59936, or visit the website at www.westglacier.com/lodge.html for further information. Reservations may be made by phoning (406) 888-5484.

The Village Inn
$$ • Apgar Village
• (602) 207-6000 Glacier Park, Inc.

Summer in Glacier is usually very temperate—temperatures in the 70s with cooler nights—but even on a hot day not many people are going to swim in Glacier's lakes.

With their origins in snow and ice, these deep lakes rarely invite more than wading. But the foot of Lake McDonald, where the water is shallow and gets a lot of sun, is a place where you might enjoy a swim—if a brief one! The pebbly beach is perfect for skipping stones, having a picnic, or just admiring the mountain vista. The Village Inn, built in 1956, sits directly on the southwest shore of Lake McDonald at Apgar. Each of its thirty-six rooms has a lake view, up toward the mountains at the head of the valley. Twelve rooms have kitchens and others are two-bedroom units. Easy access to the lakeshore—just out your door—is certainly a prime draw, but you will also find other services immediately available. Small boat rentals and a boat ramp are a few minutes' walk away. Apgar Village includes the west side visitor center, a backcountry permit office, a number of shops, a restaurant and other snack shops, and the amphitheater for evening programs at the nearby campground. A paved bike trail runs along Lower McDonald Creek back toward West Glacier, providing one of very few opportunities in Glacier National Park for biking off the roadways.

The Village Inn will be open from May 21 until September 21, 1999. Accommodations vary—1 bedroom, 1 bedroom with kitchen, 2 bedroom, and living room suite—and prices range from $90 to $142 per night for 2 people. Reservations and further information may be had by calling Glacier Park, Inc., at (602) 207-6000 (year-round) or visiting the website at www.glacierparkinc.com/.

Rising Sun
$ • Going-to-the-Sun Road, east side
• (602) 207-6000 Glacier Park, Inc.

Rising Sun Motor Inn, located on Going-to-the-Sun Road six miles west of St. Mary, catches the morning light across the biggest lake in Glacier National Park. It is nestled at the edge of the open forest that meets Two Dog Flats, a series of meadows that is home to elk, deer, and fox. Just across Going-to-the-Sun Road is the St. Mary Lake location for Glacier Park Boat Company, so that it takes only a moment to join one of their guided tours or perhaps catch a sunset cruise. Logan Pass, the top of Going-to-the-Sun Road, is just twelve miles away, and both the park shuttle and Red Bus Tours stop here. Each evening Park Service naturalists give public talks at the Rising Sun Campfire Circle.

Rising Sun Motor Inn itself consists of seventy-two rooms in a combination of three motel buildings and thirty-six cottages. In addition you'll find public showers, a campstore, and the Two Dog Flats Mesquite Grill (see Restaurants). Rising Sun Motor Inn will be open in 1999 from June 11 to September 7. Rooms are simple and economical; rates run from $81 to $87 per night for two people. Reservations and further information may be had by calling Glacier Park, Inc., at 602-207-6000 (year-round) or visiting the website at www.glacierparkinc.com/.

Swiftcurrent Motor Inn
$ • Many Glacier Valley
• (602) 207-6000 Glacier Park, Inc.

The Many Glacier Valley attracts dayhikers like few places in the National Park system because of its 5 major drainages—and their trails—which come together in the valley floor. If you look up the Iceberg drainage toward the Iceberg Notch, and then follow the jagged Pinnacle Wall a little further to the east, you'll see what's locally known as the B-7 Pillar. Tradition has it that the pillar was originally named for the Swiftcurrent cabin B-7, which the first people to climb that knob of rock stayed in while at Many Glacier. Swiftcurrent Motor Inn has long been the mainstay for many such visitors. It includes not only the Motor Inn itself, Pinetop Motor Inn, 1-bedroom cottages with bath and 1- and 2-bedroom cottages without bath, but also a campstore, laundry, public showers, and the Italian Gardens Ristorante (see Restaurants). And the long Motor Inn porch serves as a gathering place—whether for refreshments after hiking or as a sheltered place to "hang out" on a warm but rainy afternoon. Several guided hikes meet and depart from this central location. A Park Service naturalist is usually in the parking lot for an hour each evening with a spotting scope to help start the search for animals on the slopes above the Motor Inn. And each evening a naturalist presents a talk at the nearby Campfire Circle.

In short—Swiftcurrent Motor Inn is a hopping hub of activity! Rooms are simple and affordable, ranging in price from $40 per night for 2 people in a 1-bedroom cottage with no bath to between $50 and $107 per night for cottages with bath or for motel rooms. The

INSIDERS' TIP

Steep and sometimes icy snowfields, as well as unbridged stream crossings, can present extreme risks to backcountry travelers in Glacier National Park. Especially in early summer snowfields are prevalent and water runoff is high. The Trail Status Report will tell you which trails are more likely to present these hazards. The report is available at backcountry permit issuing stations. These hazards are also noted on the Trails Illustrated map of Glacier National Park. Check them out before you hike.

Granite Park and Sperry Chalets

"We crossed many passes....There was a time when I had thought that a mountain pass was a depression. It is not. A mountain pass is a place where the impossible becomes barely possible." –Mary Roberts Rinehart, *Through Glacier Park in 1915*

Granite Park Chalet and Sperry Chalet might also be said to exist where "the impossible becomes barely possible." Located respectively on the Highline Trail, just south of Swiftcurrent Pass, and on the Sperry Trail, just west of Lincoln Pass, these stone buildings are reminders of an era before the private automobile. Like Mary Roberts Rinehart, most people then came to Glacier on the train and traveled through the park on horseback. In addition to the great hotels—Glacier Park Lodge, Many Glacier Hotel, the Prince of Wales, and Lake McDonald Lodge—and horse camps at Red Eagle Lake, Cosley Lake, Fifty Mountain, and Goat Haunt—guests stayed overnight at a series of backcountry chalets. Many were elaborate wooden structures in the Swiss chalet style used by the Great Northern for its park buildings: Two Medicine Chalets, Cut Bank Chalets, St. Mary Chalets, Going-to-the-Sun Chalets, Many Glacier Chalets, Gunsight Chalet, Belton Chalets. The two most remote were Granite Park and Sperry Chalets, and these were constructed of native stone. As time took its toll on the wooden chalets in different ways (see introduction to Glacier National Park section), the stone buildings proved their durability. They continue to offer lodging today.

These two remaining backcountry chalets each boast spectacular locations. Granite Park sits on a knoll just at treeline. At an elevation of about 6600 feet, snow melts

People come to Glacier National Park to see glaciers, such as Grinnell Glacier above Many Glacier hotel.

relatively late here; those hiking into the chalet along the Highline will be treated to spring flowers even into July. The meadows around the chalet are a mass of yellow glacier lilies in the "early" season; later they will burst into a kaleidoscope of colors as summer brings the high-country flowers into bloom: penstemon, asters, paintbrush, cinquefoil, beargrass and many more. Swiftcurrent Pass is about 3/4 mile above the chalet along the Continental Divide. The hike to the pass is not difficult and offers a huge view east into the Swiftcurrent Valley and even out onto the plains. If you have energy to burn, try the Grinnell Glacier Overlook Trail, a spur off the Highline: it's only 1 kilometer to the overlook, but it's known as the longest 1 kilometer in the park! It's a steep climb to the Divide here, but when you arrive you'll be rewarded with an astonishing view of Grinnell Glacier from above, as well as of the Grinnell Valley. Like most other glaciers in North America, Grinnell Glacier is shrinking rapidly, but it is still one of the largest glaciers in the park (see Geology of Glacier National Park). And just a quick note on the chalet's name: Granite Park Chalet sits on a flow of pillow basalt, an igneous rock. This hard, dark rock was taken for granite...but there is no granite in the area.

Sperry Chalet sits high in a hanging valley, just below Comeau Pass and Lincoln Pass. Gunsight and Edwards Mountains tower over it. Mountain goats frequent the rugged terrain around the chalet. You'll have a hard time deciding how to spend your time here: trails lead in three different directions and to several destinations. Just over Comeau Pass is Sperry Glacier, about the same size as Grinnell Glacier. The hike to the glacier itself is remarkable: the trail winds its way up a series of benches, each dotted with pools and huge boulders left by the receding glaciers. No natural pass existed here, so an artificial one was created: you'll feel like you're in *Raiders of the Lost Ark* as you step up these stairs carved into the rock and steady yourself with the rope handrail! The basin offers a view not only of the glacier but also of peaks that you'll recognize from Logan Pass—but now you'll be seeing them from the south. If you choose instead to hike east, toward Gunsight Pass, you'll want to stop at stunning Lake Ellen Wilson, which glitters in a high cirque also known to produce lots of huckleberries in some years....And Gunsight Pass is a place where you're almost bound to encounter goats.

Both Sperry and Granite Park have undergone extensive renovation in the last few years. As historic structures, the original integrity of the building must be preserved, and you'll find it interesting to inspect the historic use of construction materials and methods. The building season is short, and, even in the summer, weather conditions can sometimes preclude construction work. The amount of skill, time, and money required to renovate these remarkable buildings can perhaps give us a greater appreciation for their original construction in 1913 and 1914 respectively. They do indeed exist "where the impossible becomes barely possible."

1999 season will run from June 10 until September 7. Reservations and further information may be had by calling Glacier Park, Inc., at (602) 207-6000 (year-round) or visiting the website at www.glacierparkinc.com/.

Lake McDonald Lodge
$$ •Going-to-the-Sun Road, west side·
• (602) 207-6000 Glacier Park, Inc.
Originally built as the Lewis Glacier Hotel by John Lewis in 1914, the Lake McDonald Lodge rests on the southeast shore of Lake McDonald, twelve miles in from the West Glacier park entrance. You can take a comfy seat on the veranda and enjoy views across the water, or take a seat in the lobby with its aura of an age past: Lewis's hunting trophies line the walls, and it is said that Western artist Charlie Russell drew the pictographs on the massive stone fireplace. In the early years, guests arrived at the lodge by water, and its original facade faced the lake. But now, of course, virtually all guests arrive by car or bus, and in more recent years what was once the "back" of the lodge has been adapted to present a proper welcome. As at the other

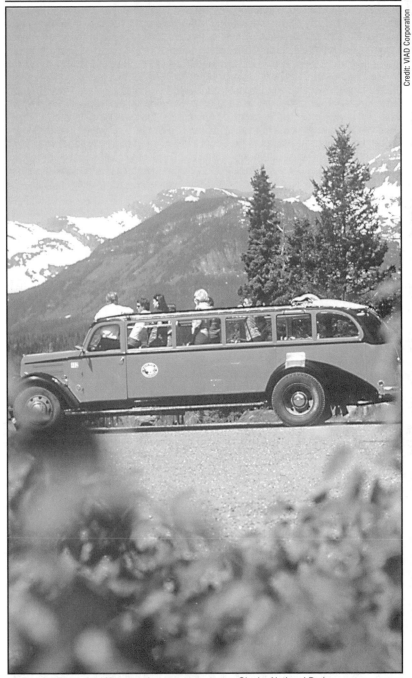

Credit: VIAD Corporation

A red bus tour is a great way to see Glacier National Park.

historic hotels, you'll find Lake McDonald Lodge brilliant with hanging flower baskets and gardens in the summertime.

Although the lodge itself has a pleasantly relaxed atmosphere, you'll find plenty of activities not far away. The Glacier Park Boat Company's *DeSmet* docks in front of the lodge; cruises are available at several times each day. Just across the Going-to-the-Sun Road are the corrals of Mule Shoe Outfitters, the park horse concession, which offers rides of varying lengths and to several destinations. If you like to hike, several trails begin here: you might pick up the trail that leads to Avalanche Creek and Lake, or try heading up to Mount Brown Lookout from the Sperry trailhead—it's one of the steepest trails in the park, but the lookout will reward you will an astonishing view of the whole Lake McDonald Valley! After a good dinner, join a Park Service naturalist at the auditorium for an evening talk.

Lake McDonald Lodge includes some 100 rooms, with lodge, motel, and cabin accommodations. The complex also includes a general store, the Stockade Lounge, and a gift shop, as well as the Cedar Dining Room and Russell's Trail's End Family Restaurant (see Restaurants). Like Glacier Park Lodge, it operates for a more extended season than some park facilities. In 1999 it will open on May 28 and close on September 27. Room rates vary by accommodation; a small cottage room for two people begins at $81 per night; motel and lodge rooms for two people range from $87 to $130 per night. Reservations and further information may be had by calling Glacier Park, Inc., at 602- 207-6000 (year-round) or visiting the website at www.glacierparkinc.com/ .

Many Glacier Hotel
$$ • Many Glacier Valley
• (602) 207-6000 Glacier Park, Inc.

Many Glacier Hotel is located at the heart of Glacier National Park, just east of the Continental Divide in the Swiftcurrent Valley. Built by Louis Hill and the Great Northern Railway in 1914-15, it is the largest hotel in the park with 211 rooms. Peaks—including Mount Gould, probably the most-photographed mountain in the park—surround the hotel, and its balcony overlooking Swiftcurrent Lake offers one of the finest mountain views anywhere. From it you may have the chance to see grizzly and black bears, mountain goats, bighorn sheep, moose, or deer—or perhaps a double rainbow arcing across the entire sky following a rainstorm.

The Many Glacier Hotel offers indoor comforts as well. The lobby's large, freestanding fireplace makes for a warm, cozy place to curl up with a book and read in the evening. Every evening a Park Service naturalist gives a slide program—on topics such as the park's history, geology, wildflowers, and wildlife—in the Lucerne Room. The hotel's staff is largely composed of college students with an artistic bent, so evenings also offer a variety of musical or theatrical performances.

In addition to the Ptarmigan Dining Room (see Restaurants), the Many Glacier Hotel houses Heidi's, downstairs in the St. Moritz Room, which offers a variety of snack foods from 8 AM to 9 PM And down the hall from the lobby is the Swiss Lounge, a fully stocked bar that features huckleberry daiquiris and Montana microbrews. If you arrive for dinner at the Ptarmigan Dining Room on a busy evening, the Interlaken Lounge is a pleasant place to wait until a table is ready. Take a moment to walk around—you'll enjoy the view of Mount Wilbur across Swiftcurrent Lake. You might also check out the paintings on the walls: look for one of some men camped out in the evening. There's a big buck in the background, and one of the men is reaching for his big, bellows-style camera. If you look more closely, however, you'll see that originally this man was reaching for a gun. You can still see its shape, long since painted out, and the gun replaced by the camera for a different type of "shooting."

Many Glacier Hotel will be open from June 4 to September 20, 1999. Accommodations range from value rooms to suites, and rates vary correspondingly from $103 to $190 per night. Reservations and further information may be had by calling Glacier Park, Inc., at (602) 207-6000 (year-round) or visiting the website at www.glacierparkinc.com/

Glacier Park Lodge
$$$ • East Glacier, MT
• (602) 207-6000 Glacier Park, Inc.

The first of the lodges to be built by the Great Northern Railway, Glacier Park Lodge continues to be the unofficial eastern gateway to Glacier National Park today. Although it is located outside the borders of the park, the peaks rise behind it in an impressive backdrop. Lovely, well-tended flower gardens line the walk as you approach the historic building. Walking through the lodge doors, you'll be impressed by the huge logs that support the lobby ceiling: immense Douglas-firs, their bark still on, imported from the Pacific Northwest to grace this hall. The neighboring Blackfeet Indians referred to the building as the "Big Tree Lodge."

In contrast with its historic past, Glacier Park Lodge also offers modern amenities in addition to its 163 rooms. The hotel features a heated swimming pool, a nine-hole golf course, a nine-hole pitch 'n' putt golf course, a gift shop, cocktail lounge (with big-screen TV), and the Great Northern Steak and Rib House (see Restaurants). The information desk will be happy to set you up with a bus tour or hayride. The talented college students that staff the hotel also provide evening performances.

East Glacier is home to many small businesses, shops, and restaurants (see Blackfeet Reservation), and you'll enjoy walking about the little town located exactly where the mountains meet the prairie. You are also within a 12-mile drive of Browning, where you can visit both the Museum of the Plains Indian and the Scriver Museum of Montana Wildlife and Hall of Bronze (see Attractions). Or you might choose to hike. The Two Medicine subdistrict of Glacier National Park is only an 11-mile drive away, with its web of trails leading to places such as Dawson Pass, Cobalt Lake, Twin Falls, or Old Man Lake. Glacier Park Boat Company also offers boat tours on Two Medicine Lake. The Lubec and Autumn Creek Trails begin along Highway 2 west of East Glacier and will lead you along the aspen-covered

INSIDERS' TIP

Just a word of warning: no food or drink are available along Going-to-the-Sun Road between Lake McDonald Lodge on the west side and Rising Sun Campground on the east side. The only pay phone in that distance is at Avalanche Campground. Logan Pass Visitor Center has wonderful exhibits, information, and book sales, but offers only public washrooms and a drinking fountain as services.

foothills. Be sure to check with a ranger station for current trail conditions.

Glacier Park Lodge has a longer season than some other GPI facilities. It will open May 21, 1999, and close on September 27. Rooms range in price from $131 to $233 per night for two people. Reservations and further information may be had by calling Glacier Park, Inc., at (602) 207-6000 (year-round) or visiting the website at www.glacierparkinc.com/

The Chalets

Sperry Chalet
$$$$ • Just below Lincoln Peak on the Sperry Trail
• (406) 387-5654, (888) 345-2649

Sperry Chalet, built by the Great Northern Railway in 1913, is one of two chalets remaining from a time earlier in the century when visitors arrived at East Glacier by train and toured the park on horseback. Even today it is accessible only by trail; you must hike or ride a horse to the chalet, which is perched on a rocky bench some 6.7 miles and 3,300 feet up from the trailhead at Lake McDonald Lodge. Although the hike to the chalet is strenuous, it is well worth the effort. Once there, you will be delighted by the craggy rock walls and waterfalls that surround the site as well as the view to Lake McDonald. The chalet is also located at the junction of two trails, so dayhikers will have to choose between going to see Sperry Glacier, Lincoln Peak, Lake Ellen Wilson, or Gunsight Pass—or staying long enough to check them all out. Those even more adventurous will find mountain climbing options here as well. Mountain goats frequent this rugged habitat.

The Sperry Chalet is actually two buildings made of native stone, a kitchen/dining hall and a two-story hotel building. There is no electricity; in the evening the dining room and kitchen are lit with propane lanterns, and you are encouraged to bring your own flashlight for use in the sleeping rooms at night. Other than that flashlight and what you need to hike in, just a "smile and a toothbrush" will be enough, as Sperry Chalet provides all bedding and three meals as well as lodging.

After a six-year closure for extensive renovations, Sperry will reopen in the summer of 1999. Reservations will be accepted for dates from July 15 to September 12; it is possible the chalet might open as early as July 1, weather permitting, and it will close September 13. As before the closure, Sperry will be offering overnight accommodations on the American plan, that is, dinner, breakfast, and lunch (or trail lunch) are included in the lodging price. Rates for 1999 are $50 room charge per room per night, plus $100 per person (additional night $90 per person). A 4% Montana accommodations tax is added to lodging charges. Sperry has seventeen guestrooms, ranging from single occupancy to rooms for four, with double and single bed arrangements. Reservations are required. Please be sure to check the policy on deposits, refunds, and cancellations. Mule Shoe Outfitters, the park horse concession, provides horse transportation to Sperry Chalet. In addition, à la carte service is available in the dining room from 11:30 AM to 5 PM, and some do choose to visit Sperry as a day trip. The Sperry Trail runs from Lake McDonald Lodge past the chalet to Gunsight Pass and then down to trailheads on the east side; a visit to the chalet can be part of this longer route as well.

Because of its remote, high-elevation setting, Sperry offers a unique opportunity to

INSIDERS' TIP

Maps are a necessity for safe, enjoyable visits in Glacier Park. A good source for maps is the Glacier Natural History Association (GNHA). GNHA offers a full selection of USGS topographic quadrangle maps and an excellent park-wide map by Trails Illustrated. GNHA sales outlets are located at the Apgar, St. Mary and Logan Pass visitor centers; the Many Glacier, Two Medicine and Polebridge ranger stations and the Apgar Backcountry Permit Center.

explore Glacier's backcountry without carrying a heavy backpack. This same remoteness requires that visitors be well informed. Please check on current trail conditions at any visitor center or ranger station before setting out. For full information on the Chalet, please write Sperry Chalet, c/o Belton Chalets, Inc., P.O. Box 188, West Glacier, MT 59936, or visit the website at www.ptinet.net/sperrychalet. Office hours are 8 AM to 5 PM weekdays, January 1 to May 14 and September 13 to December 31; from 9 AM to 6 PM daily from May 15 to September 12; phone 406-387-5654. Reservations may be made toll-free at 888-345-2649.

Granite Park Chalet
$$ • Just below Swiftcurrent Pass on the Highline Trail
• (406) 387-5555 or (800) 521-7238; fax (406) 387-5656

Like Sperry Chalet, Granite Park Chalet offers a backcountry experience with a difference: in this case, a room with a view. Built by the Great Northern Railway in 1914, Granite Park sits atop a knoll just below Swiftcurrent Pass on the Continental Divide. The historic stone building, which is just above treeline, offers magnificent views to the north, south, and west. With just a little hiking, you can stand on the Continental Divide and look east into the Swiftcurrent Valley; with a good bit of steep hiking, you can look down on Grinnell Glacier from above. The Highline Trail, one of the most popular trails in Glacier National Park, runs from Logan Pass to Canada by way of Granite Park. All in all, it's a place of incomparable subalpine beauty that will give you a sense of the sweep of the mountains.

Granite Park was recently renovated and now operates as a hikers' shelter. You must provide your own food, flashlight, sleeping bag, and water (there's a creek nearby, and the chalet does have a water filter for guest use, but it's a good idea to bring your own filter). The dining room and porch both have stunning views of Heaven's Peak, across the McDonald Creek drainage. A full kitchen is available for your meal preparation. Granite Park has twelve sleeping rooms, all with single bunk beds, with two to six people per room. If you don't wish to carry extra weight on your hike in, the chalet has an optional linen/bedding service as well as packaged meals, snacks, and soft drinks for sale.

Most people will choose to hike to Granite Park along the relatively flat 7.4-mile Highline Trail from Logan Pass, though others may come up the Loop Trail or over Swiftcurrent Pass from Many Glacier. Parking at Logan Pass or the Loop can be difficult; consider parking at lower elevation in the park and taking the shuttle up. Mule Shoe Outfitters (the park horse concession) also provides horse transportation to the chalet.

The 1999 season at Granite Park Chalet will run from July 1 to September 12. Overnight rates are $60 per person per night plus 4% Montana accommodations tax. Linens and bedding are available for $10 per person for the duration of the stay (arrangements for this service must be made at reservation time). Please be sure to read the policy on deposits, refunds, and cancellations. Before heading out on the trail, check on current trail conditions by stopping at a visitor center or ranger station. For more information on Granite Park Chalet, please write Glacier Wilderness Guides, Inc., P.O. Box 535, West Glacier, MT 59936, or visit the website at www.glacierguides.com. Glacier Wilderness Guides can be reached by phone at 406-387-5555 or 800-521-7238; fax 406-387-5656.

Campgrounds

Glacier National Park has 13 campgrounds for a total of over 1,000 sites. They offer a variety of camping experiences: some are accessible only by dirt road, have just a few sites, and are relatively primitive; others are large campgrounds on the main routes through the park. Most are available on a first-come, first-served basis, and at the height of the summer many will fill by midday (and a few by 10 AM). Two campgrounds, St. Mary and Fish Creek, have sites that may be reserved in advance through the National Park Service Reservation System at 800-365-CAMP. Operating dates vary from campground to campground; please check for up-to-date information.

Most campgrounds have drinking water

and restrooms with flush toilets and cold running water. Several campgrounds have a disposal station; there is a $2 fee to dump RV holding tanks. No utility hookups are provided. Some campgrounds will not accommodate very large RVs; others have a limited number of spaces available for large vehicles (see descriptions below). The park newspaper, the *Waterton-Glacier Guide,* and its website at www.nps.gov/glac carry complete details.

In the descriptions that follow, "primitive" means a campground with an outhouse; water is available but may need to be filtered or boiled before drinking. Several primitive campgrounds are accessible only by dirt roads not recommended for large trailers or RVs.

The fee per site per night at the campgrounds is $10 to $15. Campsites are limited to eight people and two vehicles. Apgar has eleven group sites and Many Glacier and Two Medicine campgrounds each have one group site; these larger sites accommodate parties of nine to twenty-four people. They are available on a first-come, first-served basis, for a fee of $3 per person, per night.

Most campsites have a fire grate or fire ring. Wood can be purchased at the campstores throughout the park. Collecting firewood is prohibited except along the Inside North Fork Road from 1 mile north of Fish Creek Campground to Kintla Lake and along the Bowman Lake road.

Please be sure to inform yourself about conditions in the park before your trip. Like many national parks, Glacier has regulations designed to protect both the visitors and the park itself. In particular, the presence of grizzly bears requires that food be stored properly—in a hard-sided vehicle or bear-proof food locker (provided at some sites)—whenever it is not being prepared. Pet owners should check park regulations, also. For more information, or if you are interested in backcountry campgrounds, please visit the park's website at www.nps.gov/glac, call park headquarters at 406-888-7800, or write to Superintendent, Glacier National Park, West Glacier, MT 59936.

Apgar

Apgar Campground is located at the foot of Lake McDonald. It is the largest campground in the park at 196 sites (25 sites will accommodate RVs up to 40 feet long). The campsites are in the trees but a magnificent view of the lake and the mountains is only a few minutes' walk away, and the shore of the lake is a very pleasant place to enjoy your day. Apgar Village, which includes the west side visitor center, a backcountry permit office, small boat rentals, a number of shops, and a restaurant and other snack shops, is close at hand. Evening programs are held at the campground amphitheater. A paved bike trail runs from Apgar along Lower McDonald Creek back toward West Glacier, providing one of very few opportunities in Glacier National Park for biking off the roadways.

Fish Creek

Fish Creek Campground is located just west of Apgar, also on the shore of Lake McDonald. This is one of two campgrounds where it is possible to reserve a site. Of its 180 sites, 80 will accommodate RVs up to 26 feet long. Like the Apgar Campground, the sites at Fish Creek are nestled in the trees, but there is more space between sites and

INSIDERS' TIP

Glacier Park's peak period for backcountry use is mid-July through August. Competition for coveted backcountry campsites is very keen during this time. It's important to have an alternative itinerary in mind in case your first choice is already completely booked. Fifty percent of campsites are allocated through a new advance reservation system. Applications are accepted via United States or international mail beginning April 15. Advance reservations can be confirmed for a $20 fee. Pick up the *Glacier Backcountry Guide* for complete details and application forms or call in advance for a guide at 406-888-7800.

Credit: VIAD Corporation

Equally lovely, the east and west sides of Glacier
National Park are quite different.

the campground tends to be a little quieter. A few sites are directly on the lakeshore. Park Service naturalists present an evening program each night during the height of the summer at the Fish Creek amphitheater.

Avalanche

Avalanche Campground fills early in the morning during the peak season for a number of reasons. Its 87 sites are tucked among the big trees of an old-growth cedar-hemlock forest, creating a magical atmosphere for campers. Fifty sites will fit RVs up to 26 feet long. The 1-mile, handicap-accessible Trail of the Cedars is nearby with its views along Avalanche Creek and into Avalanche Gorge. A rolling, 2-mile trail will take you up to Ava-

lanche Lake, which sits at the base of a headwall below Sperry Glacier. Waterfalls cascade down the cliffs above the lake, bringing icy waters to feed this little gem of a subalpine cirque. And Upper McDonald Creek (and the Avalanche Picnic Area) is just across Going-to-the-Sun Road. Park Service naturalists present a program at the outdoor amphitheater each night.

Rising Sun

Rising Sun Campground provides easy access to Going-to-the-Sun Road on the east side, and it tends to fill mid-morning during the peak of the season. The immediate area provides huge views up and down St. Mary Lake, but the east side wind can really blow through this valley, and you will be grateful that the campsites themselves are sheltered by trees. The neighboring Rising Sun Motor Inn complex includes the Two Dog Flats Mesquite Grill, a campstore, and public showers. Each evening a Park Service naturalist gives a campfire talk at the Rising Sun Campfire Circle. Rising Sun Campground has 83 sites, but only 3 will accommodate RVs up to 30 feet long.

Two Medicine

Two Medicine Campground is a little off the beaten track—it's not on Going-to-the-Sun Road, and it's about 12 miles north of U.S. Highway 2 at East Glacier. Because of this, it tends to fill late in the day, if at all, yet those who go there regularly report what a lovely spot it is. Two Medicine has 99 sites, 13 of which will fit RVs up to 32 feet long. The campsites are nicely spaced, and many have a view of Two Medicine Lake, which is only a minute's walk away in any case. Like the Many Glacier Valley, Two Medicine Valley is formed by the convergence of a number of drainages—which translates into many wonderful trails for dayhikers to explore. Each evening a Park Service naturalist gives a talk at the Two Medicine Campfire Circle. The valley also has its own campstore, and Glacier Park Boat Company offers scenic boat tours.

Cut Bank

For those who like to escape the crowds, Cut Bank Campground on Glacier's east side may be one place to do so. Cut Bank is a primitive campground located about 5 miles west of U.S. Highway 89 some 12 miles south of St. Mary. Cut Bank has 19 sites and is not recommended for RVs. Hiking destinations include Morning Star Lake, Pitamakan Pass,

Medicine Grizzly Lake, and Triple Divide Pass. Triple Divide Pass is just below Triple Divide Peak, which marks the three-way watershed sending water to the west through the Columbia River drainage, to the south and east through the Missouri-Mississippi system, and to the north and east through the St. Mary, Saskatchewan, and Nelson Rivers to Hudson Bay and the Arctic Ocean.

Many Glacier

Like Avalanche and Rising Sun Campgrounds, Many Glacier Campground fills early in the morning during the peak of the season. The Many Glacier Valley attracts many dayhikers who wish to explore its web of trails leading up into the mountains, and from the campground it's an easy stroll to most the major trailheads. The campground has 110 sites, 13 of which will fit RVs up to 35 feet long. The nearby Swiftcurrent Motor Inn includes a campstore, the Italian Gardens Ristorante, public showers, and a public laundry. Many Glacier Hotel is about a mile away. Each evening a Park Service naturalist brings a spotting scope to the motor inn parking lot for the nightly "Spotcheck," and campers often join the effort to spot bighorn sheep, mountain goats, or even bears on the slopes above the valley floor. Later on the naturalist will present a campfire talk at the Many Glacier Campfire Circle.

Kintla

Kintla Campground is the campground farthest north on the west side of the park—practically in Canada. Its primitive status, difficulty of access, and the fact that no motor boats of any sort are permitted on Kintla Lake makes for a remote experience that some will seek out and others avoid. Kintla Campground

INSIDERS' TIP

Glacier National Park has several sources of information available. Its website at www.nps.gov/glac includes a Virtual Visitor Center that will answer practically any question you can think of. Printed publications include the *Waterton-Glacier Guide*, a summer vacation planner, and a backcountry guide as well as more specific brochures on concession operations, lodging, and so on. Please write Superintendent, Glacier National Park, West Glacier, MT 59936, or phone (406) 888-7800.

Credit: VIAD Corporation

The dining rooms at Glacier's hotels offer rustic atmosphere and great food.

is 15 miles north of the Polebridge Ranger Station on the Inside North Fork Road. This dirt road becomes narrower and narrower as you go north—it's a beautiful drive that passes through meadows and forest, but take your time, as it's not always possible to see very far around the bends in the road (this drive is definitely not recommended for RVs). The campground has 13 sites and also has trailhead parking for hikers headed up to Boulder Pass.

Quartz Creek and Logging Creek Campgrounds

Quartz Creek and Logging Creek Campgrounds are located respectively about 4.5 and 6 miles south of Polebridge Ranger Station on the Inside North Fork Road. Both are tiny—Quartz Creek has 7 sites and Logging Creek 8 sites—primitive campgrounds that offer quiet and the opportunity to ramble through some less traveled parts of the park. The Inside North Fork Road is not recommended for RVs, and neither of these campgrounds has a site big enough to accommodate one. But the North Fork does have its own attractions—if you want to hear a wolf howl, your best chance anywhere in the park is probably between Logging Creek and Bowman Lake. If you set out to hike here—perhaps to Quartz or Logging Lake, or to Hidden Meadow—keep your eyes open for wolf tracks. You might even see the wolves themselves.

St. Mary

St. Mary Campground is one of the largest in the park, with 148 sites, 25 of which will accommodate RVs up to 35 feet long. This is one of two campgrounds where it is possible to reserve a site (see introduction). It sits near the foot of St. Mary Lake and offers views south, north, and east. The campsites are in an aspen grove that is very lovely—especially in the fall, when the leaves turn golden—but does not afford much protection from the sometimes strong east side winds. The campground lies along the St. Mary River, and the riparian habitat draws a wide variety of birds, including bald eagles. The St. Mary and Two Dog Flats are also home to a herd of elk that makes occasional appearances during the mornings and evenings all summer. The St. Mary Visitor Center is located just over a bridge across the river; Park Service naturalists give an evening program here each night during the summer. Please check for schedules and other special events. The town of St. Mary is less than a mile away.

Sprague Creek

Sprague Creek is definitely a candidate for the most crowded campground in the park: it fills up early and the sites are very close together. While these factors would seem to be deterrents to many campers, here one of the old truisms of real estate is proven again: Location, location, location! Sprague Creek is right on Lake McDonald and just off Going-to-the-Sun Road. Although the campground is crowded, the shoreline is very pleasant and offers views both up and down the lake. Sprague Creek is also strategically placed for bicyclists who want to get an early start and ride to the top of Logan Pass. Its 25 sites are small, but a few will accommodate RVs up to 21 feet long. Sprague Creek is closed to those with towed units because it's very difficult to back up in the tight loop through the campground.

Bowman Lake

Bowman Lake is another of those spots in Glacier that just seems to keep cropping up

in the picture books, its tranquil surface reflecting Rainbow, Carter, and Chapman Peaks, with Numa Ridge flanking it to the northwest. This primitive campground has 48 sites; it is at the end of the Bowman Lake Road (not recommended for RVs), which begins just north of the Polebridge Ranger Station. As at Quartz Creek and Logging Creek Campgrounds, you are in wolf territory here, so be sure to keep your ears as well as your eyes on the alert! Several good hikes leave from Bowman Campground: you might visit the lookout at Numa Ridge, do all or part of the Quartz Lake Loop, or go to Akokala Lake. This is also the trailhead for Brown Pass and parts farther north.

Restaurants

Although the lodge dining rooms are more formal than the smaller restaurants, casual dress is quite acceptable at all locations. All restaurants are designated non-smoking. Reservations are not accepted. Generally prices are higher at the lodge dining rooms than at the other restaurants.

A long-standing tradition is the hiring of college students from across the country to work at the park concessions. The wait staff, cooks, and other employees are students majoring in hotel and restaurant management, culinary arts, travel and tourism, accounting, and the performing arts.

Restaurant Rates

$	$10-20
$$	$20-40
$$$	$30-50
$$$$	more than $50

For two people, meal exclusive of beverages, tip, and tax.

Great Northern Steak and Rib House

$$• Glacier Park Lodge•East Glacier, MT • (406) 226-9311 (summer only)

A western theme dominates the Great Northern, and its menu features beef, barbecued ribs, chicken, and fish entrees. The restaurant offers a full buffet for breakfast, a luncheon carvery, and for dinner either a western buffet or a la carte options. Breakfast runs from 6:30 to 9:30 AM; lunch from 11:30 AM to 2 PM; and dinner from 5:00 to 9:30 PM

Ptarmigan Dining Room
$$ • Many Glacier Hotel • Many Glacier Valley
• (406) 732-4411 (summer only)

The Ptarmigan Dining Room picks up the "Alps of America" theme with its Swiss decor. At the same time its windows open to magnificent views of the mountains across Swiftcurrent Lake. The restaurant features a breakfast buffet, a luncheon carvery, and continental and American a la carte choices for dinner. Breakfast is served from 6:30 to 9:30 AM; lunch from 11:30 AM to 2 PM; and dinner from 5:00 to 9:30 PM

Cedar Dining Room
$$ • Lake McDonald Lodge • Going-to-the-Sun Road, west side
• (406) 888-5431 (summer only)

The Cedar Dining Room preserves the historic character of Lake McDonald Lodge with its rough-hewn beams and hunting trophies. A full buffet breakfast and a la carte lunch are served; dinner features a fine American menu with a taste of the outdoors. Breakfast is from 6:30 to 9:30 AM; lunch from 11:30 AM to 2 PM; and dinner from 5:00 to 9:30 PM

Russell's Trail's End Family Restaurant
$ • Lake McDonald Lodge • Going-to-the-Sun Road, west side
• (406) 888-5431 (summer only)

A casual atmosphere and a la carte breakfast, lunch, and dinner make this an easy stop for a meal. Open from 6:30 to 10:30 AM and from 11:00 AM to 9:30 PM Hours may vary in early and late seasons.

Italian Gardens Ristorante
$ • Swiftcurrent Motor Inn • Many Glacier Valley
• (406) 732-5531 (summer only)

The reincarnation of the Swiftcurrent Coffee Shop as the Italian Gardens Ristorante in the last few years has introduced a new era in the Many Glacier Valley: not only can you design your own pizza or specialty pasta at the restaurant, but you can get pizza to go—and it goes to the campground campers pretty frequently! Breakfast is served from 6:30 to 10:30 AM; the restaurant is open for lunch and dinner from 11 AM to 9:30 PM

Two Dog Flats Mesquite Grill
$ • Rising Sun Motor Inn • Going-to-the-Sun Road, east side
• (406) 732-5523 (summer only)

This family-style restaurant sits just across Going-to-the-Sun Road from St. Mary Lake. It features sandwiches, salads, steaks, and fish. Breakfast is served from 6:30 to 10:30 AM; the restaurant is open for lunch and dinner from 11 AM to 9:30 PM Hours will be more limited after September 8.

Eddie's Café
$ • Apgar Village
• (406) 888-5361

Eddie's Café is located in Apgar Village at the foot of Lake McDonald. It offers breakfast, lunch, and dinner, but is perhaps best remembered for the ice cream window just outside the door...featuring huckleberry ice cream among many other flavors! Eddie's is open from early June to late September. Please check for hours of operation.

Shopping

While you probably won't come to the park just to shop, it's also likely that you won't leave without having bought something—a souvenir poster, a book, or perhaps a locally made hand-thrown pot.

Glacier Natural History Association runs a considerable operation through the visitor centers, selling books, videos, tapes, maps, and posters that are specific to Glacier National Park. Proceeds from this non-profit organization go to support educational programs and publications in the park.

Glacier Park, Inc., has gift shops located in all the major lodges. They carry native jewelry and crafts, film, postage stamps, huckleberry treats, books and maps, hiking snacks, and outdoor clothing as well as a variety of souvenirs. Campstores are located at Swiftcurrent Motor Inn, Rising Sun Motor Inn, Two Medicine, and at the Lake McDonald Lodge complex, and they carry a similar selection with the addition of limited food supplies, some camping equipment, and bundled firewood.

Apgar Village also has several gift shops, each with a unique selection. The Cedar Tree offers Montana-made gifts and souvenirs as well as huckleberry products, Pendleton woolens, and t-shirts. Schoolhouse Gifts is located in a former one-room schoolhouse; Montana House features the work of Montana artists and craftspeople.

Nightlife

"Nightlife" within the park is a quiet affair, but it has its charms. Park naturalists give evening slide programs and campfire talks at many locations each night. Members of the local Blackfeet and Salish-Kootenai tribes talk about their history and culture in the "Native America Speaks" weekly program. And some special events do occur during the summer— these might include performances by Blackfeet dancers, singer-songwriter Jack Gladstone, or the actor Raphael Cristy portraying Western artist Charlie Russell. Check the park publication *Nature with a Naturalist* for current listings.

Of course, evening is a wonderful time for outdoor activities too. Stargazing is exceptional in places far from city lights, and the northern lights occasionally reward those nighthawks awake to see them. Glacier is not, however, a good place to be hiking at night, when bears may be both more active and less likely to expect people on the trails.

Quiet hours in campgrounds are from 8 PM to 8 AM Fireworks may not be used within the park, but many communities around the park have fireworks displays for the Fourth of July.

Kalispell, with a population of just more than 16,500 people, is small enough to barely make a dent on most national maps, and yet big enough to be Montana's seventh largest city.

Kalispell

Kalispell, with a population of just more than 16,500 people, is small enough to barely make a dent on most national maps, and yet big enough to be Montana's seventh largest city overall and also the largest city in the four counties of northwest Montana. It is thus a mixture of urban and rural. During your time here, you will find yourself enjoying the traditional delights of a city such as shopping, restaurants and museums, as well as those qualities that are more associated with rural Montana — the county fair, rodeo, horseback riding, and fishing, along with just the general air of peace and serenity.

Kalispell is the county seat of Flathead County, and is the business center as well. It is located at the intersection of U.S. 93 and U.S. 2, and just 45 minutes from Glacier National Park and 10 minutes from Flathead Lake. Though it does not have as much of a distinct identity as the smaller communities of Bigfork and Whitefish, it prides itself on being a town that provides a quality of life that can't be beat. The town was recently named by Mountain Sports and Living magazine as the Best Mountain Town in America, taking into account its proximity to the Big Mountain and Blacktail Mountain ski areas, as well as its superb health-care industry, its quality schools, and many recreational opportunities.

Kalispell is also, of course, rich in history. It is a frontier town that was founded in 1891 by Charles E. Conrad, a Missouri River trader who combined a colorful outdoorsy spirit with good old-fashioned horse sense that made him a rich man. Conrad's huge wooden home, built in 1895 and occupied by members of the Conrad family until 1975, has been restored to Victorian elegance and is open to the public as the Conrad Mansion (see our Attractions chapter). It is one of the city's most popular tourist stops, and provides an education on how much more civilized the frontier was than Hollywood's westerns would lead

us to believe. The mansion is one of the main stops on a self-guided walking tour of historic buildings that begins at the Hockaday Center for the Arts in downtown Kalispell.

Another exciting addition to the historic legacy of Kalispell is the Central School Museum, which opened in 1999. This impressive stone structure was built in the 1890s as a school, and later served as office space and classroom space for Flathead Valley Community College before being closed for about 10 years and nearly being demolished. The efforts of the Northwest Montana Historical Society led to the preservation of the building, which has been extensively renovated and will now be the site of exhibits, lectures and community events.

Downtown Kalispell has suffered the same vicissitudes as other Main Streets over the past few decades. The business community has expanded beyond the city limits in recent years, especially toward Evergreen, east of town on U.S. 2. This is the home of such popular stores as Wal-Mart, ShopKo, Kmart, and Staples as well as car lots, fast food restaurants, and other businesses. But today the trend is definitely toward a comeback for downtown Kalispell. Unlike many other cities, Kalispell arranged a deal in the mid-1980s that led to the building of a mall not outside of town on a highway strip, but right on Main Street, just a block or two from the city's oldest historic businesses. That anchor has proved to be important in guaranteeing a future for downtown. Today, several new buildings have gone up, housing restaurants, clothing stores, and gift shops, and Kalispell's city center is more vibrant than it has been for many years.

To the south of Kalispell, there are two communities on Flathead Lake that have distinct identities of their own, but which also are close enough to Kalispell that they should be included here. Somers is the smaller of the areas, with a public boat ramp and private marina helping to set the tone. This was a railroad town in earlier years, and many of the houses were built for railroad employees. A few of these have been converted to public use such as the Tiebuckers restaurant and saloon, which offers a mix of home cooking and gourmet meals in a rustic ramshackle house. You can also catch a ride on the *Far West* cruise boat during summer evenings at the dock across the street from the magnificent log-built Montana Grill. A few miles farther south on U.S. 93, you come to Lakeside, which in the past few years has developed into one of the most popular destinations on Flathead Lake. Several resorts and motels offer boating and fishing opportunities during the summer, and the new Black-tail Mountain ski area gives the community a year-round appeal.

All in all, Kalispell and its surrounding communities will provide days and weeks of entertainment, education and shopping for tourists, but many people find that even a long vacation isn't enough to enjoy everything Kalispell has to offer. Those are the people who move here a couple years after their vacation, keeping Kalispell and Flathead County one of the most exciting and thriving areas in Montana.

Accommodations

Hotel Rates

Keep in mind that some rates are based on availability. The average nightly rates for two adults at the hotels and motels listed in this section are indicated by a dollar sign ($) ranking in the following chart. Also, the hotels and motels in this chapter accept all or most major credit cards.

$	$25 to $49
$$	$50 to $75
$$$	$76 to $100
$$$$	$101 and more

Hotels

Aero Inn
$ • 1830 U.S. 93 South, Kalispell • (406) 755-3798, (800) 843-6114

If you pilot your own small plane, there's really only one place to land for the night — the Aero Inn, located just off the municipal airport in Kalispell. And make no mistake, this airport really is IN Kalispell: It's located less than a half mile south of the Flathead County Courthouse. The motel has 60 spacious guestrooms, along with an indoor pool, hot tub, sauna, game room, continental breakfast, handicapped facilities, and winter plug-ins for your car. There is also 24-hour front desk service at this customer-friendly hotel. Check it out on the Internet at http://www.aeroinn.com.

Bayshore Resort Motel On Flathead Lake
$$ • 616 Lakeside Boulevard, Lakeside • (406) 844-3131, (800) 844-3132

This is one of several motels located in Lakeside on the west shore of Flathead Lake about 15 miles south of Kalispell. The view can't be beat, as you look out across the lake to the majestic Mission and Swan Mountain ranges across the water. The Bayshore Resort features newer units with queen- and king-size beds. Family units feature kitchens and private decks. Take advantage of the dock and boat slips to enjoy fishing in the daytime, and then come back for a dip in the chilly waters of Flathead Lake at the beach area. Evening campfires are often lit in summer.

Blue and White Motel
$$ • East Idaho, Kalispell

This is one non-chain hotels that can compete with the more familiar names. The Blue and White gets lots of repeat business from business people and others who travel to Kalispell frequently. That's because of the friendly service, and the excellent accommodations. Rooms have double and queen size beds, with handicapped facilities available on

Montana-style interior design makes this lounge a cozy place to gather.

request. There is a free continental breakfast, and a small indoor swimming pool, sauna, and Jacuzzi. Pets are allowed, and there are winter plug-ins available for automobile engine heaters to help make it through those cold Montana nights. The large parking lots can handle RVs, trucks, trailers, or buses. Commercial, tour and winter rates are available. The Blue and White is also located next to Finnegan's, one of the few 24-hour restaurants in Kalispell.

Cavanaughs at Kalispell Center
$$$ • 20 N. Main, Kalispell
• (406) 752-6660, (800) 325-4000

This large hotel offers a perfect compromise for tourist couples who can't decide between shopping and sightseeing. After a full day at Glacier Park or on Flathead Lake, you can return to one of the 132 rooms and suites at Cavanaughs and freshen up for dinner at the Northwest Bounty Company restaurant in the hotel, and then walk into the adjacent Kalispell Center Mall for an evening of bargain hunting at the 50 or so stores. Back at the hotel, you can swim in the indoor solarium pool or relax in the sauna or whirlpools. The Fireside Lounge offers a quiet atmosphere to enjoy a drink or two before bed, or you might step across the hall to the popular casino. When you get up, you can enjoy the continental breakfast and then get back to sightseeing. Cavanaughs is a popular convention center, too, with more than 10,000 square feet of meeting and banquet space.

Hampton Inn
$$ • 1140 U.S. 2 West, Kalispell
• (406) 755-7900, (800) HAMPTON

The Hampton Inn is Kalispell's newest major hotel, and targets the business clientele in particular, but has many conveniences perfect for a family as well. All guest rooms feature an iron and ironing board, a small refrigerator, TV/VCR, video game player, coffee maker and coffee, hair dryer, HBO, and free local calls. The hotel also has a 24-hour indoor swimming pool and Jacuzzi as well as a gift shop, business center and exercise facility. Although there is no restaurant per se, a complimentary breakfast buffet featuring fresh-baked muffins and sticky buns is served every morning. Children under 18 stay free at the Hampton Inn.

Kalispell Grand Hotel
$$ • 100 Main Street Kalispell
• 755-8100, (800) 858-7422

The Kalispell Grand Hotel is a beautifully remodeled 40-room, historic hotel that is located conveniently right in downtown Kalispell. Noted writer Frank Bird Linderman leased and managed the hotel from 1924 to 1926, and he and his good friend Charlie Russell, the famed western artist, would on occasion sit in the hotel lobby's and exchange thoughts and stories of the West. Today, a complimentary continental breakfast is served every morning in the Grand Lobby, which still has the look of a luxurious frontier hotel lobby with its high, pressed-tin ceilings and golden oak staircase. The three story brick hotel also connects to the famous Kalispell Bar, where music is heard often on summer weekends, and to the Alley Connection restaurant, which serves Oriental and American cuisine. In season, you can take a carriage ride through the downtown area, or you can walk through an area that is rich with shops, restaurants and history.

Lakeshore Motel
$$ • 7175 U.S. 93 South, Lakeside
• (406) 844-2433 or (406) 251-4405

This family-owned and operated motel is close to Kalispell (just a 20-minute drive) yet you are on the water and enjoying the lovely Montana scenery. Since the 1940s, this quiet uncrowded resort has been a preferred getaway for folks on a budget. The cabins are modern with full bath and shower and offer lake views and unobstructed access to the lake. Gas barbecues are available for convenient outdoor cooking and some of the units have kitchenettes. RV hookups can be rented if you are hauling your home on wheels. For evening enjoyment there is a shoreline fireplace, and the growing village of Lakeside provides restaurants, a supermarket, banking and taverns just a minute or two away. If you want to check out the fishing on Flathead Lake, you will have plenty of opportunity here. There is a dock, with slips that can accommodate boats up to 30 feet. The Lakeshore

Motel is open from the middle of May until the end of September. You can get a look at it on the Web at http://members.tripod.com/~tendragon/lakeshore/lakeshore.html.

Lakeside Resort Motel
$$ • 7235 U.S. 93 South, Lakeside
• (406) 844-3570, (800) 348-4822

Another Lakeside motel, this one offers year-round accommodations. The Lakeside Resort prides itself on being the perfect place for family reunions, weddings or friendly gatherings. You can have your choice of one-, two-, and three-bedroom cabins or a motel room. Kitchens are equipped with microwaves, dishwashers and barbecues. A private beach with docks and boat ramps fills out the resort atmosphere. Sailing, boating, fishing, pedal boats, canoes, volleyball, horseshoes, and Ski-doos are available. A self-service laundry facility is on site along with a gift shop, hot tub, and a public restroom.

The Outlaw-A Cavanaughs Hotel
$$$ • 1701 U.S. 93 South, Kalispell
• (406) 755-6100, (800) 325-4000

The Outlaw Inn is the granddaddy of convention centers in the Flathead Valley. It is the biggest—with 220 guestrooms and suites—and the most comprehensive, with a popular restaurant and lounge and extensive convention facilities. Fitness center facilities are available along with a hot tub, sauna, tennis court, two indoor pools, and spa. The restaurant and lounge is called Hennessy's and includes a large casino area. An art gallery is also located in the building.

Red Lion Inn
$$ • 1330 U.S. 2 West, Kalispell
• (406) 755-6700

The Red Lion was acquired in recent years by the Doubletree Inn chain, and you get the quality stay here that you would expect from such a well-known name. There are 64 air-

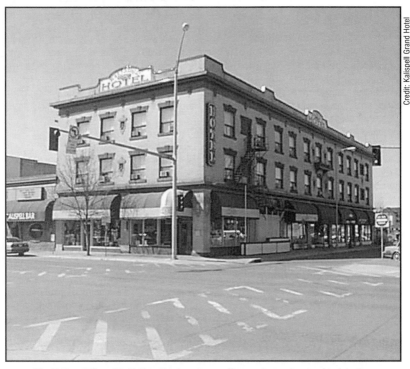

Credit: Kalispell Grand Hotel

The Kalispell Grand in Kalispell's downtown offers a chance to step back in time.

conditioned guestrooms and suites. HBO, room service, heated outdoor pool, spa, and free parking. Airport shuttle service is also available at nominal charge. Restaurant, lounge and casino are adjacent to Inn.

Somers Bay Log Cabin Lodging
$ • 5496 U.S. 93 South, Somers
• (406) 857-3881, (888) 443-3881

Despite the old-timey cabins, Somers Bay Log Cabin Lodging is one of the newer accommodations in the Flathead Lake area. Built in the spring of 1998, Somers Bay Log Cabin Lodging features both studio units and bedroom cabins. Each features a queen log bed and a queen sofa sleeper and comes equipped with a kitchenette that has microwave, stove top, refrigerator, coffee maker, and dishes. There is extra parking for boats and trailers, so you can use your cabin as the base for your lake fun. Flathead State Park Boat Access is within walking distance.

Super 8
$ • 1341 First Avenue East, Kalispell
• (406) 755-1888, (800) 800-8000

The Kalispell Super 8 motel is a safe bet for travelers who are looking for pleasant accommodations on a budget. Don't hesitate to ask for those little extras such as first aid supplies, irons and ironing boards, hair dryers and other essential toiletries you may have forgotten. The accent here is not on frills, but on friendly service, which makes it a popular choice for business travelers. There is also daily laundry and dry cleaning pickup and delivery. And a bonus for commercial truckers: Because of limited truck parking, the hotel will pay for taxi fare to and from your truck.

White Birch Motel & RV Park
$ • 17 Shady Lane, Kalispell
• (406) 752-4008

White Birch is an offbeat little motel in a park-like setting on a creek. This location, set back from Montana 35 just 3/4 mile from U.S. 2, is out of the way, but just minutes from all

amenities. All rooms have a coffeepot with complimentary coffee & refrigerator, plus three come with kitchens. A coin-operated laundry is also available on site. The motel is open year-round, and the RV park, which just opened in 1996, operates from May to October. The RV facility features modern restrooms and showers with handicapped access. No American Express.

Campgrounds and RV Parks

Campground Rates

$	Less than $9
$$	$10 to $16
$$$	$17 to $23
$$$$	$24 and more

Glacier Pines RV Park
$ • 1850 Montana 35 East, Kalispell
• (406) 752-2760, (800) 533-4029

Glacier Pines RV Park sits in a wooded location about five minutes from Kalispell. There are 30 tent sites and 140 RV sites with full hook-ups. There is no maximum size limit or time limit. Available on site are a store, laundry, showers, a heated swimming pool, horseshoes, and other recreation including a play area.

Lake Blaine Resort
$$ • 1700 Lake Blaine Road, Kalispell
• (406) 755-2891

Although the mailing address is Kalispell, this facility is actually 10 miles east of town off of Montana 35. There are 12 tent sites and 75 RV sites, along with swimming, a snack bar, playground, and skating nearby. Lake Blaine is one of many large "pothole" lakes along the eastern side of the Flathead Valley, left over from geological activity thousands of years ago. It is a delightful recreational lake and has only limited public access since there is no public ramp. The Lake Blaine area also

---

INSIDERS TIP

Kalispell takes its name from a Salish Indian group that inhabited the area, the Kalispels.

features an 18-hole golf course called Mountain Crossroads on Montana 35. The Lake Blaine Resort facility is open only for the prime summer season of June 1 to September 5. American Express is not accepted.

Rocky Mountain 'Hi' RV Park & Campground
$ • 825 Helena Flats Road, Kalispell
• (406) 755-9573, (800) 968-5637

Rocky Mountain 'Hi' is the only privately owned RV park in the Kalispell area that is not on a highway. Sign points the way from either Montana 35 of U.S. 2 toward this quiet park that features mature shade trees and cable television hookups. All sizes of RVs can be accommodated in the 59 spots, and there are also 18 tent sites. For the kids, there is a large Western-style play town and a playing field. In addition, there is a store at the site, along with camp showers, a recreation room, and pay telephone. This facility does not take American Express.

Spruce Park RV Park
$ (no credit cards) • 1985 Montana 35, Kalispell
• (406) 752-6321, 756-8288, (888) 752-6321

There are 60 tent sites and 100 RV Sites at Spruce Park, which is located near the Flathead River, and features fishing and river boat tours, along with a par 3 golf facility and a recreation room. The park is located just three miles east of Kalispell and is open year-round. Although no credit cards are taken, Spruce Park RV Park will accept personal checks from out of state as well as traveler's checks.

Bed and Breakfasts

Bed and Breakfast Rates

$	Less than $85
$$	$86 to $115
$$$	$116 to $150
$$$$	$151 and more

Blaine Creek Bed & Breakfast
$ • 727 Van Sant Road, Kalispell
• (406) 752-2519

The main level of this establishment features a large living room with a brick fireplace, cathedral ceilings, and mountain views. There are formal and informal dining areas, a cozy country kitchen and deck. The Garden Party bedroom on the main level features a queen bed with adjacent bathroom. The lower level features a large family room with a stone fireplace, pool table, and sofa sleeper. Outside on the lower deck is a redwood hot tub. The Grizzly room has twin beds and the Calico Corner has a double bed. There is a shared bath with a sauna. A full breakfast is served every day.

The Keith House

Don and Rebecca Bauder fell in love with Kalispell's historic Keith House when they stayed there as bed and breakfast guests in 1992, and five years and a massive renovation later, they became the innkeepers at the gracious East Side home.

"We were quite taken with the house at that time. It was beautiful," Don says of the enormous three-story brick house which sits on four city lots at the corner of Fifth Avenue East and Sixth Street. The nearly 12,000-square-foot home was built in 1911 by Kalispell businessman Harry Keith, and his wife, Mary, who raised their 10 children there. The

house remained in the Keith family until 1936, and since that time has been a private residence, a boarding house, a home for disabled men and a bed and breakfast.

The home was listed on the National Register of Historic Places in 1987 based on research by a previous owner.

The Bauders weren't in the market for a historic home — or a bed and breakfast business — during their five-day stay as guests, but they never forgot the house.

After they sold their Colorado business in May 1995, the Bauders wondered what had happened to the Keith House, and asked a friend to drive by to see whether it was still for sale. It was, so they wrote to the listing real estate agent asking about it.

At the same time, a former owner had suggested that the real estate agent contact the Bauders to see whether they were interested.

"I, of course, took that as a sign," said Rebecca.

Credit: Keith House Bed and Breakfast Inn

Many of the Flathead Valley's historic homes now serve as bed and breakfasts. The Keith House in Kalispell is a charming example.

They bought the house in July 1995, and a 20-month renovation project started in late August. They opened for business late in 1997 in this beautiful old house that's been restored to a grandeur that it probably never enjoyed when it was home to a large family.

The entire roof was replaced, and plumbing and electrical were completely updated.

The front porch's 450 balusters were hand-turned to exactly match the originals, using research done for the Historic Register application.

The list of repairs and improvements seems endless, and sitting in the cheery living room with its warm quarter-sawn oak woodwork, it's hard to imagine the magnitude of the renovation project.

Because the home was to be used as a bed and breakfast, bathrooms were added for each guest room, using existing closets rather than moving interior walls.

"Fortunately all the rooms had sinks, and fortunately all had nice-sized closets," Don said. Armoires were added to the rooms as a substitute for closets.

Eventually, six new bathrooms were added.

Whenever possible, the Bauders used the original sinks and the old fixtures, which were re-porcelained and replated. Tile from an upstairs bathroom was used for a hearth in the living room fireplace. The original solid-brass light fixtures were rebuilt and rewired.

Rebecca, whose background is in market research, was the interior decorator, indulging a hobby born of voracious reading of decorator magazines.

"This was a dream come true for me to have a house like this to go after," she said.

Each of the six guest rooms is designed to have a distinct personality, and each has a name.

Guests can choose her namesake "Rebecca's Suite," decorated in pine green and claret red with tartan plaids and Battenburg lace. This is the largest and most expensive accommodation, renting for $165 per night.

Three other rooms are named after her daughters, Joy, Valerie and Sara.

All the furnishings are antiques, period pieces or family heirlooms, and the house is a virtual gallery for Montana artists.

"I think every single room has at least one Montana artist in it, if not more," Rebecca says.

Rebecca did extensive research on the decor of turn-of-the-century homes, trying to keep the furnishings historically accurate.

The result is a cheery mixture of fabrics, styles and whimsy.

"If you love it, somehow or other it will all work together," Rebecca said.

The Bauders live in the third floor of the house, known as the ballroom but generally used as a playroom

The Bauders have one part-time person who helps with the housekeeping, but they work as the innkeepers and do the food preparation.

They've been pleased with their business, and are glad the work of renovation is behind them.

"It was frustrating at times and rewarding," Don said. "I'm glad it's over—or almost over. You don't restore it and that's it. I have to paint storm windows between now and the storm. There's always something to do."

Bonnie's Bed and Breakfast
$$ • 265 Lake Blaine Road, Kalispell
• (406) 755-3776, (800) 755-3778

Bonnie's Bed and Breakfast features three guestrooms. The Big Sky Room has a luxurious master room with a private bath and Jacuzzi. The Columbian Room and Alpine Room have queen-size beds. Reservations are required, but last minute inquiries are encouraged since there are sometimes unexpected openings. Bonnie's Bed and Breakfast is located a half mile from the junction of Montana 206 and Montana 35, near the Mountain Crossroads golf course and restaurant.

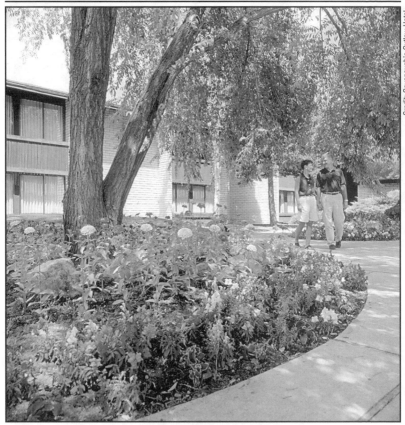

Credit: Cavanaugh's Outlaw Hotel

Summer in Kalispell is green and lush.

There is a 10 percent discount for senior citizens. Pets are not allowed.

Creston Country Inn
$$ • 70 Creston Road, Kalispell
• (406) 755-7517, (800) 257-7517

The Creston Inn is just an eighth of a mile off Montana 35 halfway between Kalispell and Bigfork. The 1920's farmhouse is situated on 4.5 acres and includes two old red barns and a large pasture and garden, with a panoramic view of the Northern Rockies and Flathead Valley. Guests can stroll the grounds along the creek, sit under the willow trees or just relax on the porch. At night, guests are encouraged to gather in the living room by the wood stove and enjoy reading, television, or parlor games. A full gourmet breakfast is served, and special diets are available upon request. Visit the inn on the Internet at http://www.wtp.net/go/crestoninn and get an idea of the amenities, whether its the Valley Vista Room with a sitting area and queen bed, or the Canterbury Room with an antique clawfoot tub and shower in the bathroom and either two twin beds or a king bed. Reservations are suggested, although last minute openings may be available. No American Express accepted, and no pets. Smoking is allowed only outside. No children under 12.

Full Circle Herb Farm
$ • 1230 Truman Creek Road, Kila
• (406) 257-8133

Not everyone wants to spend a night at an herb farm, but some of you do —and you know who you are! This is a great once-in-a-blue-moon opportunity for a truly unique vacation. As Montana's oldest herb farm, Full Circle Herb Farm is the premier source for many hard-to-find herbs as well as all the well-known favorites. The organic operation includes herb gardens, greenhouses, meadows, expansive lawns, and woods on 150 acres of scenic Montana 12 miles west of Kalispell. The guesthouse is the tenderly renovated Kila Church, which still retains its original history and charm but has been transformed into a rustic yet modern cottage in a quiet wooded setting. Amenities include queen bed (and pull-out couch), dining and living area, full kitchen, full bath, microwave, and gas barbecue. Note that this is not a true bed & breakfast, since meals are not served. Accommodations are also available for horses, which include a corral with feed bunk and water. The guesthouse is open from May 1 through November 1. For more information, visit the farm's website at http://www.ptinet.net/~herbfarm/ghouse.html. No children under 12.

The Keith House Bed & Breakfast Inn

$$$$ • 538 Fifth Avenue East, Kalispell
• (406) 752-7913, (800) 972-7913

Just when you think you've seen it all, you stumble across the Keith House, one of the largest and finest homes built in Montana during the early years of the 20th century. It has been meticulously restored and furnished with comfortable antiques, vintage linens, lovely English china and silver. Every room has a private bath, cozy chairs and lofty down comforter on a luxurious bed. Spacious common rooms invite conversation with other guests, and a secluded library with comfortable, over-stuffed chairs offers quiet reading in front of one of the home's beautiful fireplaces. A hearty breakfast is served each morning in the dining room from a magnificent Belgian antique sideboard, and a large

wrap-around veranda with wicker chairs allows you to put your feet up. Visit the rooms online at http://keithhousebb.com and then stop by on the east side of Kalispell. Even if you don't stay here, it's worth a drive-by just to admire it. Reservations are required at this non-smoking establishment.

Osprey Inn B & B

$$ • 5557 U.S. 93 South, Somers
• (406) 857-2042, (800) 258-2042

The three story home that is now the Osprey Inn is located on the shore of Flathead Lake and has a panoramic view of the lake, islands and mountains. The well-kept lawn extends to the shore of the lake with a gentle, pebbled beach and boat dock. The Osprey Inn has four guestrooms available: two rooms with private baths, a two-room suite with private bath, and a log cabin that sleeps two. All rooms have a view overlooking the lake. Your stay includes a full breakfast with fresh raspberries and sweet cherries in season. Muffins are a house specialty. The establishment is open from April 15 to October 31 and has a Web page at http://www.ospreybnb.com. No American Express.

Outlook Inn Bed and Breakfast

$$ • 175 Boon Road, Somers
• 857-2060, (888) 857- 8439

The Outlook Inn is located on a promontory across U.S. 93 from Flathead Lake in Somers. This spacious, yet cozy lodge-like home sits on seven private acres and offers all of the amenities you would expect from a fine establishment. Curl up in front of the river rock fireplace with a good book, or relax in your room with the private jetted tub or double shower. The house features a huge log deck overlooking the lake and Rocky Mountains as well as a variety of locally produced art. Walk to fine dining, dancing, karaoke, and the lake in minutes. Or step out the door and go for a walk in the wooded hills. In the winter you can cross-country ski out the door. The

Outlook is online at http://webby.com/montana/outlook.

River Rock Bed & Breakfast
$$ • 179 Schrade Road, Kalispell
• (406) 756-6901, (800) 477-0699

River Rock is located on a hill amid rolling fields of wheat and features two common living rooms, a formal dining room, sound system throughout the home and patios, hot tub, steam room, large tropical aquarium, and a modern open kitchen. The Honeymoon Suite comes with a veranda, king bed, six-foot Jacuzzi, and large shower and bath. Jennifer's Room features two queen-size beds and private bath with shower. Both rooms are oversized. There is a mixture of traditional and contemporary furnishings at this establishment, which is located north of Reserve Drive on U.S. 93 about five miles north of Kalispell. Full gourmet breakfasts are served. The River Rock closes from mid-October through the end of November.

Stillwater Inn
$$ • 206 Fourth Avenue East, Kalispell
• (406) 755-7080, (800) 398-7024

This lovely historic home is furnished with early 20th century furniture and has an air of quiet elegance and comfort. The house was built around 1900 by Gustave Gamer, who had come to Kalispell six years earlier to begin the Kalispell Malt and Brewing Company. In 1907 William Noffsinger, an attorney and businessman, purchased the home, which remained in his family until 1943. The name Stillwater was taken from a nearby river, although the inn is actually located in downtown Kalispell on one of the business-residential avenues. Guests begin each day with a delicious full breakfast. From the entrance, a gracious stairway leads up to the four guest bedrooms, two with a private bath. No American Express.

Restaurants

Restaurant Rates

$	$10 to $19
$$	$20 to $27
$$$	$28 to $35
$$$$	$36 and more

For two people, meal exclusive of beverages, tip, and tax.

Family Friendly

Alley Connection
$ • 22 First St. W., Kalispell
• 752-7077

The family that runs the Alley Connection is something of a local tradition in Flathead County. They have had a record of continuous success dating back to the 1970s when they arrived from Vietnam. Today, the Alley Connection is joined locally by four other Oriental style restaurants owned by family members, but the Alley is still the best. Specialities include Szechuan pork and chicken and egg foo yung, as well as a hearty wonton soup that includes a generous helping of pork and greens along with both fried and noodle wontons. And even if you don't usually like sweet and sour, you may want to try the sweet and sour here (our favorite is the wontons) since it has a distinct flavor that is a particular treat. There are individual combination dinners available such as Kiet's Dinner, which features soup of the day, egg roll, sweet & sour wontons, chicken chow mein, and com-

---

INSIDERS' TIP

Got a late start? Need to jump-start your drive? It seems like about every other corner in the Flathead Valley has a drive-up espresso shop: Java Joe's, Mountain Mocha, Juice 'n' Java, Java Junction, Big Mountain Buzz...they're all there, and more! Just keep your eye out...

bination fried rice for just $8.95. Lunches are even cheaper, and you can also get American menu selections for kids.

Bojangles
$ • 1203 U.S. 2 W., Kalispell
• 755-3222

This is one of those family dining establishments that locals eat at, but tourists may pass up for the more familiar McDonalds or Wendy's. Don't make that mistake. Not only is the menu full of good food, it's also full of references to the 1950s. In fact the whole restaurant is a throwback to simpler times. A cutout of Marilyn Monroe greets you at the front door, and the walls are filled with 1950s-era memorabilia such as license plates, movie tie-ins and—of course—Elvis. Hamburgers are named after pop singers such as Jerry Lee Lewis (lots of jalapenos), Neil Sedaka, Gene Vincent, and Buddy Holly (no frills, just the plain burger). Breakfast is served all day, and an added attraction for the kids is a model train that runs along a rail that is set up on beams atop the walls.

Cislo's
$ • 2046 U.S. 2 E., Kalispell
• (406) 756-7330

Cislo's is the closest thing to Mel's Diner from the old TV show "Alice" that you will find in Kalispell. It features a crew of tough but lovable waitresses, and a menu that could easily be mistaken as from the 1950s. Look for the open turkey and beef sandwiches, the chili burger, and the club sandwich, but don't be afraid to try anything on the menu. This is home cooking that won't disappoint. And be sure to save room for dessert, which usually features five or six fresh baked pies. One interesting side note: Cislo's used to be located where the Staples office-supply superstore is now situated, a bit closer to Kalispell, but when Cislo's lost their lease, they didn't lose their restaurant. They just loaded it up on top of a truck and hauled it down the highway to its current spot. Now, that's one tough little restaurant.

Charlie Wong's
$ • 2316 U.S. 2 E., Kalispell
• (406) 752-4772

Charlie Wong's is located in Evergreen, the suburb east of Kalispell's city limits where much of the business development has taken place over the past 10 years. If you get through shopping at Wal-Mart, Shopko or Kmart, it is just a short drive to this restaurant, where you can get both Asian specialities and a couple of American entrees. Always popular is the

Credit: Mackenzie River Pizza

The great outdoors even plays a part in interior design in Montana. Here rustic designs flavor the scene at a Kalispell restaurant.

kung pao chicken, but you won't go wrong on this menu. Hot entrees can be ordered mild or medium, too, so don't be shy about trying something new.

Legacy Restaurant
$ • 128 First Ave. E., Kalispell
• (406) 257-7121

The Legacy specializes in lunches, and features a complete lineup of soups and sandwiches. You can always get the soup and half a sandwich special and come away satisfied. Nothing fancy, but this restaurant has been in Kalispell for 15 years or more, and that's always a sign of doing something right. It's just a short block from Main Street, so before you load back up in the car after shopping downtown, stop here for a quick meal.

Los Caporales
$$ • 1539 Montana 35, Kalispell
• (406) 756-6300

Los Caporales features authentic Mexican food from not just south of the border, but from the region around Guadalajara, west of Mexico City, where the owners came from originally. That means some of the menu items will be a bit different than what is typically served at a Mexican restaurant, but the difference (which includes a lot of grilled foods) is a big plus. Try the carnitas de res from the beef menu for a tasty Mexican stir-fry of sirloin strips, peppers, tomatoes and mushrooms in a spicy seasoning mix. Or if chicken is your fancy, then order the arroz con pollo, which features chunks of chicken breast with onions, tomatoes and mushrooms, this time in a tasty red sauce and melted cheese, all served over a bed of rice. For the less adventurous, there is a large helping of standard Mexican fare such as combination dinners that come with one or more enchiladas, tacos, tostadas, chile rellenos, chimichangas, or burritos. Kids can get a grilled cheese and fries for $2.75 or children's sized portions of Mexican food for $3.25 to $5.25. There are also steaks and hamburgers. Los Caporales is adjoining a casino, and shares its liquor license, but the restaurant (especially the non-smoking section) is completely separate from the casino, and features Mexican music on the loudspeakers.

MacKenzie River Pizza Co.
$ • 1645 U.S. 93 S., Kalispell
• (406) 756-0060

This is one of those hip gourmet pizza joints that has become trendy the past few years, but don't let that stop you. MacKenzie River is a Montana-based company that does pizza right. You can get anything you want on top, from artichokes to garlic plus all the traditional favorites like pepperoni and sausage. There are also top-notch sandwiches and salads, and the restaurant has a beer and wine license. Meals are served at rustic-style tables or you can take your order to go.

Montana Coffee Traders
$ • 328 W. Center St., Kalispell
• (406) 756-2326

This store dares to ask, "How You Bean, Man?" It is a must stop for the coffee aficionado. Begun in Whitefish by R.C. Beall 20 years ago, Montana Coffee Traders has grown into a snug global empire, with branches in Austin, Texas (where it goes by the name Texas Coffee Traders) and Moscow (not Idaho either, but the Russian one). If you are looking for a single cup of espresso, or a complete panoply of coffee blends and supplies, this is the right spot. Even tea drinkers may find something unique here. A cafe in the store serves soup and sandwiches or desserts, and there is pound after pound of coffee to take home for an aromatic Montana memory. Our favorite is the extra strong Grizzly blend, but there is something for every taste, including organic blends from Perus, Guatemala, Sumatra and across the tropics. Montana Coffee Traders is conveniently located just across the street from the Kalispell Center Mall.

Mountain Crossroads Restaurant & Golf Club
$ • 100 Montana 206, Kalispell
• (406) 755-0111

Even though the Crossroads is on a golf course and features a large bar in the dining room, we are still including it in the family-friendly listing for a couple of reasons. First of all, the establishment has a no-smoking policy, which makes it quite unusual in Montana. Secondly, the menu features many low-priced entrees, so even though there is no

Credit: Karen Leigh, Hockaday Museum of Art

The Hockaday Museum of Art — a Kalispell Institution.

separate children's menu, there are many meals that most kids would enjoy such as spaghetti, hamburgers, or chili. Top-priced items on the menu are a New York steak at $10.95 and jumbo prawns at $9.95. You will also enjoy the appetizers, especially the "Wingers," a basket of 12 chicken wings that come drenched in your choice of barbecue sauce, smooth buttered hot sauce, or cajun sauce for just $3.95 served with either ranch or bleu cheese. The Crossroads features the best view of any non-lake restaurant in the Flathead Valley, too. You're sitting practically underneath the Swan Range of mountains at the east end of the valley. And for the family that plays together, Mountain Crossroads also features a very reasonably priced nine-hole course.

Sizzler Restaurant
$ • 1250 US 2 West, Kalispell
• (406) 257-9555

This is our favorite family restaurant in the Kalispell area. It's part of a chain, but the local owners go the extra mile for their customers, and they have been innovators throughout the years. Sizzler is a steak house, but you can get much more than the trademark sirloin steak here. For one thing, the restaurant has the best all-you-can-eat salad bar in town, with everything from fresh fruit to tacos to pasta and soups included, and a separate bar available with cake, cookies and ice cream at no extra charge. You get the whole thing for just $6.95 (less for seniors!) or just $2.95 with an entree. Kids have their own all-you-can-eat food bar featuring macaroni and cheese, pasta, chicken nuggets and fruit. This place is always packed, but they never have to turn anyone away, thanks to rapid service. You won't regret a stop here.

Fine Dining

Black Angus Steak House
$$$ • 1330 U.S. 2 West, Kalispell
• (406) 755-5341

The Black Angus is on the edge of town just as you are leaving Kalispell on the west side, but make the effort to stop here. Located in the Red Lion hotel, the Black Angus feature not just steak, but a complete line of fine dining, with nightly specials that might include a tenderloin fillet stuffed with Dungeness crab, halibut with macadamia nut butter, or lobster. You can always get the prime rib ($13.95 for a 12-ounce cut) or try something unusual like the pork tenderloin with brandy garlic sauce ($11.95). The atmosphere is quiet and low-key, and for lunch try the steak sandwich for $6.95. A full bar is available, and there's a casino one floor down.

Cafe Max
$$$ • 121 Main St., Kalispell
• (406) 755-SOUP

Cafe Max is Kalispell's undisputed leader for fine dining. Chef Doug Day is a master of presentation, as well as gastronomy, and everything in his restaurant shows the extra effort of a truly great dining establishment. Openers might include manila clams and Italian sausage or shrimp bisque, each with a dollop of creamy mashed potatoes blended in. Entrees on the menu change every couple of weeks, but might include such specialties as grilled quail marinated in soy, sake and ginger; grilled New Zealand lamb chops with zinfandel, roasted garlic and pink peppercorns; or other meat and poultry selections ranging in price from $14.95 to $18.95. The seafood choices are chosen specially each day to ensure freshness, and could include Native American-caught sturgeon or Alaskan king salmon topped with two jumbo shrimp. The service at Cafe Max is swift and efficient. Members of the wait staff circulate from table to table making sure that each customer's water glass or coffee cup is full. After dinner, your wait person will bring forth a platter of 10 desserts including peanut butter mousse pie, crème brulée, homemade ice cream, and a variety of cheese cakes and chocolates. Cafe Max serves dinner Wednesday through Saturday only, starting at 5:30 p.m. and continuing through the last seating at 9:30. Reservations are not required, but on Friday and Saturday the restaurant turns away as many as 50 people a night. For something different, try Cafe Max for lunch. The menu includes Day's specialty soups as well as focaccia sandwiches, grilled sandwiches including the Italian Meatball Grinder, daily pasta specials and a half dozen salads. Nothing on the lunch menu tops $6.95.

Fenders
$$$ • 4090 U.S. 93 N., Kalispell
• (406) 752-3000

A fun restaurant with something just a little different. The name of the establishment comes from a pair of red fenders from a 1941 one-ton Ford V8 truck that grace the entryway. The truck was actually used for 20 years on a Kalispell area Hereford ranch, and has stood guard for almost another 20. In the back of the restaurant there are also five booths that are constructed from original bench seats from vintage automobiles. You enter the booths by swinging open the car door. These seats make fine dining a family-friendly experience! As for the food, it includes a cross section of seafood, steaks and pasta, with a little chicken thrown in. Prime rib is a house specialty, and you can expect to leave a bit of the Motherlode serving on your plate. The seafood fettucini is also popular, and features a generous helping of shrimp, scallops and mussels. Try the chocolate mousse afterward to freshen your palate. By the way, this restaurant is conveniently located halfway between Kalispell and Whitefish, so it can be reached from either direction.

Hennessy's Restaurant & Lounge
$$$ • 1701 U.S. 93 S., Kalispell
• (406) 755-6860

This restaurant has been a mainstay of Kalispell dining for more than 30 years. It is located in the Outlaw Inn hotel, and also includes casino and lounge areas. The restaurant is quiet and darkly lit and makes a pleasant spot for an intimate dinner. Lunches tend to be more bustling as business men and women meet here for work and pleasure. On the evening menu, one of the old favorites here (at $14.95) is the Snowgoose, a chicken breast fillet filled with cream cheese and crabmeat and then topped with hollandaise sauce. You can also get such items as Shrimp Louie Salad for $11.95, which features lettuce, spinach, crab, tomato, hard-boiled egg and asparagus with 1,000 Island dressing. The restaurant is noted for its steaks. An unusual entry is The Gunslinger, a bacon-wrapped 6-ounce fillet topped with crab and sauce moutade ($18.95).

The Knead
$$ • 25 Second Ave. W., Kalispell
• (406) 755-7510

This is one of the newest restaurants in Kalispell, but the same crew has been cooking food for several years at Montana Coffee Traders. They moved to this larger location in 1999 because demand just kept growing. It doesn't take long to figure out why. The menu is a unique combination of health food such as tabouli and eggplant along with American deli traditions like the reuben sandwich. The restaurant has been completely remodeled and features a bright modern decor, along with a new deck for limited outdoor seating when in season. The Knead also benefits from one of Montana's new "cabaret liquor licenses," which allow restaurants to serve beer and wine without needing a costly casino license. Music is a common feature on Friday and Saturday nights, with well-known regional performers playing on a small stage, often for little or no cover charge except the price of dinner.

Montana Grill on Flathead Lake
$$$$ • 5480 U.S. 93 S., Somers

This restaurant features fine dining in fine surroundings. The restaurant and bar are housed in a timber-built structure that makes "log home" seem like a synonym for palace. And the views from the restaurant looking out across Somers Bay can't be beat. The menu, meanwhile, is varied and delightful. There are nine appetizers ranging in price from $4.95 to $9.95. Our favorites are the baked artichoke and the Spedini a la Romano, egg-batter-dipped fried mozzarella served with marinara sauce. Seafood entrees are extensive, including stuffed fillet of salmon at $18.95 and rainbow trout at $16.95. For pasta lovers, there is the blackened shrimp alfredo at $17.95. More regional dining can be found with the grilled elk steak, served in burgundy wine and mushroom bordelaise sauce. A 1 3/4 pound rack of baby back ribs runs to $23.95, but is well worth the price for the succulent flavor of the ribs cooked in plum sauce and mesquite smoked. A lighter side menu includes salmon, fettucini, and grilled eggplant. Desserts include flaming bananas for foster or cherries jubilee for two at $7.95.

Northwest Bounty Co.
$$ • 20 N. Main St., Kalispell
• (406) 752-6660

This restaurant is located in Cavanaugh's hotel at the Kalispell Center Mall. It features dining in a spacious atrium that is well-lit and decorated with many living trees. The menu is quite varied, with everything from butternut squash ravioli smothered with wild mushroom sauce and topped with asiago cheese for $11.95 to blackened salmon with fruit salsa for $17.25. There are special value entrees prices as low as $5.75 (a cheese burger) to $9.95 for chicken-fried steak. Lunches are popular here, and a specialty is the Chinese wonton salad that comes with oriental veggies, cashews and chicken stir-fried in teriyaki and sesame sauce and served on a bed of spinach inside a large golden wonton basket. After dinner, you can wander into the Fireside Lounge or across the hall to the Magic Diamond Casino.

Rosario's in Lakeside
$$ • 7125 U.S. 93 S., Lakeside
• (406) 844-2888

Lakeside has many pleasures for the vacationing family, not the least of which is Rosario's restaurant, located on the second floor of an old marina building. Through the lakeside windows, you look out over weathered docks and pilings at Flathead Lake and the Swan and Mission Mountains in the background. Turning back to the restaurant you are looking at Chef Rosario hard at work in the kitchen, keeping customers satisfied with many specials and his standard delights such as veal francaise ($17.95), four sauteed scallops of veal smothered in butter garlic lemon sherry sauce, or pollo alla rollatini ($15.95), chicken cutlets stuffed with prosciutto ham, mushrooms, mozzarella and ground veal in a marsala mushroom sauce. Plus more traditional fare like veal parmesan and fettucine alfredo. There are children's menu offerings that include chicken parmesan, burgers, and raviolli, all for $5.95.

Tiebuckers Pub & Eatery
$$ • 75 Somers Rd., Somers
• (406) 857-3335

Tiebuckers is a restaurant with a history,

literally. The building that houses Tiebuckers in Somers dates back nearly 100 years and was both a depot for the Great Northern Railway and headquarters for the Somers Lumber Co. for many years. It first housed a restaurant in the 1960s and was re-opened as a restaurant by Barry and Julie Smith several years ago. Many of the recipes pay homage to Julie's grandfather, Joe Di Cristina, such as chicken basted in Grandpa's Sauce, an oil and vinegar blend, then barbecued for an hour and steamed to retain natural juices. The 1/2 chicken is $11.25. The establishment is also noted for its pork ribs and combo platters. Dinners include focaccia, soup, salad, and baked potato or pasta of the day. Kids meals are available for those 12 and under. Dinner is served 5-9 PM Tuesday through Saturday. Music can be heard on the weekends sometimes, with jazz piano player Nina Russell performing and telling tales of her career in the big band era.

Nightlife

Finish Line Cocktail Lounge
153 N. Meridian Rd., Kalispell
• (406) 756-9116

The Finish Line is an interesting mix of blue collar, white collar, and no collar. The bar has long been a popular local hangout for businessmen, horse people (the bar is near the county fairgrounds, where horse racing is held every summer during the weekend of the fair and the weekend after), and county workers. The menu is quite varied, and includes popular burgers and steaks, as well as chicken, pasta and other selections. New in the past couple of years is a pretty steady diet of music on the weekends, and the lounge has become a standard place to hear such local blues bands as Blues Cruiser and Big Daddy and the Blue Notes.

Kalispell Bar
110 Main St., Kalispell
• (406) 752-9789

The Kalispell Bar, known affectionately to its many fans as the KB, is located in the Historic Kalispell Grand Hotel complex, which also includes the Alley Connection Restaurant and the Kalispell Casino next door. On

weekends, you have a good chance of hearing a rock band playing here, but the main reason people love the KB is its laid-back devil-may-care attitude. There is a long bar up front, and a half-dozen tall tables lining the opposite wall, so there is lots of socializing, especially during happy hour.

Montana Nugget Casino
740 W. Idaho St., Kalispell
• (406) 756-8100

The Montana Nugget is the perfect place to go if you want to acquaint yourself with the Montana casino lifestyle. The ding-ding-ding of video poker machines hitting the jackpot merges with the sounds of a sports announcer on one of the many television sets, the country tunes coming over the loudspeaker, and the waitresses calling out another order. One side of the large open building is dedicated to dining, but there is plenty of room for gambling, and there's usually a poker game in progress if you want to take your chance at beating some genuine Montana characters at their own game.

Moose's Saloon
173 N. Main St., Kalispell
• (406) 755-2337

Moose's has the reputation of being the one tavern that a visitor to Kalispell must stop in and see. It's the real McCoy, a genuine hangout, with a square bar often surrounded by customers getting to know each other or old friends. It's reminiscent of the bar on the "Cheers" TV show, complete with lots of colorful characters who are the regulars. The table area is dark and moody and the floor is covered with sawdust and peanut shells, since Moose's provides complimentary nuts to munch on with your drinks. Lots of folks in the Flathead Valley consider the pizza at Moose's to be the best in the area, and maybe the state. You can also get a variety of sandwiches, burgers and other munchies from the kitchen. Next door at Moostly Moose's, you can pick up a souvenir T-shirt.

Outlaw Inn Comedy Club
1701 U.S. 93 S., Kalispell
• (406) 755-6860

Every Friday night, the Outlaw Inn's lounge

turns into a comedy club as some of the brightest talents in the West visit Montana. There's a $6 cover charge per person, and of course since it's a bar, there's no admission for those under 21. But if you enjoy those comedy shows on cable TV, you will no doubt get a kick out of the off-color humor that prevails at this kind of club. Visiting comedians enjoy making fun of the rustic folkways of Montana, but the crowd often gets even by making fun of the urban insanity of Los Angeles, Seattle and other home cities of these comics. The Outlaw Inn lounge also features a casino, and you can get excellent food from the Hennessy's kitchen as well.

Shopping

Depot Park Square
Junction of Main Street and First St. E., Kalispell

This new complex of stores in three buildings is a delightful alternative to mall shopping, and it's just across the street from the Kalispell Center Mall, so it also makes a nice complement. Some of the stores here are The Athlete's Foot shoe store featuring gear for the sports-minded, Golf USA, a women's fashion shop called Steals, the Avalanche Creek coffee house featuring soup and sandwiches as well as a wide variety of espressos, and Boundaries Clothing featuring sportswear. The pedestrian mall quality of the three buildings and the easy parking has helped to bring a fresh attitude to downtown Kalispell, where many other interesting shops also await you, including Books West, just across First Street from here.

Finely Done & Kembali Imports
154 Second Ave. EN, Kalispell
• (406) 257-1418 and (406) 752-0905

Finely Done and the adjoining Kembali Imports are almost certain to make a sale if you stop in for a visit. Both stores are located in an old Kalispell home and the next-door annex. Finely Done features a complete line of giftware, including pottery, dishes, prints, soaps, kitchen gadgets and utensils, and linens. Next door at Kembali Imports, the mood shifts from modern crafts to New Age aura.

Incense is always burning and world music always playing at Kembali. There is a wide variety of women's clothing imported from Third World countries, as well as a large selection of handmade jewelry. A large sitting area is available for husbands, and there is a basket full of toys available for children to occupy themselves while mom is poring over the selections.

Kalispell Center Mall
20 N. Main St., Kalispell
• (406) 752-6660

It's not as big as the malls in many larger urban areas, but Kalispell Center Mall has three dozen stores to keep tourists and locals busy for more than an afternoon. The anchor stores are J.C. Penney and Herberger's, with an emphasis at both stores on clothes for all family members. Among the smaller stores that are popular are the Cherry Tree, which features eclectic style accessories and modern fashions for women; the Country Cupboard, with kitchen gadgets and necessities for sale in all price ranges; Teacher's Pet, with innovative toys for children; and International Design, which has gifts for all occasions including toiletries, crafts, and candles. There is no food court per se, but food is available at several stands such as Orange Julius, Dairy Queen, Wolfgang's Famous Frankfurters, and Anna's Greek Gyros. A distinctive feature of the mall is that it is connected to the Cavanaugh's hotel, so you can stay at the hotel by night, shop by day, and eat at either the mall or the Cavanaugh's restaurant, depending on your mood. For many, a perfect vacation.

Peppers & Pasta
8 First St. E., Kalispell
• (406) 257-4478

Some like it hot, and owners Kris and Debbie at Peppers & Pasta certainly qualify. This store specializes in hot sauces, salsas, barbecue sauces, chiles, spices, and anything else that's hot. You'll find Thai, Cajun, Creole, and Mexican specialties, along with a complete line of gifts, clothing accessories, aprons, kitchenware, books and much more. Visit on-line at http://www.cyberport.net/peppers&pasta/ for details of the Hot Sauce

Shop indoors and enjoy the sunshine at Kalispell Center Mall.

of the Month Club, Salsa of the Month Club, and other clubs that arrange for a sampling of stuff to reach you on a regular basis. Debbie also has a passion for pasta, so there are lots of pastas and pasta sauces available, too.

Sportsman & Ski Haus
Junction of U.S. 2 and U.S. 93, Kalispell
• (406) 755-6484

If you've come all the way to Montana, you may as well enjoy the great outdoors and that's where Sportsman & Ski Haus comes in. This is the department store of sporting goods stores in the Flathead, with thorough inventories for hunting and fishing, camping, and water sports, as well as an extensive line of footwear and outdoor clothing. You can get everything you need for your family expedition here, down to and including the live bait.

Strawberry Patch
404 W. Center St., Kalispell
• (406) 752-2660

This popular shopping spot was located in the Gateway West Mall for many years, but when that establishment closed recently, the Strawberry Patch send out a runner and wound up in a beautiful new facility across the street from Kalispell Center Mall. Strawberry Patch is a quintessential gift store, carrying a line of merchandise that ranges from collectibles such as Beanie Babies to local items like jellies and sauces from the Bigfork Inn, not to mention the popular selections of fudge. And if you wish Christmas was every day, you'll find the corner nook of decorations and Christmas collectibles to your fancy. There are also many brightly colored dishes and coffee cups and decorative items of every type. Prices range from hundreds of dollars for a small hand-made tabletop fountain to a dollar or two for incense or candles. And women shoppers will want to stop at the other end of this new mini-mall to visit Loretta's, which features fashions and accessories for working women.

Western Outdoor
48 Main St., Kalispell
• (406)756-5818

If you have a little buckaroo or cowgirl in tow, you might want to head on over to the Western Outdoor Store for lots of genuine western wear souvenirs that will last for years. There's a complete lineup of clothing for little pardners, from boots to cowboy hats, and there's rarely been a little one who can resist a shiny belt buckle. There are plenty of western fashions for men and women as well. This sizable store also includes a rack of cowboy hats for grownups that runs clear around the store. Up on the walls there are also hundreds of boards featuring genuine cow brands used by ranchers across Montana, some dating back into the 1800s. The store phased out saddles a few years ago, but you can still buy a full line of cowboy accessories here such as halters, bridles, saddle pads, spurs and even bullwhips. When you've spent enough money on wrangling gear, you can mosey on down the stairs to the Kalispell Antiques Market, which is located on the lower level.

For a small town, Whitefish offers a surprisingly big variety of places to stay, to eat, and to shop. It's a very busy place both winter and summer; fall and spring are quieter times to visit.

Whitefish

Originally a railroad and logging town, today Whitefish is a resort community whose residents enjoy small-town charm, many big-city amenities, and world-class outdoor recreation. The town sits at the northwest end of the Flathead valley, just south of the Whitefish Range and Big Mountain and at the foot of 7-mile-long Whitefish Lake. The town itself is a busy retail and business center that has maintained its low-key character: you'll feel at ease strolling in and out of small shops or chatting with the staff in restaurants. In the summer, flower gardens and hanging baskets ornament virtually every corner and shop; in the winter, holiday decorations add color and warmth to seasonal festivities. And Whitefish folks like to do things—just watch the vehicles going down the road. Whether they're pulling a horse trailer or snowmobiles, or carrying skis, bikes, or boats, you'll get the idea pretty quickly: Whitefish is a great place to play.

For a small town, Whitefish offers a surprisingly big variety of places to stay, to eat, and to shop. It's a very busy place both winter and summer; fall and spring are quieter times to visit. The downtown area itself is quite compact and easy to explore on foot: within a few blocks you'll find everything from the Stumptown Historical Society to the new city library and cultural arts center, small retail shops and restaurants, standard services (post office, fax, banks, etc.), and city parks. You'll find other lodgings, shops, restaurants, and larger resorts associated with Big Mountain or the golf courses, for example, but even these are only minutes from town.

Accommodations

Price Code

Lodging code per night for two people:

$	Less than $85
$$	$86 to $115
$$$	$116 to $150
$$$$	$151 and more

Hotels and Motels

Lazy Bear Lodge
$$ • 6390 South Highway 93, Whitefish • (406) 862-4020 or (800) 888-4479

Formerly a Comfort Inn, the Lazy Bear Lodge offers standard motel accommodations with one difference: kids will love the indoor swimming pool and 90-foot corkscrew waterslide. And while they're splashing and having a great time, adults can soak in one of two hot tubs—so there's something for everyone. The sixty-six rooms have color cable TV with HBO, individual heat and air conditioning. Non-smoking rooms, a handicapped equipped unit, and drive-up ground floor rooms are available. Pets are welcome (and there's a "pet comfort area")—please inquire about the pet policy. Suites may be reserved for larger groups, and some include family-sized kitchens.

Room rates for two people vary from $59 to $119 per night depending on the season. For more information, please phone, or visit the website at www.whitefishmt.com (click on lodging).

Pine Lodge
$$ • 920 Spokane Avenue, Whitefish
• (406) 862-7600 or (800) 305-7463

The Pine Lodge is neatly wedged between Highway 93 (Spokane Avenue) and the Whitefish River...which means that, while it's on the main road into town, the areas at the back of the lodge—the lobby, swimming pool, deck, and many rooms—overlook the willows and water. And should you opt for a one-bedroom suite, you'll be pleasantly surprised by the northern view as well—these rooms face Big Mountain.

The Pine Lodge offers a wide range of rooms, all including remote-controlled television, telephone, and bath. Standard rooms run from $52.00 per night in the off-season to $100.00 per night during summer. Deluxe rooms, which include a private balcony, run $52.00 to $110.00 per night. Minisuites, with one king or two queen beds, include a microwave, refrigerator, wet bar, and private balcony, and cost $79.00 to $125.00 per night. One-bedroom suites include all the above, plus a gas fireplace, VCR, separate bedroom, and private spa. All wood furnishings are handcrafted. Rates run from $140 to $150 per night. Please inquire about the executive suite if you are interested.

The Pine Lodge has an exercise room, indoor/outdoor heated swimming pool, outdoor hot tub, guest laundry, and a meeting room for up to fifty people. Complimentary continental breakfast is served each morning. Non-smoking rooms and floors are available. For more information, please phone, or visit the website at www.thepinelodge.com. The Pine Lodge is a part of the Quality Inn chain.

Rocky Mountain Lodge
$$ • 6510 Highway 93 South, Whitefish
• (406) 862-2569 or (800) 862-2569

Just opened in 1995, Rocky Mountain Lodge is the newest hotel in Whitefish. Its seventy-nine rooms include Executive Rooms and Mini-Suites, which offer a king bed and gas fireplace, wet bar with small refrigerator, sink, and microwave, jacuzzi or garden tub, a

www.insiders.com
See this and many other
Insiders' Guide
destinations online.
Visit us today!

sofa bed, and fax/modem port. Standard rooms feature king- or queen-size beds, and twelve annex rooms are located in a motel-style detached building where you can drive right up next to the room.

Other amenities include an outdoor heated pool and jacuzzi, laundry, an exercise room, and meeting and banquet facilities. A complimentary deluxe continental breakfast is available for guests each morning.

Room rates vary from a high of $159.00 per night for Mini-Suites to as little as $49.00 per night for annex rooms, depending on the season. Please inquire for rates and availability. For more information, please phone, or visit the website at www.rockymtnlodge.com.

Bed and Breakfasts

The four B&Bs listed here are all private homes which their owners have now opened up to guests. Do see also Good Medicine Lodge and Hidden Moose Lodge (under "Resorts, Guest Ranches, and Lodges"), which are small inns offering the same personal attention and full breakfast you would expect of a bed and breakfast inn.

Crenshaw House
$$ • 5465 Highway 93 South, Whitefish
• (406) 862-3496 or (800) 453-2863

Your hostess, Anni Crenshaw-Rieker, is a fourth-generation Montanan, and you'll find her personal touch throughout Crenshaw House—whether in the baby grand piano in the living room, the historic photos that decorate the walls, or the huckleberry popovers and coffee or tea at your door each morning. She'll make you welcome in this comfortable home which is yours to enjoy—except for the office and laundry room (if you come into the office, Anni says, you have to work!). In addition to the large living room, Crenshaw House has a family room, complete with games, satellite TV, VCR, video library, and bar stocked with wine, beer, and sodas. Both living room and family room have gas fireplaces for

Credit: Donnie Sexton, Travel Montana.

Charming and historic — downtown Whitefish.

warmth and atmosphere. Crenshaw House sits in open meadows and has a back deck with lawn chairs as well as a hot tub for guests.

You'll also find Crenshaw House very "kid-friendly." Children are welcome in many ways: while adults are treated to a four-course breakfast, kids will delight in decorated Mickey Mouse waffles. The family room has plush carpet and lots of space to set out a game board as well as a good supply of children's videos. There's a swing set in the yard—and lots of yard to run around in. The neighbors have horses...Anni has carrot and apple treats for kids (and adults) to take if they go visiting the four-legged friends next door. And, with advance notice, child care can be arranged for parents who'd like some time on their own.

A Crenshaw House visit includes morning popovers and coffee or tea at your room, a full breakfast in the formal dining room, and afternoon refreshments. Smoking and pets are not permitted. Rates vary from $65 to $145 per night, depending on season, your accom-modation, and length of stay. Crenshaw House is handicap-accessible. For more information, please phone or visit the website at www.whitefishmt.com (click on lodging).

Eagle's Roost

$$ • 400 Wisconsin Avenue, Whitefish, MT 59937
• (406) 862-5198 or (888) 750-6378

A high level of personal service, as well as elegantly appointed rooms, are hallmarks of the Eagle's Roost. Fine crystal, antique furniture, and English bone china complement the luxuries of your own whirlpool bathtub and in-room cable TV with VCR. Guests have their own entrance, and the comfortable sitting room features a gas fireplace and stone hearth. Upstairs you'll find the formal dining room, a deck where breakfast is served in summer, and the living room. Your hosts, Connie and Tony Davis, also display (and sell) artworks from Whitefish's The Gallery, giving guests a view of Glacier Country as seen

---

INSIDERS' TIP

To go or not to go? Find out what conditions are—call (406) 862-SNOW for the Big Mountain snow report, updated daily during ski season at 7 AM through the eyes of local painters. And, as you sip your morning coffee or afternoon wine, you'll soak up the view across the Flathead valley toward Columbia Mountain and the Swan Range. A back deck leads to the hot tub and landscaped back yard—pleasant retreats in summer or winter—and both deer and pheasants have made their appearance here.

Tucked into a hillside and nestled AMONG the pines, the Eagle's Roost is located on the road to Big Mountain. But it's also only a ten-minute walk from downtown Whitefish, so it's an easy stroll into town for dinner or entertainment. Whitefish Lake and City Beach are also only a ten-minute walk away.

When you arise in the morning, you'll find the coffee already on; a four-course breakfast follows in the dining room. After your day's adventures, you'll return to afternoon wine and snacks. And just before bedtime, homemade cookies mysteriously appear...

The Eagle's Roost takes pride in indulging its guests with warm hospitality. Rates run from $75 to $100 per night for two people. Smoking is permitted outdoors only; please inquire about off-season discounts and the pet policy. For more information, please phone, or visit the website at www.eagles-roost.com.

The Garden Wall Inn
$$ • 504 Spokane Avenue, Whitefish, MT 59937
• **(406) 862-3440 or (888) 530-1700**

"Luxurious," "gracious," and "comfortable" are three words that will spring to mind soon after you enter the Garden Wall Inn. This beautifully restored 1920s house is now furnished with period antiques; the attentive but not intrusive service will charm your stay. You'll find a rose decorating the coffee tray at your room each morning, a very civilized half-hour before the scrumptious gourmet breakfast. And after your day's adventures, you might spend some time soaking in a claw-foot tub, then sip sherry and enjoy hors d'oeuvres before the fireplace.

The Garden Wall Inn—named for the Garden Wall, the part of the Continental Divide that runs just north of Logan Pass in Glacier National Park—displays many details that reveal the owners' love of that nearby national park. Historic photos of Glacier, Blue Willow china originally used in the park hotels, first-edition copies of books about the park, even the Audubon prints on the walls all speak of Glacier (the Audubon Society was founded by George Bird Grinnell, probably the single person most responsible for creation of the park). And between owners Mike and Rhonda Fitzgerald and their innkeeper, Chris Schustrom, you'll find a tremendous knowledge of the outdoors, whether you're interested in hiking, skiing, fly-fishing, or kayaking.

They also know the Flathead Valley well, and will be happy to point you in the right direction for shopping, dining, or otherwise exploring. The Garden Wall Inn is located just two blocks from downtown Whitefish, giving you easy access to the town's services and attractions. The inn's five bedrooms range in price from $85 to $125 per night for two people; a suite may be arranged for $175 per night for up to four people. Most rooms have private baths. Pets and smoking are not permitted. For more information, please call, visit the website at www.wtp.net/go/gardenwall , or e-mail garden@digisys.net.

Gasthaus Wendlingen
$$ • 700 Monegan Road, Whitefish, MT 59937
• **(406) 862-4886 or (800) 811-8002**

America is a nation of immigrants—and Montana is no exception. Bill and Barbara Klein are both descended from Germans who entered the United States first on the east coast and then migrated further west. You'll find Gasthaus Wendlingen a fascinating mix of that German heritage and the modern West. German details—from the working cuckoo clock to imported beer steins—complement personal photographs and furniture brought from Wendlingen, Germany, where cousins still live today. Although most the cooking is American-style, special dishes do bring a taste of Europe into the menu as well.

You'll know you're in Montana, though—Gasthaus Wendlingen is located between Haskill Creek and the Whitefish River. Big views open up north to Big Mountain, east toward Bad Rock Canyon and the entrance to Glacier National Park, and south toward

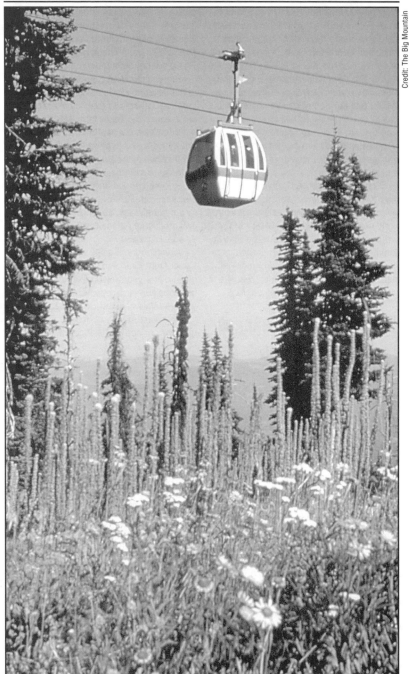

Credit: The Big Mountain

A summer gondola ride at The Big Mountain promises stunning
views and lovely wildflowers.

Blacktail Mountain. A deck overlooks the creek, where you'll enjoy watching ducks and songbirds along the water. The neighboring ranch horses add that western feeling as well.

You'll find the Kleins ready to welcome you to the Gasthaus. A large, bright living room with a river rock fireplace, gracious guest rooms, a steam room (to melt the kinks out after a day of skiing or hiking!), a long covered deck to sit out and admire the views, a full breakfast, and afternoon snacks will make you feel at home—no matter what country your family is from!

Gasthaus Wendlingen is only a ten-minute drive from downtown Whitefish, but its quiet meadows feel like a real retreat from the busy world. Room rates vary from $70 to $115 for two people, depending on season and accommodations. Pets are not allowed; nonsmoking adults are preferred. For more information, please phone, or visit the website at www.whitefishmt.com (click on lodging).

Resorts, Guest Ranches, and Lodges

Big Mountain Ski and Summer Resort

$–$$$ • P.O. Box 1400, Whitefish,MT 59937
• (406) 862-1900 or, for reservations, (800) 858-5439

The Big Mountain was, of course, initially a ski resort—but nowadays it's a good deal more too. Winter visitors still focus on skiing—and, with more than 3,000 acres of skiable terrain, the Big Mountain has something to offer for skiers of every ability. Other activities include tubing, cross-country skiing and skate skiing on the groomed track, and snowcat skiing. And summertime now brings incredible outdoor fun too—hiking, mountain biking, huckleberry picking—as well as live music and other special events (see Outdoor Recreation).

The Big Mountain central reservation office handles reservations for all the lodgings on the mountain. The different facilities cover a wide range of accommodations and prices, and all are available as part of lodging/lift ticket packages. All include a spa or sauna and laundry. Many Big Mountain businesses closely briefly in both the spring and fall, so please be sure to check dates of availability. Prices are per person per night.

Hibernation House. $. An overnight stay at this economy lodge includes a full skiers' breakfast. Shuttle to the ski hill available, or ski to your door. Rates from $32.50.

Big Mountain Alpine Homes. $. These condos, chalets, and duplexes are all within walking distance of the slopes. From $33.75.

Anapurna Properties. $. These studio to 4-bedroom condos and chalets are close to the lifts. From $37.25.

The Edelweiss. $$. These charming condos are located in the heart of Big Mountain Village. From $50.75.

Alpinglow Inn. $$. Ski to your front door at this contemporary inn. The Alpinglow dining room offers very reasonable lunch and dinner specials—and a tremendous view of the Flathead Valley. Rooms from $52.00.

Kristianna Mountain Homes. $$$. Luxurious accommodations located slope-side. From $56.25.

Kintla Lodge. $$$. Brand-new in 1999, the Kintla Lodge offers deluxe condos and shops right at the base of the ski hill. From $56.25.

Kandahar Lodge. $$$. This traditional-style ski lodge features a fine restaurant open for breakfast and dinner (reservations required) in a family atmosphere. Rooms from $62.50.

Big Mountain is a big operation! See the sections on Outdoor Recreation and Attractions for more ideas on exploring this exceptional resort. Please call for more information, or visit the website at www.bigmtn.com.

Gaynor's RiverBend Ranch

$$ •1992 K M Ranch Road, Whitefish, MT 59937
• (406) 862-3802, fax (406) 862-4158

Overlooking a bend in the Stillwater River, Gaynor's RiverBend Ranch offers a unique opportunity to enjoy ranch life in the Montana countryside—yet the four-room suite offers all the amenities of home within a 15-minute drive from Whitefish.

It's hard to explain the peace and beauty of this open valley. Although town is not far away, you'll forget it and your worries completely as you take in the quiet and big views. The river attracts songbirds and waterfowl, and mountain bluebirds nest in boxes along the fence. The ranch is set back from the road, which has very little traffic, and state forest land—with both riding and hiking trails—lies just across the way.

Whether you've spent your day exploring Glacier, skiing Big Mountain, golfing, or otherwise enjoying the area, you'll feel like you're coming home when you return to the RiverBend Ranch each evening. You'll have your own river view to the west—put up your feet and enjoy the sunset! The guest suite has its own private entrance. The kitchen is fully equipped, and coffee, tea, and spices are supplied; the living room includes a queen-size hide-a-bed sofa, a gas fireplace, and satellite TV; the cozy bedroom also has satellite TV; other amenities include phone with voice mail; washer and dryer; gas barbecue; a picnic table by the river; and a selection of books and games.

You may also choose to make the ranch itself the focus of your vacation. Sleeping in and enjoying a cup of coffee by the river is a great way to start the day, but there's plenty of exploring to do here too. Gaynor's RiverBend Ranch offers customized trail rides, tailored to your experience and limited to your own group. During your stay you are welcome to explore the entire ranch property. Its open pastures are home to eleven ranch horses as well as others that are boarded there. Those traveling with their own horses may also board them at the ranch in the spacious stalls and/or large outdoor paddocks. Your host, Don Gaynor, will be happy to help you with your plans.

The guest suite accommodates up to four. Rates vary by season from $75 to $125 per night. Children must be at least 12 years old to go on trail rides. Smoking is not allowed indoors; if you have pets traveling with you, please inquire about the pet policy. For more information please call, or visit the website at www.whitefishmt.com/lodging/gaynor/. The ranch can be reached by e-mail at dgaynor@digisys.net.

Good Medicine Lodge

$$ • 537 Wisconsin Avenue, Whitefish, MT 59937
• (406) 862-5488 or (800) 860-5488; fax (406) 862-5489

"Good Medicine"—you'll find this the perfect prescription, no matter how you take it! Location, interiors, furnishings, breakfast—every detail reflects Good Medicine Lodge's attention to your well-being. Built of cedar timbers, the lodge practically glows with the warmth of wood, accented with fabrics influenced by Native American designs. Lobby and Great Room invite you to curl up and read by the fire, help yourself to freshly baked cookies, or get ready to soak in the hot tub just out the door. In summer, you'll enjoy stepping into the garden or relaxing under the broad covered porches of the L-shaped lodge. And, summer or winter, you'll find a big buffet-style breakfast awaiting you each morning: freshly baked muffins, breads, and cobblers, cereals, granola, yogurt, sliced meats and cheeses, coffee, tea, and juice.

The nine rooms and suites all have private baths, air conditioning, phones, and custom-made log beds. Most rooms have balconies with mountain views. The rooms offer

---

INSIDERS' TIP

Technically, "alpine" refers to the terrain above the treeline; "subalpine" refers to the area right at treeline—where trees grow, but just barely; where conditions like wind, temperature, snowpack, poor quality of soil, or just plain rockiness limit them from colonizing any higher elevation. This means that Logan Pass, for example, is technically subalpine, since stunted subalpine fir trees do grow there. The climate is so tough on them, however, that they are twisted and dwarfed into formations called "krummholz"—German for "crooked wood"—a very good description of trees at treeline!

either queen or twin bed arrangements, and the largest suite can sleep five. The master suite, which has its own loft, gas stove, whirlpool tub, Swiss shower, and balcony, recently earned Good Medicine the description of one of America's ten "most romantic inns." One room is handicap-accessible. In addition, the lodge has a ski room with boot and glove driers as well as a guest laundry.

Owners Christopher Ridder and Susan Moffitt have taken Good Medicine one step further as well. The lodge is a member of the Green Hotel Association and is wheelchair accessible, smoke free, and proud to reduce, reuse, and recycle wherever possible in the effort to keep Montana beautiful.

Rates range from $85 to $115 per night for two people, depending on room and season. With just nine rooms, Good Medicine might be listed as a B&B as well. Suites vary from $145 to $195 per night. The lodge is located about 6 blocks north of downtown Whitefish on the road to Big Mountain. Good Medicine Lodge does close for the months of November and April. For further information, please call, visit the website at www.wtp.net/go/goodrx , or e-mail goodrx@digisys.net.

Grouse Mountain Lodge
$$$ • 2 Fairway Drive, Whitefish
• (406) 862-3000 or (800) 321-8822

Here is lodging in the grand style—everything you could think of, and more. With its river rock fireplaces, warm polished wood, and delicate elk-antler chandeliers, you'll know you're in Montana. The 145 rooms are stylish and comfortable, and some include jacuzzis, kitchens, or loft bedrooms. The lodge restaurant (see Logan's Bar and Grill under "Restaurants") is one of the finest in town and is open for breakfast, lunch, and dinner. The Whitefish Lake Golf Course is out your door; in the winter its fairways are groomed for cross-country and skate skiing. And the lodge has its own indoor swimming pool and hot tubs.

Grouse Mountain Lodge also has conference facilities for groups as large as 300 people. Banquet and catering services will provide just the level of support you need, whether that's coffee and rolls or a sit-down dinner.

Room rates vary by season from $72.00 to $140 per night for two people. Be sure to inquire about both ski and golf packages. For more information, please phone, or visit the website at www.grmtlodge.com.

Hidden Moose Lodge
$$ • 1735 East Lakeshore Drive, Whitefish
• (406) 862-6516 or (888) SEE MOOSE

The Great Room's log-framed cathedral ceiling and massive fireplace made of local rock bespeak the rustic yet warm feeling of the Hidden Moose Lodge. Antique skis adorn the walls for an outdoorsy feel; a mix of colors, patterns, and textures in the fabrics and custom-made log furniture add richness to the interior of all the lodge rooms. The Hidden Moose Lodge is built into the side of a hill and surrounded by pine, birch, and aspen trees. Every once in a while the "hidden moose" emerges for a stroll—and you may also see deer and the occasional bear wandering behind the lodge. But if the wilderness is at your backyard, civilization makes its presence known too—terraced rock gardens and hanging flower baskets brighten the entrance all summer long.

Your hosts, Kim and Kent Taylor, have

INSIDERS' TIP

Greg and Lori Shannon of Whitefish run Traveling Tots, Inc. a business that rents baby equipment to vacationers. Strollers, backpacks, swings, cribs, car seats, toys, and much more are available for delivery to all areas. Stop in at their location in Whitefish 276 Mallard Loop, Whitefish, 59937 or call (406) 862-3975 or toll free at 888-862-3976. If you ever thought checking the car seat or port-a-crib was a hassle but knew your vacation without it would be ruined, check with Traveling Tots before you go. Ask for anecdotes of happy customers or weird requests.

designed their lodge with all the comforts in mind. Many rooms have their own entrance, and quite a few have Jacuzzi tubs. All have their own private deck, private bath, and phone, cable TV, and VCR. Breakfast is hearty—most guests say they don't need lunch! Afternoon refreshments include wine, cheese, and non-alcoholic beverages. Guests are invited to use the lodge mountain bikes and canoe as well.

The Hidden Moose Lodge is located on the road to Big Mountain, 1.5 miles out of downtown Whitefish. With just eight rooms, the Hidden Moose can also be described as a B&B. Rates for two people range from $79 to $125 per night, depending on room size and AMENITIES. Smoking is allowed outside only; pets are allowed with prior approval. For further information, please call, visit the website at www.wtp.net/go/hiddenmoose, or e-mail seemoose@digisys.net.

North Forty Resort
$$ • Box 4250 • 3765 Highway 40 West, Whitefish, MT 59937
• (406) 862-7740 or (800) 775-1740

What could be "more Montana" than staying in a log cabin of your own? The tall pines at North Forty shelter twenty-two log cabins that combine rustic decor with modern amenities. Each of these newly built cabins has a spotless and fully equipped kitchen, gas fireplace, and its own porch, picnic table, and grill. An open-air hot tub and sauna building is centrally located. The cabins are arranged in small groups, so that North Forty would also make the perfect location to hold a family reunion or other get-together. And a walking and cross-country ski trail begins at the north end of the property.

The brand-new Snowberry Center, constructed in the same rustic log style, has just opened and is available for groups of 50 to 100 guests. With a full kitchen, large windows, gas fireplace, and large outside patio, it will provide a spacious setting for your family reunion, celebration, or other meeting.

Cabin rates vary from $89 per night for two people to $185 for a cabin that will hold as many as eight. Non-smoking cabins are available. A limited number of pet cabins are available—please inquire when you make your reservation (North Forty has four friendly malamutes in residence!). For more information, please call, or visit the website at www.northforty.com.

Credit: Wayne Mumford, The Big Mountain

Spectacular summer days are common in the Whitefish Range.

Whitefish Lake Lodge Resort and Marina
$$$$• 1399 Wisconsin Avenue, Whitefish
• (406) 862-2929 or (800) 735-8869

Whitefish Lake Lodge makes absolutely the maximum use of its beautiful waterfront location on Whitefish Lake. It is unique among commercial lodgings in being right on the water, and that gives it a special focus. The one-, two-, and three-bedroom condo suites all have private balconies overlooking the lake; and the resort's private beach has a swimming area (as well as an outdoor pool, two spas, and an indoor spa). The full-service marina also operates a boat rental service—try an afternoon picnicking on a pontoon boat! You can also or rent a speedboat for waterskiing, a paddle boat, or canoe. Ski and bike lockers as well as a guest laundry are available.

The luxurious lakeside condo suites all have full-size living rooms, gas fireplaces, fully equipped kitchens with a breakfast bar and dining room, air conditioning, and cable TV. A one-bedroom condo, for example, would rent for $125 per night in value season, $150 in regular season, and $200 in peak season. Two- and three-bedroom condos range then from $170 to $360 per night. Hotel-style rooms are also available and range in price from $65 to $85 per night.

Whitefish Lake Lodge is located on the road to Big Mountain and is about a five-minute drive from downtown Whitefish. Please inquire about ski and other special packages. For more information, please phone, or visit the website at www.wfll.com.

Campgrounds and RV Parks

Tally Lake Campground
$ • Tally Lake, approx. 14 miles west of Whitefish
• Tally Lake Recreation Report (406) 863-5420

Tally Lake is on the Tally Lake District of the Flathead National Forest and the campground is administered by that office. The campground itself is some 14 miles west of town at the far end of the lake. It has 39 sites and 1 group site. The campground is technically open all year, but the Tally Lake Road is not plowed in winter and there is no fee for those who want to snowmobile or ski into the area to camp. Full services, including running water, pit toilets, garbage pickup, and a dock on the lake, become available in mid-May. Trails will be worked and opened in late May or June, depending on snow conditions. Services end September 30, and after that time campers must again pack in their own supplies and pack out their own garbage.

Campground fees are $9.00 per vehicle per night, with $4 extra for each additional vehicle per site. A $3.00 day use fee is charged for others using the area. A covered pavilion which will accommodate up to 100 people can be rented for a $25 fee. For reservations, please call Rocky Mountain Recreation Company at (800) 416-6992.

Whitefish Lake State Park
$ • Just west of town on Highway 93 North: Follow the signs along the road beginning just west of Grouse Mountain Lodge
• (406) 752-5501

This small state park, within a ten-minute drive of downtown, is right on Whitefish Lake. Its tall trees and lakeshore offer a pleasant change of pace for those who want to day-trip or to camp overnight. Picnic tables are close to the lake. A boat ramp and parking for trailers provide access to the water. Dogs are permitted but must be on leash. The day-use fee is $4.00 per vehicle or $1.00 per person for those who bike or walk in.

The twenty-five campsites are scattered throughout the trees a little above the water. A maximum of 6 people and 2 camper units may occupy a site, where space allows. Fires may be made in provided grates only; firewood is available for purchase during the summer months. Fees for the summer season (May–September) are $12 per night, or, for those with a Montana State Parks Passport, $8 per night. Off-season rates (October–April) are $10 per night, or $6 with a State Parks Passport. The maximum stay length is 7 nights. Commercial or large groups require a permit; please call Montana Fish, Wildlife, and Parks at the number above.

Whitefish RV Park
$ • 6404 Highway 93 South, Whitefish
• (406) 862-7275

Nørskman Motel
$ • 6400 Highway 93 South, Whitefish
• (406) 862-5515 or (800) 862-3711

The Whitefish RV Park offers 57 sites, 49 of which have full hook-ups and 19 of which have pull-through parking. This new facility is just off the highway into town, yet is quiet and pleasantly landscaped with trees and grass. A dump station, new restrooms and showers, playground, and laundry will make your stay as convenient as being at home. Pets are welcome and there is a pet walking area. Cable TV hook-ups are available at all sites for free, and telephone hook-ups are available at twenty-five sites. Tent areas are also provided.

The Whitefish RV Park is open 24 hours a day, year-round. The office of the neighboring Nørskman Motel handles check-in and other management concerns for the RV park. Rates for full hook-ups are $20 per night; for partial hook-ups, $18.00 per night; plus $2.50 for each additional person over two people. Weekly and monthly rates are also available. Tent rates are $14 per night, plus $2.50 per person for each person over two people. Dump rate is $3.50 for those not staying in the park, and there is a one-time only fee of $15 for telephone hook-ups (tenant must supply outside line).

For those traveling with a mixed party— some with RVs, others looking for lodging— the Nørskman Motel provides economical lodging right next door to the RV park. The motel has 48 rooms and prides itself on its clean, comfortable accommodations. Rooms include color cable TV and air conditioning; the motel also has an indoor jacuzzi as well as an outdoor heated pool open during the summer. For two people, rates vary by season from $36.00 to $57.00. Non-smoking and handicap-accessible rooms are available.

For further information, please call, or visit the Whitefish RV Park website at www.whitefishrvpark.com or the Nørskman Motel website at www.whitefishmt.com (click on lodging).

And More...

The Non-Hostile Hostel
$ • 300 East Second Street, Whitefish
• (406) 862-7383

Recently renovated from an old Masonic Lodge building, the Non-Hostile Hostel fills a

Credit: Carl Wells, Flathead Convention and Visitors Bureau

The Whitefish Winter Carnival Parade always draws a crowd.

special niche in local accommodations. For those on the move, traveling low-budget, or interested in the social contacts generated by other travelers passing through, the Non-Hostile Hostel is the perfect solution.

The hostel has one private room available, but most hostelers will stay in one of the two dormitories. Bunks rent for $13.00 per night, and dorm lockers are available for $1.50 per night. If you haven't brought your own sleeping bag, bedrolls including towel may be rented for an additional $3.75 per night. The entire hostel, including the bath and shower rooms, is impressively clean; the facility includes a kitchen, coin-operated laundry, internet station (a small fee is charged to check e-mail), common library, TV, and music room—and a massage therapist has an office on the premises.

The hostel is also becoming something of a social center in its own right. The Wrap'n'Roll Café offers baked goods, "wraps"—burritos and burrito-like sandwiches with a variety of fillings—as well as non-alcoholic drinks including espresso. Weekends feature live music.

The Non-Hostile Hostel is located three blocks from Amtrak and one block from the bus depot. Please inquire about group rates and ski packages as well as transportation to Glacier National Park. Alcohol, pets, and smoking are not permitted. For further information, please phone, visit the website at www.ptinet.net/~hostel/ or e-mail hostel@ptinet.net.

Five-Star Rentals
$–$$$$ • 509 East Sixth Street, Whitefish • (406) 862-5994, fax (406) 863-3415

If you're planning to be in the Flathead valley for at least a week—whether it's for your honeymoon, family reunion, or small corporate retreat—you might try a different approach to lodging. Five Star Rentals offers a wide variety of listings, encompassing everything from secluded cabins in the woods to Whitefish Lake homes and condos to mountain retreats. All properties are fully furnished and equipped for a great vacation. Special amenities vary and may include barbecues, decks, fireplaces; docks and canoes at water properties; hot tubs and steam rooms. Every property is unique; some offer five-star views.

Sizes range from cozy one-bedroom cabins to spacious five-bedroom homes, and prices range from $500.00 to $2500.00 per week. Five Star's website, www.fivestarrentals.com, includes photos of properties—it's a good place to check out what's available. Or, for more, information, call or e-mail the office at fivestar@digisys.net.

Restaurants

Price Code
Restaurant price code, for two people exclusive of beverages, tips, and tax:

$	**$10 to $19**
$$	**$20 to $27**
$$$	**$28 to $49**
$$$$	**$50 and more**

Family-Friendly

The Buffalo Café
$ • 516 East Third Street, Whitefish • (406) 862-2833

The Buffalo Café truly is a Whitefish institution. Open only for breakfast and lunch, it's a favorite place for locals to get together and get caught up on what's going on around town. Despite increased competition from newer places in the last few years, the Buffalo remains the place to eat before skiing: its substantial breakfasts—whether a buffalo pie, huevos, or the pancake of the day—stand up to a good day's fun in the snow.

The Buffalo Café is open from 6:30 AM to 2 PM Monday through Friday, from 7 AM to 2 PM on Saturday, and from 9 AM to 2 PM on Sunday. Breakfast entrées generally run between $3.50 and $6.00. Half-orders of some items are available.

Café al Dente
$$$ • The Mountain Mall, Whitefish • (406) 862-3131

This unpretentious and comfortable restaurant competes with Rocco's just north of Kalispell for best Italian restaurant in the Flathead. Its quiet, relaxing atmosphere will put you in a Mediterranean frame of mind as you select from a wide variety of Italian dishes—

beef, veal, seafood, chicken, and pasta, all offered with a choice of sauces. Or try one of several combination plates, which allow you to sample two or three entrées.The house salads are reliably crisp and tasty; the breadsticks are addictive; and the dessert case is almost scary with its array of rich delights.... Dinner portions are generous, so plan accordingly!

Café al Dente is located in the Mountain Mall, on Highway 93 just south of Whitefish. Don't be put off by the mall location: the restaurant has its own entrance and is completely free of mall traffic...and there's lots of parking! Entrées run from $10 to $20; the restaurant also features a children's menu.

The Dire Wolf Pub
$ • 845 Wisconsin Avenue, Whitefish
• (406) 862-4500

The Dire Wolf bills itself as a "place for family and friends," and that's a good description. Its window booths fit six easily, and you can push together a few tables to accommodate an even bigger group. It does have a bar, but kids are welcome to the restaurant, and the atmosphere is comfortable and family-friendly. The Dire Wolf has a full lunch and dinner menu that includes appetizers, soups, salads, burgers (check out the "Stella Blue": bleu cheese and bacon), calzone, and hot and cold sandwiches. Ale-battered halibut and fries, a blackened chicken cajun sandwich, and the Wolf Den Gyros are just a few of the pub's specialties, but many come here for the great pizza—from the Garden Wall and Behemoth pizzas to the American Standard—or create your own.

The Dire Wolf is located on the road to Big Mountain—it's the perfect place to stop on your way down from the slopes, summer or winter. Hours are from 11 AM to 1 AM, Monday through Saturday, and from noon to midnight on Sunday. It is a smoke-free establishment. The Dire Wolf also features live music—see "Night Life," below.

Serrano's
$$ • 10 Central Avenue, Whitefish
• (406) 862-5600

It's true—Whitefish is just south of the border—and you'll find the best Mexican around at Serrano's! The original Serrano's flourishes seasonally in East Glacier, but here in Whitefish they're open all year round, serving "world-famous margaritas," microbrews, and fine Mexican dishes. One look at the menu and you'll see what you're in for—after perusing the list of *sopas, ensaladas,* and *aperitivos,* you'll notice that the entrées are marked with one, two, or three peppers to indicate just how hot they are...

Serrano's is open for lunch and dinner. The menu also includes several *platos americanos* for those more comfortable with the *gringo* selection. Or call in advance for a take-out order (50¢ service charge). Lunch entrées range in price from $5.00 to $8.00; dinner entrées from $7.00 to $15.00.

Truby's
$$ • 115 Central Avenue, Whitefish
• (406) 862-4979

"Truby's Wood-fired Brick Oven Pizza" is the full name of this restaurant located right in downtown Whitefish...and that'll give you an idea of what's going on: exotic pizza. Individual, entrée-size pizzas are the hot item here. Just a sampling of the menu includes Athenian, Aloha, Thai, Veggie Pie, and Rustler pizzas... If Peking Duck (!) pizza sounds a little much to you, you can, of course, "Create Your Own" pizza too. And Truby's also offers calzone, burgers, and a selection of Italian dishes as well as "kid's stuff"—burgers, pizza, or spaghetti of just the right sort for smaller customers.

Truby's is open for lunch from 11 AM to 3 PM, and for dinner from 5 PM to 10 PM, Monday through Saturday; and for dinner from 4 PM to 10 PM on Sunday. Individual pizzas run from $7.00 to $11.00; Italian entrées from $9.00 to $12.00.

Whitefish Lake Restaurant
$$$$ • Highway 93 North, just west of town at the Whitefish Golf Club
• (406) 862-5285

Also known as just "the Golf Course," the Whitefish Lake Restaurant has an authenticity to it that's hard to match. Built in 1936, the rustic, warm dining room's stone fireplace and heavy log beams give it a relaxed yet elegant feel. The service is professional but not fussy. And the food is consistently excellent—the restaurant is known for its prime rib, featured on Friday and Saturday nights, as well as for its seafood. This is a place people go to celebrate special occasions. Be sure to call for reservations—the Golf Course can be busy. Even so, you'll never feel crowded or rushed.

You'll find the restaurant at the Whitefish Golf Club, less than a mile out of town on Highway 93 North as the road heads west toward Eureka. In the winter, look for the two huge evergreens decorated with colored lights from top to bottom. The restaurant is slightly set back from the road. Entrées range from $15.00 to $25.00.

Fine Dining

Logan's Bar and Grill
$$$$ • Grouse Mountain Lodge • 2 Fairway Drive, Whitefish
• (406) 863-4700

Named for William Richard Logan, the first superintendant of Glacier National Park, Logan's Bar and Grill evokes a certain slice of western life. Just as a mountain goat oversees the Grouse Mountain lobby, so an elk keeps his eye on the dining room...as do a flight of pheasants on the far wall. The etched glass panel separating the dining room from the lobby portrays bears wandering in the meadows of Logan Pass. The menu too reflects a leaning toward wildlife: entrées include grilled duck breast, trout, venison, and Alaskan halibut. Whatever you choose, you're sure to enjoy the fine dining and distinctive ambiance of Grouse Mountain Lodge.

Logan's is open for breakfast, lunch, and dinner, from 7 AM to 9 PM Dinner entrées range from $16.00 to $23.00. Reservations are recommended.

Pollo Grill
$$$ • 1705 Wisconsin Avenue, Whitefish
• (406) 863-9400

A relative newcomer to the Whitefish restaurant scene, Pollo Grill has established itself quickly as one of the finest restaurants in town. Grilled chicken, seafood, and steak selections are the restaurant's specialty, and they are served in many ways: from the Spit-roasted Chicken Chimichanga to Potato Gnocchi with a Roasted Red Pepper Sauce to Grilled Pacific King Salmon...there's something special for every palate. The menu includes elegant appetizers and an unusual variety of optional side dishes.

Pollo Grill will also prepare orders to go. You might inquire about the "Pollo" itself—a whole roasted chicken with sauce and two side dishes ($13.95). Entrées range in price from $9.00 to $15.00.

Tupelo Grille
$$$ • 17 Central Avenue, Whitefish
• (406) 862-6136

Cajun style cooking may not be what you expected in Montana...but here it is! And Tupelo Grille (named for Tupelo, Mississippi) is one of the most often recommended restaurants in Whitefish—known for its excellence and the consistently high quality of its dinners. Just walking into Tupelo, you'll enjoy the mix of aromas. The menu features everything from seafood to duck, crawfish, chicken, sausage, and pastas...and each dinner is beautifully presented.

Tupelo Grille opens for dinner at 5:30 each evening. The restaurant is small, and reservations are requested for groups of six or more. Entrées run from $11.00 to $18.00.

And More...

Whitefish Bagel Company
$ • 10 Baker Avenue, Whitefish
• (406) 862-6383

Whitefish may not have *all* the amenities of a big city, but it does have big-city bagels....The Whitefish Bagel Company ("Ruling Bagels") serves up sesame, poppyseed, seven-grain, blueberry, garlic, whole wheat, plain, and cinnamon raisin bagels that can be compared with the best New York or Chicago has to offer. Other flavors—like cranberry—occasionally make the list too. And there's even a drive-up window for those on their way elsewhere...or come inside and sit down. Bagels are the basis for "breakfeast" and lunch too: get yours topped or filled just about any way you can imagine. Pizza, soup, sodas, juices, coffee, espresso, tea, and fruit complete the menu of this very busy establishment.

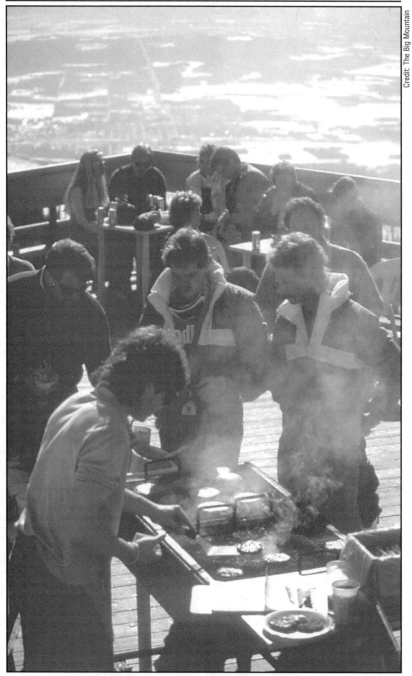

Credit: The Big Mountain

Burgers at the Summit House, a Big Mountain tradition.

The Whitefish Bagel Company is open daily from 7 AM to 2 PM On occasion they serve dinner as well—check the sign outside the building.

Trailhead Deli
$ • 234 East Second Street, Whitefish
• (406) 862-9599

The Trailhead Deli offers you an instant picnic that you can either enjoy on the premises—including two outside tables—or take with you, wherever you're headed for the day. Both hot sandwiches and cold sandwiches come with your choice of pasta salad, potato salad, or cole slaw. Or you can customize your own sandwich by ordering from a selection of ingredients. Espresso or a choice of quite a few cold beverages will complement your meal—but be sure to check out the pies, tortes, and cookies too.

The Trailhead also offers a limited breakfast menu. Winter hours are from 10 AM to 6 PM, Monday through Friday and from 10 AM to 4 PM on Saturday. Summer hours are somewhat more extended. And the Trailhead offers a unique, free delivery service Monday through Friday: within the downtown Whitefish area, if you phone in your order before 11 AM, they'll deliver your lunch to you by noon. Sandwiches range from $2.50 to $4.75.

Hellroaring Saloon and Eatery
$$ • The Big Mountain Ski and Summer Resort
• (406) 862-6364

The Hellroaring Saloon in the Big Mountain Chalet has the kind of ambiance money can't buy...only time, and many contented skiers, will make a ski-hill restaurant feel this way. Old skis grace the paneled walls (you may remember when *you* had bindings like that...), famous skiers have autographed the posters, a fire crackles in the fireplace, and Warren Miller movies play discreetly in the corners of the bar...The nachos are big, the chili is good, the beer is cold and locally brewed. And in the spring, the porch is the place to be for soaking up the sun.

The Hellroaring Saloon and Eatery also operates through the summer months, shutting down briefly during the spring and fall. A full menu of lunch and dinner entrées run from $4.00 to $10.00.

Whitefish Times
$$ • 334 Central Avenue, Whitefish
• (406) 862-2444

The Whitefish Times is a coffee house and restaurant that offers something Whitefish didn't know it was missing 'til it came along: a place to drink coffee, tea, or whatever, and hang out, visit, or read for as long as you want. The coffee house is open from 7 AM to 10 PM Monday through Saturday, and from 10 AM to 5 PM on Sunday. Lunch is served from 11 AM to 3 PM Monday through Saturday, and dinner from 5 PM to 9 PM During those specific hours, a wonderful menu featuring some fairly exotic sandwiches, soups, and quiches is offered. But all the rest of the time, the coffee house is open, serving coffees, espressos, teas, beers, and other beverages as well as delectable baked goodies and desserts. Sofas and comfy chairs invite you to pick up and peruse any of the many local and national newspapers and magazines the coffee house makes available. Upstairs in this remodeled house, you'll find the bedrooms have been converted into reading rooms where you're welcome to make yourself at home for as long as you like. One room is even stocked with a selection of children's games, books, and toys. And should the weather be warm, tables outside let you enjoy the sun while enjoying your afternoon.

Whether it's a rainy day and you want to finish that novel, you've just been to the movies and want to compare notes, or it's time to catch up with a few friends, the Whitefish Times fits the bill. Lunch items run from $3.00 to $6.00; dinners from $6.00 to $10.00.

Nightlife

Whitefish is a hopping town in a low-key sort of way. The Great Northern Bar is a landmark in its own right—you'll hear phrases like "it's just a block from the Northern" when you ask directions. Along with the Bulldog, the Palace, and the Remington—all located on Central Avenue, right downtown—you're sure to find a spot to put up your feet and enjoy a brew. And the Great Northern, Palace, and Remington all occasionally have live music on the weekends. The Dire Wolf Pub, on the road to Big Mountain, is also bringing in musical groups literally from around the world—perhaps African, then reggae, then bluegrass—so be sure to stop by and see what's happening next.

With the completion of the new I.A. O'Shaughnessy Performing Arts Center in 1998, Whitefish now has a central location for performances of all sorts. The O'Shaughnessy is the home of the Whitefish Theatre Company, which stages plays throughout the year, but it also hosts an eclectic series of musical performances. Check the marquee out front for current events.

The Glacier Orchestra and Chorale (see our Arts chapter) presents a full schedule of concerts throughout the school year. Generally the Saturday night performance is at the Whitefish Central School auditorium; call the office at (406) 257-3241 for current information.

The Whitefish Film Society brings movies to the Flathead that otherwise wouldn't make it here—the month's choice is shown at the Mountain Mall Cinema on the last Saturday and Sunday of each month at 1 PM. Check the marquee outside the mall during the previous week for the current listing.

And, in a similar vein, the Whitefish Reading Series brings both nationally recognized and local authors into town for public presentations, with usually about one talk a month during the school year. The best place to check on the current schedule is at BookWorks, located at 110 Central Avenue in Whitefish ([406] 862-4980).

Big Mountain, of course, is the source of a lot of fun...whether it's beers at the Bierstube, the end-of-ski-season furniture races, or summer concerts outdoors. Give the Mountain information center a call at (406) 862-1900.

And, last but not least—something you won't find too many other places. Late October is the off-season for the Flathead Valley, but if you do happen to be in town you'll find yourself in the midst of an incredible event: Halloween, Whitefish-style. As in other communities, you'll see the kiddies out trick-or-treating in the late afternoon. But Whitefish takes Halloween seriously: later that night, head downtown. Halloween is a huge adult party. You won't recognize anyone, that's for sure—many adults come in full head-to-toe costumes. Be sure to pick up at least a witch hat or a big nose—you'll want to feel a part of the fun!

Shopping

You'll enjoy strolling through Whitefish shops, whether you're window shopping or in search of that perfect gift. Whitefish has a

Credit: The Garden Wall Inn

Whitefish bed and breakfasts offer charming accommodations.

compact, functional downtown, where you'll find everything from a hardware store to an auto dealership to fairly upscale boutiques. What follows is just a sampling of shops that are well worth browsing through.

Artistic Touch
209 Central Avenue
• (406) 862-4813

Artistic Touch features the work of local artists and craftspeople. You'll appreciate the elegant jewelry, distinctive ceramics and painting, and fine decorative objects. This is a great place to look for gifts.

BookWorks
110 Central Avenue
• (406) 862-4980

Bookworks is an independently owned bookstore. Front tables feature local writers, books focusing on the West and western issues, and current best-sellers. The bookstore also has an excellent selection of children's books. And be sure to check the front doors for posters featuring upcoming events of cultural interest.

Imagination Station
137 Central Avenue
• (406) 862-5668

If you've discovered your child's favorite beanie baby got left at home...here's the place to go. The Imagination Station carries all sorts of great toys, games, you-name-it...and adults will enjoy looking around as much as kids.

Lakestream Fly Fishing Shop
15 Central Avenue
• (406) 862-1298

Lakestream is just what you'd expect of a fly fishing shop in Montana...all the gear you can imagine and knowledgeable staff as well. Even non-fisherfolk will enjoy strolling through Lakestream, which has a nice selection of outdoor clothing and a comfortable ambiance.

Sage & Cedar
214 Central Avenue
• (406) 862-9411

Sage & Cedar is a fun place to spend some time. The shop specializes in bath supplies—soaps, shampoo, lotions, oils, and so on. But here's the twist: you can have your own combinations mixed for you. As you walk in, there's a rack where you can smell the various scenting oils—from standards like rose, gardenia, and lavender to "western" favorites like sage, "Montana morning," or rain, to some fun food smells—try a whiff of chocolate or pear! Now you choose what sort of base you want scented—and suddenly you can have rose shampoo, sage hand lotion, and chocolate bubblebath...fun for gifts, and also for yourself.

Sportsman and Ski Haus
Mountain Mall
• (406) 862-3111

Sportsmand and Ski Haus is now the major source for most outdoor gear in Whitefish. You'll find national brands in outdoor clothing, footwear, and equipment for everything from boating to skiing and back.

Third Street Market
Third & Spokane
• (406) 862-5054

This bright little market earns a mention for the change of pace it brings to Whitefish. This health food store offers a variety of organic, locally grown, and bulk groceries. It also has a big section of vitamins and other supplements as well as books on related topics.

Do take your time to stroll around... downtown Whitefish also offers services such as banks, fax, post office, UPS and other delivery services, a brand-new public library, copy and print shops.

This little community sits at the northeast corner of the Flathead Valley, where the Flathead River flows out of the mountains through Bad Rock Canyon.

Columbia Falls and the U.S. Highway 2 Corridor

Columbia Falls is the "Gateway to Glacier," and you'll find this is true in many respects. This little community sits at the northeast corner of the Flathead Valley, where the Flathead River flows out of the mountains through Bad Rock Canyon. Since both U.S. Highway 2 and the railroad follow the river valley, if you're traveling into Glacier from west of the Continental Divide, you will almost certainly pass through this little town.

Driving through Columbia Falls, you may notice that there's no natural waterfall here. At least two different stories exist to explain the town's name: the more interesting one has to do with the expansion of the Great Northern Railway. As investors began buying up land along the projected route, they anticipated that J. J. Hill would put the next depot west of Belton (West Glacier) at a town then known as Columbia, Montana. On hearing of the land rush, in a fit of perversity Hill decided to have the next depot at Whitefish, and turned to his employees and roared, "Columbia falls!"

While the railroad may not have chosen Columbia Falls for its operations, other major industries have. Both the Columbia Falls Aluminum Company (CFAC) and Plum Creek Timber Company (see the story about Plum Creek House B & B) employ many people

here. Tourism is growing as an industry here too—many visitors choose to stay in this part of the valley because of its easy access to Glacier National Park. And so more restaurants and accommodations are springing up each year.

The U.S. Highway 2 corridor is a scenic drive in its own right. Leaving Columbia Falls and heading east, you'll start by driving through Bad Rock Canyon. Take a few moments to pull over at Berne Park along the cliffs and read the roadside markers about the wilderness and this old, old route through the mountains. The road is right by the water for a few minutes; soon you'll cross the bridge over the South Fork of the Flathead River—water running out the Hungry Horse Dam (see Attractions) from the Hungry Horse Reservoir. As you drive through Coram, you'll get your first glimpse of the peaks along Lake McDonald: Stanton Mountain appears briefly right over the highway. Once you reach West Glacier, U.S. Highway 2 follows the Middle Fork of the Flathead River through a beautiful gorge and valley up to the Continental Divide and out onto the Great Plains (see the scenic loop drive described under Attractions). You'll find lots to explore all along the way.

Within this Columbia Falls and U.S. Highway 2 Corridor section, businesses are listed by category, beginning with those in Columbia Falls and then from west to east, as if you were driving the highway from Columbia Falls to East Glacier.

Accommodations

Accommodation Rates

Keep in mind that some rates are based on availability. The average nightly rates for two adults at the hotels and motels listed in this section are indicated by a dollar sign ($) ranking in the following chart. Also, the hotels and motels in this chapter accept all or most major credit cards.

$	Less than $85
$$	$86 - $115
$$$	$116 - $150
$$$$	$151 and up

Hotels and Motels

Glacier Park Super 8
$ • 7336 U.S. Highway 2 East, Columbia Falls
• (406) 892-0888 or (800) 800-8000

You may think all Super 8's are alike—but walk into the lobby at this one! The entrance displays a remarkable collection of mounted animals—if you didn't see it in the woods, you'll probably find it here.

But, as across the country, Super 8 sup-plies clean, comfortable rooms for travelers at a nominal price. The thirty-two rooms here include some special rooms with Jacuzzis or kitchenettes. Both non-smoking and handicap accessible rooms are available.

The motel includes a spa, copy machine, fax, and meeting room; all rooms have their own television with HBO, ESPN, and DISNEY channels. Complimentary continental breakfast is served each morning. Room rates range from $43.00 in the winter to $83.00 in the summer for two people per night, depending on the size of the room and included amenities.

The Glacier Highland
$ • U.S. Highway 2 East, West Glacier
• (406) 888-5427 or (800) 766-0811

The Glacier Highland has undergone some major renovations in the last few years—if you stayed here ten years ago, it's time to do it again. For those making their first trip to the area, the Highland provides a great base for exploring all that the area has to offer. It's located right at the west entrance to Glacier National Park, with easy access to hiking, rafting, horseback riding, and everything else along Going-to-the-Sun Road as well as Amtrak and Highway 2. In the evening you'll want to come home, mellow out in the hot tub, have dinner at the restaurant, and head for your queen-size bed. Knotty pine panels the rooms, giving a warm glow to these very affordable lodgings.

All rooms have satellite TV. The summer rate for a room with one queen-size bed is $59.00; two queen beds, $69.00; and two queen beds and a twin, $75.00. Winter rates

INSIDERS' TIP

Wolves were once the most widely distributed animal in North America, but were exterminated throughout much of the continent. In Montana, the last wolf was shot in 1930. Although occasionally individual animals wandered through the state, not until 1986 was there pack—or family—activity here again. In that year, a female wolf crossed south over the border from Canada and gave birth to a litter of pups in Glacier National Park. It was the beginning of a naturally occurring recolonization of the area that continues to this day. Your best chance of seeing—or hearing—wolves is up the North Fork of the Flathead River. A fair number of people will see tracks in this area; some will hear the wolves howling, and a very few lucky folks will actually see them.

are even less; please inquire. The Glacier Highland also handles car rentals during the summer months. For more information, please call, write, or visit the website at www.cyberport.net/resort

Bed and Breakfast Inns

Park View Inn
$–$$ • P.O. Box 567, 904 Fourth Avenue West, Columbia Falls
• (406) 892-PARK

"Victorian country" says it all—the lilacs and flowering trees, the lace curtains, antiques, even the teapot collection all fit perfectly with this graceful 100-year-old home. You'll find a perfect fit too, because the Park View Inn includes not only the two suites and two rooms in the house, but also two cabins and a honeymoon cottage on the property.

www.insiders.com
See this and many other **Insiders' Guide** destinations online.
Visit us today!

Downstairs, the house includes a living room and dining room open to the guests as well as "Granny's Room"—complete with rocker—and "Grandpa's Room" with its high ceiling and vintage details. Upstairs are the Rose Suite and Garden Suite, each with one bedroom, a kitchen, living area, and shared bath. A full breakfast is served each morning for these guests.

The Park View Inn has a large back yard where you can play volleyball, croquet, or pitch horseshoes—or just sit back and relax. Across the lawn you'll find the Native American Cabin, which sleeps 4, and the Western Cabin, which sleeps 6, each appropriately decorated. These cabins have a kitchen, living room, and bath; breakfast is not included—but the Sunrise Bakery is just next door.

Last but not least—the Park View Honeymoon Cottage. This tiny cottage is big on the inside, and would be the perfect hideaway for two just wanting to leave the world behind. It has its own complete kitchen with china service, a charming living room, and a bedroom suite that includes the bedroom, bath, and an adjoining jacuzzi room. This is a honeymoon cottage indeed—a wonderful place to come back to after a great day outdoors.

The Park View Inn is kid-friendly too. In addition to its own spacious grounds, the Pinewood Park is just across the street with a swimming pool (summer only), basketball court, playground, and picnic tables. Please inquire about the pet policy. Smoking is not permitted in the buildings. Rates range from $59.00 per night for Granny's and Grandpa's Rooms (each with one double or queen bed) to $69.00 for the two suites, all including breakfast. The two cabins rent for $75.00 per night. The honeymoon cottage rents for $110.00 per night without breakfast, or for $120.00 per night including breakfast. For more information, please phone, write, e-mail halls@digisys.net or visit the website at http://www3.bcity.com/parkviewinn/.

Plum Creek House
$$ • 985 Vans Avenue, Columbia Falls
• (406) 892-1816 or (800) 682-1429

If a spectacular view of mountains, valleys, and a wild river is your idea of Montana, Plum Creek House has it. This B & B sits high atop a bluff above the Flathead River as it leaves Bad Rock Canyon and heads into the Flathead Valley. Columbia Mountain dominates the view, and you can see east up the canyon to peaks in Glacier National Park.

Plum Creek House will introduce you to local history as well. D. C. Dunham operated Plum Creek Timber in Minnesota—near Plum Creek—but because of labor troubles moved his whole operation to Montana in 1946. So many Minnesotans came with him that part of town was called "Little Bemidji." Dunham prospered. On his marriage, his new wife didn't want to live over the office, so he built Plum Creek House in 1957 at this magnificent location. Plum Creek Timber Company is still a major employer in Columbia Falls today, and you'll see Dunham's portrait as you enter Plum Creek House.

Once the Dunham home, Plum Creek House is now a splendid bed and breakfast. The six guestrooms offer a variety of arrangements, including a family suite and a suite

Credit: Plum Creek House

Visiting a bed and breakfast means being right at home.

complete with kitchen. The 600 feet of riverfront property give ample room for balcony, deck, swimming pool, and Jacuzzi. Your host, Caroline Stevens, provides a full, hot, all-you-can-eat breakfast each morning on *your* schedule. The formal dining room has the full view of the river—ask her about Chair #1! In summer you'll want to enjoy breakfast on the covered porch.

All rooms have queen beds, private bath, phone, TV, VCR, and access to the video library. Smoking is allowed outdoors only. All rooms are $75.00 per night for two people between September 15 and June 1; between June 1 and September 15 they range from $105.00 to $150.00 per night. For more information please phone, write, e-mail plumcreek@in-tch.com, or visit the website at www.wtp.net/go/plumcreek.

Bad Rock Country B&B
$$$–$$$$ • 480 Bad Rock Drive, Columbia Falls
• (406) 892-2829 or (800) 422-3666

Your hosts, Jon and Sue Alper, invite you to enjoy this elegant Big Sky home. Bad Rock Country B & B sits on open meadows framed with towering pines, and every window offers huge views to the Swan and Whitefish mountain ranges.

Beautifully appointed with antiques dat-

ing back to the 1870s, the main house is full of wonderful details that make every room inviting. The bedrooms are large; one has its own balcony for sunset views. The living room offers a fireplace and comfortable sofas and chairs for reading or spending time with other visitors. Many guests to Bad Rock come to explore Glacier National Park, so the living room also houses a collection of books on the park. Jon has a special interest in grizzly bears, and you'll find lots to read about that remarkable local resident too. Downstairs you'll find a "gathering room" with satellite TV and a guest bar stocked with juice, wine, beer, and snacks.

A little back from the main house across the lawn, you'll find Bunny Junction—the two new log buildings with a rustic feel that complements the turn-of-the-century elegance of the house. These four rooms, each named for a lake in Glacier National Park, feature handmade lodgepole pine furniture, gas fireplaces, and large private baths. Each has its own entrance.

A full breakfast is included with all rooms. Breakfast is hearty—you'll be treated to some of Sue's creations such as Grizzly Big Bite (eggs, cheese, and chorizo served on a jalapeño biscuit), wild rice-sausage quiche, or Montana potato pie. Guests have enjoyed her breakfasts so much that she's compiled a

Mountain Goats and Bighorn Sheep

Looking for animals is a great pastime while visiting Glacier, and with just a little effort you're almost certain to see mountain goats. "Goat" is something of a misnomer; these animals are more closely related to the chamois of Europe than to any domestic goat. They can look ragged in the early summer, when they are shedding last winter's extra fur, but by August or so they will be sparkling white with their new, trim summer coats. Some Native Americans called them the white buffalo. Even today, mountain goats sometimes trigger reports of polar bears at Logan Pass!

A symbol of the mountains (and of the Great Northern Railway), the goat is perfectly adapted to its high mountain home. Its hooves are sharp on the rim, for good purchase in soft rock and snow, but they are spongy on the inside, giving the goat traction on hard, flat rock. Its shoulders are massive, allowing it to climb and descend slopes approaching almost 90 degrees vertical. Its fur is dense, with an outer layer for protection from rain

and snow and an inner layer for insulation. Goats live in the cliffs which are their safety—few predators can follow them along the steep faces and narrow ledges that they traverse with such apparent ease. When winter comes, they may move to lower, lee-side cliffs, but they continue to prefer the steep terrain. With the summer grasses gone, goats lick lichens from the rocks with tongues as rough as sand paper: as one naturalist liked to teach "kids," "goats like lickin' lichen"!

Look in the steep, rocky cliffs of Glacier to see goats. Logan Pass, Many Glacier, and Two Medicine all have the rugged terrain these mountain creatures prefer.

Bighorn sheep often overlap in range with mountain goats. While goats tend toward the higher cliffs, sheep favor the open, grassy slopes just below them. They depend on their speed to outrun predators. Sometimes goats and sheep will graze close together, and their young will play together at an early age.

Bighorn sheep are brown with a cream-colored rump patch; the rams carry their namesake curling horns. The bigger the curl, the older the ram. Females are smaller and sport spike horns, similar to those seen on goats of both sexes. Sheep are more of a herd animal than goats are; in the summer time, the ewes form bands and go off to have their young; the rams form bachelor bands that often move to the high country. As fall comes on, however, all groups reconvene and move to lower elevations where the winter is just a little bit milder.

Currently there is no precise count of sheep or goats in Glacier National Park. Clearly, though, there are quite a few more goats than sheep. Good places to look for sheep include Logan Pass, across from the visitor center on the slopes of Pollock Mountain; the slopes of Piegan Mountain, just up from Siyeh Bend on Going-to-the-Sun Road; Many Glacier Valley; the Highline Trail between Logan Pass and Granite Park; and Two Medicine Valley.

Bad Rock Country B & B Cookbook at their request!

After a full day in Glacier country, you'll enjoy the luxurious outdoor hot tub. Each party reserves its own private time for soaking. The tub has a view of Big Mountain, and you'll enjoy relaxing in the hot water and fresh mountain air: the thirty acres of Bad Rock Country B & B are reserved for non-smoking guests.

Rates vary with the season. Rooms in the

house range from $108.00 to $139.00 per night for two; rooms at Bunny Junction run from $134.00 to $169.00. A two-night minimum stay is required from July through September. All rooms have private bath and telephones. A two-room suite combination is available in the house. For more information, please phone, write, or visit the website at www.badrock.com. And about those bunnies… they're very subtle, but once you start looking you'll notice them everywhere!

Glacier Bed and Breakfast
$ • P.O. Box 1900-10, U.S. Highway 2 East, Hungry Horse
• **(406) 387-4153**

Just visiting the Glacier B & B is an experience in itself. The yard is edged all around with tulips, poppies, peonies, and lots and lots of roses—you'll hardly have to bend over to smell the fragrance! Indoors you'll find yet more flowers, but also an impressive array of mounted fish and game trophies. Your host, Bob Johnson, is a fisherman and hunter of many years' experience. You'll be fascinated by the collection—elk, lynx, bobcat, buffalo, even a wild turkey—as well as many fish—and every one has a story behind it. Bob's lived in Montana for many years and knows the state and its backcountry well.

This log home also offers very comfortable and gracious accommodations. The five units each have their own bath. One includes a king-size bed and Jacuzzi; two others rent as suites with their own kitchenettes. The common living room and dining room are brightened with skylights by day and the fireplace in the evening. And a big deck overlooks the yard and gardens. A full breakfast is served each morning between 6:00 and 8:00 AM

The Glacier B & B is open year-round. In the summer, rooms rent for $75.00 per night for two people, with a $10.00 charge for each additional person; the suites rent for $60.00 and $80.00, with a $10.00 charge for each additional person. Winter rates for rooms are $40.00 per night; please inquire about rates for suites. For more information, please phone, write, or visit the website at www.centric.net/montanarec/glacier.htm.

A Wild Rose
$$$ • P.O. Box 130396, 12080 U.S. Highway 2 East, Coram
• **(406) 387-4900**

Your hosts, Brenda and Joseph Mihalko, came to the bed and breakfast business after years of traveling, and A Wild Rose is the bed and breakfast they always wished they'd found. You'll find their high standards and touch for luxury reflected in every detail: exquisite mattresses, all natural fabrics, delicious and healthful foods beautifully presented, plush robes and a hair dryer in your private bathroom. And A Wild Rose is full of flowers—rose bushes along the pathway to the front door, fresh flowers in your room, and a delightful use of floral patterns in the decorating. The Victorian style is both elegant and comforting—this is a place where you'll enjoy each day and sleep well at night.

A Wild Rose is located just 6 miles west of West Glacier, so you have great access to both the national park and the wilderness areas south of the Middle Fork River. In the evening you'll return to one of four unique rooms. The Whirlpool Suite—favored by honeymooners—includes a large bathroom with whirlpool and separate shower; the Private Balcony Suite has its own entrance, and can accommodate up to four people. The Country Rose and Victorian Manor rooms are beautifully decorated with Victorian furniture. On a sunny day, take a chair on the front porch and enjoy listening to the birds—or, later, watch the sunset colors fade from the sky. In the living room you'll enjoy browsing the library and the flicker of the firelight. (Ask Brenda about the rocking chair.) Out back you'll find a therapeutic spa that can seat seven—the perfect place to unwind in the evening. Or talk to Joseph, who will be happy to arrange a time for massage.

A Wild Rose is open year-round. Rates for one or two people range from $110 to $150 per night; each additional person is $25.00. Reservations are recommended. Pets and smoking are not allowed on the premises. A Wild Rose also offers a Romantic Evening package that includes hors d'oeuvres, candlelight dinner, massage, your room, and breakfast; please inquire for details. For more information, please phone, write, e-mail wildrose@cyberport.net, or visit the website at www.cyberport.net/wildrose.

Guest Ranches, Resorts, and Lodges

Meadow Lake Resort
$$$–$$$$ • 100 St. Andrews Drive, Columbia Falls
• (406) 892-7601 or (800) 321-GOLF

Located on Meadow Lake Golf Course, this large resort maintains inn rooms, condo suites and one- and two-bedroom condos, as well as two- to five-bedroom vacation homes. It is built on gentle hills and many trees grace the fairways, so that it feels almost like a very pretty neighborhood. The 18-hole golf course sets the tone, but, in addition to the pro shop and market, you'll find a recreation center with Nautilus and aerobic machines, pools, and spas. "Troop Meadow Lake" provides supervised children's activities throughout the week, and there's a children's playground too. The Sunset Grill offers lunch and dinner throughout the year, with service on the patio during the summer months. Meadow Lake Resort also features meeting and banquet facilities for small to mid-sized groups.

Meadow Lake does provide a good central location from which to explore Glacier Country. Glacier National Park is about a 25-minute drive to the east, the Big Mountain Ski and Summer Resort is about 25 minutes to the west, and Flathead Lake is about 30 minutes away to the south.

Rates vary by season. A room at the Meadow Lake Inn runs from $79 to $129 depending on time of year. Condos range from $89 to $229 depending on size and season. Vacation homes, with two to five bedrooms, run from $159 to $439 per night. There is a two-night minimum stay requirement for condos and vacation homes. Please call or write, e-mail at mdwlake@meadowlake.com, or visit the website at www.meadowlake.com for more details.

Timber Wolf Resort
$ • P.O. Box 190800, 9105 Highway 2 East, Hungry Horse
• (406) 387-9653 or toll-free at (877) 846-9653

RV sites, tent sites, rustic and deluxe cabins, and B & B—the Timber Wolf Resort is doing everything, and doing it in style. This twenty-acre property is a small town in the

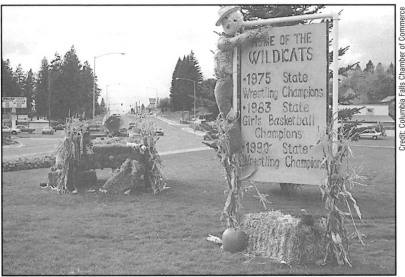

Credit: Columbia Falls Chamber of Commerce

Harvest time still results in special community projects in northwest Montana.

The majestic elk, or wapiti, are most impressive durning the fall rut.

Credit: VIAD Corporation

middle of the summer—complete with its own convenience store and gathering room—but the grounds are so spacious, hilly, and nicely wooded that no one will feel crowded.

Flowers line the drive into the Timber Wolf Resort. If it's an RV site you're looking for, the resort has twenty-four, some with full hook-ups for $20.00 per night, and some with just electric, for $16.00 per night. Both pull-through and back-in sites are available. Tent sites cost $14.00 per night.

Sleeping cabins are either rustic or deluxe. Rustic cabins rent for $29.00 per night. They have a double bunk bed but are otherwise unfurnished; bring your own linens or sleeping bag, or rent from the resort. Deluxe cabins are furnished and have a double bunk bed with linens, heat, and electricity. These cabins rent for $39.00 per night.

And your hosts, Tracy and Rob Elek, also operate two rooms as a bed and breakfast. Queen-size beds with handmade quilts will keep you cozy, and you'll wake to a breakfast basket of fresh coffee, muffins or bagels, and fruit. B & B rooms rent for $54.00 per night.

The Timber Wolf Resort also offers some beautiful views toward Glacier National Park and Columbia Mountain in the Swan Range. You'll find the practical details fall in place too: the resort includes showers, laundry, gift shop, a gazebo with three barbecue grills, a children's play area, and picnic tables. All rates above are based on double occupancy; please add $3.00 per day for each additional person. Please inquire about the pet policy. All buildings are non-smoking. The Timber Wolf's heated cabins and B & B rooms are open all winter; the full resort operates for the summer months. For more information, please phone, write, e-mail at elek@timberwolfresort.com or visit the website at www.timberwolfresort.com.

Silverwolf Chalets
**$$$ • P.O. Box 115, West Glacier
• (406) 387-4448**

"Designer log cabins for two"—ten log chalets tailored for two make up the Silverwolf. You'll find each perfect little cabin has its own queen-size log bed with handmade quilt, gas fireplace, private bath, and a cupboard that tastefully conceals your own microwave, small refrigerator, and coffee maker. Breakfast is brought to your cabin; if you don't want to stay indoors on a beautiful day, step out and enjoy your coffee on your own porch.

The cabins are nestled in a landscaped forest setting that fosters privacy and quiet. Pets are not allowed, and smoking is allowed only in the picnic area or away from the cabins. One cabin is handicap accessible, and one has two oversized single beds. The Silverwolf is open from May 15 until October 15. Rates vary by season and range from $83.00 to $134.00 for two people per night; a two night minimum stay is required between July 1 and August 20.

Great Northern Resort
$$-$$$$ • P.O. Box 278, West Glacier • (406) 387-5340 or (800) 735-7897

You won't miss the Great Northern Resort—the bright red caboose and Swiss log chalets will draw your attention immediately. The resort is located just one mile west of West Glacier, providing easy access to everything the area has to offer. The chalet balconies offer beautiful views of Desert and Strawberry Mountains, as well as the little nubbin known as Chocolate Drop—it's about the shape of a Hershey's Kiss! The charming log chalets are fully furnished and have kitchens equipped with service for six or eight. The three larger chalets have gas fireplaces. All are non-pet and non-smoking.

The Great Northern also is headquarters for all sorts of outdoor activities. Full and half-day whitewater raft trips, kayak clinics, and fishing trips can all be arranged. Fly-fishing "school" is an option for those just getting their feet wet. If you're looking for a longer trip, the Great Northern offers extended two- and three-day whitewater trips. And—at the end of your adventures—you can relax in the swim spa back at the resort. Please phone, write, or visit the website below for more details on outdoor activities.

The chalets will accommodate six to eight (with two or three queen-size beds and a sleeper sofa) and vary in price according to the season. The smaller chalets, Two Bear and Osprey, range from $110.00 to $175.00 per night. The larger chalets, Wapiti, Moose, and Tatonka, range from $160.00 to $250.00 per night. During the peak of the season, July 1 to September 15, a three-night minimum stay is required. For more information, please phone, write, e-mail at whiteh20@digisys.net, or visit the website at www.gnwhitewater.com.

Belton Chalet
$$-$$$ • U.S. Highway 2, West Glacier • (406) 888-5000 or (888) BELTON-5

The original Belton Chalet was completed in 1910, the same year that Glacier National Park was created by Congress. The balconies and gables typify the Swiss-chalet design of the Great Northern's train stations and hotels throughout the park. Originally a railroad inn, the Belton Chalet also served as the park's first winter headquarters. It closed as a hotel during World War II, and only now has been fully renovated and restored to its original beauty.

The "chalet" now consists of four buildings, all completed by 1912: the main chalet, the upper chalet, and two smaller cottages (named Lewis and Clark). As a result, the chalet offers a wide variety of lodgings: from chalet room with communal bath to main lodge with private bath and balcony, to honeymoon suite or private cottage. The chalet also in-

INSIDERS' TIP

The fastest route from East Glacier to Many Glacier (or the Canadian border at Carway)—and the straightest one, for those with long vehicles or trailers—is U.S. Highway 2 from East Glacier to Browning and then Glacier County Highway 464, the Duck Lake Road, to Babb. This paved, well-maintained road heads due north over the prairie. As it swings to the west and back toward the mountains, it also gives a huge view of the park's eastern front. You'll join U.S. Highway 89 about 6 miles north of St. Mary and 2 miles south of Babb.

cludes the Tap Room, serving beer, wine, and cocktails, and a restaurant, game room, and gift shop.

And the location… the Belton Chalet is located right in West Glacier, just a step across the road from the West Glacier Amtrak depot and a two-minute drive from the west entrance to Glacier National Park. Hiking, horseback riding, bus tours, whitewater rafting, cross-country skiing, and snowshoeing are all in your front yard.

The Belton will be opening for business on June 1, 1999. Rates for two people per night run from $60.00 to $175.00. The Belton also offers a Winter Weekend for Two: two nights' lodging plus five meals, from Friday night to Sunday morning, for $150. For more information, please phone, or visit the website at www.beltonchalet.com/index.htm.

Izaak Walton Inn
$$–$$$$ • P.O. Box 653, Essex
• (406) 888-5700

History comes alive at the Izaak Walton Inn, originally built in 1939 to house Great Northern Railway crews working the trains that traveled over Marias Pass. Located right on the rail line, today the inn's guests enjoy waving to Amtrak passengers as the trains pass by…and the only flag stop on Amtrak's Empire Builder route—Seattle to Chicago—is at Essex, just a few moments from the inn's door. The association with the railroad is evident throughout the inn—in the bar downstairs, for example, you'll be fascinated by the photos of historic engines, avalanches over the tracks, and even train wrecks. And the whistle and rumble of passing trains will bring you back to the present.

But, all rail history aside—the Izaak Walton Inn is as cozy a getaway as you'll find anywhere. When you see the very comfortable lobby, you'll want to find a good book and curl up by the fire, or perhaps spend some time chatting with other guests. The dining room, open for breakfast, lunch, and dinner, is charming and bright. All rooms have been remodeled in recent years to include a private bath, but the original character of the inn has been well maintained.

And the Izaak Walton Inn offers its own groomed cross-country ski trails during the winter, which become hiking trails in the summer. It's right on the edge of the Great Bear/Bob Marshall Wilderness and just across the river from Glacier National Park…there's literally millions of acres to hike, ride, snowshoe, and ski through. The inn's trained guides will show you the backcountry on skis or snowshoes in the winter, and the inn will be happy

BE "BEAR AWARE"

Glacier National Park is the core of a large wilderness ecosystem, which provides one of the last remaining refuges for the grizzly bear. Numerous risks and rewards are associated with a visit to this area. An encounter with a wild animal—including a bear—

is always possible. Bears are naturally wary of humans, but they are also unpredictable and may attack without warning.

Visitors have been injured and killed by bears, and in some cases, their careless actions have resulted in the bears' removal. Your knowledge of bear habitat and behavior can help reduce your chances of a dangerous encounter.

The following practices are well-accepted means to increase your margin of safety in bear country:

—Never Hike Alone. Solo hikers have been involved in a number of tragic bear encounters. Hiking in a group may make you less likely to be attacked.

—Make Noise. The human voice is easily carried along with you—use it when you are hiking or camping to alert bears and other wild animals of your presence. Bear bells also warn a bear of your approach and can be purchased locally. Use extra caution in brushy areas, on blind curves and when wind or running water masks the sounds of your approach.

—Stay on the Trail. Visibility is usually better on the trail, and human activity generally more frequent, thus giving you a greater margin of safety.

—Hike When It Is Safest. Bears can be active both day and night, but tend to be out and about more at dawn or dusk.

—Avoid Bears' Prime Food Sources. Bears will vigorously defend food sources. Never approach a smelly animal carcass and beware of other areas with abundant food sources such as berries, bulbs, grasses and flowers.

—Be Alert for Bear Sign. Fresh bear scat (dung), tracks, or signs of digging may indicate a bear is in the area. Be extra careful.

—Enjoy Wildlife at a Distance. Never intentionally approach or feed wildlife. Beware of one of the most dangerous scenarios—a sow with cubs. Immediately leave the area. If you have to, go back down the trail.

—Secure Food, Garbage and Cookware Properly. These items should be hung out of reach of bears at all times except mealtimes. Check with the National Park Service or USDA Forest Service for specific regulations.

—Respect Closures. Trail and campground closures resulting from bear danger are common in Glacier. It is unsafe (and illegal) to enter a closed area, so heed the signs for your own safety.

to help you arrange raft trips, bus tours through the park, or guided hikes during the summer.

Basic double-occupancy rooms are $98 per night. The inn also offers family rooms beginning at $150 per night. Four "caboose cottages"—renovated cabooses with heat, full kitchen, and bath—are available, beginning at $475 for a three-night stay. The Izaak Walton Inn also offers 3-, 5-, and 7-day packages that include two or three meals per day plus a choice of outdoor guided activities. For more information, please phone, e-mail izaakw@digisys.net, write, or visit the website at www.izaakwaltoninn.com/.

RV Parks and Campgrounds

Columbia Falls RV Park
$ • P.O. Box 2031, 1000 Third Avenue East, Columbia Falls
• (406) 892-1122 or (888) 401-7268

Columbia Falls RV Park really is at the Gateway to Glacier...right on U.S. Highway 2

where it leaves Columbia Falls and heads up toward the park. The RV park itself includes a laundry, showers, bathrooms, store, and a gift shop featuring local crafts, but if there's something you can't find here, Columbia Falls is right out your back door with both retail and dining establishments.

This facility, just five years old, is open from June through September. It has 50 65-foot pull-through RV sites. All have water, sewer, and electric hook-ups and rent for $20.00 per night (double occupancy), with a 2.00 charge for each additional adult. Cable is available at some sites. Pets are allowed on leash, and owners must clean up after their pets. Reservations are recommended.

Timber Wolf Resort
$ • P.O. Box 190800, 9105 Highway 2 East, Hungry Horse
• (406) 387-9653 or toll-free at (877) 846-9653

Flowers line the drive into the Timber Wolf Resort. If it's an RV site you're looking for, the resort has twenty-four, some with full hook-ups for $20.00 per night, and some with just electric, for $16.00 per night. Both pull-through and back-in sites are available. Tent sites cost $14.00 per night. If you are interested in an off-season visit, the campground water is turned on in May and off in October depending on weather, but with advance notice the owners will even plow a spot for your RV! Please inquire about winter rates.

The Timber Wolf Resort offers some beautiful views toward Glacier National Park and Columbia Mountain in the Swan Range. You'll find the practical details fall in place too: the resort includes showers, laundry, convenience and gift shop, a gazebo with three barbecue grills, a children's play area, and picnic tables. All rates above are based on double occupancy; please add $3.00 per day for each additional person. Please inquire about the pet policy. All buildings are non-smoking. For more information, please phone, write, e-mail elek@timberwolfresort.com or visit the website at www.timberwolfresort.com.

Mountain Meadows RV Park and Campground
$ • P.O. Box 190442, 9125 U.S. Highway 2 East, Hungry Horse
• (406) 387-9125

The literature for Mountain Meadows RV Park and Campground describes it as "Montana's Most Beautiful Campground"— and, once you drive in, you may well agree. RV sites are spacious for those with slide-outs and awnings, and will accommodate motor homes up to 40+ feet long. The individual tent sites are roomy and private. But the setting is what makes it: the campground is on a gently sloping hill with many trees, yet looks out over the valley. A lovely little pond (stocked with rainbow trout) and meadow area have a big view toward Columbia Mountain, Teakettle Mountain, and the Bad Rock Canyon.And Mountain Meadows provides about every conceivable service. All sites have picnic tables and campfire/barbecue grills. Restrooms and hot showers are clean. The laundry room is open 24 hours a day. A dump station and mobile pump-out service are available. The campground store sells souvenirs, ice cream, snacks, milk, pop, ice, firewood, and fishing tackle, as well as camping and RV supplies. You can even rent a fishing pole. Leashed pets are OK.

Mountain Meadows is open from May 15 (or, if the weather is nice, May 1) until October 31. Reservations are strongly recommended for July and August. Full hook-ups are $23 per night; water and electric hook-ups are $20 per night; and tent sites are $16 per night. The seventh night is free if you reserve for one full week. Rates are based on 4-person occupancy per site; each additional adult is $3.00, each additional child is $1.50 per night. For more information, please phone, write, e-mail camp@mmrvpark.com, or visit the website at www.mmrvpark.com.

Canyon RV and Campground
$ • P.O. Box 7, 9540 U.S. Highway 2 East, Hungry Horse
• (406) 387-9393 or (800) 337-9393

Canyon RV and Campground is located just east of Hungry Horse, Montana, and its property runs right along the Middle Fork of the Flathead River, providing both views and fishing access. The campground has quite a variety of sites— "No rig too big" is their way of saying that Canyon can accommodate any RV. Ten tent sites are available, and Canyon also has six 12 x 12 sleeping cabins (bring-your-own-bedding). Hot showers, a dump station, and a small store are available.

Canyon is open from May 1 to September 30. Tent sites run $14 per night; the fifty-one RV sites range from $15 with no hook-up to $20 with full service. Sleeping cabins rent for $30 per night and accommodate up to four people. Pets are permitted on leash; owners must clean up after their pets. Reservations are accepted. Please phone, write, or visit the website at www.montanacampground.com for more information.

Devil Creek Campground
$ • At mile marker 190, U.S. Highway 2 • Hungry Horse Ranger District, Flathead National Forest, Hungry Horse
• (406) 387-3800

The 13 sites of Devil Creek Campground are open from around Memorial Day (depending on snow conditions) to mid-September. Drinking water and vault toilets are available, and a campground host is in residence during the summer. Forest Service Trail #167 (Devil Creek) is nearby. Some double-wide or long sites will accommodate RVs, although there are no hook-ups. There is no garbage pickup, so all campers must pack-in, pack-out. Because this is grizzly habitat, all food (including pet food and garbage) must be kept in a hard-sided vehicle whenever it is not being prepared. Horses are not permitted in the campground.

For late-season visitors, however, the campground is open without charge until closed by weather, but water is not available and outhouses are not regularly cleaned.

A fee of $8 per night is charged during the summer. Reservations are not accepted. Mile marker 190 is approximately 8 miles east of Essex and 7 miles west of Marias Pass along U.S. Highway 2.

Three Forks Campground
$ • Between mile markers 191 and 192, U.S. Highway 2 East
• (406) 226-4479

This large campground occupies a beautiful meadow but also nestles into the trees—offering both sun and shade throughout the summer months. Campers of all sorts are welcome. Three Forks has wide, long pull-through sites, sites with electric and water hook-ups, back-in sites with electric only, and tent sites. It also welcomes groups of all sizes—up to 1000 people. A playground, shower house, dump station, and covered pavilion will make your stay comfortable and convenient. A small store sells propane and ice.

Three Forks Campground is open from May 20 to September 15, weather permitting. Rates run from approximately $12.00 for tenters to $13.00 and $15.00 for RVs, depending on hook-ups. Because this is grizzly habitat, all food (including pet food and garbage) must be kept in a hard-sided vehicle whenever it is not being prepared. Pets are permitted on leash; owners are expected to clean up after their pets. Reservations are recommended, especially for groups.

Summit Campground
$ • Marias Pass, U.S. Highway 2 • Rocky Mountain Ranger District, Lewis and Clark National Forest, Choteau
• (406) 466-5341

This small Forest Service Campground is conveniently located at Marias Pass, 12 miles west of East Glacier on U.S. Highway 2. The site is wooded, which you'll be grateful for, as the Continental Divide can be a windy place to camp, even at comparatively low elevation (5216 ft.)! Nevertheless, it's a wonderful site—not only for Memorial Square and its monuments, but for the imposing peaks just across the highway: Summit and Little Dog Mountains. If geology is your interest, take a few moments to scan these peaks: you'll be able to pick out the Lewis Overthrust Fault, where younger rocks rode up over the older rocks beneath. The fault line looks like a dark band in the side of the mountains, almost as if there were a road halfway up the slope. North of U.S. Highway 2 you're in Glacier National Park. Three Bears Lake is an easy hike in from the road, and the trail then continues both east and west below the mountains. Be sure to make lots of noise—although you're not far from a major highway, this is bear country.

Summit Campground has 17 sites. It's generally open from about Memorial Day (depending on the snowpack) to Labor Day, and a campground host is on-site to help visitors. Several sites will accommodate RVs up to 35 feet long. Drinking water and vault toilets are available. There are no hook-ups. Because this is grizzly habitat, all food (including pet food and garbage) must be kept in a hard-sided vehicle whenever it is not being prepared. Sites are $8 per night. Summit Campground can be very busy and often fills between July 4 and Labor Day. Reservations may be made for a $25 reservation fee at the phone number above.

Restaurants

Restaurant Rates

$	$10 to $20
$$	$21 to $40
$$$	$30 to %50
$$$$	more than $50

For two people, meal exclusive of beverages, tip, and tax.

Cimarron Deli
$ • 420 Nucleus Avenue, Columbia Falls
• (406) 892-1490 or (800) 811-0539

This full-service deli includes a small seating area, but it's also a great place to pick up a picnic "to go"—the variety of fresh sandwiches made up to your order, hot sandwiches, and homemade soup will give you lots to choose from. For example, check out the section on chicken—the "chicken coop"— which includes seven different kinds of "hot chicks": Monterey, Lorraine, BBQ, Chipolte, Malibu, Southwest, and a chicken breast sandwich with lemon pepper...or the equally long list of salads.

Prices run from $3.75 to $5.00, and the deli carries a selection of beverages and desserts. Cimarron Deli also caters and creates party trays.

The Back Room
$ • Behind the Nite Owl, U.S. Highway 2 East, Columbia Falls
• (406) 892-3131

The Back Room is definitely a local spot— no fuss, no muss. But if you're ready for chicken and ribs, this the place to go. Spare ribs, country ribs, baby back ribs, rotisserie chicken, broasted chicken, pizza, seafood, steak, burgers—and most dinners come with the Back Room "trimmings": baby red potatoes, cole slaw, baked beans, and fry bread with whipped honey butter. This is not for the faint of heart! And the portions are generous—lots of folks will be taking home doggy bags and enjoying the leftovers tomorrow.

Back Room dinner entrées run from $4.25 to $10.00; 7", 13", and 15" pizzas run from $7.00 to $14.00 or so. Sunday brings the "all you can eat" pizza, salad, and dark chicken bar, which is $5.75 for adults and less for kids. Chicken and ribs can also be ordered to go—as can the Back Room barbecue sauce. Both a senior and kids' menu are available.

And about that address—the Back Room is located behind the Nite Owl Restaurant, in the same building. Both are located on the south side of U.S. Highway 2, between Fourth and Sixth Avenues West.

Charlie Wong's
$ • 329 Ninth Street West, Columbia Falls
• (406) 892-9664

Charlie Wong's is like the Chinese restaurant you frequent back home—not fancy, but the food's great and it doesn't take long to get it. Here in Columbia Falls, it's located right on U.S. Highway 2 (Ninth Street is the highway as it goes through town), so it's easy to stop in on your way home from a day of exploring, or call in advance and pick up your order to go.

Lunch is from 11 AM to 3 PM and features a variety of specials—standards like Kung Pao Chicken or Lemon Chicken, but also Charlie Wong's Lunch, Asian BBQ Chicken or Beef, and Vegetarian Lunch. Appetizers, Soups, and quite a few a la carte items can also be ordered. And the menu includes burgers for those who prefer to leave their chopsticks at home. Specials cost between $4.00 and $6.00.

Dinner is from 4:30 to 9 PM, Sunday through Thursday, and from 4:30 to 9:30 PM on Friday and Saturday nights. The dinner menu is quite a bit more extensive than the lunch menu, and includes beef, pork, chicken, seafood, and combination plates. Appetizers, soups, wonton, egg rolls—and hamburgers—are available, but Charlie Wong's also offers "international selections," which are preset dinner menus meant to be ordered for the whole table and priced per person. A small dessert list finishes the menu—and, of course, a fortune cookie.

Dinner entrées run between $7.25 and $11.95; international selections are priced at $8.95 or $9.50 per person.

Spruce Park Café
$ • U.S. Highway 2 East, Coram
• (406) 387-5614

The Spruce Park Café is in a category of its own—yes, it's located at the Coram Exxon station, right on U.S. Highway 2. It's not fancy. But the food is homemade and consistently fresh and well prepared—which is why you'll see it's often a busy spot. They make their own biscuits, rolls, pies—which you can buy whole or by the slice, to go—and the menu offers a good variety of choices for breakfast, lunch, and dinner. Now, the nitty-gritty: check out the Mexican. The burritos are great, and the Spruce Park makes its own salsa and pintos. Or, for a hot summer day in Glacier Country, try a huckleberry milkshake. The Spruce Park makes a huck shake that stands up to a straw—as a matter of fact, you'll need a spoon, because the real huckleberries will plug the straw!

The Spruce Park Café is open 7 days a week, all year.

Heaven's Peak Dining and Spirits
$$$ • 12130 U.S. Highway 2 East (just west of West Glacier)
• (406) 387-4754

The recently opened Heaven's Peak restaurant has brought a more upscale dining experience to the West Glacier area. "Rustic elegance" is the watchword here—white linen tablecloths, yes, but your t-shirt and shorts are welcome. The menu features regional specialties—fresh fish, buffalo, and Flathead cherries all make their appearance. The dining room is lovely, but on a beautiful day you'll want to dine on the porch, admiring the tremendous view of the peaks of Glacier National Park.

Heaven's Peak is open for lunch and dinner from the summer solstice to the autumn equinox! —or, roughly, late June to mid-September, with live music on some weekends. The restaurant is handicap accessible. Entrées range from $12.00 to $22.00. Reservations are recommended for dinner.

Belton Chalet
U.S. Highway 2, West Glacier
• (406) 888-5000 or (888) BELTON-5

As of this writing, the details have yet to be determined—but the Belton Chalet, with its Tap Room, expects to open on June 1, 1999. This beautifully renovated, historic lodge will be well worth stopping to see...so consider taking a few moments to check out the final arrangements! Call ahead, perhaps, to learn whether drinks and sandwiches or a full menu will be available.

The Glacier Highland
$ • U.S. Highway 2 East, West Glacier
• (406) 888-5427

The Glacier Highland's restaurant offers home-cooked food at affordable prices. Open for breakfast, lunch, and dinner from May through October, breakfast treats include the famous cinnamon rolls. Lunch and dinner feature sandwiches, soups, burgers—and hand-tossed, homemade pizza. If you have any room left afterward, you'll have to top off your meal with pie—or maybe pie is a reason to stop in, all by itself...

The Glacier Highland is located directly across from the Amtrak station in West Glacier and minutes from the west entrance to Glacier National Park.

West Glacier Restaurant and Bar
$ • West Glacier
• (406) 888-5403

After a great day rafting the Middle Fork—or hiking to Apgar Lookout, perhaps—you'll enjoy not having to drive far to find a good dinner. The West Glacier Restaurant—often called the West Glacier Café—is just outside the park boundary in West Glacier, ready with breakfast, lunch, and dinner. The relaxed, family atmosphere makes it a great place to start up or wind down. And you're sure to find a huckleberry treat to complete your day in Glacier Country! The West Glacier Restaurant will be open from late May to late September.

Izaak Walton Inn
$$ • P.O. Box 653, Essex
• (406) 888-5700

Staying at the Izaak Walton Inn may not be part of your itinerary, but if you're driving U.S. Highway 2, you may want to plan to stop here for a meal. The dining room is open for breakfast (7–11 AM), lunch (11 AM–5 PM), and dinner (5–8 PM), and serves as a great reason to stop and explore this fascinating historic inn.

The dining room offers a limited but choice menu for each meal. Breakfast ranges from the basic—oatmeal or cold cereal—to fancier dishes such as the "portabella, asparagus, and gouda cheese omelette with hashbrowns." Lunch always includes a burger selection and pasta as well as heftier choices. Dinner menus offer one dinner sandwich plus three entrées—perhaps buffalo kabobs, salmon filet, or vegetable lasagna. Dinner prices run from $7.50 to $18.25. A children's menu is available for lunch and dinner.

Nightlife

Nightlife isn't too complex in this neck of the woods—but there are a few spots where you're sure to enjoy putting your feet up for a bit. Frieda's—the bar adjacent to the West Glacier Restaurant—will often have a crowd on the porch in the evening, perhaps rafters just off the river who want to swap stories about the whitewater. The newly renovated Belton Chalet will be opening its Tap Room on June 1 and looks highly likely to develop into a pleasant place to stop for a beer. After a day of cross-country skiing, you might want to check out the Flag Stop lounge at the Izaak Walton, once again a fascinating place for its railroad history.

If you're down in the Flathead valley and feeling adventurous, try the Blue Moon. For starters, it's a landmark—located at the junction of U.S. Highway 2 and Montana Highway 40, about halfway between Columbia Falls and Whitefish, which everyone here refers to as the Blue Moon junction. This grill, casino, and night club has live music, karaoke, various specials, and, on Wednesdays, line dancing, with lessons. Here's a slice of Montana life!

Shopping

Breath-taking views and outdoor activities probably take priority for most visitors to this area, but you won't want to miss these places:

Glacier Natural History Association (GNHA)
U.S. Highway 2, West Glacier
• (406) 888-5756

Located in the historic Belton depot in West Glacier, GNHA is a cooperating association of Glacier National Park. It sells books, videos, and posters on subjects related to the park, and profits are used to enhance the park's educational programs. All that serious stuff said—GNHA is a great place to shop! For anyone who's enjoyed their time in the mountains, this beautiful store offers a huge selection of books covering geology, history, Native American culture, plants, and animals—everything from *Alces alces shirasi* to *Zigadenus elegans*. Books include field guides, photo books, and children's books. And you'll have a hard time deciding which beautiful poster you're going to take home... be sure to stop in! GNHA is open from 8 a.m. to 4:30 p.m., Monday through Friday.

Izaak Walton Inn
P.O. Box 653, Essex
• (406) 888-5700

The Izaak Walton Inn has a small but selective gift shop with an enticing variety of items—all related to Glacier National Park, the inn itself, or the Great Northern Railway. You'll find all sorts of teddy bears, quality locally crafted silver and antler jewelry, Christmas ornaments, maps and books, ball caps, t-shirts, and outerwear. The inn has even arranged for the reproduction of the Great Northern's "Glory of the West" china pattern, used on the Empire Builder route from 1940 to 1957. This is a fun place to spend some time...the owners have been ingenious in choosing the souvenirs they offer.

Bigfork offers a splendid variety of diversions, from canoeing to bowling, horseback riding to live theater, jet skiing to shopping.

Bigfork

Bigfork, located on the northeast corner of Flathead Lake, is a combination of the perfect Montana small town, the perfect lakeside village, the perfect tourist town, and the perfect artists' colony. When you get right down to it, what visitors and residents all seem to agree upon is that Bigfork is perfect.

The town is located on Montana Highway 35, which hugs the eastern shore of Flathead Lake from Polson in the south to just north of Bigfork. The community is located at the mouth of the Swan River where it empties into Flathead Lake, the largest natural freshwater lake west of the Mississippi. That lake and the river provide the crux of the recreational opportunities in Bigfork—with fishing for mackinaw, rainbow, cutthroat, perch, bass and northern pike available nearby—but the town is also just 17 miles south of Kalispell, and 45 miles southwest of Glacier National Park, so there is much more to do in a day than boating or fishing. East of Bigfork is the 950,000-acre Bob Marshall Wilderness, a favorite of local backcountry hikers. The Jewel Basin Nature Area is also nearby, with 38 miles of nature trails that are easy for almost anyone to navigate. The east shore of Flathead Lake is also noted for its cherry orchards, which provide lots of raw material for roadside stands in July and August.

The population varies considerably depending on the time of year. Summertime is the high season here, and with Flathead Lake at full pool, the population in this little town soars from 3,500 to as many as 10,000. But in any case, with its economy supported by tourism, Bigfork offers a splendid variety of diversions, from canoeing to bowling, horseback riding to live theater, jet skiing to shopping. Eagle Bend is a world-class golf course not far from downtown. It was rated the second best new public course by *Golf Digest* in 1989.

And there's always a new restaurant to try in what must surely be considered the culinary capital of the Flathead.

The transformation of Bigfork into something of an artistic mecca probably coincides with the opening in 1960 of the Bigfork Summer Playhouse. That repertory company, which was then housed in a rustic building but now performs in air-conditioned comfort in the Bigfork Center for the Performing Arts, started to draw creative people to Bigfork. The tourist trade built up steadily as well, leading to many opportunities for new businesses. Today, Electric Avenue— Bigfork's main commercial street—is a bustling row of artist's studios, galleries, gift shops, bookstores, and restaurants. The playhouse's repertory company puts on shows from late May through early September. And during one of the annual festivities such as the Fourth of July or the Bigfork Festival of the Arts, the atmosphere is truly electric, although even on a standard day in summer the street lives up to its name, which comes from a small power plant nearby. Sliter Park, located at the end of Electric Avenue and across the old steel bridge, is the site of live outdoor performances such as the Riverbend Concert Series during the summer.

Believe it or not, Bigfork is also a good spot to plan for winter recreation. For one thing, the lake regulates the climate, so most winters are milder than typical for a latitude this far north. There are also breaks on rates at resorts and other lodging facilities during the "off season." And you have the same access to the Flathead Forest for cross-country skiing and snowmobiling that you would have from elsewhere in the valley. The Big Mountain Resort and the new Blacktail Mountain ski area are both less than an hour away.

Also of note is the scenic drive from Bigfork to Seeley Lake and Swan Lake on Montana

Highway 83. This trip through the Clearwater and Swan valleys typically results in quite a bit of wildlife viewing, especially at sunset when deer are frequently seen crossing the highway. The southern lakes both offer excellent recreational opportunities as well, but use caution in traveling the road.

Accommodations

Hotel and Motel Rates

Keep in mind that some rates are based on availability. The average nightly rates for two adults at the hotels and motels listed in this section are indicated by a dollar sign ($) ranking in the following chart. Also, the hotels and motels in this chapter accept all or most major credit cards.

$	$25 to $49
$$	$50 to $75
$$$	$76 to $100
$$$$	$101 and more

Hotels and Motels

Bigfork Timbers Motel
$$ • 8540 Montana Highway 35
• (406) 837-6200, (800) 821-4546

The Timbers Motel is the only moderately priced motel in Bigfork. It is within walking distance of the village, and very near to Wayfarer's state park. There is also trolley bus service to the village during the summer season. The Timbers offers 40 rooms, along with continental breakfasts, cable and HBO, and complimentary in-room coffee. There is an outdoor pool available in summer, and a sauna and hot tub year round.

Holiday Resort Motel
$•17001 E. Lakeshore Dr., Bigfork
• (406) 982-3710, (800) 421-9141

The Holiday Resort Motel is located on Yellow Bay about a dozen miles south of Bigfork on Flathead Lake. This is a waterfront motel and includes guest moorage, and boat or personal watercraft rentals. There is a private beach for guests, along with a dock for easy access to the lake. The motel is also home to "The Little Cafe on Yellow Bay," featuring waterfront dining, fresh seafood and homemade desserts as well as complimentary moorage. Breakfast lunch and dinner are served at this local favorite.

Woods Bay Resort
$ • 26481 E. Lakeshore Dr., Bigfork
• (406) 837-3333

Woods Bay is a small lakeside community located on Flathead Lake just four miles south of Bigfork, and this small facility offers six motel rooms, five cabins with kitchens, and six RV spots with full hookups. Hosts Don and Karen Sikes promote the friendly atmosphere, clean and comfortable accommodations, and beach access. Cabins are available on a monthly basis in the winter. To see some pictures of the location, visit their web page at www.ptinet.net/~wdsbayrv.

Resorts and Guest Ranches

Guest Ranches Rates

$	$70 to $120
$$	$121-$170
$$$	$171-$220
$$$$	$221 and up

Bayview Resort Marina & RV
$ • 543 Yenne Point Rd, Bigfork
• (406) 837-4843, (800) 775-3536

Bayview Resort has everything you need for a perfect economical fishing vacation: Fully furnished cabins with kitchens, dockside service, fishing tackle, groceries, beer, and boat rentals. Owners David and Sharon Young say the Flathead Lake resort specializes in family gatherings. A three-bedroom home for a little more money and motel style rooms for a little less are also lodging options. The marina can outfit you with boat rentals for any kind of recreation possibility Ñ skiing, fishing, pontoon or paddle boats, aqua cycle, and three passenger Sea Doos. There's also a private beach, and a nightly lakeside bonfire in the summer. Bayview is just four miles south of Bigfork. The resort is on the internet at www.cyberport.net/bayview and can be reached by e-mail at bayview@cyberport.net.

Flathead Lake Lodge

$$$$ •P.O. Box 248, Montana 35, Bigfork • (406) 837-4391

If you are looking for a Western adventure, try Flathead Lake Lodge, a famous 2,000-acre family operated dude ranch that attracts celebrities, wealthy businesspeople from around the world, as well as ordinary families that save up for an extraordinary vacation. The rate for an adult for a week is almost $2,000, but for that money you get much more than lodging. All meals and recreation are included in the package, and in the case of Flathead Lake Lodge that means three superb meals a day plus horseback riding, rodeo action, cookouts, water sports, use of sailboats, canoes, fishing boats, water-skiing, lake cruises, a heated pool, tennis courts, volleyball, hiking wilderness and primitive areas and· many other ranch activities. The Averill family has operated the resort for more than 50 years, and there hasn't been a complaint yet. This is a real Western vacation in a setting of unmatched luxury and beauty. The ranch offers one or two-week vacations with everyone arriving and departing on the same day, but you can't just call up and get in the next week. Reservations are often made years in advance, and the lodge boasts a 50-60 percent return of guests year after year. It has been featured by *Better Homes & Gardens, Sunset, Travel & Leisure, Bon Appetit* and *Good Morning America,* among others.

Marina Cay Resort

$$$ •180 Vista Lane, Bigfork • (406) 837-5861, (800) 433-6516

This resort is a deluxe facility on Bigfork Bay, just up the hill from the village. Accommodations range from an economy room for one or two people only with no view to a waterfront marina suite with king-size bed and private Jacuzzi. One, two and three bedroom condo rentals are also available. The resort features an outdoor pool and whirlpool, as well as a full-service marina where you can rent a ski boat, jet ski, canoe or other watercraft. Guided fishing charters will escort you to just the right spot to catch "the big one." After you come back for the night, you can enjoy one of three restaurants and several bars and lounges. Visit Marina Cay on the off-season for significant savings. Rates are discounted 50 percent or more from the last week of September to the middle of May.

Bed and Breakfasts

Bed and Breakfast Rates	
$	less than $85
$$	$85 to $115
$$$	$116 to $150
$$$$	$151 and up

Cherry Way Inn

$ • 26400 East Shore Route, Bigfork • (406) 837-6803, (800) 837-6803

This is a very reasonably priced, small alternative to the hotel and resort lifestyle. Think of this as staying with a friend. There are only two rooms for rent in the summer, both with private baths and a view of Flathead Lake. Rustic cabins are also available for extra guests. The house itself is 60 years old, and it has been in service as a B&B for seven years. A full breakfast is served, with guests selecting their favorites from the menu the night before. Swedish pancakes are a favorite.

Coyote Roadhouse Inn & Riverside Cabins

$$ to $$$ •602 Three Eagles Lane, Bigfork • (406) 837-4250

This seasonal bed and breakfast establishment is an offshoot of the Coyote Riverhouse Restaurant. Owner and chef Gary Hastings decided he wanted to offer intimate dining experiences to guests, so he started the Roadhouse Inn, which takes maximum advantage of the woodsy setting and adds fine food of a high order. The Coyote Roadhouse Inn is located near Ferndale off Montana Highway 209 on a scenic portion of the Swan River. This is a great place to get away if you enjoy quiet walks along the river.

O'Duachain Country Inn
$$$ • 675 Ferndale Drive, Bigfork
• (406) 837-6851, 800-837-7460

Best known for total comfort and Montana charm, this three-level log home and two-story guesthouse is located on five acres just five miles from Bigfork. The grounds include many rustic features as well as wild game. Bird watchers will enjoy the exotic birds such as peacocks and waterfowl, which can be seen on the pond. Bill Knoll and Mary Corcoran Knoll are the owners of The O'Duachain (pronounced O-Do-CANE), which was established in 1985 by Tom and Margot Doohan. The breakfast menu still includes Margot's Stuffed Irish Toast, as well as homemade maple nut cereal with fruit puree, and lots of different teas and coffees. The facility offers suites and rooms with private baths. The guesthouse also has balconies and patios with incredible views. If you're looking for stiff European charm, the Knolls warn, this is not the place for you. They make you feel right at home.

Swan River Inn
$$$ • 360 Grand Drive, Bigfork
• (406) 837-2220

The Swan River Inn has just three rooms, but they occupy a choice location in downtown Bigfork, where there are few accommodations available of any kind. The inn is affiliated with the Swan River Inn Cafe, but under different ownership. Room service is available, so you can take advantage of the elegant and healthy menu at the restaurant. There are antiques in the rooms, which have different themes such as Victorian, Art Deco and rustic Western. Each room has a separate entrance and private baths, with one room offering kitchen facilities.

Campgrounds

Campground Rates

$	$4 to $9
$$	$10 to $16
$$$	$17 to $23
$$$$	$24 and up

Bigfork Timbers RV Park and Campground
$$ • 8540 Montana 35, Bigfork
• (406) 837-6200, (800) 821-4546

The Timbers RV Park and Campground is affiliated with the Timbers Motel and is within

The Bigfork Summer Playhouse offers exceptional entertainment.

Backcountry Cooking

Cooking and eating are some of the most pleasurable aspects of a backcountry outing in Glacier Park and the surrounding wilderness. The scenic grandeur alone provides a backdrop that can rival the ambiance of the finest five-star restaurant. Backcountry meals facilitate enjoyable social interaction, but more importantly they provide the energy and sustenance to fuel rigorous activities.

Backcountry menus will be influenced by the personal preferences and dietary needs of your group. During a typical backcountry trip you need not worry over-much about eating an excess of sugar, starch or fats. Strenuous activities and higher elevations demand extra amounts (within reason) to provide needed energy. Preference should be given to high-energy producing foods such as pasta, rice, beans, nuts, cheese and wheat products.

Dried veggies and meats, or meat substitutes, are lightweight and add substance, color and taste to perhaps otherwise bland pasta, rice or potato dishes. A spice kit is a must for any backcountry connoisseur.

Food and cookware weight and bulk will impact your packing, particularly on extended trips. Lightweight freeze-dried food offers an attractive option and the advantage of quick preparation. You can reduce some weight and bulk by repacking food into reusable plastic bags. This also reduces litter to pack out.

Trail snacks are important to backcountry travelers. Dried fruits, nuts, crackers and cheese, candy and energy bars all provide helpful energy boosts.

Glacier Park is the domain of black and grizzly bears. Your menu and cooking techniques must take this into account. Select rations that are low-odor and avoid strong food odors that may attract bears. Try not to spill food in the cooking area.

Proper food and garbage storage are important in bear country. Regulations require you to hang food, garbage and cookware on food-hanging devices in backcountry campgrounds at all times except mealtimes. Never cook, eat or store food in your tent; it may attract a bear into your camp. Wastewater from clean up should be strained of food scraps and scattered. Food scraps should be packed out.

Campfires are permitted in approximately one-half of Glacier's backcountry campgrounds. Cooking over an open fire can be enjoyable; however the "Leave No Trace" program strongly recommends that backpackers use a lightweight campstove.

An important advantage to carrying a campstove is that you can boil water and prepare hot drinks and food quickly during inclement weather or an emergency situation.

Backcountry rangers are perhaps the greatest culinary experts roaming Glacier's wildlands. Here is a favorite dinner entree from an anonymous backcountry ranger:

Vigo brand Santa Fe pinto beans and rice with corn. (Available in the Mexican section at the grocery.) Boil contents in three cups water for one minute. Simmer 20 minutes. Add two tablespoons butter or margarine. Garnish with grated cheese. Serve with pita bread. Feeds one hungry ranger.

walking distance of Bigfork Village. Guests of the RV park and campground have access to the motel complex's outdoor pool in summer and the sauna and hot tub year round. There are five tent spaces available for $7 per person or RV hookups available for $18 per night for two. Laundry facilities and free hot showers are available. The RV park and campground is only open for the summer season.

Flathead Lake State Park
$ • 490 N. Meridian Rd., Kalispell
• (406) 752-5501

The park consists of six scenic units bordering Flathead Lake, two of which are on the east shore near Bigfork. With the exception of Wild Horse Island, all units feature economical camping, fishing, boating and swimming. Closest to Bigfork is 69-acre Wayfarer's (phone 837-4196 in summer) just outside of town, which features 30 campsites, including seven tent-only sites. The park has flush toilets and a group picnic shelter, as well as trailer and boat sewage dump stations. The Yellow Bay facility is 15 acres and the campground has six sites, including five walk-in tent sites. Flush and vault toilets and coin-operated showers are available. All individual campsites are available on a first-come, first-served basis. Plan to arrive early, as most fill up by 4 PM on weekends during July and August. Maximum stay is seven days.

Outback Montana
$$, no credit cards • 27202 E. Lakeshore Dr., Bigfork
• (406) 837-6973, (888) 900-6973

There are 40 RV sites at Outback Montana, including many pull-throughs, and 10 tent sites. There is more of an emphasis on privacy than at many RV parks, with fenced terraces, patios and picnic tables at each site. Restrooms are available, but you pay extra for showers or pets. Families will enjoy such activities as tetherball, badminton and horseshoes in the delightful outdoor setting. Although credit cards are not accepted, owners Carol and Bill Matthews take out-of-area checks.

Woods Bay Marina and RV Park
$$$ • 624 Yenne Point Rd, Bigfork
• (406) 837-6038

From May to Oct. 1, you can drive your RV right up to Flathead Lake at the Woods Bay Marina and enjoy a lake vacation for just $20 a night (full hookup) or $15 a night (partial — just water and electric). If you are pulling a boat, you have the advantage of having the boat docked within feet of your hookup. There are also three tent sites at $10 per site for one person and $5 for each additional person. Free hot showers and a laundry facility are nearby. For family reunions, ask about the four-bedroom house rental. Gas and repairs are available for boats on site, and a market sells food and tackle. Fishing and lake tour guides can be hired from the marina as well.

Restaurants

Restaurant Rates

$	$10 to $19
$$	$20 to $27
$$$	$28 to $35
$$$$	$36 and more

For two people, meal exclusive of beverages, tip, and tax.

INSIDERS' TIP

The Forest Service rents out a number of cabins on National Forest land. Most are quite remote and need to be hiked or skied to, but some can be reached by car. Season of availability is restricted in some cases. Call Cabin Rental Reservations on the Hungry Horse and Glacier View Districts of the Flathead National Forest at (406) 387-3809 for further information. These cabins are often booked well in advance; make reservations early.

Credit: Bjorge's Gallery

Bigfork lights up for the holidays

Family Friendly Dining

Brookie's Cookies
$ • 191 Mill St., Bigfork
• (406) 837-CHIP, (800) 697-6487

Just around the corner from Electric Avenue near the Swan River is a place to stop for all kinds of munchies, from chocolate chip cookies to gourmet desserts, baked fresh every day in small batches. One of our favorites is "The Bigfoot," a hearty chocolate chip cookie made with nuts, oats, and more. Brookie's Cookies owner Greg Bloom came up with this hearty cookie when he was out cross-country skiing with his wife Karen, and wanted an extra-energy treat. The store, which is on-line at www.brookiescookies.com, features a large selection of coffees and other beverages. There's also a helping of merchandise on hand such as clothing and coffee mugs with the Brookie's Cookies logo. And keep the name in mind when you are traveling elsewhere in the Flathead, because the "cookie van" takes Brookie's Cookies to a variety of stores and restaurants throughout the area.

Champs Sports Pub and Grill
$$ • 180 Vista Lane, Bigfork
• (406) 837-5861, (800) 433-6516

Though Champs is a sports bar, it is also a perfect place to have a family meal because it features a fun kids' menu and large lunch and dinner specials. There are large televisions for sports coverage and trivia games, and the bar serves local microbrews for mom and dad to enjoy. Champs is part of Marina Cay Resort, and you will find other listings under Fine Dining and under Nightlife.

Del Norte
$ • 355 Grand Drive, Bigfork
• (406) 837-0076

A great place to go with the kids is Del Norte, located right across the street from the bay in Bigfork. The menu features plenty of authentic Mexican specialties as well as burgers and other American food and take-out. Try the buffalo burger for something unique to Montana. If the kids don't like the Mexican cuisine, they will definitely enjoy the ice cream, which comes in both the hard and soft varieties and in lots of flavors, including huckleberry. Del Norte is open daily in the summer only.

Swan River Inn Cafe & Dinner House
$$$ • 360 Grand Drive, Bigfork
• (406) 837-2220

This is a great compromise for families looking for something in between fine dining and diner food. The Swan River Inn's European and American menu caters to a healthy diet, but with plenty of specialties to pique the appetite. You can get steak and eggs for breakfast to prep you for a busy day fishing on the lake, and then come back and have a gourmet dinner. On Sundays, brunch is served from 8 AM to 3 PM all year round, and Sunday evenings feature a prime rib and red king salmon special. There is also outdoor seating available in one of the best views possible of Bigfork Bay. The restaurant opens at 8 a.m. and is open for breakfast, lunch and dinner. All meals are made from scratch, and you'll enjoy the homey atmosphere and emphasis on service. There are rooms available for rent in the same building.

Wild Mile Deli
$ • 435 Bridge St., Bigfork
• (406) 837-3354

The Wild Mile Deli, which serves breakfast and lunch as well as offering gourmet food items, wine and beer, is best known for its homemade bread and pastries. There is always a long line for the thick, rich soups such as the cream of potato, and there are pasta dinners available year-round except on Sundays and Mondays. The restaurant is named after the famous Wild Mile of the Swan River, which runs near the restaurant and is the scene of a popular kayaking race every year.

Fine Dining

Bigfork Inn
$$$ • 604 Electric Ave., Bigfork
• (406) 837-6680

The Bigfork Inn is one of the defining spots in this lakeside community. It was built in 1937 after a fire destroyed the Bigfork Hotel and features a mountain chalet style that is associated with Glacier National Park. The Inn, which serves dinners only, is open year-round seven days a week, with fine dining from an extensive menu that features pasta, veal, prime rib, fresh fish, and steak. There is an outdoor patio that's open in the summer, and dancing on Friday and Saturday nights to the traditional jazz sounds of The Company Brass. The restaurant and bar open at 5 PM daily.

Bridge Street Gallery & Cafe
$$ • 408 Bridge Street, Bigfork
• (406) 837-5825

Bridge Street offers a unique combination of art and delectables. Brunch, lunch and dinner are served daily. During the summer, you can eat on the deck or inside, but it's inside where the action is. That's because the walls of Bridge Street are covered with art that is for sale. A rotating series of exhibits is featured throughout the year, including the annual Christmas wreath contest, which includes a prize for best edible wreath. The cafe also features a large selection of wines by the glass or bottle, including a selection from the Chateau Montelena winery in Napa Valley owned by Bridge Street's proprietor, Laura Barrett. A private dining room is available for larger parties, and reservations are suggested.

Coyote Riverhouse
$$$ • 600 Three Eagle Lane, Bigfork
• (406) 837-1233

Owner and chef Gary Hastings has a reputation as a perfectionist. He certainly deserves it, according to anyone who has ever eaten at the Coyote Riverhouse. This is a world-class restaurant that features a highly trained staff and a gourmet menu in a backwoods setting. You have to drive a little ways from Bigfork toward Ferndale on Montana Highway 209, then follow the signs from Ferndale to the Riverhouse, which is located on a remote and scenic portion of the Swan River. Make a reservation before you show up at the front door, because it is a very popular spot and often fills up in spite of its somewhat remote location. Most nights look for such Cajun specialties as blackened redfish and many European

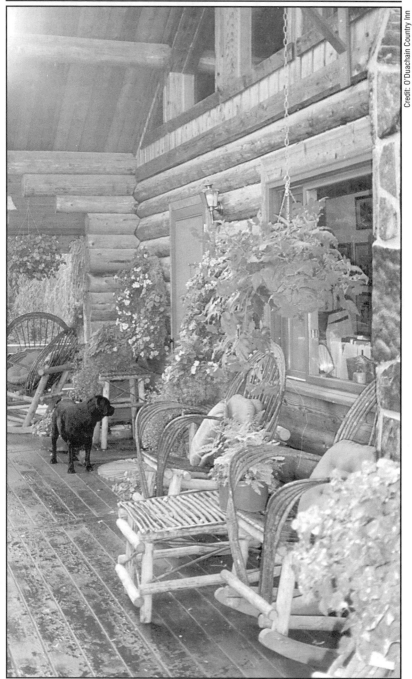

Log-house living at its most gracious.

specialties as well as fresh fish. Rooms are also available (see listing under Bed & Breakfasts for Coyote Roadhouse Inn).

Quincy's at Marina Cay Resort
$$$ • 180 Vista Lane, Bigfork
• (406) 837-5861, (800) 433-6516

Quincy's offers award-winning contemporary cuisine with an emphasis on seasonal products and fresh ingredients. Try the Kentucky bourbon steak for a variation on a familiar theme, and look for the daily specials such as pheasant or duck along with fresh seafood. The restaurant overlooks Bigfork Bay and features indoor and outdoor seating. During the high season, breakfast, lunch, and dinner are all available, plus Sunday brunch from 10 AM to 2 PM Quincy's is part of Marina Cay Resort, and you will find other listings under Family Friendly Dining and under Nightlife.

ShowThyme
$$$ • 548 Electric Ave., Bigfork
• (406) 837-0707

The ShowThyme restaurant is located next door to the Bigfork Center for the Performing Arts, which explains the pun in the name. But whether or not you are making a stop before watching a show put on by the Bigfork Summer Playhouse, you can't go wrong stopping here. ShowThyme, located in an historic building that formerly housed a bank, is simply one of the best restaurants the Flathead Valley has to offer. Every night, a variety of specials are available, from the featured rack of lamb to a variety of fresh fish and shellfish. The wait staff is trained to recite specials from memory and to take orders without benefit of a notepad. It makes for a nice challenge for the highly professional staff, and they've never gotten our order wrong yet. Save room for dessert, though you will be hard pressed to choose between the simple delight of the creme caramel and the decadent double-chocolate cake. Reservations are appreciated and sometimes necessary at this busy restaurant, which serves lunch and dinner.

Nightlife

Garden Bar
451 Electric Ave., Bigfork
• (406) 837-9914

Lots of folks park themselves in the Garden Bar after work and just hang out there for hours. Why not? There's great food from the grille, a pool table, pinball, electronic darts, TVs for sports coverage, live music on summer weekends, and video poker and keno machines for the amateur gambler. In the summer, don't forget to poke your head out back and see why the bar got its name. The outdoor patio and garden is a delightful place to sip a beer and kick back. The Garden Kitchen does a great job with burgers, but you can also get chicken, fish, salads, and hot dogs. By the way, if you aren't sure about whether the Garden Bar is right for you, this sign on the wall should be a good clue: "This establishment serves no drinks with little tiny umbrellas." A Montana tradition for 17 years, and one that shows no sign of ending.

Marina Cay
180 Vista Lane, Bigfork
• (406) 837-5861, (800) 433-6516

There are two popular night spots at Marina Cay Resort. The Tiki Bar features live entertainment 3 or 4 nights a week. A frequent contributor is Denise Sterhan, a karaoke performer with a wide range. Lunches and dinners are also available from the kitchen.

INSIDERS' TIP

Pepper spray to defend against bears has gained in popularity for both park rangers and visitors. Be aware that wind, rain and spray distance all influence the spray's effectiveness, as does the spray's product shelf life. Don't let carrying pepper spray give you a false sense of security, however, and don't substitute it for safety precautions in bear country. Some pepper sprays aren't allowed to be taken into Canada.

Quincy's Piano Lounge and Casino offers an upscale mellow atmosphere with live piano music. You'll be able to get your favorite cocktail, rare whiskey, or aromatic cigar here. Look for other listings for Marina Cay under Family Friendly Dining and Fine Dining.

North Shore Lanes and Casino
116 Holt Dr., Bigfork
• **(406) 837-5381**

This is a perfect spot for families looking for entertainment in Bigfork. It's not far from downtown, there plenty of parking, and it's open year-round. There are eight bowling lanes, available at least part of every day for open bowling. There is also a lounge area, where musical entertainment is sometimes scheduled, a restaurant (try the North Shore Burger) with a great view of the lake, and an arcade area for kids that is kept separate from the bar. The North Shore is open for breakfast, lunch and dinner.

Sabo's Pub & Eatery
260 River St., Bigfork
• **(406) 837-5251**

Another popular night spot is Sabo's, owned by the same folks who run Hap's restaurant at Eagle Bend. Here you can get pizza, sandwiches, chicken wings, burgers and more, along with a selection of microbrew beers. There's a roof deck where you can drink under the stars during the summer season, and live music downstairs on the weekends. Pool, pinball and ping-pong make for alternative entertainment, and there is keno as well. Sabo's closes down in February.

Shopping

Bigfork Bay Gift & Gear
491 Electric Ave., Bigfork
• **(406) 837-5850**

This is a good place to start your shopping, since they cram a lot of merchandise into the store. You'll find a large selection of toys, lotions, stationery, T-shirts and gift items. There are also a couple of indispensables — a Jelly Belly jelly bean counter and a wall full of Ty Beanie Babies. The prices are reasonable and the faces are friendly.

Bigfork Station
470 Electric Ave., Bigfork
• **(406) 837-2332**

One of the most recent additions to the downtown Bigfork panorama is the Bigfork Station, a collection of shops in a new building that harks back in appearance to the old-style architecture of a turn-of-the-century railroad station. Don't let it worry you that the railroad never came to Bigfork, just enjoy the ride. First stop is Roma's Eclectic on Electric, a funky shop full of delightful "don't-need-but-must-haves." Whether you are looking for, glassware, gadgets or gourmet cookware you can find it here, right down to the moose-shaped cookie cutters. The shop is brightly lit and a pleasure to the eye. We've included their phone number on this listing, since there's someone there seven days a week. Next stop is the Buffalo Trails Gallery featuring the work of sculptor Bob Stayton and other Western art and craft collectibles. Next door is the Rocky Mountain Chocolate Factory, where your purchases may not last till you reach the door. But oh, are they ever tasty. Around the corner, you'll see the Buffalo Creek Clothing Company, where you can pick up that rugged leisure apparel to fit in with the mountain chic crowd. Next up is our favorite stop, Pufferbelly Toys, which bills itself as selling "Classic toys for Playful People." Your kids will love this store, where they provide ample opportunity to sample the wares before a purchase. Trains, planes, dinosaurs, fish, games —if a kid has ever dreamed of it, it's here. Before you leave the Bigfork Station, you can get refreshed at The Cup and Saucer, serving espresso, coffee, drinks and ice cream.

Electric Avenue Books
490 Electric Ave., Bigfork
• **(406) 837-6072**

Electric Avenue Books is one of Montana's most eclectic bookstores, offering a selection of titles from contemporary to classics and everything in between. This isn't an independent equivalent of Waldenbooks by any means. Owner Katie Callan and her staff go out of their way to make you comfortable, with lounge chairs and other surprises scattered throughout the store. The shop's back room, for instance, is set up as an old-timey parlor and features an upright piano where customers or guest artists may perform. Musical events are held at the store regularly on Sunday afternoons in the summer and less frequently throughout the year. The store has one of the best selections of literary authors in the Flathead Valley, but that's just the beginning. They also have extensive offerings of Montana history, Western lore, arts, crafts, and the offbeat. In a central room upstairs, there is a children's reading room, with a kid-size table and chairs, inviting toys, and lots of books to get your youngsters interested in

reading. Head downstairs and work your way through a series of rooms until you get to the one that features a mountain cabin theme, with canoes, wooden skis, and rustic cabinetry serving as a backdrop for outdoors and adventure reading.

Kehoe's Agate Shop
1020 Holt Drive, Bigfork
• **(406) 837-4467**

Kehoe's shop lies just off the bank of the Flathead River in old Holt, an early settlement that lasted from the 1880s to the 1920s. Just across the road from the shop is the old Holt

INSIDERS' TIP

The fires of 1988 brought national attention to the effects and ecology of wildland fire. The North Fork subdistrict of Glacier National Park has sustained naturally occurring wildfires of different intensities in 1988, 1992, 1994, and 1998—all part of a long history of burns in this area. If you're interested in fire ecology, try driving the Inside North Fork Road for about 3 miles south of Polebridge to Lone Pine Prairie, or take the road to Bowman Lake (neither is for RVs)—you'll see the burned, still-standing lodgepole pines with a new crop of young trees growing up beneath them. Wildflowers are thick in the ash-fertilized soil. If you'd like to hike, try taking the northern arm of the Quartz Loop from Bowman Lake over to Quartz Lake: you'll enjoy the vistas opened up by the fires as you move in and out of the burned area on Cerulean Ridge.

general store, crumbling quietly as the years pass, and a little farther down the road are the remnants of an old ferry crossing. But Kehoe's Agate Shop actually looks much further back than the 100 years or so represented by the passing of Holt into history. The store features a variety of gemstones, agates and fossils that date back as much as millions of years. Many of them were collected from around the world and ground or worked into a variety of shapes by James Kehoe Sr., a gemologist who built the shop in 1932 from planks from the steamboat *Helena*. Today, Kehoe's children, James Jr. and Leslie, tend to the store. He also designs jewelry with gold and a variety of gemstones. A sign next to the shop explains a little of the history of Holt, the ferry, and the *Helena*. Remnants of the *Helena*, including the pilothouse, are also on display. To find the shop, all you have to do is keep your eyes open. Almost every major highway in the area of Bigfork has a sign pointing you in the right direction.

Eva Gates Homemade Preserves
456 Electric Ave., Bigfork
• (406) 837-4356, (800) 682-4283

Walk in the door of Eva Gates Homemade Preserves and you'll feel like you're back in grandma's kitchen 50 years ago. In fact, for half a century the Gates family has been creating the aromatic and tasty preserves and syrups that are today highly prized. Back in 1949, Eva used her own grandmother's recipe, and today it is her grandchildren and great-grandchildren keeping up the family tradition. When you walk in the front door, you will see Pam Siess or her assistants actually doing the cooking. They welcome questions, and love to share the secrets of their success. The syrups and preserves are made in five pint batches without additives or preservatives to keep them as fresh as possible. January through March, the store is closed on Sundays.

Twin Birch Square
459 Electric Ave., Bigfork
• (406) 837-4994

Another location where you can centralize your shopping in Bigfork is the Twin Birch Square. An "anchor" in the two story complex is Electric Avenue Gifts, where you can stop to purchase an assortment of candles, toys, Gund Bears, ceramics, lotions, T-shirts, etc. We've included the phone number for Electric Avenue Gifts to give you a starting point for your shopping. But don't forget to look further. Also downstairs is Larry Janoff's gallery, which features aviation art, and the Cherry Tree with a selection of women's clothing. Upstairs, there are two "niche" stores — The Stone Chair, which features a mix of old and new items for the country home, and Architectural Innovations, which specializes in Old World antiques and art objects. These and a variety of other galleries and retail stores will keep you occupied at Twin Birch Square for the better part of an afternoon.

Tour boats depart from the Polson dock for sight-seeing on Flathead Lake, including trips to Wild Horse Island, which is the lake's largest island and is home to bighorn sheep and other wild animals, as well as the small horse population that gives the island its name.

Polson

At the south end of Flathead Lake, midway between Kalispell and Missoula, sits the town of Polson, the first community in the area to be settled by whites. In fact, Polson is in the middle of the Flathead Indian Reservation, but you would never suspect that at first. Although the Confederated Salish and Kootenai tribes have jurisdiction over some aspects of life here, everyday matters are handled just as they are anywhere else in Montana. There is a sheriff and a county commission for Lake County, a city council for Polson, and people pay taxes to the state of Montana just as they do elsewhere. But there are a few exceptions. The tribal authorities here, for instance, negotiated a separate gambling compact with the state government that allows somewhat higher payouts for gaming machines and a higher total of machines than is allowed on non-reservation land. There is also a separate tribal license for hunting and fishing, although efforts have been made to end that authority.

Polson, which was named after pioneer rancher David Polson and was incorporated in 1910, is the largest city on the reservation, but it still only boasts a population of about 3,500 people. The city's early claim to fame was its steamboats, which for many years were the only means of reaching the north end of the lake and Kalispell. Today, Polson offers a wide variety of activities, especially for those who want to take advantage of the scenic wonders of Flathead Lake. Tour boats depart from the Polson dock for sight-seeing on Flathead Lake, including trips to Wild Horse Island, which is the lake's largest island and is home to bighorn sheep and other wild animals, as well as the small horse population that gives the island its name. The fishing is, of course, remarkable throughout Flathead Lake, with sizable lake trout and whitefish being popular catches. When you're on the lake, keep an eye open for the legendary Flathead Lake Monster, an American cousin of the Loch Ness Monster, which, like its more famous counterpart, is often written about but rarely spotted.

If you travel south of Polson toward Missoula on U.S. 93, there are some must-see spots. Just south of town is Kerr Dam, which the Montana Power Company built on land leased from the tribes. Whitewater rafting is a popular activity on the Flathead River below the dam. There are also scenic vistas and a picnic area. In the tribal capital of Pablo, you can stop at the People's Center to learn about local history and native traditions. A little farther south, you can witness the profound influence of the early European settlers on the area at the historic Mission Church at St. Ignatius, which features remarkable murals. Not far away, there is also a highway loop that brings you to the National Bison Range at Moiese, where bison, antelope, and other creatures big and small are plentiful and much easier to photograph than at Glacier National Park.

If it is late summer, you can drive north of Polson on either U.S. 93 or Montana 35 and enjoy the produce of the area's famous sweet cherry orchards at roadside stands. The trip to Glacier Park from here is under two hours.

Life in Polson is even more low-key than in many other cities in Montana—perhaps because of the combined influences of the majestic lake, the Native American traditions, and the temperate weather. In any case, while you stay here, plan on being enchanted by the downtown shops—which are heavy into arts and antiques—and by the unassuming restaurants and taverns. Everyone is just a local here. You can blend in easily as you play golf at the recently expanded Polson Country Club, watch the ensemble work of the Port Polson Players at a theater in the clubhouse, or enjoy the Montana State Fiddlers Contest, which is held annually at the Polson High School on the fourth full weekend in July.

Accommodations

Hotel & Motel Rates

Keep in mind that some rates are based on availability. The average nightly rates for two adults at the hotels and motels listed in this section are indicated by a dollar sign ($) ranking in the following chart. Also, the hotels and motels in this chapter accept all or most major credit cards.

$	$25 to $49
$$	$50 to $75
$$$	$76 to $100
$$$$	$101 and more

Hotels and Motels

Cherry Hill Motel and Cabins
$$ •1810 U.S. 93, Polson
• (406) 883-2737

The Cherry Hill is indeed built on a hill once noted for its cherry orchards. The motel overlooks the highway and the Polson Country Club golf course as well as Flathead Lake. Owner Glen Lack says the Cherry Hill was built in 1943, but it was completely remodeled in 1996. Now it has the best of both worlds, the quaint roadside motel look of the mid-century, and the amenities of the modern day. The motel is actually a series of buildings that each house a couple of rooms and two cabins. Accommodations range from two bedrooms with a kitchenette to just a simple room. In addition to the large, grassy yard, there is an outdoor hot tub for use in summer, and gazebos and benches for a comfortable perch for a picnic with a great view. The Cherry Hill doesn't take American Express, but dogs are welcome!

Days Inn of Polson
$$ •914 U.S. 93 E., Polson
• (406) 883-3120, 800-735-6862

The Days Inn provides all the comforts of a modern motel. Built in 1984, it features queen-size beds, a lake view and a view of the distant peaks of Glacier National Park, usually snow-covered well into summer. Some of the 25 rooms include a microwave and refrigerator, so if you will be staying in Polson for several days, make sure you request them. A continental breakfast is provided, and the motel is within walking distance of a full-service restaurant. Pets are allowed.

Port Polson Inn
$$$ •502 U.S. 93, Polson
• (406) 883-5385, 800-654-0682

Before KwaTaqNuk (see Resorts and Guest Ranches) came to town, this was the most popular lodging spot, and it's easy to see why. The rooms look out across the highway right onto Flathead Lake and the Mission Mountains beyond. There are 44 rooms in all, along with indoor and outdoor hot tubs, an indoor sauna, and an exercise facility. Although the outside of the motel has a 1960s look, the owners work to give the rooms a B&B feel, with flowers provided in the summertime and a continental breakfast offered. There are also a couple of theme rooms, so plan ahead and you can stay in either a cowboy-style room or one dedicated to Mickey Mouse.

INSIDERS' TIP

Mountain streams may look beautiful and clean, and they sometimes are, but they can also carry giardia, a nasty parasite that will give you untold intestinal distress. Always boil water for at least a minute before drinking it, or use a filter approved for giardia.

Schiefelbein Haus
$$ • 6395 East Shore Route, Polson
• (406) 887-2431

The Schiefelbein Haus is the farthest out of town of any of the motels in this list, but don't let that deter you. It's only 6 1/2 miles from Polson on Montana 35, which circles Flathead Lake's east shore. Look for two large blue Bavarian-style buildings. The owners go all out to provide an atmosphere similar to alpine Bavaria, including music, posters, pictures, steins, flags and decorations. The motel, restaurant, beer garden, and RV park are located on 10 acres with tall pine trees, colorful flowers and wild animals such as deer and turkeys. During the summer, a restaurant serving American, German and Cajun food is open Wednesday through Sunday.

Super 8
$$ • Junction of Montana 35 & U.S. 93, Polson
• (406) 883-6266, 406-883-6251,
• 800-800-8000

The Polson Super 8 offers all queen-size beds, continental breakfast, bus/truck parking,

Camp Tuffit

The word "rustic" could have been coined especially for Camp Tuffit, an old-style fishing resort on Lake Mary Ronan that's been run by the Thomas family for 85 years.

Lake Mary Ronan, named after the wife of an early Indian agent who stocked the lake with cutthroat trout in 1892, traditionally has had about the best fishing in the Montana. Charlie Thomas came to Lake Mary Ronan in 1914 and established the fishing camp that's now run by his grandchildren and great-grandchildren. Generations of fishing enthusiasts have come to the camp, and return year after year to the rough-hewn cabins built by Charlie and named whimsically for radio-show personalities, famous gold mining camps or celebrities. Mention Camp Tuffit around Northwest Montana, and chances are someone will wax eloquent about the beauty of the spot, the quality of the fishing and memories of the good times shared with friends and family.

The camp looks much the same as it did in old photographs that show the cabins and the lodge in the early days. A quality of timelessness may be one of the enduring appeals of Camp Tuffit. The personality of the founder still can be seen throughout the camp—in the cabins he built, newspaper clippings about him and his wife's old piano, where modern fishing enthusiasts still pound out a tune.

Charlie Thomas built wooden boats for fishing: at one time 65 hand-built boats that plied the lake. The wooden boats have been retired now, replaced by aluminum craft, but some of Charlie's creations are still being used as flower planters. Charlie was quite a marketing agent, too. He built colorful cutouts of mannequins sitting like fishermen in flat-bottomed boats. The signs, which said "Follow the boats to Camp Tuffit" at one time were posted on roads in Nevada, Idaho, Washington and Montana. The Thomases maintain handmade signs on the road to the camp, and some of the originals are now in a storage shop, along with some of Charlie's hand-built boats.

Camp Tuffit got its name after a Kalispell physician told Charlie to take his ailing wife out into the woods to "tough it" for the summer. When the doctor planned a fishing trip at the lake, Charlie wrote "Camp Tuffit" on a piece of cardboard to guide him to the spot, and the name stuck. Charlie started building boats and cabins and welcoming guests, who rented a boat for $1 a day.

The heart of Camp Tuffit is the main lodge, where guests come after a day of fishing to swap stories around the campfire and relive their adventures. The cabins have been maintained and modernized through the years, but they still keep the old rustic flavor that the guests seem to love. The camp has 33 cottages, 20 trailer hook-ups and 18 privately owned permanent mobile homes. Guests return year after year, and often reserve their favorite cabin by name.

Jerome Thomas, Charlie's son, returned to Camp Tuffit after World War II with his wife, Ruth, and the couple ran the camp with Charlie, then took over management. They're mostly retired now, and their sons and their wives have taken over the active management. It's definitely a family operation. Children, grand-children and great-grandchildren work at Camp Tuffit, or return to spend time with family there.

Jerome and Ruth spend winters down south now, while sons Gary and Mark and their wives are the active managers of the camp. But come summer, Jerome and Ruth are there to help as the family traditions continue summer after summer.

Though the future of fishing at Lake Mary Ronan has been clouded by a "bucket biologist" who illegally dumped perch in the lake a few years ago, Camp Tuffit retains its loyalty and its charm: a charming, rustic place where "progress" is suspended and the smiling presence of Charlie Thomas seems to linger as new generations tell fish stories around the campfire.

To reach Camp Tuffit, turn off U.S. 93 at Dayton, about 40 miles south of Kalispell, and travel about 6.5 miles on a paved road until you see one of Charlie's signs directing you to the camp.

and many nearby conveniences. It's across the street from the 4Bs restaurant, the Safeway grocery store and a Wal-Mart. It's also within walking distance of the golf course and two lounge casinos. Pets allowed with permission.

Resorts and Guest Ranches

Guest Ranches Rates

$	$70 to $120
$$	$121 to $170
$$$	$171 to $220
$$$$	$221 and up

Best Western KwaTaqNuk Resort
$$$ •303 U.S. Highway 93, Polson
• (406) 883-3636, 800-882-6363

This hotel and conference center is owned by the Confederated Salish and Kootenai Tribes, and is one of the greatest success stories of the tribal economy. It is the jewel in Polson's resplendent tourism crown. KwaTaqNuk Resort features 112 rooms, restaurant, lounge and casino, convention facilities, indoor and outdoor pools, indoor whirl-pool, gift shop, art gallery, and a full-service marina. Unlike most of the hotels in Polson, KwaTaqNuk is built right on the lakeshore. The *Port Polson Princess* cruise boat sails from its docks during the summer. The convention facilities can accommodate groups up to 300 people.

Big Arm Resort and Marina
$ • P.O. Box 99, Big Arm
• (406) 849-5622

If you are looking for a low-cost family vacation that is strong on lake fun, you might consider the Big Arm Resort & Marina, located about 11 miles north of Polson on U.S. 93. The resort is located right on the lakeshore and features cabins and rental trailers as well as RV hookups. A small grocery store on site sells refreshments and picnic supplies, as well as outboard fuel and oil. They also stock lures, tackle and bait. You can, of course, rent a boat from the marina, or just rent a boat slip if you have your own vessel. Evenings, when the boats pull in, you might enjoy a sing-along around a campfire or roasting some marsh-mallows. The resort specializes in family reunions, and you will need to get your reservations in early to make sure there is space available.

Mission Mountain Resort
$ • 257 Fulkerson Lane, Polson
• (406) 883-1883

This low-cost getaway is located on an 80-acre sanctuary just three miles from Polson in the Mission Mountains. You can see Flathead Lake and the rest of the valley from this scenic perch, but you will enjoy pine-scented air and mountain living. The accommodations are new and feature Western motifs. There are two guestrooms, and three guest cabins (the biggest of them sleeps six), along with a hospitable lodge where you can kick off your boots and relax. Another speciality of the house is the Antique Emporium, featuring knickknacks of the olden days, along with local artwork and gifts. The grounds include miles and miles of nature trails. Pets are not allowed.

Bed and Breakfasts

Bed and Breakfast Rates

$	less than $85
$$	$85 to $115
$$$	$116 to $150
$$$$	$151 and up

Finley Point Lodge
$$$ • 636 Georgia Road, Polson
• (406) 887-2051, (406) 887-2081, 888-558-8080

Finley Point is located 15 miles north of Polson on Montana 35. This rustic lodge features log beams, posts, railings, timbers and river rock for a true feeling of Montana living. Suites are available on and off the waterfront, with or without Jacuzzis, and breakfasts come either gourmet or continental. The multi-level decks on Flathead Lake give a great view of the Mission Mountains, and with your own boat or the lodge's canoe, you can visit eight forested islands nearby. Wildlife viewing, fishing the lake, or just lounging on the dock are popular options for guests. The lodge has a piano, too. No American Express.

Mission Meadow Farm
$$, no credit cards •1868 South Shore Route, Polson
• (406) 883-5970, 888-806-3236

Mission Meadow Farm sits on 20 scenic acres overlooking the East Bay of Flathead Lake. There are two in-house suites (one with a flora theme and one with a fauna theme), and a two-bedroom East Bay Overlook Guesthouse (perfect for families with children since it includes a full kitchen, cable TV, washer/dryer, and a large deck). Guests are encouraged to relax, read and enjoy the flowers, fruit trees, walking paths, hot tub, seasonal pond and abundant birdlife. The grounds are home to donkeys, goats, llamas and cuddly cats, which is why visitors are not allowed to bring pets. Mission Meadow Farm is also a non-smoking facility. Nearby attractions include Bird Point, a secluded fishing access and waterfowl habitat only one-quarter mile from the driveway. Mission Meadow is officially open from Memorial Day to Labor Day, but welcomes reservations all year long as well. Cash, personal and traveler's checks, or money orders are accepted.

Swan Hill Bed & Breakfast
$$ • 460 Kings Point Road, Polson MT 59860
• (406) 883-5292, 800-537-9489

This bed and breakfast, located in a red-wood home five miles from Polson, prides itself on being a mix of modern amenities and Western hospitality. The gourmet breakfasts change daily and are served in your choice of the dining room or under an umbrella table on the deck overlooking the Mission Moun-

INSIDERS' TIP

Driving conditions around the Treasure State can vary widely and suddenly. Poor visibility, snowpacked pavement, and black ice are particularly of concern in the mountains and in winter, but it's always good to check road conditions. Call the Montana Department of Transportation at 1-800-226-ROAD for a daily update of driving conditions around the state.

tains and Flathead Lake. Of particular note is the presence of a large indoor pool and sauna, along with the availability of a rental boat. Because the facility is located on Flathead Lake, it is perfect for the guest who enjoys boating, windsurfing, fishing or wildlife viewing. Three bedrooms have queen beds and one has twin beds, all with private baths. Swan Hill is a non-smoking facility and handicapped accessible. Children over 12 are welcome. No American Express.

Campgrounds and RV Parks

Campground Rates

$	$4 to $9
$$	$10 to $16
$$$	$17 to $23
$$$$	$24 and up

Eagle Nest RV Resort
$$$ • 259 Eagle Nest Drive on Montana 35, Polson
• (406) 883-5904

Eagle Nest RV Resort has seven acres of lawn and trees, offering spacious, shady, quiet campsites. There are six tent spaces and 57 RV spaces with full hookups, 50-amp service and roomy pull-throughs. The facility, which is near Polson's 27-hole public golf course, was built in 1993 and includes free showers, a rec room, laundry, gift store, a horseshoe pit, a playground and lots, lots more. Eagle Nest is open from April 15 through October 1 and features daily, weekly, monthly and seasonal rates. No American Express.

Flathead Lake State Park
$ • 490 N. Meridian Rd., Kalispell
• (406) 752-5501

The park consists of six scenic units bordering Flathead Lake, two of which are within 15 miles of Polson. With the exception of Wild Horse Island, all units feature camping, fishing, boating and swimming. Finley Point is on the east shore of Flathead Lake on Montana 35, and has four tent sites and 12 RV sites. The use fee is $15. Big Arm is 14 miles north of Polson on U.S. 93. At this facility, yurt rental is available year round, partially furnished, at $39 per night in summer or $25 per night in winter. The camping fee in season is $12.

Polson/Flathead Lake KOA
$$$ • 200 Irvine Flats Road, Polson
• (406) 883-2151, 800-KOA-2130

This campground, with its national KOA affiliation, can be counted on for a quality ex-

Accommodations in Polson offer gorgeous lake views.

perience. The grounds are well kept, and there is a tenting area with 15 tent sites that are well shaded and divided by tall honeysuckle bushes. The 58 pull-through RV sites are hard-surfaced and can handle large units. An extra plus is that there are 12 cabins at the campground that have some of the features of a hotel at an economical price. The single-room cabins are $35, and there is one two-room cabin for $40. In addition to a view of the mountains and lake, there is a store, coin laundry, free showers, a game room, pool, spa and barbecue grills. The facility, which is located about a half-mile north of Polson on U.S. 93, is open from mid-April to mid-October. No American Express.

Rocking-C-Ranch
$$$ • 6913 E Shore Route, Polson
• (406) 887-2537

A year-round facility, the Rocking C Ranch is located 7 miles north of Polson on Montana 35. The main building, which dates to 1930, was at one time a dairy barn. Today it is the centerpiece of a lovely 40-acre RV park that also includes dining and a casino. From the deck, you have a great view of the Mission Mountains. There are lots of added attractions, too, everything from a game arcade to an 18-hole miniature golf course. In summer, you can expect to enjoy live music on the outdoor stage, free hayrides, and more. There is also a 1948 Great Northern caboose on the property. There are 60 RV sites and 40 tent sites, and in winter there are still 20 RV sites available. Pets are allowed, and there are free showers, a coin laundry, and a gift and candy shop. If you want to rough it, a rental tipi is available nightly.

Restaurants

Restaurant Rates

$	$10 to $19
$$	$20 to $27
$$$	$28 to $35
$$$$	$36 and more

For two people, meal exclusive of beverages, tip, and tax.

Family Friendly Dining

Charlie Wong's
110 Main Street, Polson
• (406) 883-9402

This is Polson's version of a popular Kalispell restaurant. The menu is mostly Asian food, but you will find that they have a couple of American entrees for the picky eater. Among the most popular specialties are the kung pao chicken, which is best if ordered hot but will still do nicely even in the mild and medium forms, and the won ton soup, which is filled with pork, won tons, fried won tons, and greens. Two people can eat quite comfortably on one order of the won ton noodle soup ($4.95), which adds noodles to the mix and goes in a much larger bowl. The Polson version of Charlie Wong's definitely boasts the best view of the three restaurants in the chain (the third is in Columbia Falls): Located in the Salish building next to the bridge over the Flathead River, the restaurant looks out over Flathead Lake and the Mission Mountains.

The Driftwood Cafe
$ • 1202 Second Ave. E., Polson
• (406) 883-2558

You can get breakfast all day at the Driftwood, which is a longtime local favorite. There's nothing fancy at this cafe, but they usually get it right, and there are lots of choices on the menu. For breakfast, don't overlook the Hungry Man Special, which offers three eggs, three pieces of toast, hash browns, and choice of six sticks of bacon, six ounces of ham, or sausage links for just $6.45. There are also a variety of omelettes and a kid's menu. For lunch and dinner, don't overlook the burgers, which are available with buffalo meat for just 75 cents extra.

4Bs Restaurant
$ • Junction of Montana 35 and U.S. 93, Polson
• (406) 883-6180

The 4Bs restaurants are a Montana tradition. The first one started in Missoula many years ago, and now they are in almost every major city in Montana, as well as one in New

Mexico. The specialty here is friendly service, fast food (without being "fast food") and a family-oriented setting. The children's menu is generous to a fault, with lots of selections—everything from hamburgers to pizza—and a price that can't be beat ($1.35 for a grilled cheese sandwich with fries and Jello). The grown-ups eat almost as cheaply, with a tasty prime rib special selling for just $6.95, including choice of potato or rice, soup or salad, and a roll. The 4Bs is Polson's only restaurant open 24 hours a day.

Schiefelbein Haus
$$ • 6395 East Shore Route, Polson • (406) 887-2431

An eclectic menu is one of the delights of the Schiefelbein Haus, where the Bavarian theme leads to German specialities, but there are also American and Cajun delights—everything from sour braten and pork schnitzel to Alaskan coho salmon and Cajun prime rib, catfish, and shrimp. They also fashion themselves as the home of "the world's best Belgian waffles." Certainly, they can't be far wrong. And on a summer night after a long drive, don't forget to sample the brews at the outdoor beer garden! The restaurant is only open in summer.

Fine Dining

The Pemmican
$$$ • 303 U.S. Highway 93, Polson • (406) 883-3636, 800-882-6363

The restaurant at the Best Western KwaTaqNuk Resort is one of your best bets for fine dining in Polson—whether it's breakfast, lunch or dinner. There's prime rib every night, as well as a variety of beef and seafood selections. Friday night, you can enjoy a spectacular seafood buffet, and in the summer the best seats are on the outdoor deck right above Flathead Lake and the resort's marina. Also during the summer, you may enjoy the Sunday brunch. Hotel guests can take advantage of the restaurant's offerings through a room-service menu.

Rancho Deluxe
$$$ • 602 Sixth Street W., Polson • (406) 883-2300

This restaurant is proof that you can't just dine at spots on the highway and Main Street and expect to find the best a town has to offer. To reach Rancho Deluxe, turn off U.S. 93 at Main Street and drive up to Sixth Avenue, then hang a right, and drive six blocks to Sixth Street West right at the edge of the Flathead River. The building looks more like a bowling alley on the outside, but this is a grand supper club, featuring a gourmet menu, with everything from filet mignon at $17.95 to a grain & vegetable "steak" made out bulgur wheat, zucchini, sun-dried tomatoes, basil, and pine nuts for $10.95. There is also a light menu with burgers, prime rib sandwiches and a yellow-fin tuna sandwich. Desserts are irresistible at just $3.95 and include Key Lime pie, rich chocolatey mud pie, and our favorite—pecan brittle sundae. The wine list has everything up to and including Dom Perignon at $99.95 a bottle.

Nightlife

Best Western KwaTaqNuk Resort
303 U.S. Highway 93, Polson • (406) 883-3636, 800-882-6363

The casino in KwaTaqNuk is a bit closer to big-time gambling than most of the casinos in Montana. That's because the Confederated Salish and Kootenai Tribes own the facility, and the tribes negotiated an agreement with the state of Montana that allows more gaming machines in KwaTaqNuk than are usually allowed. There are more than 40 machines in the casino/lounge, and that means there is always something to do for adults at the resort. The full-service bar is open 24 hours a day. There's also a lounge overlooking Flathead Lake, with deck seating in the summer.

Diamond Horseshoe Lounge & Supper Club
820 Shoreline Dr., Polson • (406) 883-8111, 406-883-2048

The Diamond Horseshoe has it all, a popular bar with gaming machines, occasional live entertainment, and a great view of Flathead Lake, along with a restaurant that serves food for all tastes. You can stop in here for a quick drink or a long rest stop. On Monday night or Sunday afternoon, you'll find the televisions tuned to the football channels, and there is always plenty of sports talk. The bands here play anything from country music to current rock sounds.

Shopping

Alpine Tipis
306 Main Street, Polson
• **(406) 406-883-3500**

This is a one-of-a-kind store. You can't miss if you want to find a surprising made-in-Montana gift for the folks back home, but these are pricey gifts. There is a wide range of tipis available for several hundred dollars each, including the lodgepole frames and the outer canvas. Walk into the showroom and you will see everything from a full-size tipi that reaches to the ceiling to a child's size tipi that is perfect for a back yard all the way down to a more economical bird-feeder tipi that's just a foot tall. A map on the wall shows locations across the U.S. where children's tipis have been shipped, and Alpine does most of its business by mail order, so remember to pick up a catalog while you are in the store. If a tipi is too big for your yard, you might consider a windsock, another specialty item produced by Alpine.

First Resort
219 Main Street, Polson
• **(406) 883-2129**

This shop is worth a visit, partly because it offers a full-range of clothing for men and women, but perhaps even more so because of its unusual design. The shop was formerly known as the Flagship, and it retains the nautical design that was instituted then. There's a captain's wheel on the entryway, and inside the seagoing motif continues, with changing rooms done up as ship's cabins and the walls decorated with barrels, port holes, and gangplanks. In between, you'll find Pendletons and other brand names, along with a healthy helping of sale merchandise.

Three Dog Down Outlet
61545 U.S. 93 N., Polson
• **(406) 883-3696, (800) 364-3696**

This little store just across the Flathead River from downtown Polson is a national phenomenon. It's been written up in *Glamour* magazine, *Entrepreneur* magazine, the *Chicago Tribune*, and many other national publications, including the travel magazines published by Delta and American Airlines. Owner Bob Ricketts, a former opera singer, can only be considered a world-class eccentric, and his bizarre vision of an all-down outlet store in Polson, Montana, has proved to be something the world WAS ready for. The store buys wholesale directly from many of the top down manufacturers in the world, and there are also products manufactured right in Polson. Custom orders such as pillows, comforters, and even medical bedding are handled on a regular basis. The store's name, by the way, comes from the same Inuit folk saying that gave the name to the band Three Dog Night. It refers to the Inuit tradition of describing the temperature on a cold night by how many dogs you need to sleep with to stay warm.

Wild-Side Chocolates and Gifts
6 Second Ave. E., Polson
• **(406) 883-1722**

Owner Geri Greenwood and her husband opened this small shop just two years ago, but it's worth a stop for anyone who's in the market for a mouth-watering treat, and who isn't? The chocolates come in a variety of shapes and sizes, including the Flathead Monster and the Grizzly Paw. There are also a variety of huckleberry products as well as preserves and popular treats such as Jelly Belly beans. On several walls, there are also Montana-made gift items, including jewelry and novelties. And don't be confused by the address: U.S. 93 becomes Second Avenue East for several blocks in downtown Polson.

The mountains have always influenced the Blackfeet, who recognize them as sacred places. In more practical terms, the mountains create the wind and weather that sweep across the northern plains and touch every living thing on them.

The Blackfeet Reservation

East Glacier, Browning, and St. Mary

The Blackfeet Reservation is home to the 14,000 enrolled members of the Blackfeet Tribe. It's beautiful, open prairie, land where the Blackfeet hunted buffalo for thousands of years. From every vantage point you can see the peaks of what the Blackfeet call the Backbone of the World—the Continental Divide. The mountains have always influenced the Blackfeet, who recognize them as sacred places. In more practical terms, the mountains create the wind and weather that sweep across the northern plains and touch every living thing on them.

The towns of East Glacier, Browning, and St. Mary will probably be the focus for most visitors' stay, and listings in each category of service are arranged in that order.

East Glacier is home to many small businesses, shops, and restaurants, and you'll enjoy walking about the little town located exactly where the mountains meet the prairie. Or you might choose to hike. The Two Medicine subdistrict of Glacier National Park is only

an 11-mile drive away, with its web of trails leading to places such as Dawson Pass, Cobalt Lake, Twin Falls, or Old Man Lake. Glacier Park Boat Company also offers boat tours on Two Medicine Lake. The Lubec and Autumn Creek Trails begin along U.S. Highway 2 west of East Glacier and will lead you along the aspen-covered foothills. Be sure to check with a ranger station for current trail conditions.

Browning is the center of the reservation, and you'll find all basic services here. It's also the home of both the Museum of the Plains Indian and the Scriver Museum of Montana Wildlife and Hall of Bronze (see Attractions). One excellent time to visit Browning is the weekend after the Fourth of July—North American Indian Days. This large powwow draws not only Native Americans from tribes across the west but also from Canada and as far away as Florida. The combination of food, dancing, music, native dress, and the mix of people from across the continent create a remarkable event (see Annual Events). Or tour the reservation with a Blackfeet guide—Sun Tours will be pleased to share Blackfeet history and culture through the local perspective with you (for more information, see the Closeup, "Bus Tours in Glacier National Park").

St. Mary is a tiny community that grows

significantly in the summer season. It's located right at the eastern end of Going-to-the-Sun Road; every square foot of this little town has a magnificent view of the mountains. And you'll have access to the whole east side of Glacier National Park without too much of a drive—Many Glacier is 40 minutes away, Two Medicine 45 minutes away, Cut Bank 20 minutes away—not to mention Going-to-the-Sun Road. St. Mary has a huge array of services available in the summer but very few in winter—please read descriptions carefully if you're planning to travel in fall, winter, or spring, as many businesses close down altogether.

The Blackfeet Tribe does require a $5.00 Conservation and Recreation Use Permit for those not members of the tribe who wish to recreate on the reservation, whether that be hiking, mountain biking, or otherwise exploring off the paved roads. The permit can be purchased at local businesses, as can the tribal fishing license. For more information, please call Blackfeet Fish and Wildlife at (406) 338-7207. And do take the time to explore—the Blackfeet Reservation has a beauty all its own.

Accommodations

Please note: In addition to the 4% state accommodations tax, all lodgings on the Blackfeet Reservation must collect an additional tribal accommodations tax of 6%.

Accommodation Rates

Keep in mind that some rates are based on availability. The average nightly rates for two adults at the hotels and motels listed in this section are indicated by a dollar sign ($) ranking in the following chart. Also, the hotels and motels in this chapter accept all or most major credit cards.

$	Less than $85
$$	$85 to $115
$$$	$115 to $150
$$$$	$150 and up

Hotels and Motels

The Whistling Swan Motel
$ • P.O. Box 318, 512 U.S. Highway 2, East Glacier
• (406) 226-4412

A little worn on the outside, the Whistling Swan is quite charming—and tidy and clean—on the inside. One step into the lobby and you'll start to absorb the unrushed, comfortable feeling that pervades this little motel. Each of the eight rooms has color cable TV, and your night's lodging includes free coffee the next morning at the Two Medicine Grill just down the street. The Whistling Swan also handles U-Save car rentals during the summer.

The Whistling Swan has the great merit of

INSIDERS TIP

If you drive between St. Mary and Waterton Lakes National Park in Canada, or come in to Babb over the Duck Lake Road from Browning, you can't help but notice a looming, flat-topped peak that seems to lead the other mountains out onto the prairie near the border: Chief Mountain. Chief Mountain has a long history as a significant spiritual site. For thousands of years the Blackfeet have held sacred ceremonies here, and they continue to do so today. The Chief Mountain Highway—Montana Highway 17—affords many striking views of this imposing peak. A few miles northwest of Babb, pull off the road at the scenic overlook to enjoy the panorama of both mountains and prairie.

being open all year. If you've ever been caught in a blizzard, you'll appreciate how nice it is to have a good spot to wait out the weather. Summer rates are $40.00 per night for single rooms and $54.00 for doubles; please inquire about reduced winter rates. For more information, please phone, write, or e-mail mchowser@3rivers.net.

The Warbonnet Lodge
$ • P.O. Box 638, U.S. Highways 2 and 89, Browning
• (406) 338-7610

When you're staying in Browning, this is the place to be. Just on the edge of town, the Warbonnet is conveniently located for those traveling north, south, east, or west. Don't be too intimidated by its warlike name! The staff is friendly and helpful. You'll find the 35 rooms large, comfortable, and clean; both smoking and non-smoking rooms are available. All rooms have satellite TV, phone, and air conditioning. Some have VCRs, and you can rent movies from the lodge's extensive collection. The lodge also includes a small restaurant and lounge.

The Warbonnet is open year-round. A room for two people runs $58.60 per night during the summer, and $50.00 per night in winter.

Guest Ranches, Resorts, Lodges

Glacier Park Lodge
$$$ • East Glacier
• (602) 207-6000 Glacier Park, Inc.

The first of the lodges to be built by the Great Northern Railway, Glacier Park Lodge continues to be the unofficial eastern gateway to Glacier National Park today. Although it is located outside the borders of the park, the peaks rise behind it in an impressive backdrop. Lovely, well-tended flower gardens line the walk as you approach the historic building. Walking through the lodge doors, you'll be impressed by the huge logs that support the lobby ceiling: immense Douglas-firs, their bark still on, imported from the Pacific Northwest to grace this hall. The neighboring

Blackfeet Indians referred to the building as the "Big Tree Lodge."

In contrast with its historic past, Glacier Park Lodge also offers modern amenities in addition to its 163 rooms. The hotel features a heated swimming pool, a nine-hole golf course, a nine-hole pitch 'n' putt golf course, a gift shop, cocktail lounge (with big-screen TV), and the Great Northern Steak and Rib House (see Restaurants). The information desk will be happy to set you up with a bus tour or hayride. The talented college students that staff the hotel also provide evening performances.

Glacier Park Lodge has a longer season than some other GPI facilities. It will open May 21, 1999, and close on September 27. Rooms range in price from $131 to $233 per night for two people. Reservations and further information may be had by calling Glacier Park, Inc., at (602) 207-6000 (year-round) or visiting the website at www.glacierparkinc.com/

Two Medicine Teepee Adventures
$$$–$$$$ • P.O. Box 1510, Browning
• (406) 338-7574 or (800) 890-2209

You'll ride your own horse, sleep in a teepee village, choose which steak you want for dinner—perhaps buffalo, elk, or venison—and watch the sun rise and set over the Great Plains as others have for thousands of years. Two Medicine Teepee Adventures is an Indian-owned business that will introduce you to a different way of life in Montana. You'll ride between six different teepee camps, spend a night or two at each, and explore different parts of this beautiful country as you go. Your guides will introduce you to riding, fishing, and moving cattle, and you'll explore hills and ponds, ancient Indian camps, buffalo jumps, and old teepee rings. (Your belongings will be shuttled by stagecoach!) And, if the saddle is new to you, you'll really enjoy the luxuries of camp—all locations have showers, sauna, Jacuzzi, and toilet facilities. Each teepee village has a dining facility, but you may prefer to eat outdoors. If game isn't your fancy, native trout and whitefish as well as Montana-raised beef are part of the plan, and vegetarian meals are available on request.

Two Medicine Teepee Adventures operates from June 1 through September 30. An

Adventure can be arranged as either an overnight trip or as a package vacation. The rate for a 1-night stay, including transportation to and from the teepee site, horseback riding, cattle drive, fishing and sightseeing, is $150.00 per person. If you'd like to just stay the night in a teepee camp, that fee is $65.00. Please inquire for more options and details.

For a more extended trip, the weekly rate is $1800 per person, from ages 6 to 106, and includes your lodging, meals, horses and guide, transfers to and from the airport in Great Falls, Montana, and all camp activities. Please inquire for full details on fees. Riding age is 6

years old minimum. Optional side trips can also be arranged for fly-fishing, skeet shooting, tours of Glacier National Park, whitewater rafting, golf—whatever you'd like. For more information, please phone, write, or e-mail twomedtp@3rivers.net.

Wagner's Duck Lake Lodge
$ • P.O. Box 218, Duck Lake Road, Babb • (406) 338-5770

If you're looking for accommodations a little more off the beaten path, consider Wagner's Duck Lake Lodge. Wagner's caters to fishermen who frequent the nearby Duck

Massacre on the Marias

If the great Indian battle of the West fought by the U.S. Army was the Battle of the Little Bighorn, perhaps a lesser known but more typical event was the Massacre on the Marias. This encounter between the U.S. Army and a band of Pikuni Blackfeet occurred in the winter of 1870; it took a long time for the truth about the event to make its way to Washington. In many ways its tale of revenge, mistakes, and alcohol is all too familiar in this era, as was their result.

It's hard to say where such stories begin, but let's start this one in 1847. A trader for the American Fur Company, Malcolm Clarke, married a Pikuni, Cutting-off-head Woman. She was a member of the Many Chiefs band, as was her cousin, Owl Child. This band was led by Mountain Chief, a leader who had resisted the incursion of whites into Blackfeet territory. With this union,

Clarke secured his position as a trader among the Blackfeet and gained the respect of the tribal elders to whom he was now related by marriage. Sometime later, Clarke retired from trading and settled on a ranch on Prickly Pear Creek, north of Helena. He was able to live quite comfortably and was well established in the Helena community.

Owl Child, previous to Clarke's marriage to his cousin, had become something of an outcast from the Many Chiefs band. He'd been involved in a killing for which he was ostracized, and although he spent some time with the band, he often roamed, growing bitter toward both the whites and his own tribe. But in 1867 he, with some other of Cutting-off-head Woman's relatives, visited the ranch. During the night, Owl Child's horses were stolen. He blamed Clarke and in turn stole some of Clarke's horses.

Clarke and his son Horace soon pursued the stolen horses to Mountain Chief's camp, where they found Owl Child. "Horace struck Owl Child with a whip and called him a dog. Clarke called him an old woman, and the men left with their horses. Now it is not good to insult and beat a young Pikuni in front of his people. Such an action requires revenge...." (Welch, *Killing Custer*, p. 27). On August 17, 1869, Owl Child and 25 young warriors attacked the Clarke ranch. They left Clarke dead and Horace seriously wounded.

In an area already tense with hostilities, this was the last straw for the whites. The most powerful men in Helena demanded total annihilation of the "savages." They demanded the army. Initially General Philip H. Sheridan—the first to say "the only good Indian is a dead Indian"—delayed, saying he didn't have enough forces to attempt an attack against the Blackfeet. But at the same time he had a plan: a new tactic, tried in 1868 when Indians were attacked unprepared in their winter camp on the Washita River. No longer was war confined to warriors: women, children, and old men were driven from their tents and gunned down in the open.

On New Year's Day, 1870, General Alfred Sully met with four Blackfeet peace chiefs: Heavy Runner, Little Wolf, Big Lake, and Grey Eyes. He wanted to speak with Mountain Chief, who did not show up. Nevertheless Sully informed the others that to avoid war, they must deliver the dead bodies of Owl Chief and his party—within two weeks. The chiefs agreed, knowing they were incapable of meeting this demand; and Sully also recognized the futility of the agreement. He returned to Sheridan.

When the two weeks were up, Sheridan's plan went into effect. Scouts reported that Mountain Chief's band was wintering on the Marias River. Colonel E. M. Baker, stationed at Fort Shaw on the Sun River, was ordered to attack the band. Sheridan's telegraph read, "If the lives and property of the citizens of Montana can best be protected by striking Mountain Chief's band, I want them struck. Tell Baker to strike them hard." (Welch, p. 30)

Just before dawn on January 23, 1970, the army soldiers were in place above the Indian camp. One of Baker's scouts, a half-white, half-Pikuni named Joe Kipp, suddenly recognized by the designs on the tipis that this was not Mountain Chief's camp, it was Heavy Runner's. Clearly Mountain Chief had gotten word of the army's intentions and had cleared out; Heavy Runner's band had moved into the desirable location. Scouts and troops from the expedition alike, as well as Horace Clarke, who accompanied the expedition, later stated that Colonel Baker was drunk at the time of the attack—perhaps not an uncommon state for those leading hard and dreary lives. But when Kipp informed him that this was the wrong band of Blackfeet, Baker replied, "That makes no difference, one band or another of them; they are all Piegans [Pikunis] and we will attack them." He then threatened to have Kipp shot if the scout moved from the spot.

When the gunfire began, Heavy Runner ran from his lodge, waving a piece of paper—the safe conduct signed by General Sully at the New Year's Day meeting. He was shot dead. Most able-bodied men were out hunting, and when, at the end, 173 had been killed, most of them were women, children, and the elderly, still in their lodges. Many of them were totally helpless—smallpox had hit the band that same winter too. Ironically, at the same time Owl Child was dying of the disease in Mountain Chief's camp some seventeen miles away.

The Blackfeet never took up arms against the United States again.

Lake, known for its excellent fishing, and offers a restaurant, rooms to rent, RV spaces, and tenting on acres of beautiful land.

The lodge contains nine bedrooms which share two common bathrooms. Rooms rent for $68.50 per night in the summer and $50.00 per night in the winter, based on double occupancy. Please inquire about rooms for three or four. The unpretentious living room downstairs showcases a collection of game trophies, and the dining room is open each night serving chicken, steak, and fish specials. And if you're overdue for some really good pizza, here's one place to get it.

Ten RV sites have full hook-ups, available for $18.50 per night. And, as Bob Wagner puts it, there's acres of dry camping. Those who set up closer to the lodge can use its bathrooms and showers; for those who head further out, portable toilets are located around the property. Tent sites cost $10.00 per night. Pets are allowed. For more information, please phone, write, e-mail waglodge@3rivers.net, or visit the website at www.babbmt.com/wagners/index.htm .

St. Mary Lodge and Cabins
$$–$$$$ • St. Mary
• (406) 732-4431 (summer)
or (800) 368-3689

St. Mary Lodge is located right at the eastern end of Going-to-the-Sun Road, just outside Glacier National Park. This complex of guest facilities includes cabins, lodge rooms, and luxury cottages as well as several eating establishments, an outdoor store, gift shop, grocery, and gas station. Most services are open from May 15 to October 3, 1999.

Lodge rooms are standard motel-style accommodations with queen-size beds, private bath, and air conditioning; they run approximately $95.00 per night for two people. Glacier Cabins have a living area with breakfast table, microwave and small refrigerator; they have a queen bed in an adjacent sleeping area and a separate bedroom with two single beds and a private bathroom. These cozy cabins are newly remodeled and cost about $140 per night for two people.

St. Mary Lodge also operates three specialty cabins: the Sun Cabin (sleeps 4), the Kootenai Cabin (sleeps 5), and the Guest House (sleeps 6). These larger cabins feature a variety of amenities including full kitchens and gas barbecues. Please inquire for more details.

The Pinnacle Cottages are the latest addition to the lodge facility. The six luxury cottages are located on a bluff above the town of

Credit: U.S. Department of the Interior, Indian Arts and Crafts Board.

Step back in time at the Museum of the Plains Indians.

St. Mary, offering spectacular views of St. Mary Lake and Glacier National Park. Each cabin has two bedrooms, a complete kitchen, full bath with tub, spacious living room with fireplace, and a private deck with barbecue grill. A three-night minimum stay is required.

The Lodge itself houses the Snowgoose Grille (see Restaurants), Mountain Lounge (with satellite TV), and an extensive gift shop offering everything from teddy bears to Native American jewelry to huckleberry products and home-made fudge. For more information on St. Mary Lodge, please phone, write to the address above (or, in winter: St. Mary Lodge, P.O. Box 1808, Sun Valley, ID 83353), e-mail at stmary@glcpark.com, or visit the website at www.glcpark.com.

RV Parks and Campgrounds

St. Mary KOA
$ • St. Mary
• (406) 732-4122 or (800) 562-1504

St. Mary KOA is on the shores of the St. Mary River and Lower St. Mary Lake, just moments from the town of St. Mary and Going-to-the-Sun Road. It could probably call itself a resort—this KOA offers not only tent sites, a group tent site, RV sites, and "kamping kabins and kottages," but also canoe, paddle boat, and mountain bike rentals, a playground and game room, an evening barbecue, outdoor hot tubs, a grocery store and gift shop, and U-Save car rentals (perfect for those with RVs too long to go over Going-to-the-Sun Road). And, of course, beautiful views of the mountains, river, and lake.

St. Mary KOA will be open from May to October 1999.Tent sites are $19.95 per night. RV sites range from no hook-up for $19.95, electric hook-up for $21.95, water and electric for $25.95, to full hook-up for $29.95. "Kamping kabins" range in price from $46.95 to $56.95; these sleeping cabins have electricity and heat but no running water or bath. Bring your own bedding; water is available nearby, and each cabin has its own picnic table and grill. "Kamping kottages" run $119.95 per night, and include a bath, shower, and fully equipped kitchen. All prices are based on two-person occupancy; there is a $4.50 fee for each additional adult. Kids and pets stay free. For more information, please write, phone, or visit the website at www.goglacier.com. Reservations are highly recommended for the "kamping kottages" in particular.

Johnson's RV Park and Campground
$ • HC 72-10, Star Route, St. Mary
• (406) 732-4207
Red Eagle Motel
$ • P.O. Box 896, Browning
• (406) 732-4453

The Johnson family has quite a few enterprises going in St. Mary—all located with a view overlooking the St. Mary Lakes and the mountains. But you'll be glad for the hill and trees that shelter the campground from the east side wind...and the grassy sites, picnic tables, and fire rings make for a very pleasant stay.

All RV sites are pull-throughs. Sites without hook-ups are $16.00 per night. The 40 sites with electricity and water are $18.00 per night, and the 42 full hook-ups are $20.00 per night. Please inquire about monthly rates. Johnson's also has 50 tent spaces which cost $14.00 per night. The campground has a covered pavilion, hot showers, a laundry, and a store.

If not everyone in your party is interested in camping, the Red Eagle Motel is right next door. The 22 modern units have the same big view as the campground. For more information, please phone, write, or visit the website at www.babbmt.com and click on the appropriate business.

And More...

Brownie's Hostel
$ • P.O. Box 229, 1020 Montana Highway 49, East Glacier
• (406) 226-4426

Brownie's Hostel offers low-cost, basic lodging for those traveling through the East Glacier area. This two-story log building has twenty-five beds (linens provided), a kitchen, laundry, baggage storage, parking, and bike rentals. It's located just a bit over a mile from U.S. Highway 2, and the hostel will pick up guests from the Amtrak station by arrangement. Private rooms are also available. A bakery and convenience store operate in the first floor.

Brownie's is open from May 2 to October 14, weather permitting. Lodging is $12 per person per night; reservations are essential between July 4 and August 15. Groups are welcome but must make reservations. During the off-season, reservations are accepted by mail. For more information please write, phone, or visit the website at www.hostelweb.com/montana/.

Jon's House
$$–$$$ • East Glacier, MT • Inquire at the Mountain Pine Motel, Montana Highway 49, East Glacier
• (406) 226-4403

Have you always wished for a vacation home in the mountains? Jon's House might be the place. This privately owned home in East Glacier is rented out by the night from June 1 through Labor Day. Just five years old, its spacious living room has a wonderful view of the mountains of Glacier. It's within walking distance of "downtown" East Glacier and the Glacier Park Lodge and golf course. And it sleeps up to eight: there's a master bedroom with queen bed and private bath downstairs, four twin beds in the bedrooms and loft upstairs, and a queen-size sleeper sofa in the living room.

Jon's House also has a living-room fireplace, a fully equipped kitchen with service for eight, telephone, washer and dryer, a barbecue, and even a ping-pong table. In addition to the master bath, there are full bathrooms upstairs and down. Jon's House rents for $175.00 per night; please contact the Mountain Pine Motel at the number above.

Ye Olde House
$ • East Glacier, MT • Inquire at the Mountain Pine Motel, Montana Highway 49, East Glacier
• (406) 226-4403

Ye Olde House is located in the woods just off Montana Highway 49 in East Glacier. This nice, clean older house can be your home-away-from-home—and at very reasonable rates. Each of the two bedrooms has a queen-size bed, and one also includes a twin. Downstairs the queen-size sleeper sofa will accommodate two more, making room for a total of seven people. Two full baths, your own kitchen and living room will give you all the privacy of having your own place.

Ye Olde House rents for $70 per night for two people, plus $5.00 each for each additional person. Please contact the Mountain Pine Motel at the number above for more information.

Rising Wolf Ranch

$$$–$$$$ • 907 Clark Drive, East Glacier
• (800) 654-3704

The Rising Wolf Ranch sits right at the edge of East Glacier. This large house borders Midvale Creek and offers a huge mountain panorama: Mt. Henry, Squaw, Bison, Bearhead, and Calf Robe Mountains fill the western horizon. Even if you never leave the house, you'll have seen the mountains...

Two living areas are available to rent. Downstairs is a fully furnished one-bedroom, one-bath apartment. The living room sofa is a sleeper that accommodates two, for a maximum occupancy of four. It rents for $125 per night with a three-night minimum stay during the summer.

Upstairs, living is deluxe. A master bedroom with bath, guest bedroom with bath, and a loft that sleeps four accommodate a maximum of eight people. You'll have your own gourmet kitchen, fireplaces in both the living room and master bedroom, and vaulted ceilings. Or step out onto the deck to soak up more of that mountain light! A washer and dryer are supplied. Upstairs rents for $165 per night, with a three-night minimum stay. For more information, please inquire at the phone number above.

Restaurants

Restaurant Rates

$	$10-20
$$	$20-40
$$$	$30-50
$$$$	more than $50

For two people, meal exclusive of beverages, tip, and tax.

Two Medicine Grill

$ • 314 U.S. Highway 2, East Glacier
• (406) 226-5572

The Two Medicine Grill isn't just a restaurant, it's the social hub of East Glacier. The counter in front and the seven or so tables in back are the meeting place for everyone in town, especially during the winter months when this is the only restaurant open. Breakfast, lunch, and dinner are all reasonably priced. Cinnamon rolls, soups, and chili are homemade—and be sure to check out the buffalo burgers and sour-cream-and-chive French fries! The Two Medicine Grill is open from 6:30 AM to 7 PM, seven days a week. The website at www.babbmt.com/2medgrill/ carries the diner's menus, so you can start thinking now about what you're going to order!

Great Northern Steak and Rib House

$$ • Glacier Park Lodge • East Glacier
• (406) 226-9311 (summer only)

A western theme dominates the Great Northern, and its menu features beef, barbecued ribs, chicken, and fish entrees. The restaurant offers a full buffet for breakfast, a luncheon carvery, and for dinner either a western buffet or a la carte options. Breakfast runs from 6:30 to 9:30 AM; lunch from 11:30 AM to 2 PM; and dinner from 5:00 to 9:30 PM

Serrano's

$ • 29 Dawson, East Glacier
• (406) 226-9392

This, the original Serrano's, occupies a historic log house that's been refitted to serve as one of East Glacier's favorite restaurants. Somehow the mix of western log building and Mexican restaurant works out just right—and you'll find this is often a busy place. Serrano's serves just dinner, but dinner runs from 3:30 to 10 PM, seven days a week. Like the larger Serrano's in Whitefish, this restaurant has a full menu of Mexican delights, from soups, salads, and a la carte items to full dinners.

Serrano's in East Glacier is open from May 1 to October 1.

Snowgoose Grille

$$$ • St. Mary Lodge • St. Mary
• (406) 732-4431

The Snowgoose Grille mixes fine dining with a wonderful view for a distinctive dining experience. As you settle into your chair, you'll admire Red Eagle, Little Chief, Mahtotopa, and Dusty Star Mountains as they march up the shore of St. Mary Lake. A few moments later, the menu will tempt you with its unique combination of buffalo specialties—prime rib, steaks, sausage, burgers—local St. Mary Lake

Credit: Donnie Sexton, Travel Montana

The 1998 North American Indian Days at Browning.

whitefish, pasta, wild game, and nightly specials. While you wait, a basket of sourdough scones and honey butter will occupy your attention. And then there's dessert—huckleberry delights and others will finish the evening with just the right touch.

The Snowgoose Grille serves breakfast, lunch, and dinner from May 15 to October 3.

The Park Café
$ • U.S. Highway 89, St. Mary
• (406) 732-4482

The Park Café will attract your eyes from the road—this little restaurant is bordered all about with a beautiful garden of columbines, poppies, lupine, and big, blue delphinium. Inside you'll find eight tables and a counter, though on a sunny summer day you might go for one of the three tables on the porch. A few minutes of looking at the menu and you'll realize you can't go wrong, because whatever you choose, it'll be excellent. The Park Café prides itself on the quality of its ingredients, and every breakfast, lunch, and dinner is fresh, wholesome, and homemade.

But whether you choose a sandwich, burger, nachos (great salsa), or salad (check out the "gallinaceous green" salad)—be sure to save room for pie! The Park Café always has a great selection—from fruit to berry to pecan or ice cream pies—and they're all homemade and delicious.

The Park Café is open from around Memorial Day to September 20, 1999, from 7 a.m. to 10 p.m. The café doesn't take reservations, but when it gets busy in the evening they do keep a waiting list—and a few minutes on the porch with the delphinium is pleasant in itself.

The Two Sisters
$ • U.S. Highway 89, about 4 miles north of St. Mary
• (406) 732-5535

Whether you're coming from Babb to the north or St. Mary to the south, you won't miss the Two Sisters—this is the brightest paint job on a building in probably the whole state! Inside you'll find a comfortable little café known for its excellent big breakfasts, homemade soups, dinner specials, cake and pie. This year they've added an espresso machine too, so stop for a latté if you're about to hit the road for the Midwest, Calgary, or Yellowstone. Tuck in your napkin...

The Two Sisters is open for breakfast, lunch, and dinner from May 7 to early October. And don't forget—if you're not ready for a full meal, there's the ice cream shop next door, ready to make you a summertime sundae, shake, or banana split.

Shopping

Two places you'll want to stop and explore are the gift shop at the Museum of the Plains Indian in Browning, which features Native American crafts and jewelry, and the gift shop at St. Mary Lodge, which carries a wide variety of high-quality gifts and souvenirs from the region. For those who might be missing certain amenities from home, try the Two Badger shop in East Glacier (308 Washington; open from 2:00 to 7:00 PM Monday through Saturday) for organic foods, body care products, gifts, herbs, and books for a healthy life.

The Swan and
Mission mountains
soar to rugged 8,000
to 9,000 foot heights
stretching for nearly
100 miles without a
road crossing them.

Swan Valley

Travel the Swan Valley and you step back a century in time to lands nearly as wild and pristine as when the first homesteaders took root, loggers began eyeing the virgin timber and the Flathead Indian Tribes freely hunted its abundant game.

Its grandeur and beauty have captivated residents and regular vacationers who lovingly call it "The Swan." While they welcome you with old-fashioned Montana hospitality, they passionately guard their valley's isolation, undeveloped character and simple, unhurried lifestyle.

It is bounded by official wilderness areas—the 73,887-acre Mission Mountains Wilderness to the west and the 1,009,356 acre Bob Marshall Wilderness to the east. Most of the mountain and valley lands belong either to the Flathead National Forest and Plum Creek, a large timber company. The remainder belongs to the State of Montana and private landowners. The Swan and Mission mountains soar to rugged 8,000 to 9,000 foot heights stretching for nearly 100 miles without a road crossing them. When you enter the Swan on its only paved road—the two-lane, north-south Montana 83—there's no turning off midway. But traffic is much less than on the major north-south highways to the east and west, and many pleasurable stops await you.

The River and Lake

The ice age's magic touched the landscape carving Swan Lake and more than fifty others. These crystal-clear snow-fed lakes drain by creeks into the Swan River as it winds northward from headwaters near the Swan-Clearwater divide. It is interrupted by Swan Lake's nine-mile length then empties into Flathead Lake at Bigfork. Nearly every mile a sparkling creek gurgles under the highway bridges toward the river.

Swan Lake is bounded on the east side by the highway and many privately owned vacation homes and on the west by mostly national forest where trees come right down the to the shores. Tremendous biological diversity exists here with the convergence of three main forest types: the northern boreal, Rocky Mountain and Pacific maritime forests, with larch, Douglas fir predominating, along with ponderosa, lodgepole and other pines and Engleman spruce. Major predator and prey species abound, and it is a birder's paradise. Keep a sharp eye out for deer crossing the highway, especially in early spring, and mornings and evenings.

The People, Then and Now

Archaeologists assume people began hunting and camping in the valley on the heels of the receding glaciers about 10,000 years ago. Excavations have unearthed evidence of human presence believed dating back 5,500 years. By the 18th Century Indian tribes used the area for religious gatherings and sweat lodge ceremonies giving the Swan River its original name Sweathouse River to the lower stretch. The Flathead tribes—the Salish and Kootenai—retained treaty hunting privileges in the Swan when they moved to their present reservation from the Bitterroot valley in 1872. They also peeled the ponderosa pines to harvest the sweet cambium layer under the bark for food. Scarred trees from the 1800's can still be seen in the forest including one at the Pony Creek campsite reached by forest road 10651.

Fur trappers who had gleaned beaver and marten pelts since the late 1700s for the Northwest and Hudson's Bay companies had severely diminished that resource by the mid-1800s. Gold prospectors had also explored the Swan after gold had been discovered elsewhere in Montana, but no significant mining was done.

The first decades of the 20th Century brought many changes as timber cutting intensified, settlers began constructing cabins and the wealthy discovered the Swan as a vacationing ground. By the late 1800s much of the land had been brought into the Forest Reserve System, precursor of the U.S.D.A. Forest Service, and the first ranger station was built at Holland Lake. Later stations, log structures built at Swan Lake and Condon, remain standing in good condition. In 1937 these stations were consolidated at Bigfork in a compound of buildings constructed by the Civilian Conservation Corps.

The largest timber sale in the history of the Flathead National Forest took place in the Swan Valley during this time, according to Joe Yates, of the Swan Lake Ranger Station. From 100,000 to 150,000 board feet of mostly western larch, with some Douglas- fir and pine, were cut by the Somers Lumber Company. They barged a steam engine on Flathead Lake

www.insiders.com

See this and many other **Insiders' Guide** destinations online.

Visit us today!

to a point south of Bigfork. From there they laid tracks just ahead of the engine, drove it onto the tracks, then lifted the tracks behind it and repositioned them in front, leapfrogging this way until reaching the present forest recreation area near the village of Swan Lake. The engine served the logging operation between 1914 and 1919. Some folks say it was purposely sunk in Swan Lake and remains there today, but others claim it was taken out the same way it was brought in, was used in other logging operations and was retired to its present site in at the old depot in Columbia Falls. The village of Swan Lake began during this early period with the establishment of a store, post office and schools.

Kootenai Lodge, a luxurious vacation resort built during the teens and twenties on the north shore of Swan Lake, stood in marked contrast to the simple lives and dwellings of the loggers and homesteaders. The purchase of 137 acres of land on the lake's north shore by Anaconda Copper Company attorneys Lewis Orvis Evans and Cornelius Francis Kelley initiated the first development and several decades of incomparable opulent living and entertaining. Kelley became Anaconda president and Evans its general counsel, and the compound, that had groups of separate cabins for each family, as well as the massive main lodge, became known locally as "Kelley and Evans." They lavishly entertained the copper company elite, royalty and other wealthy or famous people including Charles Lindbergh, Holland's Queen Wilhelmina, Will Rogers and Montana artist Charlie Russell. The resort engaged local craftsmen over more

INSIDERS' TIP

Swan Lake, which lies at the valley's north end, separates the "upper" and "lower" river sections. These designations can get confusing because upper refers to elevations at the headwaters, which lie at the valley's southernmost part. Likewise, when people refer to the "head" of the lake they are talking about the southern end, while the "foot" is the northern end.

than a decade to construct the buildings of native stone, larch, cedar and copper. During its heyday Kootenai Lodge employed up to local 70 people as cooks, housekeepers, butlers, chauffeurs, gardeners, bartenders, launderers and in other occupations. Many area residents descend from those Kootenai Lodge workers and carry on in memory the Kelley and Evans legend.

The lodge and 42 acres are now privately owned and closed to the public. The rest of the acreage was logged and subdivided after the Kelley descendants sold the place in 1968. A visible reminder of that glittering age remains in The Rock House built in 1930 on the lake's west side by Evans wife, Martha. Reached only by boat, it provided a retreat from the hustle and bustle of the main compound. The Evans' entertained guests and held an annual party for lodge employees there. The house is also a registered historic site. You can see it perched above a large rocky point from the first pullout going south on Montana 83 that takes you to the lakeshore.

Today's Swan Valley retains its simple rural character, despite modest population growth and subdivision of most of the old homesteads. Many retirees have settled here bringing a diversity of skills and backgrounds to community life and contributing to the area's economy, which still largely depends on its natural resources and tourism. Traditional timber cutting on state and federal lands has slowed drastically as concerned citizens have become involved in forest management decisions and as philosophy and policy has begun to change regarding how to maintain forest health.

Facing polarization of the community by these issues, a group of upper-valley residents in 1990 formed the Swan Citizens ad hoc Committee to pursue collaborative ways of involving all interest groups and finding solutions to environmental, economic and social problems. In 1996 the group established the Swan Ecosystem Center, a research and education center based in the Forest Service Condon Work Center. Its Visitor Information Center provides a wealth of information about the Swan Valley's diverse natural environment and is well worth a stop. It offers hands-on interpretive exhibits, take-away educational materials and accurate Insider's information about the recreational and other activities in the national and state forests. They also provide an interpretive demonstration forestry project and a self-guided nature trail that explains the changing forest ecosystem.

Public lands provide hundreds of miles of roads and trails for biking, horseback riding, cross-country skiing, snowshoeing, dogsled touring. Camping is permitted free of charge on all forest lands except in developed fee areas. Use of state lands for any recreational purpose requires a recreational license, which can be obtained from the state forest unit headquarters at milepost 58 on Montana 83 or the Kalispell Unit on U.S. 93 in Kalispell.

Accommodations

Accommodation Rates

Keep in mind that some rates are based on availability. The average nightly rates for two adults at the hotels and motels listed in this section are indicated by a dollar sign ($) ranking in the following chart. Also, the hotels and motels in this chapter accept all or most major credit cards.

$	Less than $85
$$	$85 to $115
$$$	$115 to $150
$$$$	$150 and up

Hotels, Motels, and Resorts

Holland Lake Lodge
$–$$$ • 1947 Holland Lake Rd., Swan Valley
• (406) 754-2282, (800) 648-8859

"This is old Montana at its best," declares co-owner John Wohlfeil. "No golf courses, no condominiums, no luxury homes, no televisions and cell phones don't work here." There's just this awe-inspiring wilderness setting right on beautiful Holland Lake in sight of Holland Falls tumbling down out of the Swan Mountains. Built in 1925, the main lodge houses nine guest rooms, bar, restaurant and common room with a brand new fireplace of local river stone. Guest cabins with bath sleep four to six guests have been restored and improved. The lodge restaurant serves breakfast, lunch and dinner. The dinner menu features premium center cut filet mignon and other beef specialties as well as chicken and dumplings, Yankee pot roast and lighter vegetarian cuisine. The full bar stocks a collection of specialty premium California wines. Winter and summer there's lots to do here including hiking, horseback riding, canoeing, cross-country skiing, ice skating, and snowshoeing. They groom nine miles of cross-country ski trails and there is unlimited backcountry skiing on national forest roads and trails. Dog sled rides round out the winter opportunities. They rent canoes, skates, snowshoes and other equipment. Located at one of the major gateways to the Bob Marshall Wilderness they provide a selection of pack trips into the Bob, fall hunting trips and winter ski touring packages. The Holland Lake turnoff is at the south end of the valley and is well marked with large signs. The lodge is open year-round except between April 15 and May 15.

Swan Lake Guest Cabins
$ • Montana 83, Milepost 78, Swan Valley
• (406) 837-1137

This resort features new log cabins with handmade log furniture, kitchenette and gas barbecues. It is located on a hill overlooking Swan Lake, in a secluded, private wilderness setting. There are lake views from the property but the cabins face toward the woods with glimpses of the Swan Mountains. Besides cabins with a maximum capacity of six, there is a furnished teepee for rent. They require a three-night minimum stay. Small children are not encouraged because of the heavily wooded setting and the presence of bears and mountain lions. This is a non-smoking resort.

Swan Valley Super 8 Lodge
$ • Montana 83, Milepost 46.5
• (406) 754-2688, (800) 800-8000

The ten-year old rustic log buildings on the north edge of Condon are a welcome sight for travelers during the winter months when

---

Mountain Lions and Safety in Lion Country

Much of Glacier Country and the Swan Valley is mountain lion country, so it's good to inform yourself about these felines. You'll find that bears get a lot of press here, while mountain lions get relatively little. Lions in general are extremely secretive and so are rarely seen; yet, unlike bears (which generally attack only when surprised or when they have learned to regard people as a source of food), mountain lions do on occasion stalk people as prey. In particular, children and small adults need to be cautious. Children should not be allowed to play alone, and they should not be allowed to run ahead of adults on the trail. Hiking alone even by adults is not advised for many reasons, lions being one. Something to keep in mind is that cats like cover for stalking prey; treed or cliffy areas are good habitat for them, but you are less likely to find one out in a meadow. Consider too that some things people do may attract cats: small pet dogs, for example, look like lunch to a cat, and may not be the best hiking partner for this country. Some residents have been known to put out salt licks or hay to attract deer—and then are surprised when the deer attract lions.

People have been jumped by mountain lions here in recent years. In one case, a boy was jumped midday in Apgar Campground at the foot of Lake McDonald. In other instances cats have been found within the limits of Flathead Valley and Swan Valley towns. If you should find yourself being stalked by a cat, remain calm and remember first that cats are curious, indeed, and the animal may be just checking you out. Talk quietly to the animal but look big and unafraid: if you have a small child with you, pick the child up and carry him or her on your shoulders—you'll both look bigger, and you'll know where your child is. Back slowly away. Should attack seem imminent, find something you can defend yourself with—a stick, a rock—or something you can throw from your backpack. Do not run. Should you actually be rushed, yell and fight back; cats can be intimidated (note this is quite different from the advice given for dealing with bears). Once again, an ounce of prevention is worth many pounds of cure.

The chances of seeing a mountain lion are slim—if you do, more than likely, it will be a quick glimpse of magic as a long tail disappears before your eyes. Bobcats and lynx also inhabit Glacier Country but are even more rarely seen.

many other lodgings are closed. Open year-round this motel stays very busy during summer with tourists and in the fall with hunters and loggers until the snow blocks road access. They have both non-smoking and smoking rooms, disabled access and pets are permitted. They also provide two trailer hook-ups and corrals for horses.

Campgrounds and RV Parks

Swan Village Market and Post Office
Montana 83, Milepost 71, Swan Lake
• (406) 886-2303

In addition to the full grocery, prepared sandwiches, local crafts, T-shirts, magazines, paperback books, household supplies and stove fuel available at this community gathering place, there is a small campground with tent sites, full RV hookups, showers, and laundry. See page XXX for more information

Swan Valley Centre
Montana 83, Milepost 42, Condon
• (406) 754-2397

Swan Valley Centre is one of those places that can boast if they don't have it, you probably don't need it. There are water and electric hookups for campers, but no septic service, and they provide monthly parking for

Credit: Frank Miele

The Holland Lake Lodge offers a peaceful retreat.

RV campers. Showers and a laundry await the tired and dirty backpacker or equestrian just off the trail. Or if you're in need of a tow and auto repair, this is a good choice because it's the only one on this 50-mile stretch. While you're there, you can stock up on groceries, fishing supplies and have a deli picnic at the tables. Visitors and locals are welcome to fish from the Smith's property along the Swan River behind the center. See page XXX for more information

Restaurants

Restaurant Rates

$	$10-20
$$	$20-40
$$$	$30-50
$$$$	more than $50

For two people, meal exclusive of beverages, tip, and tax.

Holland Lake Lodge
$•1947 Holland Lake Rd., Swan Valley
• (406) 754-2282, (800) 648-8859

The wilderness setting of this fine restaurant at Holland Lake Lodge (see page XXX) and the views of Holland Falls make the breakfasts, lunches and dinners an experience for the senses. And the food lives up to the promise of the surroundings. The dinner menu features premium center cut filet mignon and other beef specialties as well as chicken and dumplings, Yankee pot roast and lighter vegetarian cuisine. The full bar stocks a collection of specialty premium California wines.

Hungry Bear Steak House
$ • 6287 Montana, Milepost 38-39, Swan Valley
• (406) 754-2240

Outside and in, this restaurant welcomes you in old-fashioned Montana style. The imposing 20-year-old log structure houses a high-ceilinged dining room, separate bar with pool table and dance floor. Mounted animals and trophy heads of local game adorn the high walls of both rooms including elk, moose, mountain lion, bison and beaver. Its special-

ity is beef but it also serves chicken seafood and, its patrons come from area cities to dine. If you've always wanted to try rocky mountain oysters, here's your chance. Also known as "bull fries," these are on the list of appetizers. They serve breakfast, lunch, and dinner.

Montana Charlies
$ • 6042 Montana 83, Milepost 36.5, Condon
• (406) 754-2229

Insider's tell us not to be fooled by the "regular" menu of Italian food, burgers, and chicken because the food is much better than regular. Charlie's pasta features unexpected original touches. The separate lounge is a typical Montana bar with gaming machines, pool table and dance floor where bands sometimes perform. RV hookups and camping are available on the grounds.

Shopping

Mission Mountains Mercantile
Montana 83, Milepost 45-46, Condon
• (406) 754-2826

If you've forgotten something for your camping or fishing trip, you have a good chance of finding it here. On the site of an early trading post known as Buckhorn Camp, this store now houses a mini-super market with a full range of groceries, produce, household supplies, hardware, pet, auto and picnic supplies, cosmetics, toys, greeting cards and Falcon guides. They make baked goods on the premises and cut their own meat. They also carry horse feed, propane and gasoline.

Swan Valley Arts and Crafts
Montana 83, Milepost 36, Condon
• (406) 754-3077

This partnership of local artisans features arts and crafts produced in the upper Swan Valley and Seeley Lake areas. The gallery is small, but displays an amazing variety of items including pottery, stained glass, baskets, wood furniture, jewelry, rugs, candles, paintings, sculpture and clothing. The shop is open Wednesdays through Sundays.

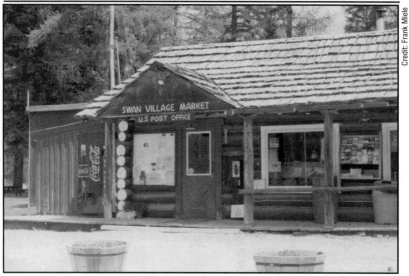

Credit: Frank Miele

The Swan Valley combines local charm with basic conveniences.

Swan Valley Centre
Montana 83, Milepost 42, Condon
• (406) 754-2397

The words "Beer Beans Bacon," in wood-block letters on the outside wall of this general store don't do justice to the variety of products and services owners Pat and Mike Smith offer. The original 1930s frame store has been enlarged over the years to accommodate other functions. Showers and a laundry await the tired and dirty backpacker or equestrian just off the trail. Or if you're in need of a tow and auto repair, this is a good choice because it's the only one on this 50-mile stretch. While you're there, you can stock up on groceries, fishing supplies and have a deli picnic at the tables. They also have freshly-made take-and-bake pizzas. There are water and electric hookups for campers, but no septic. They provide monthly parking for RV campers. Visitors and local are welcome to fish from the Smith's property along the Swan River behind the center.

Swan Village Market and Post Office
Montana 83, Milepost 71, Swan Lake
• (406) 886-2303

Established in 1926, where the southbound road ended, this general store and post office originally ran the telephone switchboard for the area. Today it serves as a gathering place for summer and year-round residents who come to get their mail and share a cup of coffee. It offers a full grocery, prepared sandwiches, local crafts, T-shirts, magazines, paperback books, household supplies and stove fuel. They have a small campground with tent sites, full RV hookups, showers, and laundry.

We arrived here once in anticipation of great things. We were not disappointed. Living in Montana is like an adventure that starts anew each morning.

Relocation

We include this chapter with special pleasure, for it was the lure of Montana's mountains, rivers, and skies that brought us or our families to this "Last Best Place," and the love of this land that made us want to stay, just like you. Perhaps it was only months ago that we were tourists or curious armchair travelers dreaming pioneer dreams. Or maybe it was generations ago that our families put down roots here, giving children the chance to discover the beauty of wilderness in their own backyard. We arrived here once in anticipation of great things. We were not disappointed. Living in Montana is like an adventure that starts anew each morning. No matter whether your day includes a routine of office, kids, home, or whether it's full of the horizon— miles of driving, hours of wilderness, acres of farm or ranch land—the life you live here is unlike any other. Start to think of the Flathead Valley as home: glaciers, grizzlies, glistening streams. Then get started making your dream come true. And though the scenery dominates this special place, you won't be moving to a cultural wasteland. One standout feature of the area as a whole is the abundance of arts and entertainment. Local and regional theater companies, an excellent orchestra, smaller musical groups, resident artists and writers all contribute to an exciting mix uncommon for an area with such a small population. The weekly entertainment section of the newspaper is chock-a-block with choices year-round, and most folks can't keep up with the dizzying array of activities, especially around the holidays. Sound like paradise? A note of caution: Consider what kind of environment this is for a long-term relationship, not just as a summer romance. If you're moving from a warm, sunny place, talk to others who've come before you. Remember that the Flathead Valley records an average of 71 sunny days per year (days when 3/10ths of the sky or less are covered by clouds) and that gray skies are often the norm in winter. Make sure you have a good job or enough retirement income to support you in a place where wages are generally low and the cost of living is above the national average. It's a magical place, but practical planning is needed to make your dreams come true. Visions of happily ever after aside, you probably can use some guidance for some of the challenges you may face in the first weeks and months of your relocation. Let the sections of this chapter offer some "mile markers" to get you started on the right track. Welcome to the Flathead!

Real Estate

Location, Location, Location (Part I)

One of the hardest decisions you may have when moving to the Flathead Valley is deciding which view you'll wake up to each morning. Mountain, river, or both? Forest or meadow? Lakeshore or golf green? With so many choices and each vista more beautiful than the last, the home search can feel overwhelming. Try to stay calm and remember the things you need most to feel comfortable. Do you want to live in town? It feels more central, more convenient, more social—and sometimes more crowded, more complicated. On the other hand, living miles out of town sounds great—pristine, tranquil—and fine until your multiple trips to school, the sitter, and the supermarket make you feel like you spent the whole day in the car. If you're moving from a place where long commutes are common, but snow isn't, adjust your thinking to reflect local conditions. A half-hour drive over winding roads may seem like no big deal in the summer, but think about that drive twice a day during the winter, when the roads may be icy and a deer could pop up in front of you on the road without warning. No matter how beautiful the view and peaceful the solitude are at the end of the day, they may not seem worth it after a white-knuckle trip in a snowstorm. Winter is a force to be reckoned with when making your plans. Another nuts and bolts factor to consider is water and sewer. Many homes built outside of the city limits are on septic systems and pump their water from individual wells. If you're planning to build, this is an especially critical factor. Drilling wells can be expensive, and septic failure catastrophic, so do your homework. Choices for heating and cooling your home also need to be considered. Natural gas is available in many areas of the valley, but other places— even some quite close to town—don't have gas. Extending utilities to new homes also can be expensive. Don't let the gorgeous view from a piece of mountaintop property blind you to the complications of building there. Some practical thinking now will save you a lot of headaches later.

Try to picture your new home in each of the four seasons. Think about that long, scenic quarter-mile driveway to your home. Then think about shoveling snow off of that long, scenic quarter-mile driveway. Who's responsible for plowing and maintaining the access roads? If you're not on a city or county road, the homeowners must bear those costs. Some subdivision roads are pitted with potholes because residents won't agree to pay their share for repairs. Take a hard look at those mountaintop hideaways. The views may be breath-catching, but you've got to get up and down the mountain in the winter. Think about fire protection. If you want to settle in the country, where is the nearest volunteer fire department? Privacy may not seem so appealing in case of an emergency. Do you want room to

expand on your property to keep stock and add outbuildings, or will you be content with the limitations of a standard city lot? If you're very social, will you feel lonely or isolated with no neighbors in a two-mile radius? Consider each option carefully and you'll avoid going too far in your quest to get away from it all.

Now add a buyer's market to the mix. New arrivals are initially amazed at the number of homes for sale and their reasonable prices, like a three-bedroom, two-bath historic home in downtown Kalispell for less than $150,000 or gorgeous lakefront homes for less than $300,000. They get jumpy, thinking of markets in Washington and California where homes sell in two days or less and buyers have to move quickly to make a deal. Here in the Flathead, however, the pace is a bit slower. Statistics from the Northwest Montana Association of Realtors showed that 1,544 houses were listed for sale in January 1999. During 1998, half of all homes sold were on the market for more than 120 days. Homes priced $180,000 and up stayed on the market an average of 286 days. Homes costing more than $500,000—24 of these homes were sold in 1998—were on the market for an average of 420 days before they sold. A total of 1,311 homes sold during 1998, with about half the sales clustered in the price range between $70,000 and $140,000. Low interest rates and a good selection made it a good time to buy real estate in the Flathead Valley.

The good news is that the Flathead Valley offers the presence of both nationally known and locally respected real estate offices whose agents can help you in your search. These agents are up to date on local trends and the latest developments in the market. Take your time and find one who specializes in your area (lakefront, homes with acreage, etc.) and who picks up on your interests and style. Real estate is big business in the Flathead. Sales of single-family homes totaled nearly $186 million during 1998, not small change by anybody's standards. Personal recommendations are always a good way to find a Realtor. Ask your friends and acquaintances who they used when they bought or sold a home. Your search will be more enjoyable and more successful with an agent who can help match you with the right property. Then grab some of their publications, go on-line to scout out some possibilities, and you'll soon be home!

Real Estate Companies

Northwest Montana Association of Realtors and Multiple Listing Service
690 N. Meridian Road, Suite #105, Kalispell
• **406-752-4197**
• **http://www.nmar.com/**

This agency can provide you with statistics on real estate transactions and general information about companies in the Flathead Valley. The association represents 110 real estate firms in Flathead and Lake Counties— a total of about 500 Realtors—and while it can't make recommendations or referrals to individual real estate firms, it can give the names, addresses and phone numbers of its members. Check out the real estate listings on the MLS web site.

Better Homes and Gardens Lakeside Sales Company
7254 U.S. 93 S., Lakeside
• **406-844-0100**
• **www.montanarealtors.com**

Lakeside Sales Company has six licensed agents and focuses on the area just north of Somers to the Lake County line. The company, established in 1994, handles all types of real estate, including lake frontage and other residential property, commercial and acreage. Lakeside Sales has sold a number of parcels of commercial property for a new bank, hardware store and office buildings in Lakeside.

Better Homes and Gardens Glacier Real Estate
135 W. Idaho, Suite B, Kalispell
• **406-752-1555**
• **glacierrealestate.com.**

The oldest real estate firm in the valley, established in 1939, has operated under just three owner/brokers during that time. The company has 17 agents who specialize in residential transactions; the company also handles commercial and undeveloped land throughout the Flathead Valley.

Credit: ERA 1st Choice Realty

In the Flathead Valley you can find your Montana dream home.

Century 21 Home & Investment Center
284 Fourth Ave. WN, Kalispell
- 406-755-2100
- www.century21montana.com.
- c21hi@digisys.net

This firm has been in business for well over 20 years and consists of seven owner/ brokers, with no sales associates. "We have the knowledge and integrity of experienced brokers and the power of Century 21," says owner/broker Edna Hellickson. The firm handles all types of transactions, with Individual agents specializing in areas such as farms and ranches, commercial and residential property.

Century 21 Whitefish Land Office
110 East Second St., Whitefish
- 406-862-2579 or 800-933-9155
- Big Mountain: 800-858-4146
- 406-862-1910
- www.c21whitefish.com

Established in 1978, this company is the exclusive sales agent for Big Mountain Development Corporation, a subsidiary of Winter Sports, Inc., which owns the Big Mountain Ski Resort. Big Mountain subdivisions include Sunrise Ridge and Wood Run, along with the 20-unit Kintla Lodge a luxury condominium project completed in 1998. The company also handles a variety of other real estate properties, primarily in the Whitefish area, including many resort properties that are second homes for the buyers. Whitefish Land Office has 12 real estate agents and was the No. 2 Century 21 office in Montana for closed sales in 1998. Owner/broker Wink Jordan describes his office as "a friendly down-home bunch of folks."

One interesting piece of property listed by this firm is a lakefront equestrian estate with miles of riding trails, a private beach, a 7,000 square foot manor home, surrounded by a state forest. This could be yours for a mere $3.9 million.

Coldwell Banker Wachholz & Company Real Estate
Kalispell: 1205 S. Main, Kalispell
- 406-751-4300
- www.cbwwachholz.com
- cbwckal@digisys.net

Whitefish: 105 Baker Ave., Whitefish
- 406-862-4200

Columbia Falls: 1123 Highway 2 W., Columbia Falls
- 406-892-5200

Lakeside: 7215 U.S. 93 S., Lakeside
- 406-844-3100

Bigfork: 710 Grand Dr., Bigfork
- 406-837-1234

This is the largest real estate firm in Northwest Montana, with 64 agents in five real offices throughout the Flathead Valley. Former banker Paul Wacholz established his original office in Kalispell in 1981 and affiliated with Coldwell Banker in 1985. Since then, the company has been the top-producing Coldwell Banker office for the state of Montana and was in the top 3 percent of the 2,000-plus Coldwell Banker offices nationwide for 1991-93 and 1995. The company has expanded throughout the valley, beginning with the Whitefish office in 1986. Wacholz and Company moved into Lakeside in 1998, buying out the Century 21 office there, and in 1999 bought another adjacent Lakeside real estate firm. The company

INSIDERS' TIP

A small first aid kit is essential for backcountry outings in Glacier country. Your first aid kit should contain enough items to control bleeding and to fashion and secure dressings and splints—athletic or duct tape is useful here. Moleskin or duct tape can effectively treat blisters—a common occurrence on the trail. Be prepared to improvise, using the contents of your backpack or other gear. For example, a trekking pole can easily convert into a splint. It's always a good idea to obtain first aid training before you travel to learn how treat injuries in the field.

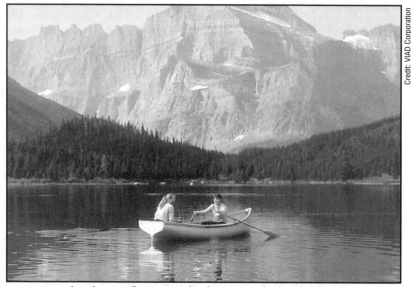

Credit: VIAD Corporation

Imagine spending your weekends on our cool mountain lakes.

handles all types of real estate, from commercial property to high-end homes. One of the firm's most-expensive listings is a custom home on 59 acres of land near Bigfork with an elaborate home theater, complete with plush seats and a snack bar. The price: $5.8 million.

Chuck Olson Real Estate Inc.
Bigfork: P.O. Box 672, Bigfork
• 406-837-5551
Kalispell: 241 Main St. Kalispell
•406-752-1000 • 800-555-5376
• montanaweb.com/homes/
Whitefish: 567 Spokane, Whitefish
• 800-775-3250 • 406-862-5536
• www.whitefishmt.com/chuckolson/
• property@digisys.net

Chuck Olson Real Estate is a locally owned, independent firm established in 1971. It's the only "major player" in the valley that's not affiliated with a national franchise and touts itself as the "home team." Each of its three offices is independently owned and operated, although the offices cooperate and share advertising. The biggest office is in Kalispell, which has 16-18 real estate agents, including nine owner/brokers. According to owner/broker John Badger, the firm consistently ranks among the top agencies for overall gross sales.

Edgewater Realty, Inc.
13 Second Ave. W., Polson
• 406-883-5393

This company has been in business for nearly 50 years, with a name change or two along the way. Current owner Gerald Newgard has been selling real estate in Polson since 1970, and his company has eight real estate agents. As its name implies, Edgewater specializes in lake properties, mostly in the area between Polson and Rollins. "We serve who comes through the door—that's the boss," Newgard says.

Montana Brokers, Inc. Realtors
685 Sunset Blvd., Kalispell
• 800-933-3177
• www.montanabrokers.com
• mtbroker@digisys.net

Owner Rick Doran is a self-described "local yokel" who grew up in the Flathead Valley and has been in the real estate business here since 1978. Montana Brokers was established in 1986, and currently has nine or 10 agents, all brokers with an average of about 15 years of experience. The firm handles all types of real estate throughout the valley and was one of the first companies to go "on line." Although a number of the agents are natives, Doran says the firm also welcomes people from other places, because "We all came here from somewhere, sometime." One interesting piece of property listed is a castle-like home, complete with turret, on about 200 acres of land.

RE/MAX Glacier Country
1 Main St., Kalispell
• 406-257-8900

"Have fun and make money" is the motto at RE/MAX Glacier Country, a company that's in "major growth mode," according to owner/ broker Doug Denmark, after purchasing and refurbishing an historic building in downtown Kalispell. The firm had eight Realtors in early 1999, and planned to add several more experienced agents. Denmark said his firm is the No. 2 RE/MAX office in sales, and two of his agents are members of the RE/MAX hall of fame. Glacier Country sold the property and is the marketing agent for "The Willows," an 87-lot subdivision being developed just southeast of Kalispell on Willow Glen Drive. Denmark says he's especially proud of this project because it's turning a 30-acre tract of land that had been blighted and an eyesore with rusted equipment into an attractive subdivision of moderately priced homes.

RE/MAX Land & Lake
P.O. Box 582, Lakeside
• 406-844-3500
• http://www.montanaland.com

Land & Lake has been in business for 25 years and specializes in lakeshore and residential property. Owner Bruce Young says

he's one of the few real estate agents who often shows and sells property by boat, even in the shoulder months of April and November. The firm uses advanced technology, but does business "the old-fashioned way, with integrity," Young says. Among the interesting properties Land & Lake handles are islands or parts of islands, such as Wild Horse Island, a 2,700-acre state park which is home to big horn sheep, deer and bald eagles. The island also has 52 private lakeshore lots, one of which occasionally goes up for sale.

Trails West Eagle Bend Realty
420 Electric Ave., Bigfork
• 800-976-6682 • 406-837-7050
• www.montanaweb.com/trailswest

Owner/broker Katie Brown says a major goal of the seven full-time agents in her firm is to make the buying/selling process "fun or at least a comfortable experience." Trails West, which has been in operation since the early 1970s, merged with Eagle Bend Realty in 1997 to form the existing company. Trails West Eagle Bend works with many second-home buyers, who are interested in lake frontage or acreage, primarily in Bigfork, the Swan Valley and the Eagle Bend development. A number of the company's listings have been featured in national magazines such as *Architectural Digest*.

Real Estate Publications

Home Seekers
• 1-800-882-9044

Published by Century Publishing Company 13 times a year, this magazine features properties in Kalispell, Whitefish, Columbia

Falls, Bigfork, Lakeside, Eureka, Libby, and Polson. Listings from more than 30 agencies and brokerages are included.

The Montana Land Magazine
Real Estate Publications, Inc.,
P.O. Box 30516, Billings MT 59107
• 406-259-3534
• www.montanalandmagazine.com

The Winter 1999 issue of this quarterly publication contained 175 pages of statewide and Rocky Mountain listings of which about 10 percent covered the greater Flathead and Seeley/Swan area.

Homes and Real Estate
The *Daily Inter Lake*, 727 E. Idaho, Kalispell
• 406-755-7000

Published by the Daily Inter Lake monthly, this is a very comprehensive guide to current listings around the valley, with most prominent agencies represented.

Northwest Montana Real Estate
Milestone Publications, Inc, Ronan
• 800-696-2804
• http://www.milestonepublications.com

Published five times a year, this real estate guide lists properties on Flathead Lake, in the Mission Valley and surrounding areas.

Northwest Real Estate Guide
RE Guide/Brady Graphics & Printing,
P.O. Box 794, Lewistown

Published quarterly, and available as subscription (four issues for $12.50), you'll find here homes and land from Helena to Sandpoint Idaho, including properties on the edges of the Flathead Valley in Libby and Missoula.

Polson and Lake County Homes and Real Estate
The *Daily Inter Lake*, 727 E. Idaho, Kalispell
• 406-755-7000

Published four or five times a year, this guide gives a comprehensive listing of property for sale in the southern part of the Flathead Valley.

In addition to these periodicals, some individual real estate firms publish booklets listing their properties. Some of these booklets appear as newspaper inserts, and others are available on the racks of free publications that are maintained at various locations outside grocery stories, motels and shopping malls.

Building

New construction is not only an important marker of the valley's economic well being, it can be the way for you to get exactly what you want in your home. Whether your dream is to build it yourself, to choose from the models in a new neighborhood community, or to have a custom-built log home with river-rock fireplace, contractors in the valley are prepared to deliver. The Flathead Building Association, 1702 Fifth Avenue East, Kalispell, 406-752-2422, can refer you to a builder who specializes in the type of home you desire, or answer questions about the particular contractors bidding on your job. The association publishes a directory of members each March in conjunction with their annual trade show. Residential construction was booming in 1998, while commercial building permits declined substantially. Flathead County issued 653 building permits for single-family homes in 1998, a 33.5 percent increase from the previous year. The value of the permits totaled $79.8 million, up from $70.7 million in 1997. In Lake County, residential construction increased by 21.5 percent from 1997 to 1998, to a total of $29.2 million.

Home Rentals

Resist that urge to buy the first house you see, say locals, and rent for the first year—or at least through your first winter. Even if you've visited here before, this advice makes good sense. Renting gives you the chance to test your instincts on neighborhoods, landscapes, and other practicalities of Montana life before making a commitment to a particular property. You'll gain a sense of how much home you need to feel comfortable, a chance to prioritize the fireplace versus the hot tub. Then when you're ready to buy, you'll have more information on what truly attracts you and what to avoid. Some rentals are beautiful homes that are languishing on the market or even vacation properties not used during the off-season. Their owners prefer to have these homes lived in than sit vacant. So now can be your chance to live in a great setting without homeowner's headaches like fixing the roof or the furnace.

Whether it's an apartment in a large complex, a privately owned rental home, or a professionally managed property, interview a prospective property manager or landlord carefully before signing any paperwork. Ask them to describe what their services to you will include. Some landlords can be very attentive to the needs of renters, especially dependable, long-term ones. The cost of an average three-bedroom rental unit runs from $550 to $700 per month, and lovely places can often be found for a reasonable cost. Some agencies can even help you secure a temporary place to stay when you first arrive. But remember that an agent's primary customer is the property owner, not you. Overall, renting may not be the best option for people who like to feel "settled," but it works for a great many newcomers to the Flathead. Check your yellow pages for listings under "Real Estate Rental Service" or look for classifieds in the local papers or Mountain Trader.

Rental Agencies

Corental
1046 S. Main, Kalispell,
- **406-752-5600**

Corental, established in 1983, provides professional management for apartments, houses and commercial property. Services offered are a full-time licensed real estate broker, free advertising, tenant screenings, 24-hour telephone service.

Eagle Bend Rental & Property Management
836 Holt Dr., Bigfork,
- **406-837-0323**
- **800-239-9933**
- **http://www.mtvacationrentals.com**
- **info@vacationrentals.com**

This firm specializes in vacation homes on Eagle Bend golf course and other areas of the Valley, including Flathead Lake, Swan Lake and Swan River.

Flathead Property Management
282 Fourth Ave. WN, Kalispell
- **406-752-5480**

This licensed property management firm

has been in business since 1981 and offers a variety of services to landlords. It also rents a variety of storage units.

Flathead Valley Property Management
101 Lakeside Blvd., Whitefish
• 406-862-6074

Offers professional, full-service management of seasonal and long-term residential rentals. Owner Peter F. Elespuru is a Montana native who owns rental properties and has "over 35 years of professional experience as a key member of corporate management entrusted with fiduciary responsibility and trust."

West Shore Property Management.
P.O. Box 42, Lakeside
• 406-844-2137
• www.relaxMT.pair.com
• westshor@digisys.net

Specializing in weekly rentals (Saturday to Saturday) of fully furnished lakefront homes. The company also will assist with advance bookings, help plan an itinerary and provide maps information about highlights of the valley.

Location, Location, Location (Part II)

The great spots in the Flathead Valley are many. The rugged sportsman, retired couple and the growing family all find their places here in an eclectic and exciting mix. Neighborhoods may not be as clearly delineated as they are in some cities, and exclusive parkside and waterside properties are located throughout Northwest Montana. But each major center of the Flathead enjoys a personality of its own. Other standard criteria for selecting a home will still apply, so ask a reputable agent for current information on the community resources, schools, and services in your area of interest.

Bigfork & the Flathead Lake

Quiet and quaint, Bigfork Village is home to delightful artist's galleries and fine shops

Credit: Marina Cay Resort

Spectacular scenery can be found all over Glacier and the Flathead.

and restaurants. In the summer, the single main street is abustle with visitors enjoying the ambiance that sometimes can make Bigfork seem like a stage set rather than a real, living town. One of the best things that happened to Bigfork seemed like a disaster at the time—the highway bypassed the town. As a result, Bigfork was spared the through traffic that's plagued Kalispell and Lakeside, and its downtown retains a village feeling, without a single stoplight downtown. Parking is another matter, though, as summer visitors vie for the limited number of mostly angle-in spots. Homes and cherry orchard properties extend along the eastern shore of Flathead Lake down to Woods Bay with summer cabins and year-round home retreats reaching along the Swan River out into Ferndale. You'll find newer homes on large wooded lots at the edge of the mountains along Foothill Road, near Echo Lake, and in the Many Lakes development, while west of the highway you can find older farm homes and estates with views of the Flathead River, fields of hay, mint, and dill, and marshes full of wildlife. If you must live where you golf and golf where you live, Eagle Bend golf community is just west of Bigfork Village. On the western shore of the lake, the community of Lakeside is booming with mid-priced homes with lake views and proximity to the new ski resort on Blacktail Mountain. And all along the lake small summer cabins are being turned into year-round residences. Farther south is Polson, a pretty little town at the foot of Flathead Lake. The view of the lake coming over the hill on Highway 93 from Missoula is almost unbeatable. Polson is located in a relative banana belt, and residents boast they can play golf all year.

railroad tracks continue to hold much of their charm from the town's early days. Stately maple and chestnut trees line the boulevards in the older sections of town, and the fall colors are striking. Many of the historic and larger homes are found on the east side near Woodland Avenue, while newer homes have developed north of the downtown near Lawrence Park and south of town near the city airport. Building lots within the city are rare, and many people opt for remodeling an existing home rather than building a new one. Living within the city limits provides many conveniences. Residents can walk to Woodland Park, shops on Main Street, to the Kalispell Center Mall, movie theaters, museums, concerts and art galleries. The downtown is experiencing a commercial revival, with development of several small shopping malls and restoration of the KM Building, a historic landmark that dates back more than a century. A special note about Woodland Park, which was donated to the city of Kalispell in 1903 by the widow of the town's founder, Charles E. Conrad. This 40-acre park is a treasure enjoyed by residents and visitors year-round. A flock of ducks, geese and swans delight park visitors and beg for handouts, and generations of children and their parents have kept them well fed. You can purchase a healthy snack of cracked corn at the convenience store across the street from the park and delight the resident waterfowl population. Flower gardens are a popular spot for summer weddings, a skating rink is open in the winter, and youngsters can splash in the municipal pool on hot summer days. Families wander across the wooden bridges and business people take a lunch break in this beautiful spot, even on chilly winter days.

Kalispell

The commercial center and seat for Flathead County, Kalispell is the largest municipality in the valley and in Northwest Montana, making it popular for those who like to be close to services and community resources. In 1998, *Mountain Sports and Living* magazine picked Kalispell as the best mountain town in the nation based on quality of life criteria. Streets in the historic central part of town south of the

Whitefish

Popular as a resort for many years among skiers, a fur trading, logging and railroad town in its early days, Whitefish was once known as Stumptown because buildings were erected over stumps from downed timber. Little of its blue-collar past now remains in this upscale town. Whitefish is growing as a community that offers year-round outdoor attractions like Big Mountain and Whitefish Lake, as well as community resources like a new theater and new public library. With a downtown core full of restaurants and shops, and a slate of special events, Whitefish has developed and identity as a lively, entertaining community. Real estate in this area can be pricey. Lakeshore on Whitefish Lake sell for up to $3,000 a front foot, and lakeshore view property sells for up to $20,000 an acre. In 1998, the average price of a home was $182,623.

Columbia Falls & Glacier Park

The gateway communities to Glacier National Park have no trouble attracting residents who want to live just a few spare minutes from the park's boundaries. Columbia Falls has long been a home for generations of employees of Plum Creek Timber and the Columbia Falls Aluminum Company. But like all areas of the Flathead, secluded wooded or riverside lots attract dream house homeowner/builders. The communities of Hungry Horse, Martin City and Coram lie beyond, and fro those who really want to get away from it all, they can travel up the North Fork Road into the remote Polebridge area near the boundary of Glacier National Park.

Living in Grizzly Country

The forests and wilderness areas of Northwest Montana comprise one of the largest expanses of grizzly habitat in the country. As greater numbers of homeowners settle in outlying areas of the Flathead, reports of contacts between humans and bears have increased. And in years when bears encounter food shortages (1998 was a particularly bad year for huckleberries, their favorite food), the number of encounters is even greater. Rangers advise special precautions for residents who live in grizzly country and along its edges. They discourage the feeding of birds, deer, or other animals, and recommend that garbage and pet food be secured inside, not on porches or in sheds. Bears that sniff out and win these "food rewards," they advise, are essentially learning to return to human settlements for an easy meal. Once this behavior is learned it is very difficult to train a bear to only seek berries in the forest. A bear that learns this lesson too well will probably wind up causing property damage, and even being destroyed. Prevention rather than correction in advised so that sightings of animals might continue with few unfortunate consequences.

Living in Forest Fire Country

Your home nestled amid the tamarack trees brings with it a special responsibility—wildfire control. Large forest fires take on historic significance as they take out the trees that make up the livelihood of residents and support the local economy. Everyone takes the risk of fire seriously. For homeowners, this means taking care of forested areas on your property, and keeping underbrush—a source of fire fuel—controlled. Prevention of chimney fires through regular cleaning of stovepipes and flues is another important precaution. Make sure firefighters can find your hideaway. Efforts to quench recent fires at two remote homes near Kalispell were complicated by the fact that no house numbers were posted on access roads. Fire can quickly wipe out your dreams, so take all the precautions you can.

A Note on Recycling

Moving to an area where I had to haul my own trash to the county landfill took some getting used to. (We were living in the country: garbage pickup service is available in most places in the valley). Giving up access to a comprehensive household waste recycling program came next. I have learned to adjust. Materials that are currently recycled in the Flathead include: newspaper, aluminum cans, cardboard and mixed paper, Styrofoam egg cartons and plastic pop bottles. Large sorting containers for these materials can be found outside most of the major grocery stores, and some stores individually collect plastic shopping bags and Styrofoam egg cartons. A successful program for glass does not currently exist.

Retirement

Since this is a place where many families live for generations, you often find families that tell you how they all came to move to the valley over time. It is important to know what facilities exist to care for older family members. Retired "empty nesters" comprise a relatively large segment of newcomers to the valley, so housing options will be increasingly important to them in the future. Seniors make up a significant portion of the population and many activities and services are available for them, and lots of volunteer opportunities exist in the community as well. Flathead Valley Community College offers a popular "Senior Fridays" program in the winter, with classes ranging from computer training to ceramics. Lunch and transportation from area senior centers are included in the reasonable fee.

Agency on Aging
723 Fifth Ave. E., Kalispell
• 406-758-5730

This agency offers a variety of services to seniors, including a meals program, transportation, information and assistance for a variety of problems, a newsletter, reference library, homemaker program and companion care.

Eagle Transit
723 Fifth Ave. E., Kalispell
• 406-758-5728

Adequate transportation is necessary for a comfortable life in this valley, and bus service can be a godsend for seniors who no longer can drive. Buses operate Monday through Friday from 9:15 AM to 5 PM and early morning Dial-A-Ride is available from 7 AM to 7:30 AM and from 9 AM to 9:30 AM Arrangements for Dial-A-Ride must be made a working day in advance. Eagle Transit provides special transportation for passengers with disabilities.

Senior Citizen Centers

A number of senior centers offer a variety of activities. Here are some of the centers in the area: Bigfork, 639 Commerce Street, 837-4157; Columbia Falls, 205 Nucleus Avenue, 892-4087; Kalispell, 403 Second Avenue West, 257-1598; Lakeside, Lakeside Baptist Church, 844-3006; Polson, 504 Third Avenue East, 883-4735; Whitefish, 121 Second Street, 862-4923.

The Summit
205 Sunnyview Lane, Kalispell
• 406-751-4100

The Summit, a full-service health and fit-

INSIDERS' TIP

To add a special focus to your visit to Glacier Country, try a field seminar with the Glacier Institute! Outdoor education classes cover many topics, ranging from outdoor photography to medicinal plants to geology to predator-prey relations. Classes may last a single day or stretch over several days; some are tailored for children. Hike levels are rated for each course. The Glacier Institute is affiliated with Flathead Valley Community College and college credits can be arranged for many courses. For more information, check the website at www.digisys.net/glacinst or write The Glacier Institute, 137 Main Street, P.O. Box 7457, Kalispell, MT 59904. The office phone is (406) 755-1211 year-round; the summer field camp at Glacier National Park is open from June to August at (406) 888-5215; and the Big Creek Outdoor Education Center is open from April to October at (406) 758-8516.

ness center, offers a variety of activities for non-members through its Successful Aging Program, including free health education lectures on the first and third Wednesdays of each month, a Cribbage Challenge on the second Thursday, and a Scrabble Mixer on the fourth Thursday of each month. A Summit staff member also conducts a Mall Walk program for seniors on Monday and Fridays from 9:30 to 10:30 AM at Kalispell Center Mall. The Summit also conducts low-cost cholesterol screenings once a month and every few months has a $1 day for seniors.

Nursing and Retirement Centers

Brendan House
350 Conway Dr., Kalispell
• 406-752-5460

Skilled nursing facility operated by Northwest Healthcare, which also owns Kalispell Regional Hospital. A comprehensive team approach is used to deal with the individual needs of each resident, whether they are recovering from surgery or have illnesses that are terminal. "Comfort care rooms" are available to allow terminally ill patients and families a comfortable, homey setting in which to spend time together. Adult day care is also available.

Buffalo Hill Terrace
40 Claremont St., Kalispell
• 406-752-9624

This retirement community, owned by the Immanuel Lutheran Corporation, is designed for seniors who can live independently. The 100-unit complex atop Buffalo Hill consists of studio and one- and two-bedroom apartments with kitchen facilities. Residents can eat in the dining room or cook their own meals. Basic services include two meals a day, weekly housekeeping, scheduled transportation and a full-time activities and social director.

Colonial Manor Nursing Center
1305 E. Seventh St., Whitefish
• 406-862-3557

This is a 100-bed skilled nursing facility that has both private and semi-private rooms.

It is owned by Peak Medical Corporation, a company based in Albuquerque, New Mexico, that owns 27 nursing homes. A variety of programs and services are available, including Hospice/Respite care, physical, occupational, speech and respiratory therapy and an Alzheimer's/Aging Support Group.

Friendship House
606 Second Ave. W., Kalispell
• 406-257-8375

This is a state-licensed assisted living facility for adults who can no longer live safety at home. It is located in a gracious historic home on Kalispell's west side and has a capacity of 18 residents. Adult day care on an hourly basis also is available.

Harmony House
Kalispell • 406-257-5991
• junge1@bigsky.net

This new assisted living facility provides a home-like environment to seniors with Alzheimer's or other forms of dementia. Harmony House has a capacity of six residents and opened in November 1998 in a private home on Kalispell's west side. (Owner Peggy Junge asked us not to list the exact address because "it's their home" and she'd just as soon not have people just drop by without calling.) Meals are home-cooked and unlimited healthy snacks are available. Mental and physical activities are alternated every half-hour. The family's pet cat has the run of the place.

Heritage Place
171 Heritage Way, Kalispell
• 406-755-0800

A skilled nursing home and rehabilitation center that's part of the Lantis Living Network, which operates four facilities in the valley. Lantis, a family owned corporation based in Spearfish, South Dakota, operates 22 assisted-living and nursing homes in five states. Heritage Place specializes in the needs of the elderly, both for long-term residency or short-term care after surgery, illness or an injury. It has 31 semi-private rooms, six private rooms, five "premier" rooms, eight skilled care rooms and 28 special care beds. Services include transportation, beauty and barber shop, a lounge and dining room. An Alzheimer's Unit has employees especially trained to care for the needs of residents with Alzheimer's and other dementia conditions.

Immanuel Lutheran Home
185 Crestline Ave., Kalispell
• **406-752-9622**

The oldest private nursing home in the valley, established in 1957 under the auspices of the Evangelical Lutheran Church of America. The capacity is 149 residents, housed in private and semi-private rooms. The home offers nursing services that range from minimal assistance to skilled care. Registered nursing care is provided 24 hours a day. Immanuel has a special care unit for persons suffering from dementia diseases, such as Alzheimer's.

Lake View Care Center
1050 Grand Ave., Bigfork
• **406-837-5041**

Lake View Care Center is a state-licensed nursing home and rehabilitation center operated by Lantis. It has 36 semi-private and seven private rooms, a beauty and barber shop, lounge and dining room. On-site apartments are available to those who are able to

live alone but need meal service. Housekeeping, laundry, maintenance and transportation services are available. Residents also can participate in community outings and social activities.

Prestige Assisted Living at Kalispell
125 Glenwood Dr., Kalispell
• **406-756-1818**

Residents pay for the personal care services within the system at this assisted-living facility with various levels of care determined by individual need. Studios and one- and two-bedroom apartments are offered, and three meals a day are included, along with scheduled transportation, apartment maintenance and availability of personal care staff. Size of apartments varies from 377 to 835 square feet. A variety of additional services are available for an additional monthly fee. Small pets are welcome upon approval.

Montana Veterans Home
P.O. Box 250, Columbia Falls
• **406-892-3256**

Nursing and assisted living home for honorably discharged veterans and their spouses who are unable to earn an income. The home

Credit: Buffalo Hill Terrace

Retirement communities are a growing part of
the Flathead Valley.

was authorized by the Fourth Montana Legislative Assembly in 1895, just six years after Montana joined the union, and the first building was dedicated in 1896. The latest addition is a 50-bed nursing home dedicated in May 1984. The home has 150 beds, including 90 in the nursing home. Members pay on the basis of their ability.

WEL-Life at Kalispell
156 Three Mile Dr., Kalispell
• **406-756-8688**

This assisted-living home operated by Lantis offers a variety of levels of assisted living. Accommodations include studios, deluxe rooms, one- and two-bedroom apartments. Personal assistance and residence services are geared to individual needs.

WEL-Life at Windward Place
245 Windward Way, Kalispell
• **406-257-2549**

Assisted living for senior citizens including 24-hour attendants, linens, meals and medication monitoring. Transportation, activities and social events, weekly housekeeping and laundry and a library are among the services offered. WEL-life at Windward Place is located just north of Kalispell, near Kalispell Regional Medical Center. This is another Lantis facility.

Healthcare

The Flathead Valley boasts a load of top-notch physicians and surgeons and its medical facilities are among the best in the state. The 1999 community profile published by the Kalispell Chamber of Commerce says the community has 142 medical doctors, or 197 doctors per 100,000 population. The beauty of the area and opportunities for outdoor recreation have been a major drawing-card for medical professionals. Three full-service hospitals, Kalispell Regional Medical Center, North Valley Hospital and St. Joseph Hospital meet the regular needs of valley residents. Sports medicine is of course a specialty, in an area that attends to the knees and backs of golfers, skiers, and hikers. Occasionally, for extensive or rare medical problems, residents are referred to larger cities like Seattle or Missoula or Spokane to seek further treatment or a second opinion. Naturopathic practitioners, acupuncturists and chiropractors also enjoy the support of clients seeking non-traditional treatments.

Kalispell Regional Medical Center
310 Sunnyview Lane, Kalispell
• **406-752-5111**

Kalispell Regional Medical Center is a 110-bed, acute-care hospital with a fully equipped intensive care unit, inpatient rehabilitation, free-standing birthing center, hemodialysis, home health, physical occupational therapies, the latest CAT Scanners, MRI, diagnostic heart cathertization and a cancer treatment center equipped with a Varian linear accelerator. The Northwest Healthcare Medical Campus is located on Buffalo Hill, adjacent to many medical and professional offices and a pharmacy. Northwest Health Care, the corporation that owns the hospital, also operates a number of other services, including Home Options/Hospice, the ALERT helicopter, and the Summit fitness center.

North Valley Hospital
6575 U.S. 93 S., Whitefish
• **406-863-2510**
• **http://www/nvhosp.org**

North Valley is a full-service facility with 44 acute-care beds and 56 long-term-care beds. The hospital provides care to a service area of approximately 20,000 people, including the communities of Whitefish, Columbia Falls and Eureka. Services include obstetrics, emergency care, same-day surgery, geriatric services and a number of wellness programs. Expansion plans call for 1999 construction of a 36-apartment assisted living complex on the hospital's northwest campus overlooking the Flathead River.

St. Joseph Hospital
P.O. Box 1010, Polson
• **406-883-5377**

St. Joseph is a full-service hospital licensed for 22 beds that provides a full range of medical services, including Home Health Care and an assisted-living center. A fundraising drive is under way for a new hospital building, with groundbreaking in March 1999 and completion scheduled for late 2000.

Education

The Flathead Valley continues to attract top educators to the region, who come here for adventure and stay for the quality of life. The benefit of these highly skilled and enthusiastic teachers and administrators translates into the quality of education and care given to valley schoolchildren. In the public school system, you will find a good balance of basic skills with access to athletics, art and music, and computer resources. More than half of graduates continue on at four- and two-year colleges. Growth in the valley has put strain on the public school system, especially at the high school level, but to date initiatives to build another high school in Bigfork or Kalispell have not succeeded. Both Bigfork and Kalispell hired new school superintendents for the 1999-2000 school year, and those administrators are sure to bring new energy and direction to their districts. Strong support for homeschooling is also found in this region, a correlation to the independent streak shared by many Montanans. Statistics from the Flathead County school superintendent's office show a 275 percent increase in home-schooled elementary students between 1989 and 1998. During the same period, total elementary school enrollment increased by 11 percent. High school enrollment increased by 38 percent. Flathead High School, with about 1,750 students in grades 10-12, is the largest high school in the state. Public schools in Flathead County are divided into many local school districts. The smallest public elementary school in the county is Pleasant Valley, which had just eight students registered for the 1998-99 school year. By contrast, the largest school in Kalispell's school district 5 was Edgerton, with 547 students. Enrollment in public schools in Flathead County totaled more than 13,500 for the 1998-99 school year. To the south, about 1,700 students are enrolled in Polson's two elementary schools, middle school and high school.

Flathead Valley Community College
777 Grandview Dr., Kalispell
• 756-FVCC
• http://www.fvcc.cc.mt.us

Established in 1967 and fully accredited by the Northwest Association of Schools and Colleges, FVCC offers more than 600 day and evening classes annually, including transfer, occupational and non-credit programs, and operates an extension campus in Lincoln County. More than 2,000 credit and 4,000 non-credit students enroll each year at the two campus and nearby community sites. FVCC offers the Associate of Arts and Sciences and Associate of Applied Sciences Degrees as well as certificates in business management, office technology, medical assistant, criminal justice, computer applications, accounting, hospitality, human services, professional goldsmithing, surveying and natural resources. Montana State University and FVCC have a dual admission agreement that admits qualifying students to both institutions at the same time. Through a number of partnerships with other institutions of higher learning, FVCC offers four-year and advanced degree opportunities

Glacier Institute
137 Main St., Kalispell
• 755-1211
• glacinst@digisys.net

Educational adventures in Glacier Country are offered through the Glacier Institute, an organization that provides high-quality, well-balanced educational experiences for children and adults of all ages. Courses emphasize a hands-on, field-oriented approach to learning, and highlight the diverse natural and cultural resources of the Northern Rockies Ecosystem. Many popular courses are offered each year, but still fill quickly. Facilities of the Glacier Institute include the Glacier Park Field Camp, a rustic facility located within the park which is the site of summer field courses for adults and children. Also used is the Big Creek Outdoor Education Center, a full-service residential center situated along the Wild and Scenic North Fork of the Flathead River in the Flathead National Forest, home to youth field science programs, Elderhostels, and special workshops.

Private Schools

A number of private schools, both religious and secular, offer parents an alternative to the public education system. Private school enrollment at the elementary school level totaled 1,251 for the 1998-99 school year, according to the Flathead County school superintendent's office, while enrollment in private high schools totaled 171. Enrollment in private schools, including home schooling, is on the increase in Flathead County at both elementary and secondary levels. You'll find a variety of choices of schools for your youngsters.

Cross Currents Christian School
820 Ashar Ave., Whitefish
• **406-862-5875**
The mission of Cross Currents is to "assist parents in educating their children in a manner honoring Jesus Christ." The school promotes spiritual growth, academic excellence, sound family relationships, responsible citizenship and moral and ethical values guided by biblical teaching. The evangelical, interdenominational school was established in 1978 and moved into its own building in 1989. Enrollment in grades pre-K through 8 is about 140. Expansion plans include a gymnasium, a multi-purpose room and other classrooms. The full-time faculty are all certified teachers. A new elective enrichment program allows students to expand their horizons in areas of particular interest. Guest professionals teach band, drama, foreign language, chemistry, computer applications, art, music and literature.

Education Recovery Foundation Inc.
322 Second St. W., Kalispell
• **406-756-6645**
Education Recovery is a free program for individuals from 16-20 who have dropped out of school, helping the individual establish educational goals, and prepare for the GED.

Flathead Valley Christian School
1251 Willow Glen Dr., Kalispell
• **406-752-4006**
• **http://www.fvcs.k12.mt.us**
• **fvcs@digisys.net**
Founded in 1980, this Christian school has an enrollment of 320 in grades K-12. School facilities include a library, computer lab, cafeteria and gymnasium. The school is accredited by the Association of Christian Schools International and draws students from a 30-mile radius. More than 50 churches of various denominations are represented in the school's enrollment. The school has 25 full- or part-time teachers, with a student-teacher ratio of 16.4 to 1. Average SAT scores for the three most recent years are Verbal, 557, Math, 534, and Composite, 1096. The school maintains a local chapter of the National Honor Society and is a member of the Montana Christian Athletic Association (MCAA). High school teams compete in the MCAA as well as playing area public schools as schedules permit.

Flathead Valley Association of Homeschoolers
P.O. Box 7661, Kalispell
• **406-881-4178**
This organization provides support to families who homeschool their children. Bob and Linda Heffernan are the contact people for this group. A Home Learning Center offers curriculum support and the association publishes a newsletter monthly from September through May. The association also coordinates support group meetings for parents, sports and music programs. A detailed voice mail message gives a variety of information about activities and numbers to call.

Glacier Christian School
80 E. Railroad St., Columbia Falls
• **406-892-4798**
Glacier Christian School is an independent, non-denominational Christian school with an enrollment of about 60 students in pre-kindergarten through eighth grade. The adult to student ratio is about 1-10. The school uses the Abeka curriculum in K-8 and Bob Jones reading and spelling. The curriculum includes a formal Bible class for each age

group, and Christian principles of honesty, courtesy, kindness and morality are stressed throughout the school day. "Our school was established as an extension of the Christian home, affirming parental authority and reinforcing Godly principles taught in the home and church."

Kalispell Montessori Center, Inc.
5 Park Hill Road Kalispell
• 406-755-3824

The Kalispell Montessori Center "fosters the natural spirit of inquiry and thrill of discovery within each child by upholding the Montessori philosophy that learning is best achieved within a social atmosphere that supports each individual's unique academic, physical and emotional development." The school serves children ages 3 to 12 years of age, from pre-school to sixth grade, and enrollment is about 150 students. Expansion into a new building was planned for the fall of 1999, and consideration is being given to adding a junior high program. Parental involvement is a key part of the Montessori philosophy and one of the program's goals is to create a partnership between home and school. Montessori Administrator Sally Welder says the best way to understand the Montessori philosophy is to come visit the school while classes are in session. Please call ahead to schedule a time to observe.

North Valley Music School
P.O. Box 4446, Whitefish
• 406-862-8074

Started in 1998 to provide string training to students outside of the Kalispell School District, this school was organized by musicians and parents. Instruction includes the Suzuki method for violin and piano, Kindermusik, guitar, and voice classes for children as young as five. Recent classes also included Celtic Music Group, Madrigals Group and the Whitefish Xylophone Ensemble.

St. Matthew's School
602 S. Main St., Kalispell
• 406-752-6303

This Catholic school was established in 1917 and has an enrollment of 160 students from kindergarten through sixth grade. The kindergarten program is all-day or morning only. The program includes both academics and religious instruction. St. Matthew's also provides before-school playground supervision starting at 7:30 AM and childcare in-house from 7:30 AM to 5:30 PM. Pre-school programs, after-school care are also provided.

Trinity Lutheran Elementary School
495 Fifth Ave. WN, Kalispell
• 406-257-6716

The school, founded in 1958 by Trinity Lutheran Church (Lutheran Church Missouri Synod), combines strong academic studies with religious education and has a good reputation for solid academics. Teachers are state-certified and many hold advanced degrees. Music, fine arts and sports programs are available. The school's motto is "excellence in education in a caring Christian environment." A chapel service is held weekly. Various classes, school staff, guest pastors and Trinity's ministerial staff lead these services on a rotating basis. A hot lunch is available at noon for students and staff. Eligible students may receive a free or reduced rate. Enrollment is 220 students, K-8.

Valley Adventist Christian School
1275 Helena Flats Rd., Kalispell
• 406-752-0830

This school for children grades 1-8 is affiliated with the Seventh-Day Adventist Church. The school provides a Seventh-day Adventist education for the youth of the church and any others who want a Christian education and agree to abide by the school's standards. The educational program is based on the Bible. The curriculum includes weekly art classes, music classes and physical education in addition to academic studies. Enrollment is 16-25 students.

Childcare

Finding high-quality childcare is a top priority for working parents, and a variety of options are available, ranging from large daycare centers to stay-at-home moms who want to care for an extra child or two. Weekend and evening care, along with care for infants, are the hardest to find, but good choices do exist. Ask your friends and neighbors for recommendations, or take advantage of special help that's available for parents.

The Nurturing Center
146 Third Ave. W., Kalispell
• **406-756-1414**

This agency serves as a referral center for childcare, matching parents with appropriate providers. A total of 66 child-care providers in Kalispell are registered with the Nurturing Center, while eight are listed in Bigfork, 12 in Columbia Falls and 11 in Whitefish. A basic referral to two providers is free, and an "enhanced referral" tailored to individual need costs $15. The Nurturing Center also offers other support to families, including parenting classes, a reference lending library and support groups.

Bear Grass Club and Montessori Children's House
1301 E. Seventh St., Whitefish
• **406-863-4685**

The Bear Grass Club, Children's House and preschool provide before- and after-school care for children in grades 1-4 and Montessori education and child care for ages 2-K. Hours are from 7:15 AM to 6 PM Total enrollment is about 60 and maximum class size is 16 children per two adults. A summer camp program is offered for grades 1-4.

Bigfork Montessori Children's House
195 Old Bridge St., Bigfork
• **406-837-3885** • **406-837-6786**

This is a Montessori program for children ages 3-6. Half-day and full-day programs are offered. Class sizes are 8-10 children, with total enrollment of about 14. Owner Lori Henes previously operated a Montessori program in Hamilton, moved to Bigfork to "retire" and soon found herself involved in Montessori education again in her new hometown.

Discovery Developmental Center
985 N. Meridian, Kalispell
• **406-756-7295**

A non-profit organization offering inte-

grated child care for children 18 months to 6 years, programs include Playgroup, preschool, pre-K (morning and afternoon) and Kindergarten enrichment. Transportation is available. Specialists in Speech and Language Therapy, Physical Therapy and Occupational Therapy are available on site for children with special needs. The center is licensed for 40 children. All staff members have degrees in elementary education or early childhood development.

Kalispell Parks and Recreation Department
City Hall, Kalispell
• **406-758-7718**

After-school sports camps are available throughout the school year through the parks department at a reasonable cost. These camps are for first through sixth grades and feature indoor activities such as indoor soccer, basketball, floor hockey and new games and outdoor excursions for ice skating, sledding, cross-country skiing, baseball, bike riding and exploring city parks. A spring break offers another child-care option for parents of 6 to 11year olds, featuring indoor/outdoor activities, games, skits, arts and crafts and field trips if the weather permits. "I'm bored" ranks high for most parents as a least-favorite phrase, and, let's face it, after the novelty of no school wears off, summers can be, well, boring. The parks department also conducts a series of summer day camps at Woodland Park for children ages 3-12. The week-long camp sessions run from mid-June to late August.

Moms Program
Trinity Evangelical Lutheran Church, 400 W. California St., Kalispell
• **406-257-5683**

Moms of children of all ages are welcome at this support group, which meets from 9:30 to 11:30 AM the first and third Wednesdays of each month from September through May. Guest speakers, including doctors, lawyers, attorneys, teachers and nurses, are featured at each meeting, along with a craft project once a month. The program is free and childcare is provided.

Smith Memorial Day Care Center
329 Second Ave. E., Kalispell
• 406-755-9224

This was the first childcare center in Kalispell, established in 1966 through a bequest from a member of the First United Methodist Church. The center, which is licensed for ages 2-12, has room for about 50 children and is generally at capacity. The center is located on the top floor of the Methodist Church. Activities include music, exercise, stories outside play time, nap time and snacks. Hours are 7:30 AM to 5:30 PM, Monday through Friday.

Sugar N' Spice Learning Center
255 Summit Ridge Dr., Kalispell
• 406-752-8050

Preschool for ages 3-4, pre-K, kindergarten and pre-first. Day care from ages 6 weeks to 12 years, up to 14 with special needs, with transportation to area schools, and a summer enrichment and after school program. It is licensed for 115 children.

The Summit
205 Sunnyview Lane, Kalispell
• 406-751-4100

A variety of programs for children are offered at the Summit, including "No School Fun Camps" from 7:45 AM to 6:30 PM on school holidays. The camps are designed to provide a safe place for children ages 6-12 who want to participate in sports-related activities and learn how to live a healthy lifestyle. The Summit also operates "S.P.A.R.K." (Sports, Physical Activity and Recreation for Kids) programs for children ages 4-6 on weekdays over the noon hour and after school for kids ages 6-12 from 3:30 to 6:30 PM.

Worship

In the Flathead Valley, ministry is an important calling. The church building is an important structure — a gathering place for neighbors and friends, a source of support, education, and community service. In small communities the church is still the focal point, while in larger cities you'll find a church practically on every corner. Religious communities in the Flathead Valley developed along with the first settlers, and churches were some of the earliest buildings constructed in the towns of the Flathead Valley. For examples look at St. Richard's Catholic Church in Columbia Falls, or the First Presbyterian Church in Kalispell. Strongly Christian in many ways is this community. You'll find your friends and neighbors to be very open with their faith beliefs and opinions. As a newcomer, you'll find that folks getting to know you are genuinely concerned that you find your "church home" as you get settled. Your liberal views on certain issues may be viewed with concern by some folks, though not all, in an area where the middle of summer finds a pro-life march right down Main Street and wintertime finds carols played over community loudspeakers. Many religious communities offer more than just Sunday services — they provide living opportunities, thrift stores, transportation, soup kitchens, youth camps and schools. And although it's strongly Christian with most every denomination represented, other centers for encouragement and enlightenment are there for the seeker, including Baha'is of Flathead County and an active Jewish community. Whatever your religious preference, you'll probably be able to find a group of like-minded folks here, and you'll be warmly welcomed and drawn into your chosen family of worshipers.

Once you've unpacked the boxes . . .

You're finally settled in your new home, and ready to get involved in the life of your new community. The Flathead Valley has the usual contingent of clubs, lodges, business associations and groups for special interests. Whether you're interested in quilting, reading, photography, investments, Bible study, barbershop music, or duplicate bridge, a group of people of like interests probably exists here. If not, you can start a group of your own and ask your neighbors to join you. The *Daily Inter Lake* runs a comprehensive list of meetings every Sunday, and once a year publishes a guide called *The Answer Book*, a compilation of various community resources that also can give you valuable information. Community bulletin boards and radio and newspaper announcements also let you know what's going on in your new home. You'll find that people are generally very friendly toward newcomers, and they're happy to share their love of this special place. Many of the people you'll meet were in your shoes not so long ago: a recent study classified one in six residents of Flathead and Lake counties as newcomers. You'll find good friends and neighbors in the Flathead, as long as you're willing to be a good friend and neighbor yourself. So relax, take a deep breath of the fresh mountain air, take a look at the glories of nature that surround you, and enjoy your new home. We're sure you're going to love it here.

Ever since circuit riders carried messages by horseback, stagecoaches clattered over our rough roads, and telegraph wires were first strung overhead cutting black lines across the big sky, residents of the Flathead Valley and Glacier Country have been hungry for news and have devised clever ways of getting it.

Media

Ever since circuit riders carried messages by horseback, stagecoaches clattered over our rough roads, and telegraph wires were first strung overhead cutting black lines across the big sky, residents of the Flathead Valley and Glacier Country have been hungry for news and have devised clever ways of getting it. At the end of the 20th century, we've jumped on the information superhighway and we're zooming along on the only Montana highway that doesn't, in fact, have a speed limit. Our residents are wired into the Internet and cable and digital television, and we're still avid readers of our community newspapers. The following listings will give you an idea of the myriad fine communications opportunities we are privileged to have.

Newspapers

Major Dailies from around the State

The Daily Inter Lake
Kalispell
(406) 755-7000
This is the place to turn for daily information on the Flathead Valley. The paper has been in existence since 1889 and is a respected community business leader.

Great Falls Tribune
Great Falls
(406) 791-1444
Established in 1884 and still going strong, the circulation of the *Great Falls Tribune* is around 40,000. It is owned by the Gannett newspaper chain and is available on newsstands throughout the state.

The Missoulian
Missoula
(406) 523-5210
Part of the Lee newspaper chain, this daily has been in business since 1870 and is a fine source of information for Missoula, the Flathead Valley, and the Bitterroot Valley to the south. It is available throughout the state.

Billings Gazette
Billings
(406) 657-1200, 800-927-2345
Available at newsstands throughout the state, this is Montana's largest daily newspaper. The circulation is about 60,000. It is owned by Lee Enterprises, which owns papers in Helena, Missoula, and Butte, as well.

The Local News

Each of these weeklies or semi-weeklies is an essential part of the community in which it is located. Here you'll find fine reporting on local news events, coverage of the area's festivals and fairs, and reports of local schools and clubs. You're not "in the know" unless you take the time to peruse these local papers. Don't think that because they're small they're sub-par. Some of the finest writing and reporting in the state goes on at the local level.

Bigfork Eagle
Bigfork
(406) 837-5131

Glacier Reporter (formerly the Browning Chief)
Browning
(406) 338-2090

Hungry Horse News
Columbia Falls
(406) 892-2151

Lake County Leader
Polson
(406) 883-4343

Seeley Swan Pathfinder
Swan Valley
(406) 677-2022

Whitefish Pilot
Whitefish
(406) 862-3505

Radio Stations

Kalispell

KALS-FM, 97.1
Christian
(406) 752-5257

KBBZ-FM, 98.5
Classic Rock
(406) 755-8700

KDBR-FM, 106.3
Country
(406) 744-8700

KOFI-FM 103.9
Country
(406) 755-6690

KGEZ-AM, 600
Oldies
(406) 752-2600

KOFI-AM, 1180
Adult contemporary
(406) 755-6690

KUKL-FM, 89.9
Public Radio

Whitefish

KJJR-AM, 880

KUFM-FM, 97.1
Public Radio

Polson

KERR-AM, 750
Country
(406) 883-5255

Great Falls

KAAK-FM, 98.9
Contemporary hits
(406) 727-7211

KEIN-AM, 1310
Oldies
(406) 761-1310

KGFC-FM, 88.9
Christian
(406) 265-5845

KLFM-FM, 92.9
Oldies
(406) 761-7600

KMON-AM, 560
Country
(406) 761-7600

KMON-FM, 94.5
Country
(406) 761-7600

INSIDERS' TIP

Mel Ruder, of the *Hungry Horse News,* won the Pulitzer Prize for local reporting in 1964 for his coverage of flood conditions around Columbia Falls. The *Hungry Horse News* is the only Montana paper to have been honored with the award.

KMSL-AM, 1450
News/talk/sports
(406) 761-2800

KQDI-FM, 106.1
Classic rock
(406) 761-2800

KXGF-AM, 1400
Adult contemporary
(406) 761-7211

Missoula

KGGL-FM, 93.3
Country
(406) 721-9300

KGRZ-AM, 1450
Country
(406) 728-1450

KGVO-AM, 290
News/information/sports
(406) 721-1290

KLCY-AM, 930
Entertainment/information
(406) 728-9300

KMSO-FM, 102.5
Adult contemporary
(406) 542-1025

KUFM-FM, 89.1
Public radio
(406) 243-4931

KYLT-AM, 1340
Oldies/Sports
(406) 728-5000

KYSS-FM, 94.9
Country
(406) 728-9300

KZOQ-FM, 100.1
Album rock
(406) 728-5000

Television Stations

Public television and all three major networks are available through local affiliates in Montana. Cable television supplements the local offerings through TCI. The stations you'll get with or without cable depend on where you are in the state. Below are the closest local stations to the Flathead Valley.

ABC

KFBB-TV, Channel 5
Great Falls

KTMF-TV, Channel 23
Missoula

CBS

KGRT-TV, Channel 3
Great Falls

KPAX-TV, Channel 8
Missoula

KAJ-TV, Channel 18
Kalispell

NBC

KCFW-TV, Channel 9
Kalispell

KGTF-TV, Channel 16
Great Falls

KECI-TV, Channel 13
Missoula

Learn more
about
Glacier and
the
Flathead.

For More Information

The following books, pamphlets, and brochures will help you explore Glacier and the Flathead to the fullest.

Books

These books are available through Falcon Publishing, Glacier Natural History Association bookstores, or other bookstores throughout Montana.

A Climber's Guide to Glacier National Park
    by J. Gordon Edwards

Alpine Wildflowers
    by Dr. Dee Strickler

Backpacking Tips, Trail-tested Wisdom from FalconGuide Authors
    by Bill and Russ Schneider

Bear Aware, Hiking and Camping in Bear Country
    by Bill Schneider

Best Easy Day Hikes Glacier and Waterton
    by Erik Molvar

Birding Montana
    by Terry McEneaney

Central Rocky Mountain Wildflowers
    by Wayne Phillips

Columbia Falls Yester-years
    by Beatrice Macomber

Family Fun in Montana
    by Chris Boyd

Fishing Glacier National Park
    by Russ Schneider

Fishing Montana
    by Mike Sample

Flathead Lake, From Glaciers to Cherries
    by R.C. "Chuck" Robbin

Flathead Valley Yesteryear
    by Lou Bain and Frank Grubb

Glacier Country: Montana's Glacier National Park, Montana Geographic Series
    by Montana Magazine

Glacier's Grandest, A Pictorial History of the Hotels and Chalets of Glacier National Park
    by Bridget Moylan

Going to the Sun: The Story of the Highway across Glacier National Park
    by Rose Houk

Growing Up Western
    by Monty Hall and
    Joe Durso, Jr.

Heart of the Trail
by Mary Barmeyer O'Brien

Hiking Glacier and Waterton National Parks
by Erik Molvar

Hiking Montana—20th Anniversary Edition
by Bill and Russ Schneider

It Happened in Montana
by Jim Crutchfield

Kalispell, Montana, and the Upper Flathead Valley
by Henry Elwood

Logan Pass: Alpine Splendor in Glacier National Park
by Jerry DeSanto

Looking Back: A Pictorial History of the Flathead Valley, Montana
by Katheryn McKay

Man in Glacier
by C. W. Bucholtz

Mark of the Grizzly
by Scott McMillion

Montana Bird Distribution.
by P. D. Skaar, published by the Montana Natural Heritage Program.

Montana Campfire Tales
by Dave Walter

Montana Wildlife Viewing Guide
by Hank and Carol Fischer

More than Petticoats: Remarkable Montana Women
by Gayle Shirley

Mountain Lion Alert
by Steven Torres

Paddling Montana
by Hank and Carol Fischer

Rock Climbing Montana
Randall Green, editor

Rocky Mountain Berry Book
by Bob Krumm

Scenic Driving Montana
by Sarah Snyder Schneider

Somers, Montana, the Company Town
Henry Elwood, editor

Stump Town to Ski Town: The Story of Whitefish, Montana
by Betty Schafer and Mabel Engelter

Trail Riding Western Montana
  by Carellen Barnett

Trains, Trails, and Tin Lizzies: Glacier National Park 1932-1934
  by Glacier National History Association

Western Trees: A Field Guide
  by Maggie Stucky and George Palmer,

When You and I Were Young, Whitefish
  by Dorothy Marie Johnson

Wild Country Companion
  by Will Harmon

Wild Montana
  by Bill Cunningham

Wilderness First Aid
  by Gilbert Preston, MD

Brochures

NatureWatch, a brochure describing this national program that that fosters conservation of wildlife, fish, and plants and their habitats and provides viewing opportunities for the public.

"A Checklist of Montana Birds." Available from Montana Audubon, P.O. Box 595, Helena, MT 59624, 449-3949 or Montana Fish, Wildlife and Parks, 1420 East Sixth Avenue, Helena, MT 59620.

Index